DAVID FOSTER WALLACE'S BALANCING BOOKS

DAVID FOSTER WALLACE'S BALANCING BOOKS

FICTIONS OF VALUE

JEFFREY SEVERS

COLUMBIA UNIVERSITY PRESS
NEW YORK

Columbia University Press
Publishers Since 1893
New York   Chichester, West Sussex
cup.columbia.edu
Copyright © 2017 Columbia University Press

Library of Congress Cataloging-in-Publication Data
Names: Severs, Jeffrey, 1974– author.
Title: David Foster Wallace's balancing books : fictions of value / Jeffrey Severs.
Description: New York : Columbia University Press, 2017. |
Includes bibliographical references and index.
Identifiers: LCCN 2016019208 (print) | LCCN 2016030061 (ebook) |
ISBN 9780231179447 (cloth : alk. paper) | ISBN 9780231543118 (e-book)
Subjects: LCSH: Wallace, David Foster—Criticism and interpretation.
Classification: LCC PS3573.A425635 Z864 2017 (print) | LCC PS3573.A425635 (ebook) | DDC
813/.54—dc23
LC record available at https://lccn.loc.gov/2016019208

Columbia University Press books are printed on permanent and durable acid-free paper.
Printed in the United States of America
Cover design: Archie Ferguson
Cover image: © Gary Hannabarger

CONTENTS

NOTE ON THE TEXTS

THE FOLLOWING texts by David Foster Wallace are cited parenthetically with abbreviations. Full bibliographic information is in the bibliography.

NOVELS AND SHORT STORY COLLECTIONS

The Broom of the System	*B*
Girl with Curious Hair	*GCH*
Infinite Jest	*IJ*
Brief Interviews with Hideous Men	*BI*
Oblivion	*O*
The Pale King	*PK*

ESSAY COLLECTIONS, NONFICTION, AND INTERVIEWS

A Supposedly Fun Thing I'll Never Do Again	*SFT*
Both Flesh and Not	*BF*
Conversations with David Foster Wallace, ed. Stephen J. Burn	*CW*
Consider the Lobster	*CL*

ACKNOWLEDGMENTS

THANK YOU to the University of British Columbia for grant and leave support and to my colleagues in the English Department, especially Ira Nadel. Thanks to the library staff at the Harry Ransom Center at the University of Texas–Austin; to the editorial staff at Columbia University Press, especially Philip Leventhal, and the anonymous reviewers of my manuscript; to my research assistants, Angus Reid, Madeline Gorman, and especially Jeff Noh and Jae Sharpe, who were both indispensable to the book's completion; to the students in my seminars, who spurred many insights herein; to Eric Bennett, Brian Bremen, Ralph Clare, Siân Echard, Matt Gartner, Jeff Hoffman, Chris Leise, Linda Meng, Geordie Miller, Travis Miles, Jason Puskar, Matt Rubery, Adam Seluzicki, Charles Seluzicki, and Jeff Waite, who each helped with conversation and support at crucial moments; to Steve Moore, who gave me and my archival research a Texas home; and to the staff and management of Vancouver's City Square Shopping Centre Food Court, where many of these pages were written.

Above all, I thank my mom and dad, my sisters, and my entire family for loving me and educating me. And thanks beyond thanks to Christina Seluzicki, for showing me what value and gifts can be.

An earlier version of portions of chapters 2 and 5 appeared as "Collision, Illinois: David Foster Wallace and the Value of Insurance," *Modern Fiction Studies* 62, no. 1 (Spring 2016): 130–150. Copyright © 2016 The Johns Hopkins University Press. An earlier version of parts of the introduction and chapter 6 appeared as "'Blank as the Faces on Coins': Currency and Embodied Value(s) in David Foster Wallace's *The Pale King*," *Critique* 57, no. 1 (2016): 52–66. This article, published on December 30, 2015, is available online: http://www.tandf Col/ online.com/doi/full/10.1080/0011 1619.2015.1019397. Reprinted by permission of the publisher. All quotations from the Wallace Papers at the Harry Ransom Center are published with the permission of the David Foster Wallace Literary Trust.

DAVID
FOSTER
WALLACE'S
BALANCING
BOOKS

INTRODUCTION

A LIVING TRANSACTION

VALUE, GROUND, AND BALANCING BOOKS

WHEN DAVID Foster Wallace committed suicide on September 12, 2008, amid the tragedy one of the most surprising details to emerge was news of the project he had left unfinished: a novel on the unlikely subject of the Internal Revenue Service. Mentioning in its opening pages bookkeeping's "double-entry method" (*PK* 9) and featuring a section rendered in doubled columns, *The Pale King* proved to be thematically and formally concerned with balance books—perhaps it constituted a kind of ledger for American culture, assessing its credits and debits.[1] That Wallace would take consuming interest in the balance sheets of a federal agency should not have come as a shock, though. He had throughout his work been subtly invested in images of balance and reciprocity, as well as mutuality and the socially shared. He pursued balance on levels that extended from the bodily and the interpersonal to the spiritual, sociological, financial, geopolitical, and cosmic. Wallace showed characters struggling to place two feet on the ground and restlessly sought to balance the books for a chaotic culture (and determine the moral authority on which one could do so). Seeing him as such casts new light on the reasons his writing has signaled a sharp turn against postmodernist tenets and a galvanizing new phase in contemporary global literature.

In this book, finding unifying motifs for aspects of his work that have gone largely unexplored, I detail Wallace's quest for balance in a world of excess and entropy; show him probing the unbalanced ledgers that ideas of gift, contract, and commonwealth raised at breakthrough moments in his career; and, adding a third area of his collegiate interests to the portrayal of him as the philosopher-novelist, pose him as at bottom a rebellious economic thinker, one who not only satirized the deforming effects of money but threw into question the logic of the monetary system, often acting as a historian of financial markets, the Great Depression, and the precarious fate of the social-welfare achievements of the New Deal. Fusing readings of metaphysical, existential, and moral themes with this sort of historicization, I demonstrate the great relevance his work has to the neoliberal nation that he tragically left behind in 2008, just as it started to feel the impact of a tremendous crisis in what the accountant's double ledger ideally helps maintain: the connection between price and value, one of Wallace's continual subjects.

In one of the last essays he published in his lifetime, Wallace invokes "value" as his standard in selecting *The Best American Essays* of 2007 —"which, yes, all right, entitles you to ask what 'value' means here" (*BF* 311). Wallace's polymath mind was always asking what "value" meant in numerous contexts. Our understanding of his transformation of contemporary fiction gains new dimensions through reading his dialogical efforts to juxtapose mathematical, metaphysical, monetary, moral, linguistic, and aesthetic meanings of value, a word he always saw on the Wittgensteinian "rough ground" of its contextual uses.[2] For Wallace, value, kept loose and polysemous, could connect depression's internal discourse of low self-worth and spiritual impoverishment to larger cultural formations of financialization and economic crisis under neoliberalism. Through value he redefined both the currency of human exchange and the act of calculation within postmodernity, with huge ramifications for his fiction's moral force. Value, balance, and ground are the governing motifs of this study, all interconnected at the root of Wallace's philosophically educated imagination. Together these topics make his works axiological fiction, a term I explain fully later in this introduction, along with the varying definitions of value he continually compared.

Many of Wallace's individual works have already been well examined by critics for their treatments of solipsism; therapy; technological mediation; philosophical and literary influences such as Wittgenstein, Kierkegaard, and John Barth; and the relationship of irony and sincerity (a topic I examine in greater detail later). But needed now is a synthetic reading, based in his whole career and archive, of Wallace's deep engagement with more traditional social and political problems. What can now be performed is a reconciling of the opposed categories in Pankaj Mishra's suggestive sense, voiced in a review of *Consider the Lobster*, that Wallace "has been an old-fashioned moralist in postmodern disguise all along."[3] Likewise, we can now see more fully why Wallace sought to pull off the seemingly contradictory feat of, as he said, championing "postmodern technique" and "postmodern aesthetic" but "using [them] to discuss very old traditional human verities that have to do with spirituality and emotion and community."[4]

Wallace used value, with its connections to both the traditional project of a moral literature and the radical critiques of commodities and computation laid out in postmodernism, to mediate these conflicting tendencies. The balance scale, I argue, was the image to which he kept returning for reconciliation of his varied ambitions, beginning from his naming of his first protagonist—an LB—after a standard unit of weight, money, and work (from the Latin *libra*, balance) and continuing through his romancing of IRS balance sheets. Computerized-systems man Claude Sylvanshine remarks in *The Pale King* about a closet full of old IRS decision-making equipment, "It's all very ancient and scuzzy and I wouldn't be surprised if there were monkeys with abacuses and strings inside" (*PK* 371). With the balance scale Wallace vivified human acts of valuing in a technologized age, liberating the ancient, scuzzy devices of decision making from other models of computation and sorting that were ascendant at his 1985 IRS and in postmodern culture. The balance scale speaks to the "monkey" inside, making primitive measurements, often simple and binarized, perhaps in the attempt becoming human—and fiction is, in an often-quoted Wallace remark, "about what it is to be a fucking *human being*" (*CW* 26). These calls back to the ancient indicate that Wallace's dependence on past virtues has been underestimated—that, in calling for the "outdated" and "anachronistic" power of sincerity (*SFT* 81) with a fervor (as Adam Kelly says) "not seen since modernism," Wallace also invokes a much, much deeper past on the subject of value.[5]

There is a consistent tension in Wallace's work: the distance between manipulations of values and variables at the highest levels of (often technologized) calculation and some more primitive impulse to reckon with what can be seen and counted at hand—the monkey inside the human, evoked in what Stephen J. Burn shows is Wallace's frequent attention to the "reptilian brain" and the "deep time" of evolutionary development.[6] As Wallace writes in *Everything and More* about the "concrete" origins of even higher math, "Consider the facts that numbers are called 'digits' and that most counting systems . . . are clearly designed around fingers and toes. Or that we still talk about the 'leg' of a triangle or 'face' of a polyhedron" (*EM* 29). Writing moral fiction within a postmodern United States is for Wallace a matter of restoring readers' sense that beneath what has been sold to them as infinite choice lies an ancient moral image: the balance scale, a primitive computer with two options, clearly seen and objectively weighted. Modern computing, high finance, and advertising-driven capitalism are ultimately all aligned for him because each proposes, in its own way, *many* values, much randomness, alongside the overload of "250 advertisements a day" (*LI* 9). The effect of such forces is, for his characters, enervating—often to the point of questionable morality and nihilism, sometimes to the point of psychological instability.

Wallace stands, the dominant argument goes, as the paragon of literary sincerity and, by virtue of that, herald of a movement beyond postmodern irony and metafiction's self-consciousness, whether in periodizing accounts of a "New Sincerity" (Kelly's term), "Postironic Belief" (Lee Konstantinou's), or a "Post-Postmodern Discontent" (Robert L. McLaughlin's).[7] These are characterizations of Wallace that I hardly dispute on the whole, but I do document their limits in evoking his true range as a creative artist and cultural critic, especially in relation to history and political economy.

While varied in their conclusions, the postpostmodern readings most often turn on coordinating the rhetorical, self-reflecting author and his fictional enactments in a (in light of his total output) small collection of texts from the 1990s, usually beginning from his 1993 manifesto, "E Unibus Pluram: Television and U.S. Fiction," passing through *Infinite Jest* (1996), and taking in the short story "Octet" (1999). Sincerity may have proven ultimately unachievable to Wallace: Kelly, calling "true sincerity" an "aporia," says that "even the writer him- or herself will never know whether they have attained true sincerity" ("New Sincerity," 140), while A. O. Scott (in a review that Wallace himself found illuminating)[8] calls his writing "less anti-ironic than . . . meta-ironic."[9] But a sincere move beyond a postmodernism shackled by irony has emerged as the primary dynamic of Wallace's career.

Essential versions of Wallace tend to go missing in this critical attention to ideas voiced by the author as rhetorician, that part of him supremely skilled with the broad, persuasive statement that Jonathan Franzen described when he called Wallace, in his obituary, our "strongest rhetorical writer."[10] Burn, reviewing *Consider David Foster Wallace* in 2011, was among the first to call for scholars not "to hang on the master's words" about anti-irony in "E Unibus Pluram," claiming that it "belongs to a particular moment in Wallace's early career."[11] Lucas Thompson also laments critics' "overemphasis" on the TV essay and Wallace's oft-quoted 1993 statement-of-purpose interview with Larry McCaffery.[12] Tore Rye Andersen, finding precedents for Wallace's later turn to ethical attention in writers (Nabokov and Pynchon) criticized in the McCaffery interview, describes scholars "struggling to break free from the interpretational framework established by Wallace himself."[13] More work is needed in this vein, more reading of the tales against the teller's precepts.

Reading for value, I describe a Wallace more attuned to the history of political economy than previous critics have noticed—a historicized Wallace who ranged well beyond 1960s art and culture and 1980s and 1990s anomie in finding his narratives' bases. I also reveal his strong thematic continuities between 1987 and 2008: what may seem like Wallace's sudden leap into mature themes between 1989 and *Infinite Jest*, or his shift in focus to civic life in later books, masks an ongoing value project. Interpretations of Wallace in relation to the debilitating effects of capital, finance, and neoliberalism have recently appeared, but they remain largely focused on his posthumous tax novel, whose attention to value I find hidden throughout earlier works. Richard Godden and Michael Szalay, who also link the timing of Wallace's suicide to the 2008 financial meltdown, find that *The Pale King*'s characters "engender abstract equivalents of themselves, and become thereby objects of exchange."[14] Stephen Shapiro, deploying Marx and Tocqueville, calls *The Pale King* "an American communist novel" whose sinuous temporal form simultaneously evokes the "general derangements of capitalism" that go back to America's founding and "the more period-specific" effects of post-1970s neoliberalism.[15] But taking a wider view of Wallace's oeuvre uncovers his many far more oblique and uncanny engagements with U.S. fiscal crises reaching back to the Depression, as well as far broader meditations on the deracinating effects of financial abstraction. My readings also demonstrate that Wallace continually sought illustrations of his central philosophical and spiritual themes through economic thought—and well before he made accountants his central cast.

My theoretical approach is synthetic, mirroring Wallace's own eclecticism, which took in everything from Western philosophy and Eastern religions to mass-market fiction and self-help books.[16] At key moments I find this consummate synthesizer to have much in common with the amalgamating outlook of a neopragmatist who was, for one semester in 1989, his philosophy teacher: Stanley Cavell.[17] Writing on *Hamlet*, a play of great importance to Wallace, Cavell summarizes a dynamic of selfhood that the fiction writer returns to repeatedly, rooted in the famous "To be or not to be" soliloquy:

> I see Hamlet's question whether to be or not, as asking first of all not why he stays alive, but first of all how he or anyone lets himself be born as the one he is. As if human birth, the birth of the human, proposes the question of birth. That human existence has two stages—call these birth and the acceptance of birth—is expressed in religion as baptism, in politics as consent, in what you may call psychology as what Freud calls the diphasic character of psychosexual development. In philosophy I take it to have been expressed in

Descartes's *Cogito* argument, a point perfectly understood and deeply elabo-rated by Emerson, that to exist the human being has the burden of proving that he or she exists, and that this burden is discharged in *thinking* your existence, which comes in Descartes (though this is controversial) to finding how to say, "I am, I exist"; not of course to say it just once, but at every in-stant of your existence; to preserve your existence, originate it. To exist is to take your existence upon you, to enact it, as if the basis of human existence is theater, even melodrama. To refuse this burden is to condemn yourself to skepticism—to a denial of the existence, hence of the value, of the world.[18]

Wallace claims that his generation suffers from a "congenital skepticism" that matches up with the skepticism Cavell describes (*CL* 272). And the art of *"thinking* your existence" at every moment has echoes in *This Is Water*. In his essay on David Markson, which begins with an epigraph from Cavell, Wallace also argues that literary texts are ideally engaged with proving ex-istence: Markson's *Wittgenstein's Mistress* should have been titled "I EXIST," which Wallace says is the "signal that throbs under most voluntary writ-ing—& all good writing" (*BF* 83). Cavell sees the embrace of existence and removal from skepticism as a process of acknowledging "value": being born a second time is inextricable from accepting the value of self and world, a process that fails for so many of Wallace's nihilists and skeptics.

A writer who resisted mightily giving readers closure for his narratives, Wallace designed texts that lead up to the precipice of this bracing Cavel-lian choice to accept birth and be born a second time. His fictions therefore not infrequently end with a greeting to this new self that can only now be-gin the real struggle, rather than walk off into a presumed state of maturity that obviates the reader's action. A fear-drenched Bruce, for instance, hears "welcome" from a therapeutic voice at the end of "Here and There" (*GCH* 172). Don Gately lies on the beach at his lowest point in the last lines of *Infinite Jest* (as though he might rehearse the birth of the entire species, emerging from the sea). The "Hello" in the last line of "Forever Overhead" marks a dive into what Cavell would see as a baptismal pool (*BI* 16). To say "I exist" at "every instant" also involves, in Wallace's drama of images, trying to achieve balance and a relationship to stable ground. These are the signs, far from easily granted by Wallace, of life at a point of calm and mental peace—that moment at which his voice could say, in the surrender ending "Good Old Neon," "'Not another word,'" before the mind could go on another of the "inbent spiral[s] that keep[] you from ever getting any-where" (*O* 181).

While the accountant's balance book is an analogue for *The Pale King*, I title this study *Balancing Books* because balanced states were never truly reached in the works of Wallace, who, keenly attuned to poststructuralism, believed that final reconciliations, whether for self or text, were not only philosophically untenable but even potentially fascistic. The progressive participle, balancing, is thus quite important. Balance was for Wallace a sought-after spiritual and psychological state; the yin-yang symbol from Taoist philosophy, usually out of whack, appears frequently in his books as a way of discerning the right relationship between self and other.[19] How-ever, sensitivity to symmetry also left him ready to forge baggy encyclo-pedias and point out the ragged, the unreciprocated, and (in a word that recurs throughout the late work) the "incongruous," formal features that often suggest just how few human relationships achieve a balance of trade, the economic term through which he frequently understood the interper-sonal (*O* 197).

At the same time, these conceptions of balance are too abstract to serve as a guide to Wallace's visceral fictions and their attention to the fact many of his characters forget or refuse: in the words of the last section of *The Pale King*, spoken to a "you" who does "not feel your own weight": "You do have a body, you know" (*PK* 539). The "inbent" body trying to balance, to find its feet, to feel and be aware (but not debilitatingly aware) of its weight, is the pervasive subject of Wallace's phenomenological work, the concept informing the particular ways he forms and deforms his characters, from paraplegia to bad spinal health. Growing up, Wallace was excellent at ten-nis, in which maintaining a ready balance for motion in multiple direc-tions is paramount. He writes in praise of Roger Federer "wrong-foot[ing]" (*BF* 6) his opponent (a strategy also described in *Infinite Jest* [1032n184]). Perhaps Midwestern landscapes are another source for Wallace's attention to ground: "The native body readjusts automatically to the flatness," but "you can start to notice that the dead-level flatness is only apparent," he writes about returning to rural Illinois. "It's like sea-legs: if you haven't spent years here you'll never feel" the ground's "gentle sine wave" (*SFT* 84). Playing surfaces "bare of flaw, tilt, crack, or seam" were "disorienting" to him as a youngster, he writes in "Derivative Sport in Tornado Alley" (*SFT* 14), and in this essay that led him into the writing of *Infinite Jest* lies an allegorical *ars poetica*.[20] Wallace's fiction is a metaphorical playing space that eschews perfectly even topologies in favor of the "rough ground" of contextualized language that Wittgenstein calls for.

From Lenore Beadsman's obsession with feet and footwear to Chris Fogle's "nihilistic ritual of the foot" in *The Pale King* (187), to be of interest to Wallace's narrative gaze is often to be sensitive to ground and to alienation from it. Of the many freshly and grotesquely described body parts in Wallace, the only one more crucial than the foot is the spine: across his career he uses the spine as a locus for exploring humans' often frustrated attempts to lay claim to ontology and say "I EXIST," constantly addressing how humans stand up and balance, how they rise up from flatness to inhabit (it is implied) a third dimension, whether the force keeping them down is a gunshot wound or the effects of endless desk work. Such are Wallace's highly physical means for illustrating problems of metaphysics and ontology and seeking space beyond the playful acceptance of uncertain ontologies that Brian McHale, in a seminal argument, finds definitive of postmodern fiction.[21] Standing up in Wallace's work is almost inevitably associated with the moral life, with having values and being able to share value with others. As *Infinite Jest* says, in a line that applies not just to the deformed like Mario, "People who're somehow burned at birth, withered or ablated way past anything like what might be fair, they either curl up in their fire, or else they rise" (*IJ* 316). How to rise, in spite of all (and to do so with passion and without arrogance), is Wallace's major subject.

Images of weight and balance stoke Wallace's phenomenological imagination because their creation leads to an existential fiction—unique in contemporary writing—that addresses itself not to the realist's dramatic incident but what Wallace calls throughout *This Is Water* our "default settings": those assumptions about existence that, like the immanence of the water through which a fish swims, are so naturalized as to go wholly unnoticed (*TW* 113). Wallace has a persistent concern for philosophical grounds, those overlooked terrors of "abstract thinking" that he dramatizes on the first page of *Everything and More* as "getting out of bed every morning without the slightest doubt that the floor would support you"—and suddenly descending one day into tormenting doubt (*EM* 13). Weight, balance, ground, and, as we will see, value and work are among those "most obvious, ubiquitous, important realities" that prove "the hardest to see and talk about"—but not if we tune in to the thoughts about these subjects subtly progressing on nearly every page (*TW* 8). With Wallace, the taken for granted is where we must look; he wants to expose—and often move—the ground beneath our mental feet.

VALUE, VALUES, EVALUATION: AXIOLOGICAL FICTION

What does value "mean" in this book? The potency of the word arose for Wallace from the variety of contexts in which he could locate it and, playing an expected meaning off an alien one, cause productive dissonance for his reader. The student of mathematics and its extensions into philosophy never lost his sense that the exactness of enumeration—values as they appear in equations—might inform areas of greater vagueness in the human experience, morality chief among them. There was, after all, that overlap in wording: the values of 7 and 8, the moral values parents instill in children (or ought to, this traditional mind thought). Wallace took seriously the fact that we use the same word for the enumerated and the seemingly incalculable—values—without suggesting the two meanings could ever be merged. Another point of linguistic overlap lies in economic value, the type at the front of most minds in an advanced capitalist society and my readings' most frequent subject. But economic, monetary, mathematical, semantic, aesthetic, and moral meanings of value all interact here, as they do in Wallace's inventions of character and his idea of fiction's capacious mission.[22]

A guide appears in the blurb Wallace provided in 2007 for the twenty-fifth-anniversary edition of Lewis Hyde's *The Gift*, a work whose optimistic claims about the ability of art to confound commerce Wallace both championed and wrestled with throughout his career. That blurb (excerpted on the book but published in full on Hyde's website) observes: "No one who is invested in any kind of art, in questions of what real art does and doesn't have to do with money, spirituality, ego, love, ugliness, sales, politics, morality, marketing, and whatever you call 'value,' can read *The Gift* and remain unchanged." A careful description transcending what Wallace calls "formulaic blurb-speak," these words seem to offer "'value'" as the synthetic summa of the wide-ranging list of subjects associated with "real art," but at the same time value is utterly flexible in this role, taking the lead-in "whatever you call" as a challenge to the reader of even just this blurb to consider what *she* calls "value."[23] That reader is then provoked, in Wallace's work, to determine for herself "the real, no-shit value of [a] liberal-arts education" (*TW* 60) or what it means to "endorse single-entendre values" (*SFT* 81).

Some critics have already attributed Wallace's distinctiveness within postmodern writing to his desire to preserve traditional values. Hence Paul Giles sees Wallace expressing "a residual attachment to traditional American values, even within a globalized world."[24] Conley Wouters points to "earnest midwestern value systems that Wallace seemed alone among contemporaries in embracing."[25] Two of the Wallace critics most dedicated to searching his work for guides to a life of noninstrumentality and moral value, Nathan Ballantyne and Justine Tosi, demonstrate that value and irony are naturally opposed stances for him, writing, "Once in the grip of irony . . . we don't value anything at all," a state that even Richard Rorty's view of the liberatory potential of ironism cannot salvage.[26] In his own essays, Wallace often approaches questions of value through the language of a social accountant, suggesting that equations, even huge ones, *can* be balanced when arbitrating large-scale social problems. He frequently weighs the "cost" of social phenomena, particularly of the freedoms of choice he had seen explode with consumer capitalism and sexual liberation. When faced with a difficult social problem, Wallace seeks not to consult favored ideologies but to consider tradeoffs. In 2007, in his final magazine publication, for instance, he refers daringly to the victims of 9/11 as "sacrifices" to the cause of "freedom," writing, "what if we decided that a certain minimum baseline vulnerability to terrorist attack is part of the price of the American idea?" (*BF* 321). Was this fundamentally different from a culture desiring cars' "mobility and autonomy" considering a certain number of highway deaths per year "worth the price" (*BF* 322)? Wallace was, as the title says, "Just Asking," and there were rarely easy answers to his sobering questions about cost, rarely any easy reduction of human lives to the symbolism of math or money.

None of these accounts of values, though—not those of critics, not Wallace's broad metaphors—describes in adequate detail the means by which his fiction arrives at, displays, and wields moral values, an area where, even as he pursued sincerity, he feared slipping into a mode of preachy moralism that he *did* prize postmodernism's ability to dissolve. This book builds toward a concluding view of Wallace's embrace of a technical moral authority, a mode of writing that maintained faith in a flood of details sharpening readers' moral attention, specifically through the dry, unremarked skill of small-scale, comparative valuation. Such was the unlikely, indirect means by which Wallace brokered, line by line, his postmodern moralism. In such authority, Wallace tried to offer what his ironic predecessors, in the thrall of negation and rebellion, had not. Irony had "an almost exclusively negative function" of being "destructive, a ground-clearing" (*SFT* 67); something new had to be built, something "morally passionate, passionately moral" (*CL* 274)—though what exact form that morally authoritative stance might take, beyond these pithy remarks, could confound a writer who heeded tenets of postmodernism such as Jean-Francois Lyotard's era-defining question: "Who is the subject whose prescriptions are norms for those they obligate?"[27]

While staying open to many meanings, let me provide a few specific philosophical markers for the types of value that guided Wallace's explorations. First, Wallace criticizes, and depicts subjects in radical departure from, value as construed by logical positivism, that method in which he trained at Amherst. This philosophy, embodied by Wittgenstein's *Tractatus Logico-Philosophicus*, takes as foundational an absolute distinction between fact and value, between language that refers to the empirically verifiable and language, such as ethical statements, based in subjective feeling. The Wallace beacon John Barth summarizes the spirit of many thinkers' rejection of logical positivism when the narrator of *The End of the Road* complains of "the fallacy that because a value isn't intrinsic, objective, and absolute, it somehow isn't *real*."[28] In his rereading of U.S. literature from the 1940s to the 1970s as a long engagement with logical positivism, Michael LeMahieu quotes that piece of Barth in demonstrating that this much-denigrated philosophical stance was received by fiction writers as "a threat to aesthetic representation" but also (therefore) a productive opportunity.[29] As he examines the key Wallace influences Barth, Pynchon, and the De-Lillo of *End Zone*, LeMahieu finds logical positivism erased in U.S. fiction by 1975—but Wallace carries into the 1980s and beyond the legacy of building a fictional vision around the need to both seriously entertain and aggressively undermine *Tractatus*-style thinking.

In this engagement, Wallace makes moves like the opening heading of the 1989 novella that first sketched many of his mature themes, "Westward the Course of Empire Takes Its Way": that heading, "BACKGROUND THAT INTRUDES AND LOOMS: LOVERS AND PROPOSITIONS," puns on positivism's atomized "propositions" by introducing sexual connotations and the most slippery of value judgments, love. As Charles B. Harris summarizes—thinking perhaps of the narrator of "Westward," Bruce in "Here and There," and Hal in *Infinite Jest*—most of Wallace's "lost characters are trapped in a *Tractatus*-like state of emotional solipsism, their language entirely inner directed."[30] Wittgenstein eventually left the *Tractatus*'s precepts behind, according to Wallace's reading of the philosopher's career, which turned dramatically, in the posthumously published *Philosophical Investigations*, toward an antisolipsistic vision: while words' referents may indeed still be "out there" and inaccessible to human minds, Wallace summarizes, we are at least "all in here together," "in language" (*CW* 44). Wittgenstein's movement away from a cold logic and into a social language—the movement traced by many Wallace characters, too—means that the working definition of value must expand into interpersonal territories, often illustrated by Wallace through the economic and transactional.

Placing a value on human satisfaction and the good and thus mathematicizing moral decision making are the domains of utilitarianism, a second philosophical context I keep in view. Utilitarianism prescribes "a whole teleology predicated on the idea that the best human life is one that maximizes the pleasure-to-pain ratio," Wallace rails to McCaffery (*CW* 23). In *Infinite Jest* Marathe echoes Wallace by designating Steeply "the classic . . . *utilitarienne*. Maximize pleasure, minimize displeasure"—a principle without logical purchase in an age of self-murderingly pleasurable technologies (*IJ* 423). Robert C. Jones identifies Wallace's "distaste" for utilitarian arguments in a reading of animal rights and "Consider the Lobster" but leaves out the greater role utilitarianism had as an object of critique in the fiction.[31] Human minds for Wallace were inevitably calculating, and as he pursued possible intersections of morality with math, Wallace carefully distinguished his own analysis of quantified moral value, giving it a humanity and complexity utilitarianism lacked. The ratios of one's pleasure and another's pain that structure the utilitarian mindset also inherently depend, on a larger scale, on the divisibility of social goods. But Wallace draws attention to objects that are not easily divided, as in Marathe's fable of soup two people both deserve: to Steeply's "maybe we divide" it, Marathe replies that solipsistic capitalism gives us "the ingenious Single-Serving Size," "notoriously for only one" (*IJ* 425). The theme grows more grand in *The Pale King*'s account of 1977 Illinois and its "Subdividable!" slogan for a progressive sales tax (*PK* 198). Indivisible goods (often tax-funded "public good[s]" [*CL* 342]) become Wallace's way of highlighting the intertwining of utilitarianism, consumerism, and neoliberalism, pathological American triplets.

My third and most important philosophical guidepost on value is axiology. Wallace defines axiology in the sample of his dictionary notes in *Both Flesh and Not*: "**axiology**—philosophy: the study of values and value judgments" (*BF* 34–35). Seeking values' roots, axiology is a natural opposite of nihilism, and Wallace's fiction is a grand means of defining and dramatizing axiology, which exposes the less-than-apparent connection among key elements in my analysis: value, ground, and weight. The link lies (as do many for the dictionary-reading Wallace) in etymology: both axiom and axiology derive from the Greek *axios*, meaning worthy or of value, of weight; that which is self-evident, the basis on which to build a philosophical system, is so because it stands out as worthy or fit. Wallace's texts often operate like highly imaginative and compellingly lucid versions of the claims of Heidegger, who, as part of his call to return to the ancient question of Being that had been abandoned by modernity, sought a language in which ground could truly be ascertained. Explicating the lecture "The Ground Principle" and distinguishing its ideas from logical positivism's, John Caputo writes that, for Heidegger, terms other than *axioma*

> contain nothing of the original force of that Greek word. *Axioma* is derived from the Greek *axio*, a verb meaning to value or appreciate something. . . . Thus an axiom is that which is held in the highest esteem. However, the Greeks had no "theory of values" in which a "value" is something added on to a "fact" by the representational (*vorstellend*) thought of the ego. . . . For the Greek a thing stands in the highest regard, not because man has conferred a value upon it, as in modern theory, but rather because it stands forth of itself.[32]

While I refer at times in this book to Heidegger's calls back to ancient, unpostmodern foundations, I am far from claiming Wallace to be consistently a Heideggerian in his depictions of ground and groundless subjects.[33] Nonetheless, these understandings of ground, value, and the axiomatic form a significant model for understanding many signature Wallace images. In his mental dramas of *axios*, Wallace frequently catches his characters as they apprehend phenomena that glow with an apparent worth, often manifestly embodied, and wrestle with converting that apprehension into a system of value (often externalized, quantifying, and attenuating).

The healthy "glow" of the rich Mark Nechtr in the opening paragraphs of "Westward" is a good example: regarding Mark, the narrator spends the whole novella covertly rethinking his almost automatic notion, in the second paragraph, that Mark's "monstrous radiance of ordinary health is a commodity rare, and thus valuable" (*GCH* 233–234). Are there *other* terms in which to value this person, this sinuous narrative asks, perhaps absolute ones or more morally tenable ones? In doing so "Westward" gives new dimensions to value, that term that logical positivism makes an opposite of fact and commodification makes a byproduct of supposed rarity. We readers face the question of value as well, for implicit in so many of the imperatives to decide, read, and make judgments that Wallace places in his narratives is, as at the end of a "Pop Quiz" in "Octet," the command to "Evaluate"—determine value, acting as a precise (though not utilitarian) moral mathematician (*BI* 145).

Pursuing questions of value in a rainy Illinois cornfield, Mark ends up "beseeching, soaked," and in the "mud," for grounding is inevitable in Wallace's work (*GCH* 370). In the void left by his abandonment of realist plots and resolutions, Wallace's protagonists move toward a telos of embodiment and posture (whether ending up kneeling, supine, or prone). "Whole periods of time now begin to feel to me like the intimate, agonizing interval between something falling off and its hitting the ground," Bruce says in "Here and There," which he will end on the floor, undone by an attempt to fix a stove (a symbolic self) (*GCH* 165). Wallace's axiological fictions take place *in* this agonizing interval, and readers learn that characters can only control the violence of impact by becoming aware of their ground, whether in a North Shore condo or a DePaul University accounting classroom. All these literalizations of Heideggerian ground also underscore that what some readers find off-puttingly unrealistic in Wallace (such as wheelchair-bound assassins) often results from his attempt to find physical instantiations of metaphysical states, tendencies that align him with the expressionism of Kafka.

Let me give two more contrasting examples of the intertwining of axioms, earthly ground, and lives of morality and fulfillment in Wallace. First, "B.I. #59," an axiological comedy about the gross manipulation of the self-evident: this interviewee recalls, as a boy in the Soviet bases where his father worked on nuclear missiles, trying to give scientific credibility to masturbatory fantasies of stopping time (using a wave of the hand modeled on the TV show *Bewitched*). The boy recognizes that, to maintain the logical plausibility his pleasure requires, he must uproot and reground, via systems, the entirety of the rotating earth. Now institutionalized (and apparently restrained with "belts and straps of leather" [*BI* 215]), he has a mind that has been uprooted, too. "The hand's supernatural power was perhaps the fantasy's First Premise or *aksioma*, itself unquestioned," he says, "from which all else then must rationally derive and cohere" (*BI* 218). Here is a reason for the empty Q's of *Brief Interviews*: these men become hideous by virtue of finding new, often rapaciously motivated axioms that are beyond the reach of questioning and, building from the ground up, refashion the world in fantasy terms—"*aksioma*, itself unquestioned." These characters, in an often misused phrase, beg the question—they *beggar* the question, leaving it logically impoverished to the point of disappearance ("a textbook petitio principii" [*O* 317]).

This Hideous Man has no relationship to ground as he eviscerates axiom and axis. As a counterexample, consider the man retrospecting on childhood in "All That," another narrative of unaccountable rotation.[34] His parents, while far from the worst Wallace ever created, nonetheless cruelly instill in the boy a radical ontological uncertainty by jokingly telling him the cement mixer on his toy truck rotates, though only when he is not looking. A kind of madness ensues for the boy, who employs desperate means (from looking over his shoulder to a tape marker and photography) to catch the mixer spinning. At work is an allegory of empirical and other types of knowledge: how can I know that the earth is rotating on its axis, when I do not observe the ground moving beneath my feet (issues Chris Fogle will glimpse while watching *As the World Turns*)? In this context, the title, "All That," invokes "The world is all that is the case," the famous translated first line of the *Tractatus*: here is another character due for a fall away from logical positivism, from what this story calls "skeptical empiricism."[35]

But "All That" has a sentimental ending, to use the adjective Giles shows unexpectedly contradicting Wallace's posthumanist anatomies:[36] the story's second half describes a move from radical uncertainty to superseding (and, as is characteristic of Wallace, strategically vague) belief. The boy tries on an unorthodox religious identity (he hears voices) that transforms his mental troubles into "fits of ecstasy," with him rolling on the floor in pleasure (getting reacquainted with ground?), feeling the world is conspiratorially out to make him "so happy I could hardly stand it." He attempts various explanations, but we recognize that, in addition to the satisfactions of belief, he is really describing a remembered grounding in parental love that the Soviet boy never had: the climax of "All That" describes a father-son ritual of watching TV that reconnects not only the two of them but the boy and the axiomatic ground that was so destabilized. These two connect on the couch, "my father, who read during the commercials, sitting at one end and me lying down, with my head on a pillow on my father's knees." One of the boy's "strongest sensory memories of childhood is the feel of my father's knees against my head and the joking way he sometimes rested his book on my head." In one of Wallace's always precise descriptions of bodily positioning, the boy's feverish brain is soothed by attachment to his father's legs and thus to the stable floor; the book on the head suggests a way in which certain knowledge (especially of love and happiness) bypasses the analytical brain. The title "All That" thus switches in the end to a sign of "sensory" plenitude, a feeling of fullness, no jesting infinity. This is a grounding that many Wallace characters will yearn for and, very occasionally, be granted.

ECONOMICS AND BODY HEAT, VALUE AND ENERGY

Those are meanings of ground and value on Wallace's metaphysical and moral planes. In areas more mathematical and communal, value in this book means those standard numbers according to which the common social life is measured—the governmental realm that led Wallace to depict a scale maker in the "New York State Department of Weights and Measures" in his first novel and those who decide tax debts in his last (B 181). Wallace excels at noticing those parts of culture where values in the quantitative sense are illuminatingly juxtaposed with values in the morally shared and socially binding sense—areas in which humans have long built trust and agreement out of accepting adjudication from balance scales rather than dwelling in the conflicts postmodernism emphasizes. Consider what may be Wallace's most ingenious invention, Subsidized Time: only as the reader struggles to establish a chronology in *Infinite Jest* (before getting some help from a calendar [*IJ* 223]) does it become clear that numbered years are, indeed, a shared civic measurement, a unit essential to finding one's place in the world because time itself seems to all of us a commonwealth not subject to privatization by Glad (whose contracts are made with the "O.N.A.N. Dept. of Weights and Measures Oversight Committee" [*IJ* 999]). These overlooked areas of universal agreement on values (who thinks to operate with his own definition, his own private language, of a year, pound, or mile?) appeal to Wallace as a subtle way of exposing the invisible but sturdy bonds that undergird solipsistic lives, just as recurrent motifs in the disparate narratives of a story collection can "impl[y] commonality of experience and struggle," in Mary K. Holland's words.[37] These bonds must be uncannily evoked rather than proclaimed, just as those who announce their virtue or sincerity in Wallace are unlikely to be actually virtuous or sincere. Such standard values also produce questioning of what grounds of agreement might lie in more intractable areas of civic value—such as the "*E Pluribus Unum*," "From many, one," written on U.S. currency, a major subject in my interpretation of *The Pale King*.

Value also means in this book what Wallace knows it means to most of his readers, most of the time: money, the market, and the system of price through which one determines "good value." As D. T. Max reveals, in his early years at Amherst, Wallace participated in debate, considered law school, and worked hard in his economics classes, winning a student prize in the discipline (*Every Love Story*, 28). Nuancing the predominant view of a young writer bifurcated between analytic philosophy and creative writing (a view reinforced by his own interview accounts of college [*CW* 12]), I draw throughout on Wallace's study of economics, claiming that we should grant it a critical importance equal to that accorded to his linked senior theses, in fiction (what became *The Broom of the System*) and modal logic (a refutation of fatalism published in 2011 as *Fate, Time, and Language: An Essay on Free Will*). With his economic vision, Wallace pursues images of exchange that alienate readers from the common acceptance of money as the arbiter of human value; indeed, quite often he conceives of characters themselves as coins and bills, a subject in my readings of several texts.

At times, in its effect and scope Wallace's value project resembles that of Jean-Joseph Goux, who attempts a fusion of semiotic, economic, and psychoanalytic systems by reading each as dependent on a "general equivalent," an "excluded, idealized element" by which all other elements of the system "measure their value." These general equivalents, Goux argues, function like gold in monetary systems and allow us to find a "single structural process of exchange" and substitution in linguistics, economics, and psychosexual development.[38] While he never pursues so comprehensive a theory, Wallace does share with Goux the drive to see human life as a state of constant exchange best illuminated by questioning the standards of equivalency that structure it. For Wallace, language is often a kind of currency, and a narrative is a verbal economy; he agrees with Marc Shell that in "the tropic interaction between economic and linguistic symbolization and production," a "formal money of the mind informs all discourse."[39] Interested in embodiment and affect in this link, Wallace sees fiction ideally as "a living transaction between humans," a communicative exchange he opposed to capitalist economics (*CW* 41). He contrasts "an artistic transaction, which I think involves a gift," with "an economic transaction," which he "regard[s] as cold."[40]

"Living" in the crucial formulation "a living transaction between humans" is an indirect reference to the John Keats poem "This living hand, now warm and capable," which Wallace took, Max recounts, as his standard for a text's ability to offer an embodied relationship to the reader, saying of drafts that failed this test, "there's no hand" (*Every Love Story*, 235). Wallace may see in Keats's gothic poem of the reader wishing her "own heart dry of blood" so that it might fill the writer's dead "hand" (punning on the appendage and handwriting) an aesthetic counter to Adam Smith's famous "invisible hand" of self-correcting capitalist markets.[41] Katherine Rowe makes that connection in calling nineteenth-century "dead hand" images expressions of "the uneasy ambiguity of agency [in] the relationship between individuals and the economy."[42] Certainly Wallace's living transactions often use tropes of gothicism and the abjection of blood to alienate readers from habituated acceptance of the money form and the limited types of agency and control that life in a neoliberal, market-obsessed society offers.

Always thrumming beneath Wallace's diction and imagery is the idea that human sense and perception are the only axiological standards, the only true means of valuation: hence attendees of a state fair may purchase much but are really engaged in "sensuous trade," "expending months of stored-up attention" at this communal event (*SFT* 109). We pay attention, as the metaphorical verb phrase inexorably goes—and Wallace, in *The Pale King* and elsewhere, attunes to the fact that "some of our most profound collective intuitions seem to be expressible only as figures of speech" (*CL* 63). Wallace also agrees with key claims made by the anthropologist of value David Graeber, who upends common understandings of money as a neutral medium by showing it to be grounded in moral relationships of debt, credit, and obligation, even claiming that erasing such origins was necessary to founding economics and "the very idea that there was something called 'the economy,' which operated by its own rules, separate from moral or political life."[43] A creative anthropologist of value himself, Wallace works toward the stripped-down foundations of exchange, playing with ancient economic myths and frequently underscoring the etymological origins of economics in the ancient Greek *oikos*, the household or hearth.

With his deep understanding of physical systems, Wallace also continually reduces human economies to the level of microscopic and molecular transactions, causing us to see at times an equivalence (at other times, a rivalry) between transfers of economic value and transfers of energy—often, body heat or images of fire in the household hearth. Transfers of energy possess a greater reliability for characters in spite of (or perhaps because of) the difficulty in quantifying the exchange and dealing with the inevitability of heat loss or entropy, that tax on every physical interaction. Wallace is a writer of systems novels and a major student of the form as practiced by Pynchon, DeLillo, and Gaddis.[44] Wallace's distinction from these postmodern predecessors, though, arises from the intimacy and moral urgency with which he approaches a systems-based understanding of human lives, for instance, in the aggression and masochistic mania with which his characters seek to hoard energy and operate as closed systems, from the broad satire of Norman Bombardini in *Broom* to the painful account, in *The Pale King*, of a contortionist boy who wishes "to be, in some childish way, self-contained and -sufficient" (*PK* 403). Bombardini is the first of many in his corpus who express an overarching anxiety about value in a capitalist society by making their bodies the site of an illusory primitive accumulation, imagery through which Wallace also contends with the legacy of the Protestant work ethic.

Wallace learned to take Max Weber's thesis and the history of Calvinism as subjects from Pynchon, his primary interlocutor on that fundamental means of creating value and resisting relentless consumerist forces of infantilization: work, a subject through which Wallace taps into major American cultural traditions in ways that have gone largely unnoted by critics (except Giles, who considers the traditions of the American Renaissance that Wallace occupies ["All Swallowed Up"]). Unlike Pynchon, however, Wallace does not wish to dump the legacy of Calvinism; he seeks to build fictions around work and the fervent call to work, an activity he recurrently sees not just in terms of the labor theory of value but, through the lens of Hegel, as the only way of creating a fully viable self. Whether through an executive washroom attendant, diligent cruise-ship workers, or an actuary who dies prematurely of a heart attack, Wallace consistently makes work heroic and tragic, its lack, avoidance, or meaninglessness a sign of his most lost and, in the realm of laborless capitalist value extraction, most evil figures. Absorption in work seems to be a reliable antidote to depression and feelings of worthlessness. Hegel's bondsman is a recurrent trope, as is metaphysical slavery in general. Work also marks yet another site at which Wallace can make types of value overlap: for instance, while describing *Girl with Curious Hair* as "a very traditionally moral book," Wallace says in 1993 that his "is a generation that has an inheritance of absolutely nothing as far as meaningful moral values, and it's our job to make them up, and we're not doing it" (*CW* 18). The phrasing exposes the insistence with which he turned to the rhetoric of work and slid punningly between the monetary and moral: if moral values are, like money, inherited, then so, too, may the morally impoverished of his 1980s generation, new versions of Horatio Alger, go get jobs "mak[ing] them up"—work that sounds, in metafictional terms, a lot like a career in fiction writing. Such descriptions undergird his metafictional and metaphilosophical narratives of workers in language and moral judgment, from the telephone operator Lenore Beadsman to the "moral warrior[s]" of the IRS (*PK* 548). Wallace ends his career valorizing accounting because its practical math keeps the monetary values of the balance book tethered to moral values—a job in which making up moral values could be an everyday occurrence.[45]

A key turn in the drama of this book arrives in chapter 5, which examines a time when, in the last decade or so of his career, Wallace loses some of his faith in a work ethic—his own, his readers', almost everyone's—and is led to important shifts in both style and outlook in his last two works of fiction. But across his career, we must ask about nearly every character: what job does he have, if any? How hard does he work, whether physically or mentally? What value has he earned or produced? What system of valuation accounts for his work? How does that system of value influence his moral decision making? And how is his job like art?

The denigration of work, the celebration of efficiency, and the worship of the market are all hallmarks of the ideology that has dominated the United States since the late 1970s, neoliberalism. Alissa G. Karl provides a compact definition: "Postulating that markets are organized most effectively by private enterprise and that the private pursuit of accumulation will generate the most common good, neoliberalism . . . pursues the opening of international markets and financial networks and the downsizing of the welfare state."[46] At his most political, Wallace chronicles the long-term infiltration of neoliberal ideology into the American and global scene. Reagan's union busting plays a role in my analysis of *Broom*, and the North American Free Trade Agreement (NAFTA) figures in *Infinite Jest*, which repeatedly makes ideas of freedom and trade, those neoliberal bywords, cross from political and economic spheres to the complexly interpersonal. The corporatization of health insurance becomes a significant subject in the post-2000 work (and my chapter 5). Once detected, such formations, sometimes global in orientation and often intertwined with intimate portraits of low self-worth, help challenge claims, like Adam Kirsch's, of Wallace's essential "provincialism."[47]

Wallace also constantly criticizes the assumptions of private contracts and contract language—the legal forms through which a neoliberal society claims to enforce reciprocity of value, including when civic institutions "contract out" services that were once an assumed part of a public mission of accountability. Contracts were once protections against "capitalist power" and "a metonym for the expanded version of the social contract associated with the welfare state," Andrew Hoberek argues. But, particularly within the early-2000s crisis of predatory loans, contracts are fictions; they are "putatively central to capitalism but in fact increasingly outmoded within its current incarnation."[48] Under siege in U.S. neoliberal policies are the achievements of Roosevelt's New Deal, from social-insurance programs to the financial regulatory apparatus strengthened in the wake of 1929. Wallace was a devoted fan of FDR, and he resurrects certain New Deal values in reaction to financial capital's excesses in the 1980s and 1990s. Wallace finally turns directly, in *The Pale King*, to the more proximate history of neoliberalism's reign, and there he reenvisions his early career through the lens of himself as, appropriately, a "low-value contract hire" (*PK* 415n4). Mark McGurl calls Wallace an "explicit apologist of the welfare state," based on an anonymous testimonial to state support of rehabilitation that has been persuasively attributed to the writer.[49] But subtle play with Rooseveltian liberal values marks much of the Wallace oeuvre, with important ongoing effects on narrative form and character construction.

Tying together many of Wallace's antineoliberal ideals about political economy is a concept of commonwealth, of which language, shared and unhoardable, is Wallace's ultimate example. In the preface to *Commonwealth*, the final work in their trilogy anatomizing neoliberalism, Michael Hardt and Antonio Negri, defining their title term, write that

so much of our world is common, open to access of all and developed through active participation. Language, for example, like affects and gestures, is for the most part common, and indeed if language were made either private or public—that is, if large portions of our words, phrases, or parts of speech were subject to private ownership or public authority—then language would lose its powers of expression, creativity, and communication.[50]

Wallace invents fictions in the domain that Hardt and Negri point toward —a dystopia of language and even affect and gesture that are somehow owned. Wallace weds to the perspective of Hardt and Negri a Wittgensteinian awareness that there can be no metaphor capacious enough to capture language's operations. But by insisting that the economy—a pervasive and ultracomplex network—serve as a central analogue for language, Wallace hopes to offer his reader a compelling view of both language *and* economy as unifying systems of human bonding.

Verbal exchanges constitute our true economy and the scene of our potential salvation; the hoped-for transformations are inward and conversational ones. Thus, however much we may hope for it, Wallace makes no sustained, realistic attempt to revolutionize value in a political sense. Throughout I deploy Marxist critics and basic Marxist concepts of use value and exchange value, but Wallace is ultimately (contra Shapiro and Godden and Szalay) no Marxist. There is little in his work that would help someone seeking to derive from his extensive attention to work (as he conceives it), commodity fetishism, and neoliberalism an active liberal politics, a model for solidarity, or even a consistent critique of reification. He is unlike Franzen, who began his career with an anatomy of Indian revolutionary Marxism (in *The Twenty-Seventh City*, a book Wallace admired [Max, *Every Love Story*, 115]). Wallace also lacks excitement over Pynchonian Counterforces, and in his books the global perspective on revolutionary struggles in DeLillo is absent or exists only in Quebecois caricature. Konstantinou's tempered view is right: Wallace lacks "interest in remaking society along any particular institutional lines," preferring an "idea of politics—to the degree that he articulates one—[that] rests within a tradition of symbolic action."[51]

With so many characters who cannot find alternatives to market-based value, Wallace's work does agree on nearly every page with the spirit of Fredric Jameson's benchmark 1984 claim that the totalizing force of "multinational capital ends up penetrating and colonizing those very precapitalist enclaves, Nature and the Unconscious," that once held hope for critique.[52] Yet Wallace does not follow this path of resignation to the foreclosure of "imaginable alternatives" that Alison Shonkwiler and Leigh Claire La Berge find uniting contemporary forms of "capitalist realism."[53] Wallace, unrealistic in multiple senses, instead so invests in the possibility of gifts and images of economic trade as linguistic exchange, as "living transaction," that questions of political change tend to be overwritten by ecstatic, at times utopian community, the marketplace leading not to reflection on commodities or workers but to the fleeting possibility of seeing the "sacred, on fire with the same force that lit the stars—compassion, love, the subsurface unity of all things" (and, more importantly, all people) (*TW* 93).

THE ONGOING FICTIONAL SPEECH

"I really like recursions," Wallace confesses, along with "contradictions and paradoxes and statements that kind of negate themselves in the middle" (*LI* 107). It would be foolish to use such structures as a large-scale template for a critical work—taking a later book, say, as the negation of an earlier part of the ongoing fictional speech—for as Wallace's persona in *The Pale King* says, "I find these sorts of cute, self-referential paradoxes irksome, too" (*PK* 69). Nonetheless, Wallace's works frequently refract and rework his previous output, justifying not only a single-author study of him but the looks both forward and backward that my chapters sometimes take—all while still working chronologically through the corpus. His works, especially in the later career, appear to have accreted like those of Joyce, a writer he studied closely (Max, *Every Love Story*, 316n18): Wallace's texts almost always had porous borders, the preoccupations, motifs, and (in the last three books) even plots of one bleeding into those of another. By structuring his final novel around May 1985, about the time he must have finished a draft of his first, he also sought to return to origins and rewrite his professional writing career (characteristically) from the ground up.

Chapters 1 and 2 situate *The Broom of the System* and the early short stories in the context of Reagan-era economics and the history through which it was mediated, including a mythologized Calvinism, the Great Depression, and the New Deal. *Broom* offers a covert dialogue with Reagan's consolidation of the neoliberal agenda around a revived version of the Protestant call to work in the 1980s, driven (on the surface) by fears of the effects of a service economy. I unpack this novel's preoccupation with work, other (less reliable) forms of creating and accruing value, and connected issues of language use: my foci include the leisure-based national literature represented by Rick Vigorous, the ersatz topoi of Protestantism and self-reliance embodied by a politician and a minister, and the countering force of Lenore Beadsman, whose depiction fuses an allegory of language philosophy with an economic critique. In chapter 2, in the short stories of *Girl with Curious Hair* and the uncollected "Crash of '69," Wallace becomes a creative historian of Black Tuesday, the Dust Bowl, and the New Deal policies that form the overlooked backbone of his interest in civics. What if, I ask, instead of locating Wallace's primary history in the art and media transformations of the 1960s he so often maligned, we look instead for his origins in the crash of 1929, a less predictable moment of cultural crisis in which he saw another means of developing his critique of irony?

In chapter 3, I read *Infinite Jest* as both an unforgiving diagnosis of unbalanced human beings and an encyclopedia of transactions, money, and methods of valuation, documenting its subtle engagements with the economically topical (NAFTA and neoliberalism) and the culturally embedded (ongoing perversions of the Protestant work ethic). Wallace leads us to see viewers of the title Entertainment—and their more thoroughly examined analogues, drug and alcohol addicts—as economic agents seeking a return of value that has been utterly compromised, resulting in conditions of slavery. With these terms in place, I revisit AA scenes that have driven interpretations focused on sincerity and irony and show these moments' structuring term actually to be value. Often noted for his generative exceptionality in Wallace's cast of characters, Don Gately comes to his distinctiveness through a relationship to work and the rewritten coinage in which he receives "payment." In the chapter's conclusion, I uncover an abiding Wallace claim, explored most fully in his masterpiece: that language, despite attempts to treat it as money, is the ultimate example of commonwealth, the Massachusetts place name with which *Infinite Jest* plays throughout.

Chapters 4 and 5 show Wallace seeking the inner histories of the crises brought on by neoliberal definitions of value at the turn of the millennium, from the role of the 1997–1998 Asian currency crisis in *Brief Interviews with Hideous Men* to the hidden critique of the U.S. insurance and health-care industries in *Oblivion*. Interweaving a genealogy of Wallace's probability-driven formal experimentation with a history of stochastic math's importance to modern finance, I describe in chapter 4 the dialectic of computerized complexity and balance-scale simplicity that underlies the moral vision of *Brief Interviews*. In chapter 5, in addition to finding new dimensions in his representation of numismatics, I connect Wallace's newfound skepticism about work to his increasingly intricate readings of social institutions within a neoliberal universe: I extend chapter 2's reading of the New Deal into the twenty-first century by revealing Wallace's critiques of financialized insurance in multiple stories. This chapter concludes by interpreting the workless workplace of "The Suffering Channel."

Where *Infinite Jest* explored the calculating minds of addicts and consumers, Wallace turned to taxation in *The Pale King* for its innumerable arcane terms of public valuation and reconciling, which facilitated his newly aggressive social analysis. *Oblivion*'s wariness of the saving power of work receives new accents in this novel's examination of manipulated and Sisyphean ascetics, and, in chapter 6, by elaborating anew my central terms of work, value, and political rhetoric, I add nuance to readings that have already characterized this final novel as a history of the rise of neoliberalism. This chapter addresses, first, the reenergized role of ritual, a trope adapted from DeLillo, as Wallace depicts priestly accountants at sacred work; second, central forms of value in a neoliberal society, including contracts and a grotesquely rewritten currency; and, third, a final rendition of axiology in human attention's valuing of details, explored through competing models of relevance and what the text calls "the exact size and shape of every blade of grass" in a lawn—one last image of the new ground Wallace's fiction can form (*PK* 261).

My focus throughout is on Wallace's fiction, with supporting roles played by his formidable body of essays and literary journalism. As Giles and Josh Roiland demonstrate,[54] Wallace's nonfiction calls out for literary interpretation as readily as his fiction does, and cruise-ship workers, state-fair rituals, and film analyses are all put in dialogue here with the six major works of fiction. In the book's conclusion, which leans heavily on "Authority and American Usage," I read the grocery-store scene of *This Is Water* as a fiction all its own, with symbolic roles played by the food, the wait, and the expected transaction at the cash register, a modern version of the balance scale and a prod to consider the task to which Wallace calls readers: the clear calculation of (moral) value. Wallace calls nonfiction "harder" than fiction; while the latter was "scarier," the former partakes of a "felt reality" that today is "overwhelmingly, circuit-blowingly huge and complex," as he writes in "Deciderization" (*BF* 302). I examine this essay in depth in chapter 5 to explain the alignment between Wallace's dense late style and the selection of valuable details out of that overwhelming reality. The social diagnostician, the literary critic, the historian of math, the documenter of capitalist pleasures' raw deals—my recurrent suggestion is that the many writerly identities on display in the nonfiction can be tied to an ongoing search for value in myriad forms. Thus, while no single chapter focuses on it, Wallace's nonfiction is a ubiquitous presence here.

Also active in this single-author book are some of the many fiction writers Wallace has influenced and challenged. Jonathan Lethem (in chapter 3), Zadie Smith, Teddy Wayne, Tom McCarthy (all in chapter 4), and Dave Eggers (in chapter 6) appear as interlocutors, appropriately after *Infinite Jest* made Wallace central to conversations about the direction of contemporary fiction. These comparisons allow me to nuance critics' accounts of Wallace's unexpected impact on realism (Hoberek), his inspiring of "examination[s] of freedom" (Burn), and his creation of renewed interest in "the dialogical dimension of the reading experience" (Kelly).[55]

As critics sort out his proliferating legacy, Wallace's suicide has made for more personalized tributes and roman à clefs than studies of influence usually account for. For instance, Franzen's *Freedom* (2010) features Richard

Katz, whose preference for working in dark rooms and tobacco chewing (as well as his womanizing) have been linked to Wallace.[56] Jeffrey Eugenides, in *The Marriage Plot* (2011), creates Leonard Bankhead, a science graduate student who wears a do-rag and suffers from depression.[57] Jennifer Egan's *A Visit from the Goon Squad* (2010) has a chapter written by a footnote-happy New Journalist whose hysterical, quantum physics–inspired meditations on celebrities seem indebted to Wallace's essays. Another key Wallace disciple, George Saunders, both extends his themes and is filling a cultural space—Mildly Zany, Fundamentally Decent, Earnest Writer?—left vacated by him: Saunders's 2013 Syracuse commencement address, published as *Congratulations, by the Way*, clearly echoes *This Is Water*. Meanwhile, the younger novelists Benjamin Kunkel and Chad Harbach, both editors of the groundbreaking journal *n + 1*, have given us some of the most compelling responses to *Infinite Jest*'s intellectual heft: written before Wallace's suicide, Kunkel's *Indecision* (2005), a story of the will on drugs, is narrated by a DW, Dwight Wilmerding, who thinks in great gales of Heideggerian thought and provides one of the best examples of the "hysterical realism" James Wood claims Wallace helped bequeath to fiction.[58] Harbach uses a college setting to allow Martial's epigrams and Zeno's paradox to filter into his sports novel *The Art of Fielding* (2011), and the climactic scene of exhuming a dead father's casket for reburial attempts subliminally to complete the scene, left to ellipsis, of Hal, Gately, and John Wayne digging up Himself.[59]

In this pivotal moment in the consolidation of Wallace's legacy, though, critics must balance considerations of tribute (sometimes superficial) and deeper responses that point to how Wallace's ideas are likely to survive and flourish. For most of the Wallace followers I treat in detail here, whether they work before or after his passing, extending Wallace's legacy entails recognizing the usefulness of his economic displacements and in some way responding to his understanding of value. Many of these readings begin from noticing a hidden homage to Wallace before describing the new direction the successor takes, whether in Wayne's application of stochastic art to a reading of finance and 9/11 or Smith's attention to gender in gift-based aesthetics. There will be many critical dimensions to Wallace's enduring importance, but his best "readers" are those writers who see past the books' size and surface rhetoric to his quieter reexamination of value.

In nearly every reading of this study, I identify in Wallace's work cultural teachings on what to value and how to value the self. At different times these teachings on the power of prestige take shape in sports; parental approval; the aesthetic standard of a minimalist, proficient realism; artistic success; or media culture's attractive vision of a self-centered existence. The domains of valued achievement also include success with the abstract finance of the stock market, winning streaks defined by a culture Wallace often sees as a game show—any area where point scoring or marks on paper eclipse the direct apprehension of a body and mind. In mischievously exploring these cultural expectations and often counseling detachment from their rigid definitions of individuated personal substance, Wallace opens up spaces that his reader can dwell in, learning what other forms of valuing (and thus of loving) there are. This book argues that Wallace's work is best understood as an intellectually rigorous prayer for awakening to felt value, a phenomenon that has to be protected from abstraction and mathematicization. Reading him with both the mind and the body, we can let Wallace lead us back from abstraction, bank accounts, and point scoring and toward a culture-wide redemption of value.

1

COME TO WORK

CAPITALIST FANTASIES AND THE QUEST FOR BALANCE IN *THE BROOM OF THE SYSTEM*

So here I am at like twenty-one and I don't know what to do. Do I go into math logic, which I'm good at and pretty much guaranteed an approved career in? Or do I try to keep on with this writing thing, this *artiste* thing? The idea of being a "writer" repelled me, mostly because of all the foppish aesthetes I knew at school who went around in berets stroking their chins calling themselves writers. I have a terror of seeming like those guys, still. Even today, when people I don't know ask me what I do for a living, I usually tell them I'm "in English" or I "work free-lance." I don't seem to be able to call myself a writer.
—DAVID FOSTER WALLACE (WITH LARRY MCCAFFERY),
"AN EXPANDED INTERVIEW WITH DAVID FOSTER WALLACE"

Philosophical problems arise when language goes on holiday.
—WITTGENSTEIN, *PHILOSOPHICAL INVESTIGATIONS*

A S HE became a writer at Amherst and Arizona, Wallace thought deeply about work—the work of writers and readers, the work of the artist as a job or vocation, the kinds of "living" American economics granted approval or deemed pretentious. In my first epigraph, rarely quoted lines from a much-quoted interview, Wallace suggests: *I might have been something else*, and that thought of career paths not taken will hover over his many future depictions of work environments. In the Weberian and Protestant terms his thinking hearkens back to, Wallace was a young person worried about his "calling"; in less auspicious terms, he may have been explaining to himself the working-class signifiers of his dress—bandana, "untied work boots"—when his experience of labor, particularly any menial sort, was largely a theoretical issue.[1] Whatever the origin of the values in these comments (Midwestern? Emersonian? an Oedipal impulse to step into his philosopher-father's territory, even while seeking to be "approved"?), they show a young author meditating on class image, aesthetic value, and writing as a job, as value-earning pursuit. In one sense, Wallace was unsure about whether "artist" could be a job at all: a young woman "wanted to write made-up stories for a living" in his first published story. "I didn't know that could be done," the narrator replies.[2] On a deeper level, though, Wallace seems determined in his fiction to mirror Wittgenstein's claim (in my second epigraph) that language "works" by being examined in context, not abstractly, not on "holiday." Yet Wallace is also keen to build from ideas of the writer at work a cultural critique more urgent and morally effective than an allegory of language could be.

While *The Pale King* undoubtedly surprised many by depicting workers examining endless tax returns, Wallace took interest from the very beginning in work, especially the mental kind, and the way difficulty and tediousness were defined against easy consumerist pleasures. Elsewhere in the McCaffery interview, Wallace describes his reader also in terms of work—a fellow laborer, co-creating with him. At issue is an act of painful balance and ratiocination. Wallace claims that TV and popular film are

> lucrative precisely because [they] recognize[] that audiences prefer 100 percent pleasure to the reality that tends to be 49 percent pleasure and 51 percent pain. Whereas "serious" art, which is not primarily about getting money out of you, is more apt to make you uncomfortable, or to force you to work hard to access its pleasures, the same way that in real life true pleasure is usually a by-product of hard work and discomfort.
>
> (CW 22)

These would be commonplace late-twentieth-century ideas about the aesthetic and commercial—essentially reasserting Clement Greenberg's infamous division of avant-garde from kitsch—but for the intricate mechanism of balance Wallace places at their center. The adult world he frequently invoked was a realm of tradeoffs asking people to calibrate personal balance scales; fiction could be good training for that, as suggested by this image of reality's delicate 51/49 ratio. Challenging the reader made Wallace calibrate a scale of his own: "There has to be an accessible payoff for the reader if I don't want [her] to throw the book at the wall" (*CW* 33). Whereas mass media promise a ludicrous contract to a passive audience, Wallace's fiction offers the reader-as-worker a different system of value and return. The underlying image, though, remains one of a fair economic deal: the "avant-garde pitfall," for advanced versions of the foppish aesthetes, was to "forget about making yourself accessible" (*LI* 10).

In the implicitly feckless, beret-wearing "*artiste*" and the hard-working reader dedicated to communication, Wallace also happens to describe the two central figures of *The Broom of the System*, the bad writer and the woman he wants not just to love but own, even consume: Rick Vigorous and Lenore Beadsman. Following these two and several others on their postcollege trajectories in a near-future world, *Broom* is a multithread bildungsroman that contemplates Wallace's postcollege career possibilities and, more broadly, prophesies what may become of American work and value in the late 1980s and beyond—all while also suggesting which modes of language use correspond to the philosophy of hard work and which to modes of capitalist domination.

In this chapter I read *Broom* as a thorough interrogation of work, its frequent lack in a grotesque U.S. capitalism, and elements of work's "payoff," value and value creation, that will structure Wallace's approach to American culture over the next twenty-plus years. Possessing a protagonist slyly named for a unit of work, *Broom* is itself named after an instrument of humble, domestic labor and a term from physics naming a domain, the system, the only way to raise the energy value of which is work. Another suggestion of the title is that an older, more primitive tool (the broom) exists within those technologies and schemas (the system) to which humans have largely ceded labor and production. A broom also appears in Lenore's great-grandmother's illustration of a Wittgensteinian claim about linguistic meaning being equivalent to an object's function (or, in the terms I have established, the work it does [*B* 149–150]), and Wallace revealed that the full title—not referred to directly in the novel—comes from his mother's name for roughage, that food that cleans out one's system by aiding waste removal (*CW* 12; see also Concarnadine's repeated "roughage" [*B* 362–371]). These basic definitions of work and action—grounded in the body's cycles of sustenance, in science, in pragmatist views of meaning, and on the floor—guide my consideration of Lenore's battle with a capitalism run amok in a novel centered on commodified baby food, symbol of the fateful overwriting of use value by exchange value and humans' earliest indoctrination into consumerist satisfaction. *Broom*'s fundamental questions are how humans create value, confer it on themselves and others (often via fetishization), and consume it and convert it into energy. Wallace pursues these themes through Lenore, who—a model of work, linguistic clarity, and balance, as well as someone who has chosen a low-wage job in communication—strives to return language from the holiday of philosophical obscurity on which Wittgenstein says it can go. As a character who worries her "actions and volitions are not under her control," who feels "as if she had no real existence" (*B* 66), she also provides Wallace's first model of the quest for ontology and weight, where the refrain "I EXIST" becomes intertwined with an implied ending: ". . . BECAUSE I WORK."

Wallace recognizes in work and the resistance to it a political problem wider than Amherst social types or the writer-reader relationship within an entertainment-driven culture. Published in the spring of 1987, *Broom* arrived at a moment of great anxiety over transformations in the U.S. economy and the fate of the vaunted American work ethic. Fears over competition for global economic dominance often clustered around both factory automation and the stereotypical image of superior and selfless Japanese workers, who appeared to be outstripping American laborers, in an era said to mark the end of U.S. manufacturing. Over the past ten years, the *New York Times* read in May 1987, the "service economy has fallen from grace as Americans have come to equate it with the decline of manufacturing, lower wages . . . a shrinking middle class, and low-skill, low-tech economic activity like hamburger flipping."[3] Wallace, the prizewinning student of economics at Amherst (though not, like Andy Lang, a major), incorporates analysis of this field alongside all of *Broom*'s allusions to his philosophy studies.[4] *Broom* depicts a United States where industry has met a limit (such that a company named "Industrial Desert Design" creates desert landscapes feeding a perverse tourism [*B* 54]). Characters refashion the human appetites that drive a service economy rather than admit to limits on consumption-based profit—hence the novel's interest in the biotechnology of food and an entrepreneur in that field who seeks to fill a personal void by eating everything in sight. This novel builds from shifts in American work and production a vision of a social order that, placing all its faith in consumption, does not produce much of value any more. *Broom* thus offers a bracingly Rabelaisian account of a postmodern capitalism that, enduring a crisis of accumulation in the 1970s, sought the flexible modes of a financialized economy that reshaped space and time, according to David Harvey.[5]

But Wallace also attends to forces that compensated for the anxiety over these trends in value: the mythologization of American work and the Protestant work ethic that Reagan offered the populace, even as, in realistic terms, he was promoting illusions of "welfare queens" and solidifying a neoliberal assault on worker protections and trade unions. By compensatory mythologization I mean passages such as the following, from Reagan's first inaugural, with its quasi-biblical overtones of workers "cast" out into "misery."

> Idle industries have cast workers into unemployment, causing human misery and personal indignity. Those who do work are denied a fair return for their labor by a tax system which penalizes successful achievement and keeps us from maintaining full productivity. . . . Putting America back to work means putting all Americans back to work. . . . All must share in the productive work of this "new beginning" and all must share in the bounty of a revived economy.[6]

Years before Johnny Gentle is born, *Broom*, partly in the voice of Reverend Sykes, satirizes aspects of Reagan's rhetoric. Knowing, though, from Max's revelations, that Wallace voted for Reagan twice and (in 1992) supported Ross Perot, we should view the Wallace of this period as a writer with a complicated relationship to such conservative traditions and to the broader issue of presidential speech.[7] Working out a response to neoliberalism in the years it was first solidifying, Wallace seems to have invested, at bottom, in the possibility of meaningful language arising from politicians and American traditions. *Broom*'s parodies are his awkward, youthful attempt to liberate an authentic moral force from overwrought political rhetoric and implicitly argue for a tempered acceptance of the enduring power of cultural formations like the Protestant work ethic. Such are the seeds of his forceful turn toward the political thirteen years later in "Up, Simba," about another Republican for whom he has a complicated respect, John McCain.

Wallace's career emerges during a period when Jameson is defining postmodernity in (post-)Marxist terms as, in part, the "'effacement of the traces of production' from the object itself," in favor of reification and consumers' ability "not to remember the work" embodied in their many purchases.[8] Wallace, though, portrays work under a different kind of erasure in *Broom*, where many of the key references are not to Marx but to the source for his definitions of labor and human development, Hegel, whose *Phenomenology of Spirit* is travestied in a central scene by the allegorically one-legged and ungrounded LaVache Beadsman. As we will see, his college exchanges of tutoring for drugs lie in lived contradiction of the Hegelian ideas about work he purports to explicate. To McCaffery, six years after publication, Wallace said of *Broom*'s experimentation that, "sufficiently hidden under the sex-change and . . . allusions, I got to write my sensitive little self-obsessed bildungsroman" (*CW* 41). *Broom* is indeed, as Patrick O'Donnell puts it, "an irresolute bildungsroman."[9] But Wallace does not so much produce an instance of the bildungsroman as record the subversion of those guiding assumptions about culture and personal cultivation that had made the form central in the era of and after Hegel. Wallace goes back to the form's philosophical roots and points to what shackles such a category in the mediated, abstracting moment in which he writes.

"Lenore, come to work, where I am," Rick says in what passes for an invocation of his muse as the 1990 plot begins (*B* 32). But while Rick's overture may come from upstairs in the Bombardini Building, Rick is not truly at work at all. In a book with countless misdirected communications and the suspect calls of Reagan, Rick, and a drugged cockatiel ("Go forth and do the work directed," Mrs. Tissaw thinks she hears God say through the quasi-Pentecostal Vlad the Impaler [*B* 174]), Wallace seeks to show us via parody something positive, a viable 1980s version of what Weber famously identified in Protestant theology:

> The exhortation of the apostle to "make one's own calling sure" was inter-preted as a duty to strive for the subjective certainty of one's election and justification in daily struggle. Instead of humble sinners, to whom Luther promised grace if they entrusted themselves to God in penitent faith, those self-assured "saints" were bred who were embodied in the steely Puritan merchants of that heroic age of capitalism and are occasionally found right up to the present day. And, on the other hand, *tireless labor in a calling* was urged as the best possible means of *attaining* this self-assurance. This and this alone would drive away religious doubt and give assurance of one's state of grace.[10]

Pynchon had taken from this and other parts of Weber a cynical reading of the United States' Puritan legacy that focused on the unearned election of those "self-assured 'saints'" who, taking material success for divine ap-proval, built over centuries a secular infrastructure predicated on damn-ing the preterite, the "'second Sheep.'"[11] Wallace had consumed *Gravity's Rainbow* over eight days in 1983 (Max, *Every Love Story*, 34) and, as McHale demonstrates, echoed it in his sentences and plots for the next twenty-five years.[12] But, still feeling his way toward a systematic critique of postmod-ernism in *Broom*, Wallace wants to preserve the grounding value of Ameri-can work within his literary world. This is a story I continue unfolding in subsequent chapters (especially chapter 3) assessing the fates of Wallace's workers and their relationship to value.

In the following sections I lay out the prevailing ideology and ethos of consumer capitalism in *Broom* before discussing Rick's feeble resistance to such forces and Lenore's protracted struggle against a workless social order. Lenore is led on a quest to restore balance and justice that grows particularly vivid in contrast to the wasteful work of her brother LaVache, a text-driven philosopher of the sort Wallace eschews. Lenore's varied career leads into my climactic consideration of various other attempts to accrue value, including a final contrast between the profane religious solicitations of Sykes and Lenore's answering image of a miraculous lottery win that Wallace identifies with the communicative power of the novel itself—and with the choice to gamble on the contingencies of art over the "approved" paths to economic value he foresaw in academia and other pursuits. For many narratives to come Wallace will be returning to the lottery and similar images of the chance that necessarily characterizes true choice and communication.

GREENHOUSE EFFECTS

Broom portrays capitalists in a phase of mania in which, reaching a crisis in the accumulation of money and goods, they deny entropic forces and desperately hoard heat energy and calories, those building blocks of organic order, in systems so small they include the human body. Bombardini's "Project Total Yang" (or "Tiny Yin"), his effort to "grow to infinite size," is the clearest example of this paradoxical accumulation by consumption, dependent on (in addition to cannibalism) ignoring the limits of the body as storage space and the inevitable processing of waste—all while erasing yin-yang balance (*B* 91). Growth and cultivation in *Broom* are, as they will be in *Infinite Jest*, matters of complete impatience with gradualism. Stonecipheco owns a nursing home that (in a nod to the "hothouse" images of Pynchon's *V.*)[13] offers a "greenhouse heat" in which residents "languish[]" (it is also run by a Bloemker—a false bloom? [*B* 29]). The company's language drug is called an "Infant Accelerant" (*B* 153); rather than promote growth it feeds a flame destructive to the children themselves, and the drug's use of "cattle-endocrine derivative" (*B* 149) suggests, via the etymological links between *cattle* and *capital*, the making of humans themselves into pliable capital.[14] Excess heat and light are everywhere the sign of capitalism and its concentrations of wealth: Bloemker, agent of Stonecipheco, "level[s]" at Lenore (like a gun) an evil eye that "glow[s] gold" with refracted sunlight

(*B* 35). Clarice, the one Beadsman child to do the expected and take the family money, converts it into ownership of a line of tanning salons, one of which, in a running gag, badly burns the appropriately named Misty Schwartz (*B* 268). Lenore, since her name means "light" or "bright," cannot help but take such forces personally. Her great-grandmother—in a foreshadowing of her apparent attempt to control the drug, despite her Wittgensteinian authority about language—is unable to allow for an entropic balance of molecules inside and outside her: she requires rooms be kept at 98.6 F. All these monetary and personal enterprises recapitulate the logic of capitalism reaching a dead end in the Great Ohio Desert, the space toward which the younger Lenore is railroaded by a culture that is in effect trying to burn her.

With the G.O.D., Wallace has Reagan's rhetoric in mind, building on the desert setting of DeLillo's *End Zone* and perhaps the absurdist president stories of Donald Barthelme (a major inspiration to the early Wallace [*CW* 62]). In a perverse, tone-setting call to work, we read a transcript of Ohio's Governor Raymond Zusatz's order to create the desert on June 21, 1972, a date chosen to evoke Watergate (the untranscribed eighteen and a half minutes of conversation between Nixon and H. R. Haldeman occurred on June 20, 1972) (*B* 53). But the more important reference is to another American governor of 1972, in a state with real desert. Reagan invoked the founding Puritans in many campaign and presidential speeches, especially the image of the "City Upon a Hill" from John Winthrop's 1630 sermon "A Model of Christian Charity," given onboard the *Arbella* en route to Plymouth.[15] Concluding his 1989 farewell address, Reagan schmaltzily depicted the colonizing Winthrop sailing "on what today we'd call a little wooden boat; and like the other Pilgrims, he was looking for a home that would be free."[16] In *White Noise*, writing of a "College-on-the-hill" (note the deflating effect of the definite article), DeLillo skewered Reagan in the black-robed Jack Gladney's vision of a religious "assembly" of station wagons laden with consumer goods.[17] Wallace funnels such representations of American mythology toward the issue of work. Thus Zusatz, in spite of continuing prosperity, distills the grave misunderstanding of labor throughout *Broom*, saying, "Too much development. People are getting complacent. They're forgetting the way this state was historically hewn out of the wilderness" (*B* 53), an obvious reference to the Puritans' 1630 errand into the wilderness. "There's no more hewing," Zusatz concludes (*B* 53)—hence the need to create "a wasteland," to "remind us what we hewed out of" (*B* 54).

In this mythological Ohio, Wallace begins with the residents' departure from the Shaker Heights Nursing Home to suggest the potential for return to the culture of work, artisanship, and spiritual wholeness that the Protestant Shakers embody (Shakers are also known for cleanliness, another virtue turned into distorting obsession in *Broom*).[18] Rather than the Shakers' prayerful relationship to God, the community has a relationship to a hellscape called G.O.D. Language itself has absconded with these virtues: Lenore Sr. plus "twenty-five other people" missing from the Home makes an alphabetical twenty-six (*B* 99). But as with almost everything in *Broom*'s atmosphere of linguistic attenuation, the Shaker Heights name is merely superficial, the Protestant work ethic it calls up a joke: the real Shaker Heights has that name because the town was laid out in 1912 on land formerly owned by a local Shaker church congregation.

Wallace recasts part of that land history in his invented locale of East Corinth, another Cleveland suburb, built in the 1960s by Lenore's grandfather, Stonecipher II, who has made a mockery of the social body of the community by laying out the town in the shape of Jayne Mansfield. Wallace sets up here a joking Wittgensteinian allegory of language awareness in which many "crawled and drove and walked over the form of Jayne Mansfield, shaking their fists" at lascivious airline pilots flying low and blinking their lights (*B* 46). As Wallace summarizes a claim in the *Philosophical Investigations* (advice the looming Bombardini and the roof-jumping Vance Vigorous would do well to follow), "the fundamental problem of language is, quote, 'I don't know my way about.' If I were separate from language, if I could somehow detach from it and climb up and look down on it, get the lay of the land so to speak, I could study it 'objectively,' . . . know its operations and boundaries" (*CW* 45). Given all the ways *Broom* shows the sublimation of work into pleasure seeking by men who control women, it is telling that the layout renders Mansfield's breasts (a giant bust, in multiple senses?) as "a huge swollen development of factories and industrial parks"—a perverse image, in the context of a baby-food conspiracy, of both work and human sustenance gone wrong (*B* 45).

There is no actual East Corinth, Ohio (a Corinth, Ohio, does exist, but it is more than sixty miles east of Cleveland, nowhere near Shaker Heights). In inventing this locale for his moral project Wallace invokes another spiritual reference point, the ancient Corinthians to whom Paul's epistles were addressed, including lines that will remain important to Wallace up through Chris Fogle: in the well-known King James Version, "When I was a child, I spake as a child, I understood as a child, I thought as a child: but when I became a man, I put away childish things. For now we see through a glass, darkly; but then face to face" (1 Cor. 13:11–12). *Broom* travesties Paul's wisdom when Vlad, the bird that speaks words without knowing their meaning, is seen talking while "staring dumbly at himself in his cloudy mirror" (a glass, darkly) and embodying the narcissism that rules this fictional world (*B* 97).

In the context established by the G.O.D. and extremes of heat, East Corinth, Ohio, is also another coded place name, a pun from which environmental and economic studies of Wallace ought to begin, as well as a sign of Wallace's attempt to reconcile his seemingly disparate areas of undergraduate focus. E.C. connotes "Ec," a common abbreviation for economics in school settings, while E.C.O. signifies eco-, the common root of economics and ecology and derived from the ancient Greek *oikos*, or household, home and hearth. Economy and ecology are clearly under siege in this novel, and through the otherwise entirely superfluous subplot involving Stonecipheco's testing of the infant language drug and use of a pesticide on the Greek island of Corfu, Wallace suggests many parallels: East *Cor*inth and *Cor*fu, both Greek names, are sites at which the ancient etymological origins of economic value and ecological care have been forgotten. As with the axiological, Heidegger's calls back to the foundational questions of the ancient Greeks may be offering Wallace a cue: as Caputo summarizes, the "revolution the young Heidegger wanted to start" was "to think the *ousia* of [Aristotle's] *Metaphysics* back down into factical life, into *ousia* taken as *oikos*, everyday household life, house and hearth."[19] There is a reason Lenore now lives in a building (formerly Misty's home too) with "inoperative fireplaces" (*B* 94). Depicting brooms that underlie systems, households undone (the Langs', the Vigorouses', and, most horrifically, the Beadsmans'), and the abandonment of the hearth's steady, localized glow for a capitalism of rapacious burning, this novel suggests an economic atavism is called for in postmodernity. Instead, though, signification itself is given over to insidious capitalist forms of value production and alleged guarantee.

LANGUAGE UNDER CONTRACT

Rick embodies the novel's central perversions of work and pleasure into consumptive, often misogynistic fantasies. There is little truly vigorous about this Vigorous, whose name echoes Zusatz's ludicrous, empty hewing. Rick's firm's name, Frequent and Vigorous, is a low joke about his sex life (neither frequent nor vigorous) but also a sign of the mockery Americans have made of any storied work ethic: *The Frequent Review*, supposedly a quarterly, never seems actually to publish or even to receive any outside submissions. Rick, presumably the self-obsessed creator of the stories he tells Lenore, emblematizes the dissoluteness of a leisure economy and the inability of American writers to do more than reflect the narcissistic tendencies of their consumerist environment (an idea that will structure Wallace's manifestos to come, "Fictional Futures and the Conspicuously Young" and "E Unibus Pluram"). Monroe Frequent, whom Rick suspects has bankrolled the magazine, made his fortune by inventing the leisure suit (like the beret, a one-time accouterment of cool, but now ridiculous) and is "a corporate entity interested in [the journal's] failure for tax purposes," foreshadowing the "passive-loss" tax-avoidance schemes of *The Pale King* (*B* 57; *PK* 13). The point seems clear: a literature that does the bidding of a leisure and consumerist economy will be reduced merely to embodying its principles. Rick, who makes money by writing ad copy about their pesticide, later comes under contract to Stonecipheco in the direct manipulation of Lenore, a first instance of the trope of contractualized language that I return to in subsequent chapters.

An interest in contracts, vehicles of an alleged balance, grows naturally from Wallace's instinctual focus on capitalism's distortive and privational forms of value and reciprocity. An objective illustration of Lenore's "loss of individual efficacy of will," the contract trope is also gendered: in *Broom*, juxtaposed with commodified females are the men who exert control through contracts (*B* 65). The father of the gymnast Kopek Spasova, only eight, has signed for her a "mammoth promotional and endorsement contract" with Gerber's (*B* 127). Reflecting him, Stonecipher controls his daughter by signing Rick to a contract that entails "withholding of information" from her (*B* 168). The young Wallace's vilification of family/corporate contracts and their oppression of women in particular can also be heavy-handed, as when Stonecipher makes his imprisoned wife, Patrice, play endless rounds of contract bridge, a pointed conjunction of misogynist manipulation, games, and contracts (*B* 264–266).

"For language even to be possible," Wallace remarks in admiration of Wittgenstein's transformed conclusions in the *Philosophical Investigations*, "it must always be a function of relationships between persons," "dependent on human community" (*CW* 44). But with all its contract tropes *Broom* seems to be working from Wittgenstein's more specific claim about agreement in a dialogical moment in the *Investigations*: "'So you are saying that human agreement decides what is true and what is false?'—It is what human beings *say* that is true and false; and they agree in the *language* they use. That is not agreement in opinions but in form of life."[20] Contract writers in *Broom*, much like masters of games and their rules throughout Wallace's corpus, symbolize the recurrent effort, capitalism inspired and otherwise, to override language's foundational agreement, its "form of life," with second-order rules—and thus claim a control over language's operation. Wallace's thinking was almost always about immanence—whether he was examining late-capitalist attempts at total pleasure environments (cruise ships, virtual reality) or telling the joke about fish and water.[21] Language is the fundamental immanence—"not a tool but an environment," as Wallace puts it elsewhere (*SFT* 140)—and as a consequence, as Wittgenstein showed, language is unexplainable through any metalanguage. Humans may disagree about particular meanings, but they "agree in the language they use"—they have always already signed on to the biggest contract of all, but one that can never be pointed to. In this philosophical context there is more than sophomoric humor in Lenore's opening refusal to sign her name on the dotted line of Lang and Biff's posteriors and subordinate herself to male bodies (*B* 18).

Corresponding with masculinist contract writing is the treatment of language itself as a consumable, a commodity, or a currency one can hoard. Wallace pointedly makes the major capitalist figures in the novel, Stonecipher and Bombardini, the speakers of the longest monologues, anticipating the Hideous Men but identifying hideousness with capitalist relationships to value accumulation. Sykes, who makes his money in the one-way discourse of TV, is another important monologist, as is Rick, teller of multipage stories with few breaks for Lenore's responses. Bombardini suggests language is powered by food or is food itself, in a travesty of biblical wisdom about not living on bread alone: "What a delicious series of thoughts," he says, announcing his eat-everything plan (*B* 82). Page to page in this dialogue- and phone-call-laden book, the long speeches substantiate the common drive somehow to *own* language or, paradoxically, consume it, even as it necessarily exits one's mouth.

"SEE, SHE WEIGHS ABOUT ONE POUND"

Lenore is the figure who mightily resists the novel's prevailing destinies of work, value, justice, and language use. Possessing shades of the impossibly pure heroines of nineteenth-century fiction, she is the shining exception to the pervasive acquisitiveness, and in the novel's hermeneutic depths, various males' attraction to her is explained by her representation of a value far different from the gross capitalist kind and by her moral and metaphysical grounding. Rick's R.V. initials, used often by Lang and somehow erased from their remembered spot on a bathroom door (*B* 232), translate to *random variable* in mathematical parlance, whereas Lenore often has the qualities of a constant. Marshall Boswell points out how Lenore's L.S.B. initials nearly invert Andrew Sealander Lang's A.S.L. and make him "A" to her "B," but more important to Wallace's symbolism is Lenore's L.B.[22] The initials signify the Latin *libra*, for balance, abbreviated in everyday discourse as the lb. of weight and the £ of the British pound (an identification under-scored by Lenore's minor reflection, Kopek—the Russian penny, in effect a mere fraction of her powerful father Ruble). Another significant association for Lenore, from the moral realm, is the blind justice of myth and symbol, the female figure holding the balance scales that dates back to ancient representations of Justitia, Isis, and Themis.[23] Through Lenore Wallace juxtaposes varying meanings of value as individuals interact with and embody it: value in the sense of standard measure (here, weight); value in the monetary sense; and values in the moral sense, the weighing of courses of action in "real love" (B 183), the judgment that Rick calls, in a story about a "weights and measures expert" and scale constructor (B 190), "the power to discriminate and decide whom and on the basis of what criteria to love" (B 183). Glimpsed in Lenore is a first major example of Wallace's interest in common values: weights and measures, standard units, all the fundamental (and unpostmodern) social agreements that need not be contractualized and cannot be solipsistically determined.

Lenore's identification with the balance scale underscores her role as the moral center of Broom. In Bombardini's weighty and oppressive love for her, Wallace also allegorizes a criticism he makes of peers who offer "fiction pre-occupied with *norm* as *value* instead of value's servant" (BF 61; italics mine). Norms have no necessary moral force; achieving that requires, for Wallace, choosing. As he tries to impose himself everywhere, this Norm—whose obese body was becoming increasingly normative in the United States when Broom was published—threatens to crush the L.B. of (potentially) objective value, just as he hopes to crush the Weight Watchers scale "under a weight of food. The springs would jut out. Jut" (B 82).

An even more basic meaning of pound, though—from which the unit of weight derives—is the English measure of work: in physics (that is, every-where, in every action), the foot-pound, abbreviated ft-lb, equals the energy transferred (or work performed) in exerting a force of one pound over a distance of one foot. A 120-pound person standing up and lifting her weight from a seated position, displacing her mass by two feet, has done about 240 foot-pounds of work (more, though, since the human body is an inefficient system). This foot-pound is a means by which Wallace can both get us to consider Lenore's rising and lifting and undermine capitalism's general disassociation of monetary value from the actions of persons who earn it: at root, there is no way to do real work and thus produce real value or energy, Wallace's onomastics imply, without pulling one's weight.

Lenore is also that ideal mental worker Wallace described in his thoughts on reading his challenging literature; he would pursue the fantasy of this potent worker/reader up through his portrayal of superpowers of total concentration in *The Pale King*. Thus when a procrastinating Rick intones, "Lenore, come to work," it is an admission that the book's main writer figure is useless without this woman who, as she listens to his stories throughout, becomes an image of the reader (*B* 32). Rick first notices her "reading, her legs crossed ankle on knee" (*B* 61) in Dr. Jay's office, and later, at the switchboard, "She . . . looked back down at her book" (*B* 69). But as we keep track of speakers in a book so heavy with unattributed lines of dialogue, especially at the (often jarring in media res) beginnings of scenes, we readers also recognize ourselves in her work of sorting phone calls.

"Why on earth did she work as a telephone operator?" Rick asks upon meeting Lenore. Holding back the story of her family trauma, Lenore answers that she "obviously needed money to buy food" (*B* 65). This answer, in features certainly connected to its clarity, is a baseline equation of use value and labor as a precapitalist, pre-surplus-value fulfillment of direct needs, a sharp contrast with the prevalent attempts to make language (and its infant acquisition) an object of consumption and profit. Why *on earth* does Lenore work, indeed, since Rick's questioning is really about the conditions Lenore exemplifies that tether the human body, mind, and principles to processes of struggle, entropy, and solid identity—all of which Wallace illustrates via connection to the earth and awareness of one's embodied weight, however indirectly these are gained through attention to narratives.

In this axiological novel, Lenore's communicative work is also fundamentally connected to a philosophy of attention to ground—long before it is revealed that Lenore Sr., in an act that seems sacrificial, has somehow made *herself* part of the underground telephone network beneath East Corinth. Wallace would begin his review of Markson in "The Empty Plenum" by quoting Cavell on the distinctiveness of Wittgenstein's view of language: "what other philosopher has found the antidote to illusion in the particular and repeated humility of remembering and tracking the

uses of humble words, looking philosophically as it were beneath our feet
rather than over our heads?" (*BF* 73).[24] Lenore is at heart this Cavellian-
Wittgensteinian philosopher of what lies "beneath our feet." In what seems
merely a funny first line she notes, "Most really pretty girls have pretty
ugly feet, and so does Mindy Metalman," whose calluses and "cracking and
peeling" nail polish suggest "decay" (*B* 3). There is a biblical seriousness
here: Mindy is the "Metal" goddess of this novel, and her feet of clay—to
use the codification of the image into cliché—draw on the imperial statue
with toes of iron and clay in Nebuchadnezzar's dream[25] and Shelley's echo of
same in "Ozymandias" (a poem Fogle's father will mordantly quote in *The
Pale King* [172]). To be aware of the central Wallace trope of *memento mori*
is not to take up Yorick's skull, necessarily, but to be first of all an observer
of feet, those body parts that wade through the dust we become. Lenore, "a
long-legged girl with feet larger than average," comments later on Sykes's
cowboy boots (*B* 59); "footwear, again," complains Rick, who would certainly benefit from examining grounds (for more than just the Jayne Mansfield outline of East Corinth) (*B* 283). Lance Olsen calls *Broom* "Termite
Art," after Manny Farber's term for works that eat their own boundaries,
but *Broom* is of the termites too in looking groundward and underground.[26]

Through such motifs Wallace begins constructing a code for the progress and insights of his characters within often static plots that deny them
traditional action in favor of contemplation of where they stand and what
their foundations are. In the opening scene Lenore uses the spiked heel of
her pump as a weapon against the hulking aggressor Biff Diggerence, who
bangs on the wall with his head, that abstracting extremity with which
Wallace seeks to put feet into dialogue. When she escapes the dorm, it
is as though Lenore comes into a fullness of embodiment, again from the
bottom up: after running away "in bare feet," outside "she enjoys a brief
nosebleed" (*B* 21). This rather inexplicable image only makes sense as an
amalgam of the moral injury she has suffered, the countervailing joy ("she
enjoys . . .") of self-definition and ontology, and a sign that the narrative
to come will show her dealing fundamentally with altitude, with the ab-
normal air pressure and removal from one's level that nosebleeds (a "persistent . . . problem" for Lenore [*B* 67]) can point to. When she is removed
from the ground during the flight of chapter 12, it is as though she loses

a measure of ontology: rather implausibly she sleeps as Rick tells Lang the traumatic story of her childhood, among the many narratives in which she finds herself lacking "control," equated often here with the ability to tell one's own story (B 66).

Lenore's quest for balance and ground coalesces around her association with the truth-finding techniques of analytical philosophy, the school of thought in which Wallace seeks a continuing viability rather than too readily ceding ground to the more fashionable deconstruction of the novel's era. Rick calls Lenore's "uniform of white cotton dress and black Converse high-top sneakers . . . an unanalyzable and troubling constant"—a description rife with puns from mathematical proofs (B 58). With qualities of uniformity, by acting as a "constant," Lenore is "unanalyzable," meaning that her part of any equation is not subject to dissection or transformation by the proof finder's pen. The Converse sneakers, her platform in a sense, evoke solid standing and symmetrical reversals: the converse of a statement, obtained by reversing its two parts (for the implication $P \rightarrow Q$, the converse is $Q \rightarrow P$), is a tool in balancing equations and establishing a statement's truth value (also in disentangling antinomies, which Lenore frequently explains).

While Wallace contends throughout with different relationships to language and communication, Lenore represents the alignment of clarity in speech with the moral force of truth. Indeed, her constant white dress is a kind of sacred vestment, in a novel concerned with false priests and the possibility of secular work becoming vocational. While the names seem merely corny, Wallace has a serious purpose in naming Judith Prietht (read: Judas Priest with a lisp) and the ineffectual communications repairman Peter Abbott. The Stonecipheco minion Neil Obstat Jr., meanwhile, is named for the phrase of papal censorship, *nihil obstat* ("nothing hinders"), in a corollary to legalistic control over language. By contrast, confronting the jargon-riddled discourse of Bloemker, Lenore says, "I don't think I understand what you're saying" and presses him for precise meanings (B 32). She also has instincts for restoring a sacred sense of balance, asking Bloemker about the allegorically named neighbor ("in the next room") Mrs. Yingst, who represents one half of the yin-yang symbol, Lenore Sr. the other: "She and Lenore are like this," Lenore says, her fingers obviously intertwined in illustration (B 33).[27]

But by placing Lenore under such constant pressure, even to the point of possible death, Wallace also demonstrates the limits of the mathematical precision in language that the tradition of logical positivism had promised him. In 1996, recalling (and regretting) his defense of its absent ending "word," Wallace said of *Broom* that "the entire book is a conversation between Wittgenstein and Derrida, and presence versus absence."[28] This "conversation" is the metaphilosophical means by which *Broom* earns a place alongside the many Menippean satires by Barth, Coover, and Pynchon that Wallace read as a young man.[29] Lenore, if we take her as a metadescription of language, is the *Tractatus*-era Wittgenstein side in this conversation: she is associated with constant, empirical data like the pound, the world of fact (yet, as I have been suggesting, by placing a "fact" in moral conflicts Wallace begins to undo the fact/value distinction). As for the other side, switching the double letters in Biff Diggerence yields Big Difference, the "serious" meaning of which is on the order of that of Judith Prietht. For what if we hear the French accent in Difference and connect it to Derrida's central idea? The years from 1981 to 1990 were certainly big years on college campuses for *différance*.[30] A sign of which side has the edge in the Wittgenstein/ Derrida debate, especially morally speaking, comes in Biff's acts of signification: drunk and blocking the way, he "whomps" his forehead repeatedly on the door—what Derrida's style and nonpragmatic view of language may lead to (*B* 19)? LaVache, much farther down a path of philosophical gamesmanship and moral bankruptcy in 1990, defies Wittgenstein by arranging a private language, tellingly around the communications system his sister attempts to help repair: he claims he does not have a phone because he calls his phone a "lymph node" (*B* 214). And LaVache and friends (most of them with no philosophical knowledge at all) are new vehicles for body-denying, deconstructive headaches, modeled on Biff: "This legendary guy a few years back started this tradition where, instead of getting sick, we pound our heads against the wall" (*B* 217).

Lenore's shoe-based battle with Biff thus allegorizes her role in the conflict with Derrida-inspired understandings of language, many of which are produced by Rick's perception of her. For example, in Rick's fantasizing narration—suffused with poststructuralist suggestions about linguistic constructedness—Lenore is reduced to letters and even mere punctuation:

lying asleep, Lenore, "defined by the swell of a breast and the curve of a hip" like the outline of Mansfield, "is an S," before becoming "a question mark, a comma, a parenthesis," and finally, legs spread, "a V" (one of *Broom*'s many references to Pynchon's Stencilized lady) (*B* 235). Recounting their first date, Rick keeps Lenore at the distance of reported speech (there are no quotation marks here), and in another equation of legs with ontology, Rick "sweep[s] the area under the table," "insanely curious about where her legs were" (*B* 65–66). Portrayed as a writing effect in such scenes, Lenore spends the text trying to lay claim to the legs and feet that bear her weight and thus, in Wallace's metaphilosophical game, the reality of her existence, an ontological status deconstructive readers would deny her.

If she is a figure of balance, though, why can Lenore not simply recognize her identity as the LB constant and take on both the ontological certainty and moral authority that would imply? Consider a rhyming scene to her outing with Rick, a moment in the Gilligan's Island bar in which she encounters a literally weightless version of herself, the blow-up doll "date," named Brenda, of Bloemker, a sexual fetishist like Rick (*B* 144). Brenda is an image of the hyperthin commodified female, Kopek, made newly grotesque. The little girl LaVache enchants with his leg on the Amherst hill is also named Brenda (*B* 242), a sign that he will join the novel's other males in manipulating Lenore (*B* 243). During the discussion with Bloemker, as Brenda floats upward, Lenore—again the text's grounded clarifier—questions him before exclaiming, "This isn't even a person . . . See, she weighs about one pound" (*B* 144). Lenore herself is "one pound" in a different sense, but Wallace uses the mirroring moment to reinforce her own weightiness and groundedness, through a "reading" of an-other. She is, in Cavell's terms, doing the work of being born a second time herself through the negative recognition that Brenda "isn't even a person." The Bloemker scene calls for embracing knowledge of oneself not as a constant (that seems always to be the outsider's view) but as a contingent variable. What other reason can there be for Bloemker's meandering monologue here about the Midwest, in which he asks, "How to begin to come to some understanding of one's place in a system . . . a world that is itself stripped of any static, understandable character by the fact that it changes radically, all the time?" (*B* 143). Lenore thus embodies a principle of reading and writing as the fluctuating displacement and peripheralization of personal experience (both a writer's and a reader's) in text, a method Wallace will employ, and continually transform, on into *Oblivion* and *The Pale King*.

LEGS TO SUPPORT

With one Beadsman child clarified, let me attend to the family resemblances. Wallace, still mastering the Dostoevskyan structure he will use in *Infinite Jest*, seems not to have the space, or perhaps the capacity, to take two of the siblings seriously: we get cardboard portraits of Clarice and John as two extremes. Clarice has taken the approved path of merging the familial and corporate by marrying a Stonecipheco vice president; John, a math genius, refuses not only the family money (like Lenore and LaVache) but sustenance altogether—he is another weightless figure to contrast with Lenore, who characteristically finds a balanced middle path. "Cipher" can mean a number in general or zero in particular; thus Stonecipher, the father's name, reads as a person frozen at zero—a nihilist, for whom patriarchal tradition (symbolized by statues of "Stonecipher Beadsmans I, II, and III" [*B* 38]) is the means of increasing "value" and accumulating wealth. Lenore, among Stonecipher's children, is the only one who takes on the "job" of "mak[ing] up" moral values in the face of a bankrupt 1980s inheritance that I discussed in the introduction.

The first third of *Broom* establishes the distances between Lenore's value system and those of her father and suitors, but at Amherst, by way of LaVache, Wallace explores abuses of the Protestant work ethic and the philosophical bases on which work becomes grounds for true (moral) development. Lenore and LaVache, their names soundalikes, may be bonded by rejection of their family, but they diverge strongly on the question of work. LaVache is a hard intellectual worker, but always in the service of his drug habit, rather than Lenore's self-reliance and balance. When the siblings meet, Lenore revises Rick's question about the logic behind her low-paying job, after seeing LaVache's fraudulent tutoring in action.

"You don't work, here, do you?"

LaVache smiled at her. "That was just work, what I did. I do lots of work."

"He literally does the work of like forty or fifty guys, and even more girls," said Heat. "He does all our work, the big lug."

"What about your own work?" Lenore said to LaVache.

"What can I tell you? I've got a leg to support, after all."

[B 216]

"I've got a leg to support": "me" is tragically missing from the end of LaVache's statement, which speaks instead to enslaved self-diminution. Drug addiction has literalized for LaVache a state of legless floating; through his perversion of work and "support," he has resigned himself to a radical lack in his relationship to ground and weight. When Lenore pesters him, he reduces himself to an object and embraces the logic of fetishism running throughout *Broom*: his leg is his "thing." "You have to have a thing here" (B 239). The name LaVache, his middle name and mother's maiden name, means "cow," marking him as subhuman and (given the species' legendary stomach storage) as one on a quest to accumulate (an ironic form of grass ends up stored in his prosthesis).

LaVache is also, not by coincidence, a bad philosopher, a bad educator, and, in a trope Wallace will return to, a propagator of error. The inside philosophical joke of the Amherst scenes lies in LaVache's misreading of Hegelian work and the interaction of economic value and metaphysical value. In limited space, and since, as LaVache says, "Clear presentation is not Hegel's strength" (B 239), let me rely on Sean Sayers's cogent summary of work in *Phenomenology of Spirit*:

> Work is a mode of . . . practical being-for-self and a means by which it develops. Work involves a break with the animal, immediate, natural relationship to nature. In work, the object is not immediately consumed and annihilated. Gratification is deferred. The object is preserved, worked upon, formed and transformed. And, in this way, a distinctively human relationship to nature is established. . . . By working on the world, by shaping and forming it, human beings become separated from the natural world and established as self-conscious subjects, as beings-for-self, over against an objective world.[31]

In the "being-for-self" that work "develops," Sayers cites Hegel's all-important category of *Fursichsein*—the state Wallace ironically refers to by naming the Amherst economics professor "Fursich" (*B* 215). Fursich's student Clint Wood, a tall, staid, and clueless fellow who comes to LaVache for help, plays on both Clint Eastwood and the human as undeveloped object, as automaton (echoing LaVache's status as mere animal). LaVache's advice for the first Fursich quiz is incredibly simple, a sign that Wood has done none of the work in the young term: "All you need to remember for Fursich is, when the interest rate goes up, the price of any bond issued goes down" (*B* 215). Read as part of the philosophical allegory Wallace will continue mounting, Fursich's economics class actually concerns the value of the subject: if being-for-self is the goal, a low bond price points to the state of bondage out of which Hegel's subject struggles by way of work—an idea amplified with LaVache's next customer, Nervous Roy Keller.

LaVache looks forward to exploiting Keller economically all semester through a one-on-one tutorial on Hegel with a professor named Huffman (a name suggesting the breath of Spirit, but about to be reduced to puffs of marijuana smoke?) (*B* 221). N.R.K., Keller's initials, together sound like "anarchy," and the order that philosophy might bring to this nervous boy should allow him to grow up, or somehow rise (*keller* is German for basement). But LaVache leads Keller astray: repeating Huffman's first assignment back to him on the phone, LaVache says, "Obliteration of Nature by Spirit?" and consults the text for the right pages (*B* 222). But the relevant section of the *Phenomenology* actually concerns "Observation of Nature"—quite a slip![32] LaVache may be attentive to philosophical texts in a way that makes for correct page citations and good grades; later he will refer to an exact page number of the *Investigations* with Lenore, who has left her college books in boxes and is instead living out philosophical questions. But LaVache is not one who weds philosophical insight to living a moral life: ironically, one of his tutorials is on the Bible as "moral fiction, useful . . . as a guide for making decisions about how to live" (*B* 217–218). He has technical knowledge, but it does not become embodied—a state indexed in his identification with wood, object, and the animal.

Obliterating nature, rather than observing it, is what Zusatz's G.O.D. has done to Ohio (and what Reconfiguration will do in *Infinite Jest*). "This is so fucking American, man," Wallace says in an analysis of minimalism and metafiction; "either make something your God and cosmos and then worship it, or else kill it" (*CW* 45). This denial of moderation could be applied very broadly to the American structures *Broom* illuminates, including an economy bereft of *oikos* and the scorched-earth conversion of the natural landscape into a so-called G.O.D. These are the consequences when subjects forego a program of steady work and growth in favor of an annihilating, totalizing romanticism.

HOW TO WIN THE LOTTERY

But how else to produce, accumulate, and relate to value in *Broom?* In the remainder of this chapter I array the pathways to value creation evoked in the novel's later parts, beginning with Hart Lee Sykes, a broad parody of 1980s televangelists, thoroughly lacking the "heart" and "soul" (*psyche*/Sykes) his name suggests. The call to work that Wallace represents to *Broom*'s reader receives its climactic distortion in the money grubbing of the minister (also named for a Dickensian thief), who mirrors the call of Zusatz for a parodic "hewing" and offers the novel's final trace of Reagan. Sykes says, "I stand before you tonight" (though he is, tellingly, "standing" at a televisual distance) "to say that a partner is a worker," one who recognizes the need to unite with others "in the service of" Jesus (*B* 458), himself "a *worker*" and "*partner*" (*B* 459). But Sykes is merely stuffing work into a corporatist idiom, as so many others have. By asking for this infusion of cash from the corporation-like "Partners With God," Sykes speaks a perverse version of the Protestant work ethic: "If all us partners work *together*, in the Lord's *soil*, our desires are automatically spiritually transformed into *Jesus's* desires, too" (*B* 461). Seeking a cynically pragmatic logic in spirituality, Sykes wants to reconcile God and mammon and dictate terms to Jesus. According to Sykes, one can simultaneously be a hyperconsumerist and a transcendent Christian; he perverts the otherness of divinity to identify it entirely with the acquisitive self, tellingly rendered here in the technological language of the "automatic." Indeed, he promises viewers the "100 percent pleasure"

Wallace finds endemic to entertainment, prophesying "the satisfaction of your every *need*. The fulfillment of your every *wish*" (*B* 461). Saying come to work by merely calling in, Sykes thus offers as great a distortion of the path to God as the waste land of the G.O.D. does. These late-twentieth-century forms of civic and religious authority also hold nightmare versions of the Puritans' founding hope to be a new Israel, to be brought out of the desert and into a promised land called America.

A profane minister calls forth, on the other side of the screen, a profane "Metal" goddess, the text's final echo of Pynchon's devilish clockwork goddess, V. In the concluding scenes, completing his allegory of a workless society, Wallace fuses Sykes's hand with that of Mindy, who has been, from foot criticism to tensions over Lang, a rival to Lenore. In addition to receiving money from her father, Rex (a worshiper of artificially fertilized lawn rather than actual ground), Mindy earns her value as the recorded voice in cars and grocery-store checkouts, another of the text's examples of fetishization and its replacement of human labor as the source of a product's value. As Marx writes in defining the commodity fetish in *Capital*, products are "abounding in metaphysical subtleties"; in his famous description of a table as commodity, it "evolves out of its wooden brain grotesque ideas."[33] Mindy's work as this metaphysical voice within objects contrasts with Lenore's efforts to fix the phone lines that technologize the human voice for (potential) two-way communication. In *Broom*'s revision of *Lolita* (allusions to which Boswell notes [*Understanding*, 42]), Wallace treats the adolescent Mindy, object of Rick's leering gaze, as a woodland creature, strongly associated with the baptismal wash of the lawn sprinkler (*B* 210). When Rick finally becomes her lover in the novel's final scene, though, Mindy is an electrified goddess for the age, her luminousness coming from the TV as she "kneel[s]" before it to "touch" Sykes: "Cold light comes out from between her fingers on the screen." Later, Rick sees a "flickering hand, dead and cold"—Sykes's. "It covers everything": technologized agency pervades all (*B* 466). The deeper reference, though, is to a negation of Keats's "This living hand," that Wallace standard for artistic (i.e., nontelevisual) connection. Lenore, whose apparent death in the phone tunnels Mindy is not even interested in hearing Rick narrate, has failed in her quest to become the measure of (moral) value.

Elsewhere, though, Lenore rebels against both Metalmanhood and Sykes's late-capitalist "Christian" charity by seeking out alternate forms of economic value that point to other kinds of donation and other foundations of moral value. First, in yet more sly Wallace onomastics, there is the meaning in Beadsman, notably *not* used by the nihilistic Stonecipher in naming his corporation. Here Wallace evokes the bedesmen, religious figures in medieval Scotland who solicited donations on the promise of praying for their benefactors (compare Sykes's appeal).[34] The themes of giving and asceticism are underdeveloped here, considering all Wallace will do with them in the future. But Lenore does challenge Rick's notion that gift exchange is just an occasion for reciprocity and even further demands: foreshadowing his turn to the sadomasochism of handcuffs, Rick once asked to be allowed to tie her up for Christmas, but she gave him a beret instead. As they argue about Vlad, another of his presents, Lenore sees Rick's disturbance of true gift structures, while he is stuck on an "emotional dash legal deep sense" of "technical[]" ownership (of Vlad *and* her) (B 283). Critiquing possessiveness, Lenore asks, "Why do you perceive everything in terms of having and losing?" (B 197).

Finally, there is the lottery to consider—like the gift, a symbol of an unbalanced ledger as well as an image of the contingent, communal value that Wallace will continue placing in characters' purses and wallets as he builds a vision of money's displacement. Unable to pay the high price Gerber's charges her for Kopek's performance, Lenore drops her purse, and "bright" "lottery tickets spilled out and went everywhere" (B 386). Sheepishly she tells Lang that she and Candy play often and "have all these systems, using our birthdays" (B 396), implicit challenges to the homogenized "system" that looms over the novel in the title. She insists there is more logic than luck to it: they started playing in college, and Lenore, a philosophy major, "hit on this sort of syllogism, ostensibly proving we'd win" (B 396). While LaVache disproved it, Lenore has maintained the practice. A condescending Lang asserts capitalist sense and value: "I personally majored in ec-o-nomics" (B 396). Lenore, fighting off one more act of male chauvinism, notes that though her father wanted her to major in it (read: Lang and economics echo the law of the father, in psychoanalytic terms), she only ever took one class. She then describes her burnout, similar to Wallace's own, with logicians of language, who "play their games with words, instead of numbers, and so things are even harder." But "by the end of school I didn't like it much any more" (*B* 397). Thus despite three male voices—Stonecipher, LaVache, Lang—all insisting on the stupidity of seeking value in the lottery, Lenore goes on gambling, guaranteed returns be damned. Like the axiological figures discussed in the introduction, she finds herself attracted to the "bright" tickets' glow, their contingent promise of value, their disturbance of the logic of "having and losing." Wallace, who understood the astronomical odds perfectly well, may have himself been a lottery player: "I would have loved to have gotten nominated for the National Book Award" for *Infinite Jest*, he says in 1997. "I would also love to win the Illinois State Lottery" (*CW* 81).

Considered as an ending response to the many games in *Broom* involving dire falls (Chutes and Ladders) and outright sadism (LaVache's "Hi, Bob"), the open-ended, state-run lottery is a salutary vision: in losing week after week, Lenore is actually paying into a civic fund that is not unlike taxes, a fund of commonwealth that the young Wallace tentatively steps toward here. Many U.S. lotteries have historically been legally set up to support states' public-education systems, another sign of Lenore's involvement with learning (though increasingly such claims about state lotteries are truthless advertising). Given the role played by chance in the bleeding of switchboard calls (some of her lottery tickets are stored in "one of the white switchboard cabinets" [*B* 447]), communication itself becomes a lottery of connections, a secular miracle. And by playing a game without the likelihood of "winning" it, without rationalizing it, or without delimiting each of its rules in the way that, say, a chess player does, Lenore honors tricky aspects of rule following and play in language games. As Dale Jacquette explains, drawing on Wittgenstein's many comparisons of chess and language games, with the latter "we must share in at least some of the relevant form of life in order to determine the point and purpose of the game, in order to distinguish its essential from its inessential rules."[35] Recall here the way contracts in *Broom* also expose the distance between imposed rules and the "essential" "form of life." Rick echoes the point thematically and performatively when, making multiple, semivague attempts at fashioning his metaphor of understanding, he says of the figure on whom he heaps so much language, "Lenore has the quality of a sort of game about her. . . . Lenore soundlessly invites one to play a game consisting of involved attempts to find out the game's own rules. How about that. The rules of the game are Lenore, and to play is to be played" (B 72). If the lottery is the uninstrumentalized "game" figuring language that *Broom* ultimately settles on, it is important that Lenore's dreams of winning remain unfulfilled and even irrational—for actually winning might connote that she is an owner of language or a controller of its contingencies. Language is, in actuality, commonwealth, the property of all, like the proceeds from lottery-ticket purchases (minus the winnings) ideally conceived.

The lottery, always a loss for Lenore, expands *Broom*'s references to Frank Norris's *McTeague*, where Trina's lottery winnings lead to her murder.[36] But more importantly, through the lottery Wallace partially resolves his anxiety over an "approved career" and the "*artiste* thing" in the McCaffery interview. For the real metafictive subject in the discussion of college majors—to bring this chapter full circle—is the calling Wallace did heed, over Lenore's philosophy and Lang's economics. Speaking to his college alumni magazine in 1999 (and reflecting on his Amherst creative writing project?), Wallace reinforces his association of artistic success with the lottery and suggests that his first book points to the gamble of trying to become a writer: he knows "way too many fine and serious writers who haven't been able to get anything published to be able to regard the whole process as anything much more than a lottery" (*LI* 61). Thus among the many metafictional meanings of Lenore's switchboard, lottery tickets, and poverty is Wallace's commitment to art that will only "pay" if it has the good fortune to make a connection with an audience. In the purse and cabinet of tickets also lie replies to other vessels of value and bearers of weight in the text, so many of them signs of desperation: LaVache's hollow leg in which he stores his drugs, Bombardini's massive stomach. In his essay on Kafka, Wallace would indict an idiom that convinces American college students "that a self is something you just *have*," when the truth is that "the horrific struggle to establish a human self results in a self whose humanity is inseparable from that horrific struggle"—much like LB's efforts to establish her existence, which are inextricable from the physical exertion that comes attached to her name and identity (*CL* 64). In its critique of romantic possessiveness, its many images of entropic seepage, and its insistence that there are no guarantees in the accrual of value, *Broom* begins Wallace's career-long critique of the self as an externalized object of possession or purchase.

Not long after publishing *Broom*, Wallace in 1988 would write "Fictional Futures and the Conspicuously Young," which notes, "Nothing has changed about why writers who don't do it for the money write: it's art, and art is meaning, and meaning is power: power . . . to order chaos, to transform void into floor and debt into treasure" (*BF* 68). In this chapter I have detailed the many reasons Wallace, in eschewing money as motivation for his life's work, would pair a magical production of economic value ("debt into treasure") with a magical production of stable grounding ("void into floor"), an alliance that will persist throughout his balancing books. Debt and treasure also contrast with the puns Wallace layers into the essay's title: "Futures" suggests an artistic stock market in which writing careers are somehow advanced financial instruments, and "Conspicuously" evokes Thorstein Veblen's famous phrase "conspicuous consumption," which involves competitive spending and body-deforming display that have little connection to the actual satisfaction of human needs or to the resolve of Lenore (daughter of the leisure class) to work simply to buy food.

A lifetime supply of fast food will be the payment for appearing as a child in a McDonald's commercial in "Westward," Wallace's next long work on value and a meditation on a new generation of writers contending with art's entry into the marketplace. I turn to it in the next chapter, placing it alongside important but overlooked stories about the great American moment of economic contingency, the 1929 stock-market crash and Great Depression.

NEW DEALS

(THE) DEPRESSION AND DEVALUATION
IN THE EARLY STORIES

O N OCTOBER 19, 1987, "Black Monday," stock markets around the world crashed. In the United States the Dow Jones Industrial Average dropped 508 points, a 22.6 percent loss in value, the largest one-day percentage decline in history. Some economists predicted a new Great Depression. A headline in the *New York Times* on the morning following Black Monday alarmingly read, "Does 1987 Equal 1929?"[1] and the equation of the two eras was a topic debated in the media over the next several weeks. Identifying the definitive causes of the 1987 crash is outside my scope here, but rampant overvaluation of stocks inarguably played a major role. In a thesis likely to catch the eye of a young writer who would later portray resistance to the market-driven logic of using computers to check tax returns a year or two before 1987, many economists also blamed the crash on new trading programs able to make incredibly rapid transactions, leading to automated selloffs as prices fell, without (human) regard for a communal faith in stocks' value. As Paul Crosthwaite notes, one designer of the programmed trading even feared that the crash would lead the Soviets to initiate attacks on a weakened U.S. and produce nuclear Armageddon.[2]

Wallace's continual interest in questioning the fundamental basis of value creation warns me away from suggesting a simple causal narrative in which his work of this period responds straightforwardly to the market crash. He is not that sort of writer; he is led more often by a DeLilloan urge to make work that, while conversant with daily headlines, prophesies the culture's turns and diagnoses its abiding myths in near-future settings. Still, the economic crises of the late 1980s contribute to the unorthodox view of the early short stories, in *Girl with Curious Hair* and elsewhere, that I offer in this chapter, expanding on chapter 1's historical connections to Reagan and anxieties about productive work. I draw anew on the effects Wallace's economics study had on his fiction, focusing here on his interest in the New Deal and the formation of the U.S. welfare state. The Wallace who studied economic policy and considered law school had, Max says, "inchoate" dreams of a life in politics, built on a childhood vision that he might become an Illinois congressman—a fate he would romance in "Lyndon."[3] Max also describes Wallace, upon returning from medical leave for his senior year of 1984–1985, competing with his best friend Mark Costello, who had graduated the previous spring with "two theses, one a novel, the other a study of the New Deal," a subject in which Costello had a "boundless interest," often shared around the dining hall tables at which he and Wallace held court (Max, *Every Love Story*, 39, 27). Wallace's own, less conventional study of the New Deal, I argue, continued well after college graduation. As demonstrated by *Signifying Rappers*, which he and Costello coauthored in alternating chapters in 1989, Wallace conceived of some of his writing in this period as a dialogue with his best friend, who became a lawyer after Amherst (and eventually a federal prosecutor) but would later publish novels as well.[4] The idea that writing fiction might commingle with more civically engaged (and more "approved") jobs seems often to have been on Wallace's mind in his early career.

Economic readings of the early short stories show Wallace reaching back in U.S. history to a decade when the nation relearned the meaning of monetary value and submitted to its profound intertwining with the civic, while also confronting (in an echo of *The Broom of the System*) the value of work. In the three stories of 1988–1989 I examine in the greatest detail, "Crash of '69," "John Billy," and "Westward the Course of Empire Takes Its Way," Wallace drew long arcs between the Depression and later moments

in the twentieth century when the American winning streak had met another of its periodic, catastrophic ends—busts for a culture that seemed
not so much expectant of constant boom as utterly dependent on it. Viewing Wallace's early experimentation in the light of the Depression opens
up to history fiction that has been largely viewed in terms of its relation
to postmodernist predecessors and minimalist contemporaries, whether in
Boswell's claim that *Girl* remedies the "self-satisfied irony" of writing by
"Generation X" or Kasia Boddy's treatment of the book as a response to
MFA workshop culture and popular 1980s styles.[5]

Given Wallace's much-discussed break with the ironic tradition of postmodernism in "E Unibus Pluram" and the McCaffery interview, what happens if we take as the "origin" or ground of his fictional ethos not the traditional twentieth-century breakpoint of 1945, not the 1960s and 1970s
in which so many of his key intertexts emerged, and not the Reaganite
1980s in which he began publishing but, instead, 1929? This was the date
that, especially in the period of *Girl*, provided him with a metaphorics of
economic Depression and crashes of value—all evidence of radical contingency—that he could juxtapose with crashes of self-worth and interior
states of depression. In calling readers back to the Depression, Wallace
could also chasten 1980s opulence and excess. Such is the general context
in which I read Wallace's historically unstable and multivalent economic
allegories below. Our understanding of Wallace—not a postmodernist or
postpostmodernist but, as Boswell argues, the "nervous leader of some still-
unnamed (and perhaps unnamable) third wave of modernism" (*Understanding*, 1)—benefits from situating his work specifically within the history of
the U.S. welfare state and, in Jason Puskar's words, the "grand narrative[s]
of chance collectivity" and "social and material interdependence"[6] that critics have recently used to renovate political readings of U.S. modernism and
naturalism. These histories demonstrate the intertwining of literary imagining and welfare-state achievements such as the Social Security Administration—developments that, in Szalay's words, "changed profoundly the
political valence and cultural instrumentality of existing literary conven-
tions."[7] It is precisely these state formations that are under steady attack
during Wallace's career by neoliberal principles, and here I begin an ac-

count of Wallace's engagement with the liberal tradition of social insurance that extends into chapter 5's analysis of *Oblivion* and the reactive neoliberal formation of for-profit insurance.

Anticipating an encyclopedic novel that would find states of loneliness and depression reflected in a nation's appetite for an empty popular culture, many of Wallace's early stories construct elaborate economic metaphors to connect individuals' statements about feeling worthless to issues of American poverty and the acts of communal repair that might serve to remedy both—the Depression linked to depression, the New Deal connected to the small-scale "living transaction" through which he defined the salutary exchange with his readers. The 1930s are for Wallace, if in a far more muted form, what 1945 was to Pynchon in the signal text of postmodernism, *Gravity's Rainbow*: that is, the moment of historical apocalypse that needed to be traversed and retraversed in the fictional imagination. Wallace's contentious relationship to postmodernism thus finds reflection in his choice of devaluation and Depression, elements of the modernist era, as his key moment of twentieth-century crisis. In the following sections, I trace Wallace's narratives from the crash of 1929 to varying forms of redress in his figurations of New Deal ritual, social insurance, and 1960s rhetoric of a Great Society. In the chapter's conclusion, with a historicized Wallace in place, I demonstrate his merger of impoverishment with abiding philosophical questions, returning to "Westward" for models of value not from the 1930s but the ancient world.

CRASH OF '29, '62, '69, '87 . . .

Wallace had an unerring sense that winners, examined from the oblique angles of his fiction, were really losers—not schadenfreude, but a claim that any struggle other than that Kafkaesque one to "establish a human self" was ultimately an illusory imposition of games' numbering and geometry on the flux of interpersonal experience and its essential lottery effects (*CL* 64). In terms that recall the alignment of contracts and games, U.S. culture had succeeded in laying over an inchoate and saddening phenomenal experience a grid, an archer's target, a tennis court, or a game show, such that abstract victories and valuations could erase (or try to) the dread and loss that pervaded people's bones and breath. The examples are abundant: the starving John Beadsman, who (in an allusion to Salinger's Glass family) has converted memories of his forced childhood test taking into a game-show scenario; Julie Smith of "Little Expressionless Animals," who has won more than seven hundred consecutive *Jeopardy!* matches but remains traumatized by the childhood neglect that brought her all the trivia knowledge; and Karrier, the stock-picking protagonist of "Crash of '69."

"Crash of '69" is the surreal tale of a man who is, like his father, "always wrong" in predicting successful stocks—and thus supremely valuable to financial firms, who do the exact opposite.[8] The original title was "Crash of '62," the year of Wallace's birth.[9] Despite the specificity of these titles, no 1960s stock market crash is described. The ostensible historical subject is another type of value crisis: the removal of the U.S. dollar from the gold standard and the establishment of fiat currency, dramatized in conversations between what appears to be the Federal Reserve Chairman, called "Father" throughout, and a range of advisors, including his daughter. "Crash" initiates Wallace's contention that financial value and the irrational—if not the psychotic—are aligned, as dramatized here by a wheelchair-bound Fed Chairman who, presiding from something more like a heavenly realm than the Treasury, suffers the effects of a stroke or dementia. In Wallace's philosophical allegory, he is the dead God of Nietzsche's *Gay Science*, no longer handing out Platonic forms—or a God on life support, "late in Term" (4). One line jokes, "new Nietzsche: God is Dyslexic" (7).[10] Metaphysics here is not presumed dead but fighting to stay alive, in line with Wallace's drive to stage rather than resolve philosophical conflicts in his fiction.[11] More specifically, "Crash" undoes the hegemony of the rational mind on questions of value by accounting for Father and Karrier's conditions with a "strange phrenological jut" on the back of the heads of both (4); Karrier has a corresponding "dent in [his] forehead," home of the frontal cortex and analytical logic, as if he has "been creamed with a shovel" (7). Intuition, instinct, and the senses may be all he has left, but the culture utterly distorts them.

"Crash" registers the impact of Wallace's economics study on his understanding of the poststructuralist language crisis of the mid-century. The "correct" date for this story might be 1971, when Nixon ended the Bretton Woods agreement (in place since 1944) and removed the U.S. dollar from the gold standard. But also in play are the 1930s, since the Fed Chairman conjures the wheelchair-bound FDR, whose monetary policy fought the Depression by temporarily removing the U.S. dollar from the gold standard. Given suspicions during Reagan's second term that he was suffering from memory lapses, Father could also refer to him (though Reagan's Alzheimer's disease would only be confirmed after he left office and Wallace's story was already published).[12] "This year is what year?", a question about Karrier's time on the job, applies to the whole story, for Wallace mounts a pastiche of many moments—crises of money juxtaposed with crises in meaning and the valuation of self (8). Karrier's father may or may not have committed suicide in 1929 (8), and his son, also seen attempting suicide, inherits the stock-picking ability and the genetics of depression that being "always wrong" suggests: he both is a "carrier" of the disease and feels empty, like caries or a cavity. The title "Crash of '62" identified a depressive's autobiography in which being born is an irreparable crash. But "Crash of '69," the final title, suggests the theme is the crash of balance itself—note that the 6 and 9, unhinged from reference to a year, denote yin and yang, one's head chasing the other's tail. Wallace thus projects 1929 forward and expands it into a general crash of the American psyche and language.[13]

Just glancing at its pages reveals "Crash" as an heir of Joyce's "Circe": all-capital headings announce the "speaker" of each section, and a witch-like woman seduces a callow young man. More than Joyce, though, Wallace's model is David Lynch. Wallace credited seeing *Blue Velvet* in 1986 while at Arizona with granting him an "epiphanic experience" about his artistic mission.[14] "Crash," which archival notes indicate Wallace drafted in Arizona, pays homage to Lynch's influence by naming the Fed Chairman's daughter, in a final heading, "Miss M. Lynch" (11).[15] Like Dorothy Vallens in *Blue Velvet*, this woman proves the sexual aggressor with the naïf

Karrier (analogous to Jeffrey Beaumont). In context, Miss Lynch seems to refer to the financier Edmund Lynch, one half of Merrill-Lynch, the employer of Karrier's father (5). But seeing Karrier's lover as a "daughter" of David Lynch instead makes the film director one more instance of surrealist innovation in a story that mentions, in two historical fabrications of October 1929, René Magritte and the inkblots of Hermann Rorschach: "The air hung with plummeting well-dressed forms. It was a seminal day. Magritte painted the plummeting forms. A Rorschach conceptualized the Rorschach test from his little analyst's office overlooking the sidewalk" (8). Lynch's "entirely new and original" surrealism liberated Wallace, he told Charlie Rose in 1997, from anxiety about "follow[ing] in a certain . . . tradition" of the avant-garde, and in "Crash" Wallace constructs his own "seminal" artistic history by bending surrealist benchmarks to a domain he knows well, financial value, all to expose an overvalued stock market as the scene of collective hallucination and dementia.

Let me expand on the valuing of Karrier's "always wrong" language, through which Wallace retunes his association of Lenore with analytical logic's two-valued system of truth and focuses his governing link between monetary and linguistic exchange. The crash the story evokes is the destruction of meaningful opposition itself: every Karrier "yes" becomes a "no" and vice versa. In the paradox thus pursued, financial value arises in the story at the expense of the truth value of Karrier's words. Wallace, proposing truth value as an axiomatic distinction within any logical system, plays upon common notation for the (computer-like) logical positivist, in which true statements are represented with a 1, false ones with a 0.[16] "Crash" underscores this distinction in how meaning and money are "numbered" when the elder Karrier in the 1920s claims the new company Eastman Kodak has "not even a fraction of a chance. Meaning a bare zero for potential growth" (4). His "no" has tremendous value in the market, as his employer buys up the stock, but his truth and "meaning" are converted into "a bare zero" or falsehood. Money's value and language's truth value prove wholly incompatible.

Such inversions also expose the subordination, within systems devoted to generating exchange value, of the body, use value, and the felt satisfactions connecting the two. In a return to the distorted hunger of Bombardini, the country, embodied by Karrier, has lost the sense that taste and appetite govern consumer desire. After Karrier predicts a winning horse by saying "I feel in my chest, bowels the absence of even one slim snowball's chance" for it (3), Diggs, his agent, offers him a glass of champagne, asking, "How's this for a year"—a question about alcohol's quality notorious for raising debates between consumers' instincts and the specialist's knowledge of market value. "A terrible year," Karrier answers. "Bluck." "Good enough," says Diggs, treating the judgment of Karrier's taste buds in the same way he treats his abstract judgments of money systems (4). "Crash" thus aligns the impoverished senses that some depressives experience (deficits in taste and smell, for instance) with a large-scale insensitivity to the real ground of value. In such a context, the standard of good fiction for Wallace necessarily would become, in an interview refrain he would develop throughout the mid-1990s, an appeal to a physicalized intellectual sense, that keynote of his divergence from a more cerebral postmodernism: great artists have "their own vision, their own way of fracturing reality," and "if it's authentic and true, you will feel it in your nerve endings."[17]

Wallace's unique and aggressive stance on irony and sincerity is being birthed here as well. By inverting the truth value of all of Karrier's statements and making the opposite of each sincere statement the word to bank on, Wallace finds one of his first dramatic windows into the pervasiveness of irony, which is always "based on an implicit 'I don't really mean what I'm saying,'" a lie that does not assume the stance of a lie (*SFT* 67). In his interactions with his father's old colleagues, even Karrier's familial affections face a black hole of ironic neutralization: "He was the worst, your old man, the former retired market analysts will say to me, in admiration, no rancor" ("Crash of '69," 4). These market men demonstrate the ironic distance from one's words that "E Unibus Pluram" also locates in the 1960s. In fact, reading "Crash" as Wallace's preparation for that manifesto helps illuminate a point it makes only elliptically, through the interpretation of TV's cynical ads: that irony's pervasiveness and the profit motive are aligned. And the title "Crash of '69," in this context, evokes a dead end toward which the postmodern cultural formations of that decade were headed.

Finally, the deepest subject of "Crash" is the question of how the mind values not money but the entirety of creation (or "All That"), the domain in which, Wallace often asserts, we must resist the temptation of a nihilism reinforced by a depressed perspective. "It's great" is Karrier's refrain, his remark in his first and last speeches and a masking of his depression (3, 12). The line distorts God's response at the end of each day's work in the Bible's creation story: "God saw that it was good."[18] Karrier says instead, "It's great": in "great" rather than (sufficient, full-stop) "good" is the leading edge of enumeration and comparative valuation, the mental world of greater-than and less-than (and, ultimately, the pitfalls of utilitarianism). Yes, it's great, this voice says, but might another product be greater? In this way Wallace expands the problem of use value and taste Karrier encountered: pursuing exchange value, especially as financial instruments grow more "advanced," almost inevitably leaves the body and feelings behind. On the personal level, "It's great" is the voice of a depressive denying his condition, but allowed to dictate the entire nation's conception of value, the forces of "It's great" are what produce the mania of pricing and stock-market crashes and widespread unhappiness. Wallace is preparing for *Infinite Jest*, where depression and a consumer culture of limitless, greater-and-greater choices will prove mutually reinforcing and utterly disastrous.

NEW DEAL RITUAL, ROOSEVELTVILLE, AND LYNDON'S BED

How to repair nation and self after the crash? Here I examine three stories in *Girl with Curious Hair* that lead Wallace into the 1930s and beyond as he creatively describes the New Deal and the U.S. welfare state: "John Billy," "Westward the Course of Empire Takes Its Way" (my most extensive reading), and "Lyndon." In all three, Wallace seeks a pathway through twentieth-century U.S. history that exposes visions of commonwealth, a compassionate state, and, in images that turn often to the regeneration of land for the therapeutic remaking of individual psyches, a mysticism of shared value and gifts. Across *Girl* Wallace focuses on more reliable forms of value than those decried when Karrier's father, finding an economic metaphor for the kind of self-conscious, ironic literature Wallace would later indict, "beg[s] his firm not to invest in its own stock. No more value-less paper he'd cried," speaking up for a literature in which moral value is paramount and against a wave of "profit-taking," with "no production or insight or making do" ("Crash of '69," 7, 8).

In the formally challenging "John Billy," Wallace creates a communal ritual—a choral "mythopoeum" and rain dance of sorts—that serves as a poetic embodiment of the New Deal, the social policy of renewed commonwealth that arose out of the Depression's devaluation (*GCH* 136). Wallace finds here a set of parallels between personal and national "cures" that he will continue reconfiguring into his examination of the neoliberal diminishment of the New Deal in *The Pale King*, itself a narrative of middle-American ritual. "John Billy" is an axiological narrative portraying the subject's metaphysical search for ground through the nation's literal ungrounding during the Dust Bowl of the 1930s. While the setting is the 1970s, the Dust Bowl has not really ended: in Minogue, Oklahoma, since the Dust Bowl blew his farm away and he "angled some job out of F. Delano R.'s WPA," the character "Simple Ranger," a "damaged" man, has worked "as a watcher for major or calamitous dust" (*GCH* 121). He turns out, in the *Odyssey*-like ending, to be the much younger central character himself, Chuck Nunn Junior, returned in disguise to hear his own myth of trauma and rage told—the 1930s again connected to Wallace's generation.[19] Nunn's name is a compact Heideggerian allegory: Heidegger writes in *Being and Time* that Dasein is "thrown" into existence; "thrownness [*Geworfenheit*]" is "meant to suggest the *facticity of its being delivered over* [Uberantwortung]."[20] Ejected from a car in another crash that reads as a birth, Wallace's character is "chucked" or thrown into a state of nothingness ("Nunn" as "none"), all of which depends on merely being born into existence, of being "Junior." Wallace also finds a source here for his recurrent trope of the ecological collapses, increasingly self-imposed, that punctuate capitalist economy: Dust Bowl displacements will be the unlikely historical referent for the "dust that forms a uremic-hued cloud" visible for miles around the returning herd of feral hamsters—images of hyperconsumptive Americans—after "Experialist migration" in *Infinite Jest* (*IJ* 93).

Both "John Billy" and (as we will see) "Westward," deftly philosophical narratives, begin from thesis sentences about value or hypotheses the stories are designed to test. The first paragraph of "John Billy" calls Chuck a "good luck bad luck man, who everything that hit him stuck and got valuable" (*GCH* 121). Contingency (luck) is again at issue, and note the dropping of "to" after "stuck": the words describe an elusive incorporation, with "stuck" connoting not surface adhesion (i.e., stuck *to* him) but the breaking of skin. This undoing of body and ego fortifications seems necessary to creating value; moreover, the valuable is not something accrued by the imperial individual (also to be indicted in the title of "Westward"). Throughout, developing further Lenore's critique of Rick, Wallace's quasi-Oklahoman dialect turns "got" from a word of agential acquisition to one of submission to external forces: in the final vision of community, for instance, "on that one fine dark day a pentecost's throw from Ascension, we all of us *got* levitationally aloft" (*GCH* 146; italics mine). As a more nuanced version of the satiric Sykes scenes of *Broom*, "John Billy," with a group levitation and a recitation of Nunn's myth, seeks to provide a ritual for the restoration of ground and fertility.

In making value begin in being "stuck," Wallace incorporates near the ritual ending, as the rains arrive, a paradoxical vision of vitality: "The land commenced to look wounded" (*GCH* 145). Having begun as the story of a single man of no value, "Nunn," "John Billy" grants its ritual ensemble not only a share of the commonwealth of story and language but "an everything of flora, sheep, soil, light, elements"—the world remade by the collective, agreed-upon perception undergirding language, in Wittgenstein's terms (*GCH* 147). A breakdown in such agreement on the color of "everything" will be Wallace's object in the grim flash-fiction of a couple's dissolution, "Everything Is Green." In "John Billy," though, the newly fertile scene, in a conjunction of (healthful) wound and signs of monetary value, is marked by "coins of water bright and clean" that look "like open cancres in the red light of the low hurt red sun" (*GCH* 145). In these coins a new sort of value has been established, not just of nature but of the abidingly wounded state of the human psyche. In a narrative of car crashes and invasive metal, such liquid "coins" are a welcome respite, even if their redemption is tempered with pain. The distrust of monetary value in "Crash" becomes, then, an attempt, rampant in Wallace, to remint metal and paper currency in nature's terms.

In its quasi-tall-tale idiom, "John Billy" depends on a sense that the vaunted western frontier, once a source of expanding American value, met yet another limit when the dust rose, driving the characters toward new forms of communal personhood. Working the same vein, "Westward the Course of Empire Takes Its Way" refers to Bishop Berkeley's famous phrase but more pointedly to the Emanuel Gottlieb Leutze mural, at the U.S. House of Representatives, that applies the phrase to a scene of eager pioneers enacting Manifest Destiny. This is the mythos of an eternally expansive economy that Wallace mocks by stalling his young characters at the Collision airport. While westward may lie the course of capitalist expansion, eastward is where Wallace turns in finding the ancient sources he continues to juxtapose with modern economies. In addition to the Zen influence on the story's archery imagery, there is classical mythology: Mark, a competitive archer possessing a "monstrous radiance," is the sun and archer god Apollo (*GCH* 233). But in this story his arrow is mainly a prop, and his "surgeon shirts" are a light parody of his inability to be a god of medicine and healing (Apollo's other identity) (*GCH* 236). Taking a cue from DeLillo's accenting of Joyce's legacy, Wallace takes great interest in the "survival" of mythological forms, and Mark Nechtr (named for the food of the gods) is his attempt to see how an Apollo fares in postmodern conditions, much like Lenore was Justitia placed in 1990.[21]

But despite these appeals to myth, Wallace proves no Eliotic modernist in "Westward," which thoroughly rejects Eliot's view of a sterile modernity. In this unerringly allegorical story, Mark and D.L.'s dyspeptic traveling companion *Tom Stern*berg represents *Thomas Stearns* Eliot and a bad-digestion-based reading of wasteland sensibilities, which overlook an extant plenitude and become aligned with nihilism. Sternberg's is a backed-up system (perhaps in need of the broom of roughage?), and

Wallace undermines his grim vision, consonant with Eliot's, in favor of a hopeful vision of art-driven abundance. Just as "John Billy" brought rain to a dry land, "Westward" seems to agree with Saul Bellow's Moses Herzog, who indicts in Eliot and others *the Wasteland outlook, the cheap mental stimulants of Alienation.*[22] As a consequence, Mark's development (like Karrier's in relation to valuing the creation) depends on countering the advertising mogul J. D. Steelritter's nihilistic claim that in the "verdant" landscape of Illinois lies "nothing to hold your eye, you have to pan back and forth, like a big No, your eyes so relaxed and without object they almost roll" (*GCH* 242, 244). With "pan" suggesting a camera's gaze, J.D. embodies what Wallace calls "passive spectation," the opposite of a reader's hard, open-minded work (*CW* 33).[23]

Wallace writes his response to Eliot's wasteland sensibility not through myth or allegory but, unexpectedly, Social Security—or rather, by creating a vision in which welfare-state formations are symbolized by versions of the Fisher King. An idiosyncratic, insurance-like structure calling back to the New Deal plays a crucial role in "Westward," which enshrines the grandparental generation of the 1930s—and becomes, not coincidentally, a story of social insurance—through the invented town of Collision, ostensibly named after its founding event, a car crash that kills a local farmer named Kroc. Collision is also common American shorthand for car insurance, importantly the kind that pays out when one injures another. But in Wallace's contortion of the idea, the grief-stricken, wealthy woman driving the car (revealed to be the eventual Mrs. Steelritter, mother of J.D.) instinctively offers Kroc's family, with "no litigation," a "settlement way beyond legal" as recompense. The pun on "settlement" and Collision's name suggest that the community both arises out of trauma and is inseparable from the social buffering that legal/insurance settlements represent (*GCH* 258, 259). Insurance is thus, for Wallace, community itself: this community *is* collision and the shared risk of getting struck or stuck, a political expansion of Wallace's idea that "an ineluctable part of being a human self is suffering" and that readers, by realizing their own pain is shared, grow "less alone" (*CW* 22).

Out of guilt, Mrs. Steelritter remains fixed to the spot in her car, and in a foreshadowing of the attention to fulfilling promises that Mark learns in the larger story, "her vow" to remain stationary, "plus strength of character, yielded certain implications," with "yield" figuring here as a verb of (agricultural) gain (*GCH* 258). The town's entire economy grows around this woman, who functions as a central marketplace and bank in the story's rendition of community being rebuilt within the Depression: stationary, she "wanted things, and would exchange money for the things" (*GCH* 258). Infusing what are essentially gifts into a system in which monetary exchange has utterly failed, Mrs. Steelritter is a Buddha-like god of stillness and the payment of ongoing karmic debt, or perhaps she is Cain, the Bible's first killer, who comes to be a founder of cities.

As the afflicted farmer's family takes the money and founds McDonald's with it, Wallace's narrative of a neoliberal America that has ceded community to the market is unmistakable: between the 1930s and the 1980s, shared, reparative American value went from community-founding fund to unnourishing fast-food profits, the further attenuation of a shift into an economy of advertising *about* fast food now mocking Mrs. Steelritter's initiating act. Her son, J.D.—a master of contracts who has initials evoking a lawyer's degree and has "soothed and signed" Ambrose—plans to pervert her extralegal community settlement by assembling (and then killing off, it seems) a group of TV-linked strangers in Collision (*GCH* 242). This is the culmination of his effort to make McDonald's, in a slogan that summarizes much in the neoliberal spirit to which this story is sensitive, "the world's community restaurant" (*GCH* 246).

In portraying Mrs. Steelritter turning life in a car (the fate of many in the Depression) into the founding of a town, Wallace is again romancing subjects he studied in college. "Itinerant Depressed poor, but with things, and entrepreneurial drive, flocked to" the crash site to build "shanties" around the woman (*GCH* 258). Providing money at a time of disaster, Mrs. Steelritter points to many aspects of Roosevelt's New Deal that allowed community economies to become functional again, including the old-age insurance scheme of Social Security and deposit insurance for banks. By calling this tent city a *"nouveaux-bourgeois* Rooseveltville" (a twist on the "Hoover-ville" name that satirized a previous president), Wallace suggests that not just emergency measures but the prosperous American middle class grew robustly out of Roosevelt's New Deal (*GCH* 258). Other echoes of Depression economics abound: the dead farmer represents the collapse of agriculture, and the efflorescence of agricultural "yield" with the farmer lying in the fields gestures toward not just a revamped Eliot but the Federal Crop Insurance Corporation, created in 1938 to mitigate the effects of farming disasters. The Steelritters' rose farming, begun from J.D.'s father's journeys by bicycle as (pun intended) an "itinerant peddler" of flowers, not only captures the story's spirit of Ludditism and economic atavism but recalls the reduction of many to flower selling and movement between towns for work during the Depression (*GCH* 258). These 1930s forms of value lie in contrast to the shakiness of the financial capital and loans that dominate the present, aspects of the credit economy I explore further in this chapter's conclusion.

In a move typical of the postmodernists such as Pynchon he was still prone to imitate, Wallace spatializes history and has the 1930s past survive materially in the present: in the ending breakdown scene, J.D. tells his son, DeHaven, to ask for help at three of the old "shanties," which have inexplicably survived (inhabited?) into the 1980s (*GCH* 344). Likewise, the dead farmer of Collision's founding is reincarnated as a gigantic farmer who attempts (in another evocation of Depression transactions) to pay for his car rental with a handful of grain. "What's happened to the big old farmer who's unable to trade a whole season's sweat and effort, in the tradition that made the U.S.A. . . . . possible and great, for a lousy three weeks of flashy transport?" Wallace writes in further economic nostalgia and adoration of an American work ethic (*GCH* 268). As in "Crash of '69," history proves repetitive: this farmer also gestures toward the crisis of farm devaluation in Reagan's America. The car is "for the farmer's eldest son's potential wedding to a loan officer's daughter," sign of the move from farm-based valuation to an economy of money and usury (*GCH* 268). The farmer in effect "wins" the westward march of progress, though, appearing in a final scene, carless but driving his tractor past DeHaven's stalled vehicle. While he never proves any sort of socialist or utopianist, Wallace finds much that his contemporary world has left behind in the insurance and other collective supports grounded in the New Deal, here given various magical renderings.

"Westward," as it assesses the current state of American "empire," is also anxious about the east, aware that the mythos of Manifest Destiny its title points to now has as much relevance to economic realities as Zusatz's mythical "hewing" did to 1970s Ohio. Watching an episode of *Hawaii Five-0* leads J.D. to posit that the popular TV story of "white guys flying around in helicopters restoring order to this oriental island" reflects American anxiety over the Vietnam War (*GCH* 318). That is Wallace's invitation to read his novella—and its awkward inclusion of stereotyped "Orientals" at the Collision airport (*GCH* 302)—as an allegory of 1980s east/west competition: DeHaven, wearing the Ronald McDonald suit, represents a burger-flipping service economy but also, with his broken-down, homemade car, beleaguered American auto manufacturing in the process of being overtaken, Wallace implies, by Japan. Hence the car full of Japanese people that speeds past the stranded, oilless main characters, leading to a racist rant from J.D. Note the trace of Dave in the name of DeHaven, who practices postmodern art (atonal composing) when he is not jury rigging a car evocative of a postmodernist pastiche: the franchised Funhouse discos of Barth's postmodernism will render Dave's generation of artists mere Ronald McDonalds if new paths are not found, "Westward" suggests. As with Rick's acceptance of leisure-suit funding leading to an attenuated literature, Wallace proposes that a consumer-driven economy (one that, like Mark the writer, "produce[s] little") will be sadly reflected in aesthetic values (*GCH* 233).

The ironies are succinctly summarized when Wallace, again drawing on his economics studies, shows superabundant "corn" being converted into "coin" and thus rendered worthless (astonishing given how much McDonald's food depends on the crop, from high-fructose corn syrup to hamburgers made from corn-fed animals). Collision-area farmland is "so fertile it's worthless" because of mismanaged government subsidies, as Magda explains, providing another 1980s economics lesson: they see "so much corn that it's literally worthless, oodles . . . of bushels of Supply that intersect the market's super . . . elastic Demand curve down near the base, where Supply equals oodles and Price equals the sort of coin you don't even bother to bend over to pick up" (*GCH* 299–300). Thus does the economy of Price and exchange value, abstracted from earthly abundance, come into alignment with J.D.'s nihilistic "big No," also directed at the corn.

J.D.'s economy is hamburger flipping times "billions and billions": total service, total consumption, end and death oriented, a prototype for the promise of limitless pleasures in *Infinite Jest* (*GCH* 252). J.D.'s vision, like Bombardini's, foregoes production in favor of massive, orgiastic consumption remaking the limits of human appetite. The ad man seeks to be a modern-day Dionysus (antagonist to Mark's ordering Apollo), planning a "general orgiastic *Walpurgisrevel*" saturated with McDonald's food (*GCH* 266). After the attendees' deaths, J.D. will "retire to the intersection where everything started. At peace in the roaring crowd's center. Maybe have a long-needed nap, stretched out on the intersected road" (*GCH* 310–311). J.D. thus envisions himself as another Fisher King for this dead-end narrative, laying false claim to a regenerative cycle: "in Death, [advertising] will of course become Life" (*GCH* 310). Where his Depression-era mother unconsciously created a bonded community out of her accident, J.D.'s manufactured Reunion, while also dependent on his largesse, reads as a fascistic inversion of his birthright. The Reunion is a contemporary *Triumph of the Will*, a spectacle with a "gemmed altar" under gigantic "twin arches of plated gold" (*GCH* 310).[24]

Before turning to other elements of the search for enduring value in "Westward," let me expose one other aspect of *Girl*'s view of welfare-state politics—and of its connection of 1930s values to Wallace's lifetime—by examining "Lyndon," a rare opportunity to scrutinize Wallace in terms of race, gender, and sexual identity.[25] One of Wallace's oblique political histories and an homage to Barthelme's "Robert Kennedy Saved from Drowning," "Lyndon" is subliminally about the extension of FDR's New Deal in LBJ's vision of a Great Society—in Medicare and other state stands against poverty and health crises. Filled with political apathy in the opening scene of his hiring, the protagonist David Boyd has a conversion proleptic of Chris

Fogle's and agrees to take on Johnson's "Same Day Directive" (*GCH* 83), which requires answering all constituent mail the day it arrives—an echo of Lenore's information sorting and a precursor of the Sisyphean task of human tax examination.

Boyd, a closeted gay man, works through the suicide of a male lover, a disastrous marriage to a woman, and a long-term relationship with a Haitian immigrant named René Duverger, who suffers from what Max identifies as a historically very early case of AIDS (*Every Love Story*, 84). The story is about not only the acceptance of Boyd by Lyndon but a bond of familial love, vivified by the ending's surprise connection between Johnson and Duverger. In Duverger's name I hear "diverge" or "divergent"—that is, in this multiple minority, a black, gay, working-class immigrant with a disease that will be stigmatized (when not totally ignored) for years to come by mainstream American society and government, Wallace renders a symbol of the new social movements of the 1960s pressing for awareness and change. In a sign of just how strongly he believes in the power of a state's compassion and in affective politics generally, Wallace ends "Lyndon" with the president and Duverger embracing in the White House bedroom. Might they in fact, in this story's rewriting of history, be lovers, unbeknownst to Boyd? The story leaves things highly ambiguous. Both extremely ill, the white man and the black man lie together among the policy notes Boyd fears he has lost—rhetoric of a Great Society and civil-rights legislation given flesh.

The tragedy of these imminent deaths keeps this from being any sort of utopian view of the nation, but we should still sense beneath the surface an idealism about Washington's intimate reach as well as a trust in Lyndon's patriarchal benevolence. With the identity of a "boy" who grows up emphasized in alter-ego David Boyd (read: David, boy-ed), Wallace mediates a childhood imagining of presidential virtues that may have fed his own ambitions to run someday for Congress: Johnson was, after all, Wallace's "first" president, from age one to age six, no doubt familiar from TV. Here he gets remade. Calling upon Johnson also allows Wallace to criticize the work of a postmodern ironist: Robert Coover's scurrilous *The Public Burning*, which Wallace refers to in "E Unibus Pluram," citing the scene "in which Eisenhower buggers Nixon on-air" (*SFT* 45).[26] Where Coover's "repulsive political farces exploded hypocrisy" in line with the ironist agenda, "Lyndon" is Wallace's effort to build something new and palliative from the 1960s, doing specific recuperative work in Coover's wake by giving Johnson a homoerotic experience that also projects a compassionate U.S. welfare state, an extension of the vision of "Westward" (*SFT* 66). The eloquent Lyndon—while subjected by the country to the fate of an Oedipus, the story implies—is one of Wallace's potent antidotes to the "buffoonish" fathers, "ineffectual spokesm[e]n for hollow authority," endemic to that more powerful force of the 1960s, TV (*SFT* 62, 61).

"ONLY THAT CAN BE ONLY GIVEN": VALUING COMMODITIES AND PERSONS

As a coda to this chapter, let me turn from these more historicized readings of value(s) to the connected issues of axiological fiction: deciding how to value the apparent "radiance" of other people and oneself, especially as this task intersects with the overwhelming importance placed on commodification in postmodernity (*GCH* 233). Throughout *Girl*, Wallace makes his characters reconcile with true radiance, those sources of interpersonal warmth that he faithfully shows remain beneath the layering of abstracting, cold systems. Julie in "Little, Expressionless Animals," for instance, "brightly serene" on her televised winning streak, "radiates a sort of oneness with the board's data," a pose her loved ones and the reader must try to see past (*GCH* 17). To make sense of her underlying radiance, for the seemingly commonplace name Julie Smith, we should read *joule-smith*— that is, one who works (like a blacksmith or wordsmith) in the medium of face-to-face heat energy, the realm to which *Girl* tries to move TV's hot lights. Here the joule, another unit of systems' work, plays a role similar to that of Lenore's foot-pound in *Broom*. Being a joulesmith—a generator of actual heat and, in his case, the use value of food—also befuddles Bruce, the brilliant programmer of "Here and There." Though expert with computer electronics and programming, Bruce cannot fix his aunt's stove, a means of reheating lunch for her husband, a simple act of daily love. Wallace returns once again here to a failure of the *oikos*, of the household hearth. When he tells his aunt her stove is "old and poor and energy-inefficient," Bruce is also in effect denying features of his embodied self. His aunt's reply— that the stove has "sentimental value"—summarizes the kind of alternative value that Bruce's *Tractatus*-led logic obscures (embracing a picture-theory of language, he begins the story kissing a photo) (*GCH* 169).

"Westward" also has much to say about both human radiance and value, in the voice of a largely hidden first-person narrator. Wallace says he often makes readers "fight *through*" the voice of his narrative, and in "Westward" the reader fights through the narrator's authority on valuing, especially of people (*CW* 33). At the beginning, to return to important lines quoted in my introduction, this narrator conceives of persons in commodity terms, saying Mark has "just this monstrous radiance of ordinary health—a commodity rare, and thus valuable" (*GCH* 233–234). But why should a person's health be a commodity, shining like a coin, or derive value from rarity? One's health should have absolute, not comparative or competitive value. As with external judgments of body, so too with metaphysical qualities: especially in the beginning, viewing the man from the outside before omnisciently inhabiting his consciousness, the narrator takes a knowing tone about the monetary wealth from which Mark's seemingly noble response to D.L.'s (probably fake) pregnancy must truly derive. Of Mark's decision to marry D.L. (part of the story's play with the image of Christ's father, Joseph), the narrator sneeringly remarks, "Most in the Program thought it was the kind of rare unfashionable gesture that these days only someone of incredible value could afford to make" (*GCH* 238). We linger in this sentence on the edge between monetary value and moral values; the narrator is unable to judge the latter free of the former.

Foreshadowing such tendencies, in the story's second paragraph, this narrator offers another of Wallace's (hypo)theses about value: "We in the writing program—shit, even the kids over at E.C.T. Divinity—could love only what we valued" (*GCH* 234). "Only" is a word of exclusion and rarity that "Westward" works with repeatedly in relation to solipsism (see Mark's delusion "that he's the only person in the world who feels like the only person in the world" [*GCH* 305]). "Only" is also a powerful tool for the modal logician, and it is easily misplaced syntactically. As Max notes, Wallace was fond of a classroom grammar lesson on the word's ambiguities that made sport of the major differences between "I fed *only* the dog," "*Only* I fed the dog," and "I *only* fed the dog!" (*Every Love Story*, 271). In the line from "Westward," the set of the loved is contained in the larger set of the valued—value must come first, this line claims. From the digression on E.C.T. Divinity emanates the hubris of such a position, reminiscent of the creation of the G.O.D. in *Broom*, for the narrator implies that, just as Joseph's biblical moral values are outmoded, not even the absolute love of *agape* (what the Divinity students examine) can escape his earthly valuations. Readers naturally expect that this first-person narrator's identity will emerge more fully—but it never does because Wallace is really addressing the coproduction of meaning between writer and reader in this "we": the reader is in the idiosyncratic "writing program" of this text, and its ultimate objective is for reader and writer ("we") to discern a relationship between loving and valuing, without giving into the logical-positivist view of emotional, nonempirical values as (to quote LeMahieu again) "senseless or nonsense."[27]

Surprisingly, Mark McGurl mentions "Westward" only once (very briefly, in an endnote) in his highly regarded examination of postwar creative writing, *The Program Era*.[28] But the exclusion makes sense: Wallace is working through philosophical positions here more than he is meditating directly on his MFA experience at Arizona. The novella's narrator emerges not so much from the university as social institution, the "program" in McGurl's sense, as from a "program" in the computer's sense—mathematical mindsets and logical positivism.[29] Likewise, identifying Barth's Johns Hopkins as "East Chesapeake Tradeschool" is not just a jab at an elite creative-writing program but Wallace's idealistic suggestion that fiction writing is artisanal "produc[tion]" (*GCH* 233) and, more importantly, trade, the exchange of an alternative form of economic value—his "living transaction" made ascendant again.[30]

The narrator's perspective changes dramatically over the course of "Westward," turning quite dramatically from fascism to Buddhism: judging Mark's good looks on the first page, the narrator foreshadows J.D.'s fascist spectacle by expressing nostalgia for an "ancient Aryan order" (*GCH* 233). By the last page, though, the real drama of transformed perception in the story having been his own, the narrator rejects commodity terms, exposing J.D.'s treasured market spin as the wheel of samsaric desire and referring to a third eye: "See this thing. See inside what spins without purchase. Close your eye. Absolutely no salesmen will call. Relax. . . . I want nothing from you" (*GCH* 373).

Between those two points, in concomitant developments around "value," this narrator mistakenly characterizes the transmission of the narrative itself as subject to a presumed scarcity of the reader's time and attention, taken as commodities or currency to be spent. After one of many seeming digressions, he remarks, "I'm sorry . . . I am *acutely* aware of the fact that our time together is valuable. Honest. So, conscious of the need to get economically to business, here are some plain, true, unengaging propositions" (*GCH* 235). With this voice Wallace lampoons, along with Barth's metafiction, the allegedly more "honest" and businesslike tone of the minimalist contemporaries with whom he emerged in the 1980s, particularly Bret Easton Ellis and Jay McInerney, implicitly calling their stark sentences "unengaging," productive of no bond with the reader and derived from the capitalist ethos they bemoan. But in a formal undermining of stated principles, Wallace's narrator also pens maximalist sentences arguing points about "the pained product of inglorious minimalist labor" and mounts a mock-encomium to Gordon Lish (*GCH* 265). Like the characters, the narrator, possibly looking ahead to a truly maximalist book, is working out a deep relationship to an economy of word and self—and finding that "spending" language is utterly different from spending money or time.

Mark tries eventually to depart from the precepts of value-as-scarcity, the iron law of the commodity system, into the transcendent interpersonal value of the gift. Hyde emphasizes repeatedly that the gift must *move*: "the gift keeps going"; "a gift that cannot move loses its gift properties"; "The gift not only moves, it moves in a circle," returning increase to its originator, who then passes that increase on again.[31] But Wallace registers the absence of such increase in "Westward" by making a gift of seemingly limitless value the basis on which characters remain stalled. "Mark's Dad," as a wedding gift, gives his son and D.L. "a Visa card with no limit, in the Dad's name, to help establish credit," but Avis (a name representing a failed flight from the self, into a westward frontier) requires that the card be in the renter's name (*GCH* 238). For Wallace, his 1980s generation may have inherited plenty of spending power from their parents, but again, in the realm of moral values, the children have been left with "an inheritance of absolutely nothing," with useless credit. Thus in parallel with Mrs. Steelritter's "beyond legal" indebtedness to the Krocs, "Westward" places "credit," a term of finance, in the plane of human relationships. The pedantic D.L., confronting the Avis agent, gets the point across: "'Though the credit is unlimited,' [D.L.] says slowly, 'it's not *ours*, you're saying. It's unlimited, but it's not about responsibility, and so in some deep car-rental-agency sense" (and, Wallace suggests, deep moral-philosophical "agency" sense) "isn't really credit at all?" (*GCH* 274). As with the farmer's grain evoking the Depression's devaluation of currency, Wallace ingeniously strips money away, laying bare the question of honoring not the credit card but the *credibility* of the persons themselves.[32] In this context, we should regard Mark himself as living currency: his name plays on the German mark (famous for 1920s hyperinflation), and his climactic realizations center on ideas about the "self's coin" (*GCH* 369), seemingly the medium honored in the "living transaction" of Wallace's fiction.

"Honor" becomes perhaps the most important word in "Westward" and a site at which Wallace begins constructing the famous calls to "quaint, naïve, anachronistic" sincerity that have structured his reception (*SFT* 81). Honor, kin of honesty, has clear connections to the issue of sincerity. Wallace is sketching an early draft of "E Unibus Pluram" (particularly its stirring final paragraph) when he has those identified with postmodern writing in "Westward" confront the seeming outdatedness of honor: D.L., refusing to eat the fried rose petals, feels "old fashioned . . . She does like the word *virtue*. *Honor* is even a noun to her, sometimes" (*GCH* 320); Ambrose, discussing Mark's story of Dave with the workshop, calls it "charmingly unfashionable to hear *honor* actually used as a noun, today" (*GCH* 360). Today, whether in 1989 or 2017, when we more commonly use "honor" as a verb of financial transactions (we honor legal tender, honor a debt), we draw forward into modernity aspects of the economy of "honor price" or "face" in seventh-century Ireland that Graeber reviews in his history of debt, a book that shares with Wallace a drive to strip away our assumptions about what precisely money transacts between humans. Graeber writes of the medieval Celts paying for injuries in terms of "honor price": "One's honor was the esteem one had in the eyes of others, one's honesty, integrity, and character, but also one's power, in the sense of the ability to protect oneself [and family] from . . . degradation."[33] The attention in "Westward" to the origins of the transactable in personal moral integrity draws on an idealized version of this history: a person's esteem emerges from the face-to-face interactions Wallace so often valorizes, liberating them from the quantifying, commodifying terms with which the narrator wants initially to judge Mark's "value." No bank card can be honored when this type of credit-ability—this credibility, this truthfulness or sincerity—is at issue.

The violent history of slavery and degradation in which Graeber locates honor economies also survives into modernity in criminality: honor among thieves and mobsters, often subject to a cruel enforcement when it is breached. Wallace turns to this meaning in the noirish murder story Mark writes of Dave, which turns on the latter's decision whether to "rat" on a fellow prisoner (*GCH* 367). By not doing so (and thus, in one of this story's many paradoxes, nobly telling a lie), Dave defines that alternative, person-centered currency—resistant to market fluctuations—that lies at the core of the symbolism in "Westward": "The fact that he *does not rat*: this is his self's coin, value constant against every curve's wave-like surge. Dave covets, values, hoards, and will not spend his honor. He'll not trade, not for anything the cosmic Monty's got stashed behind any silver curtain" (*GCH* 369–370).

Dave decides, "They can't take your honor. Only that can be only given" (*GCH* 369). Here, we should see a reply to the narrator's opening line, "We . . . could love only what we valued." Whereas the earlier "only" formulation supported the narrator's combination of cold logic and commodifying principles at the expense of unconditional love, Wallace crafts Dave's insight into honor so that the word of logical exclusion—"only"—now defines an outward-facing ethic of giving, defying the assumption that the self is at bottom an object of ownership. The passive verb, "given," sets us up for the ending's rejection of love statements that are more about the speaking ego than the beloved ("You are loved" [*GCH* 373] instead of "I love you"). But "given" also, quite sneakily, shows that the self-valuing Mark discovers through his story is axiological: "given" here means both gift and logical axiom. Thus "Westward," too, is an axiological fiction, one in which Wallace deftly combines economic history and philosophical poetry in a critique of American values. Against the positivist who would claim that a system's logical given must arise solely in the realm of empirical fact, Wallace proposes a model in which the given arises from the subjective, valuing self, from the ethical realm of generosity, honor, and gifts. No wonder the ultradigressive narrator of "Westward" starts over again and again and struggles with ordering events: he is confused throughout, as nearly every Wallace character is, about where to find his ground and, by extension, his values.

In closing, let me suggest as well a metaphilosophical meaning for the "Lord" of this story, Jack, the *Hawaii Five-0* star. As Mark tries to find a metaphysical value for himself outside the metaphors of monetary value, he is, finally, a Hegelian slave, a topic covered in a section of *Phenomenology of Spirit* LaVache skipped over. The name Mark Nechtr is loaded with significance: aside from German currency, the associations of Mark include the archer's target and its rings of point values, the "mark" or dupe of film noir (important to the prison story), and mere signification (like weightless Lenore, Nechtr is ultimately just a mark on a page). As for Nechtr, Boswell notes the nod to Barth's Ambrose (and ambrosia) in the homophone "nectar" (*Understanding*, 105), but Wallace also returns here to Hegel. In Mark's story of his own imprisonment (his bondage) through Dave, Wallace activates the echo in the oddly spelled Nechtr of *knecht*, German for servant or slave and famously rendered in philosophy as *Knechtschaft* in "Lordship and Bondage."[34]

In prison, Dave the bondsman encounters his lord, or Lord. Jack Lord functions here as an instantiation of his name—the distanced perspective of his helicopters, his air of lordship. Wallace makes sure with this Lord that we are quite alienated from any simple allegorical scheme in which he might stand in for a Judeo-Christian God and Mark for an orthodox believer. By rendering Mark/Dave as a slave—a seeker of transcendence, of the infinite—Wallace gives us a highly compressed preview of his more expansive ruminations on the slavery and valuelessness of the addicts in *Infinite Jest*. After spurning Jack Lord's model of heroism early on, Wallace's masterpiece, to which I now turn, will also culminate in an encounter between a quasi-mystical other and an immobilized criminal, one who will struggle mightily with what in him is gift and given.

3

DEI GRATIA

WORK ETHIC, GRACE, AND GIVING IN *INFINITE JEST*

don, *n. 2*: *Obs. rare.* A donation, gift.
—*OED*

WORKERS OF Wallace, unite; you have nothing to lose but your uniqueness. In this chapter I hardly seek to disagree with the critical consensus that *Infinite Jest*, in fusing techniques of avant-garde experimentation with elements of pathos and sincerity never before associated with postmodernism, marks a watershed in not just Wallace's career but the imperatives of contemporary fiction. At the same time, building on my first two chapters, I argue for substantial continuities between the Wallaces of the 1980s (especially in *The Broom of the System*) and 1996, including a preference for grounding his moral satires in figures associated with weight, work, and a respect for pragmatic, unintellectualized intuitions. Don Gately is the character who makes *Infinite Jest* a masterpiece: Wallace began the novel as early as 1986 and returned to it in 1988 and 1989; "none of it worked, or was alive," he writes, but then "in '91–'92 all of a sudden it did."[1] The book was catalyzed by Wallace's stay in early 1990 in Granada House, the model for Ennet House, but in particular the resident "Big Craig," a former burglar who became the basis for Gately and a major addition to the novel-in-progress.[2] Like many critics of *Infinite Jest* (Elizabeth Freudenthal is one example),[3] I describe Gately as the exception to the novel's ethos of addiction, despair, and disembodiment, a man on the rise in comparison to Hal's deepening well of denial, but I distinguish Gately in terms—of work, weight, value, and unassuming virtues of gratitude and generosity—new to the proliferating discourse on Wallace's big book. The crucial act in *Infinite Jest* is working to raise one's felt value while respecting somatic, mental, and ecological limits and thus avoiding the trap that ensnares many—a belief in false forms of self-expansion and in the joke transcendence that is one vicious valence of the book's title. Such a jesting infinity lies in the falsely transcendent skies represented on the first edition's cover and in Tavis's waiting room at E.T.A., where "the wallpaper scheme was fluffly cumuli" and "overenhancedly blue sky, incredibly disorienting wallpaper" that makes Hal (in an echo of the ungrounded Lenore) feel "high-altitude . . . and sometimes plummeting" (*IJ* 509). The antidotes lie in Wallace's gospel of work but also in the new forms of alternative economy—new forms of work and living transaction—that he finds in the recovery methods of Alcoholics Anonymous.

As required by AA, Gately gets a "humility job" (*IJ* 361) as a janitor at the Shattuck Shelter for Homeless Males, where he cleans bathrooms, some of the men gathering behind him to "watch him jet feces off the shower-tiling, treating it like a sport and yelling encouragement and advice" (*IJ* 435). Gately's sober (though also quite comic) confrontation with the consequences of overindulgence lies in contrast to the book's many obsessive-compulsive cleaners (Avril, Joelle) and the absurd toxic-waste policy practiced in the Organization of North American Nations. There are also resonances of mythological heroism in Gately's labors: Burn identifies Gately with Heracles and his legendary twelve labors but does not mention the first of the penitential labors, the cleaning of the Augean stables by rerouting rivers, comically suggested in the shower scene.[4] For Wallace, Gately's job is an important source of growth: meaningful work has largely been lost as a practice and point of ethical reference in this society, and this novel demonstrates the power of becoming the "parents" doing the work of cleaning up after the wild party of postmodernism

(*CW* 52). Gately's narrative eventually centers on this sort of parental (house)work, more community oriented and less humiliating than cleaning showers, though often more frustrating: caring for the residents of Ennet House as a live-in counselor, including soothing the child addicts when they have bad dreams.

For Gately, read Gat———y, and for Don, read don in the mafia sense—that is, *Infinite Jest* rewrites the life of another man with a mob-connected past who is shot outside his house, Jay Gatsby. In *Girl with Curious Hair*, Wallace had dispersed across several stories his ambitious echoes of *The Great Gatsby*: of Faye he writes that her "cries rang out like money" (*GCH* 4), echoing Nick's famous line about Daisy Buchanan (née Fay). The ending of "Lyndon" rewrites *Gatsby*'s, while J.D.'s arches, "inclined like a child's severe eyebrows" over the horizon, rework T. J. Eckleburg's billboard eyes in "Westward," which also features a land speculator named Gatz (*GCH* 311). On the larger canvas of *Infinite Jest*, though, bidding to join the tradition of the Great American Novel (a capitalized cultural "dream" Lawrence Buell dissects using *Gatsby* and *Infinite Jest* as examples),[5] Wallace offers a positive outcome for his Gat———y: reconceiving the American story of opulence and inevitable crash, Wallace allows Gately to lay partial claim to a vast, redeeming wealth of a nonmonetary sort, centered on taking up the identity more thoroughly played on in his first name—the "don" as gift, the seventeenth-century definition given in my epigraph (again, "outdated," like the virtue of sincerity and the meaning of bedesman). Building on Mark's association with honored value, Don's payment for his humility takes the form of living currency that I unfold in this chapter around coinage and the galvanizing new Wallace subject of grace, the *Gratia* of my title. Through that idiosyncratic form of value Wallace seeks to counter the kinds of poisonous exchange that characterize not only the circulation of his title film but geopolitical and market formations in the neoliberal vein.

On the level of form, reading for value I also find partial confirmation for the bold claims Wallace made about the cohesiveness of his baggy monster. Of reviews calling the book excessive, he says, "There's nothing in there by accident."[6] "If it looks chaotic, good, but everything that's in there is in there on purpose" (*CW* 64). Echoing its author, Joseph Conte is right to class *Infinite Jest* among postmodern novels that, rather than embracing chaos, "propose that out of the vortex of their disorderliness a capacity of self-organization may emerge." Such works "exhibit [great] surface complexity" but ultimately "reveal their principles of organization."[7] The dogged search for value production and a viable, sustainable model of self-expenditure—especially in relation to felt forms of nourishment and warmth—is an organizing principle allowing us to draw compelling through-lines from Hal's opening contortions to Gately's work and Fackelmann's ending windfall and Dilaudid binge. Moreover, as I argue in the chapter's conclusion, *Infinite Jest*'s meditations on its verbal economies and those of its characters give way to a vision of language as not just something encyclopedically weighty but as shared asset, as indivisible good.

Especially now as he vies for comparison to encyclopedic postmodern classics, mundane work, whether at Shattuck or Ennet, represents for Wallace a significant gap in the work of the predecessors who cast long shadows on the subject of Protestant America: Gaddis and Pynchon. In *Gravity's Rainbow* Pynchon, showing malignant incursions of the Puritan vocabulary into American life, had pointedly named his protagonist Tyrone Slothrop, for sloth, a rejection of the Protestant call to work. Further credence comes in Pynchon's 1993 essay on sloth as a deadly sin, which almost entirely disregards the real impact of melancholia in a way Wallace never would, interpreting the state of *acedia* in terms of its anticapitalist and Luddite potential.[8] Luc Herman and Steven Weisenburger write, "Calvinism's gospel was that, in [*Gravity's Rainbow*'s] phrasing . . . 'we are meant for work and government, and austerity.'"[9] The rest of the line they quote is even more critical of the call to work: work, government, and austerity "shall take priority over love, dreams, the spirit, the senses," all things "found among the idle and mindless hours of the day."[10] Wallace, differing in his resistance to the capitalist order, sees such rebellious claims as exemplary of a 1960s social-liberation discourse that may have succeeded in "explod[ing] hypocrisy" but could not retain a positive value for the square values of discipline and work, which he continues to prize as fictional subjects (*SFT* 65).

Gaddis offers Wallace a more positive model on the possibilities of work. John Lingan, sounding as though he is analyzing *The Pale King*, writes that for Gaddis, "work equaled an individual effort . . . to sort through the swarming cultural ephemera and create, with monastic persistence, something that no machine or business could adequately reproduce."[11] In an essay on American culture, Gaddis approvingly quotes Ernst Troeltsch's indictment of capitalism "'steal[ing] into the Calvinist ethic'" and distorting its meaning by regarding "'profit . . . as the sign of the Divine approval'" and of assurance of one's election.[12] Sykes in *Broom* spoke this language of profitable Christianity in only slightly exaggerated form. Characters in Gaddis's *J R* extend the argument with greater satiric force: "God damned Protestant ethic can't escape it have to redeem it," says Gibbs,[13] and another character laments that the "whole Protestant work ethic" has fallen prey to a "General Motors" philosophy of "utilitarian pragmatism" (*J R*, 530).[14] Wallace, too, I suggest here, sets out to redeem the Protestant ethic, though he does so by reinscribing the issues of American industriousness and utilitarianism (and the sadness of the slothful) in areas rarely touched on by Gaddis and other predecessors: psychological health in a pharmacological age, the spiritual implications of entertainment choices, and the general denigration of sentiment.

In chapter 1 I argued that Lenore embodied a baseline definition of work, energy, and weight lifting that could not be gainsaid, even by a decadent society. In *Infinite Jest*, the questions of how to rise and to lift (one's own) weight are endemic: how to grow, how to generate heat, how to be agential in a way objects are not. The story of a trainer dying locked in a sauna room, recounted ten pages from the end, recalls *Broom's* greenhouse motif and alludes to the warp-speed cultivation of young people attempted at E.T.A. (*IJ* 971). As we will see, unbalanced and disabled figures drive the narrative, and a weight room is a key locale for wisdom and therapy. James's father counsels his son at the start of a devilish monologue to "see just how much force you need to start the [garage] door easy, let it roll up out open on its hidden greasy rollers and pulleys in the ceiling's set of spiderwebbed beams" (*IJ* 157). *Infinite Jest* looks intently at those dark, spiderwebbed spaces, trying to see precisely how the mechanism of the self and its rising (its opening up) works. A doppelgänger to Gately who also ends up hospitalized at St. Elizabeth's, Doony Glynn (read: D——on—— Gly——), provides a negative example on this score. He first appears in the text as the filer of a fraudulent worker-compensation report, a Buster Keatonesque story (based on a decades-old joke) of lifting a load of bricks that testifies to his fall back into addiction (*IJ* 138–140). To establish the self, avoid relapse, and truly rise, one must actually work.

For his part, Hal believes that, rather than pulling on the pulley rope to lower one's emotional flag to half-mast, one can raise the pole itself, "to like twice its original height" (*IJ* 42). But with this unlikely feat, involving a signifier of the nation-state, he maintains a fantasy of feral growth, of manipulating the scale rather than actually changing the self, just as his country has Reconfigured the territories over which its flag flies rather than scale back. There are always in Wallace's corpus many paths to avoiding embodied relationships—their heat, their limits on derivable value, the work needed to sustain them—and nowhere is this more the case than in this sprawling novel.

In the first of this chapter's three major sections, I again, as with *Broom*, define the fictional world's prevailing relationships to value, and the economic ethos—for both persons and continents—aligned with abstracted and mathematicized value. This section culminates in an analysis of neoliberal "free trade" and another view of slavery according to Wallace. In the second major section I define the countervailing force of Gately and his connections to coinage, gifts, chance, and grace—all linked to elements of his work life that have been neglected in criticism focused on sincerity, irony, and limited aspects of the novel's spiritual themes. I then turn to Jonathan Lethem's gift aesthetics to complete this argument. In the concluding section I characterize the novel, major parts of which take place *on* Commonwealth (the Boston street), as a novel *of* commonwealth, unpacking Hal and Don's contrasting relationships to language as object of value, consumption, and inflation.

IN-FIELD AND ECONOMICS: VALUE AS A FOREIGN LANGUAGE

Let me enter into this book's philosophical conundrums by first mapping the ground. Enfield, an invented locale, is "one of the stranger little facts that make up the idea that is metro Boston," a "kind of arm-shape extending north from Commonwealth Avenue and separating Brighton into Upper and Lower, its elbow nudging East Newton's ribs and its fist sunk into Allston" (*IJ* 240). Showing Enfield to be grounded not in space but the *Tractatus*esque "little facts that make up . . . idea[s]," the description registers the reduction of the body to two dimensions that runs rampant here as well as a sadistic aggression of fists, elbows, and an arm suggestive of the players' hypertrophied limbs at E.T.A., used in pursuit of the next "plateau" of their ranked value (*IJ* 116). For Enfield, we might read "In-Field," with field signifying the gaming arena or—as in *Everything and More*'s mentions of "number-fields" and "field theory" (216, 218)—an abstract collection of data, say, the set of complex numbers or rational numbers (in my terms, values). In this context, Erdedy comes first in the main plot sequence because his name, combining the German for earth (*erde*) with morphemes suggesting "already" and "dead," summarizes the Field- and addict-driven destruction of the lived-in world: as with LaVache's misreading of Hegel and J.D.'s panning "No," nature's ground has been obliterated by perception. Eschaton, which lays a map on top of a map, is another example: it depends, a long endnote says, on calculus's "Mean Value Theorem" (*IJ* 323), which can deal "with anything that varies within a (*definable*) set of boundaries"—including (in a telling contrast between mathematical and moral values) "a certain drug's urine-level range between Clean and Royally Pinched" (*IJ* 1024n123).

Hal is the spokesman for the intimate stakes of In-Field sorts of value. In one of the most pithy descriptions of depression that Wallace ever wrote, Hal, contemplating the disjunction between embodiment and math, "finds terms like *joie* and *value* to be like so many variables in rarified equations, and he can manipulate them well enough to satisfy everyone but himself that he's in there, inside his own hull, as a human being—but in fact he's far more robotic than John Wayne" (*IJ* 694). Burn notes that *joie*, happiness, is ironically evoked by the initials of Hal's suicidal father, James O. Incandenza (*Reader's Guide*, 55), but "hull" here is also a near-homophone of "Hal." In the gap between "Hal" and "hull" is the suggestion that his hull is in fact empty, a mere shell, containing no "human being." "*Value*" is, like "*joie*," invoked as mention rather than use through the distancing power of italics, and the foreignness of "*joie*" (which would call for italicization anyway) subtly marks "*value*" too as distant and strange. *Value*, in sum, is a foreign word in *Infinite Jest*: it ought to be a stabilizing term, naming what fills the hull of the self. Yet, as with Lenore's weight, value slips away from being a felt state and into abstraction; self-worth becomes a mere number. The younger players at E.T.A. suffer in these same terms, though with less self-awareness: "The idea that achievement doesn't automatically confer interior worth," Wallace writes, "is, to them, still, at this age, an abstraction, rather like the prospect of their own death—'Caius is Mortal' and so on" (*IJ* 693).

Tracking the terms of value tells us Hal's inner narrative, his sad passage through external forms of achieved ranking. Winning a school competition rife with Field-type valuations (and recalling Julie on *Jeopardy!*), Hal feels "an LSD afterglow . . . some milky corona, like almost a halo of approved grace, made all the milkier by the faultless nonchalance of a Moms who made it clear that his value was not contingent on winning first or even second prize, ever" (*IJ* 999n76). "Almost a halo" plays on his name, and the almost-halo's "milky" makeup is an embodied doubling of the "value" that Avril, the unnourishing mother, clearly *is* withholding and making "contingent" (see here as well the students' correct suspicions that the milk at E.T.A. is a powdered substitute). As we see in these densely poetic examples and in what I termed the (hypo)theses of value in "John Billy" and "Westward," Wallace frequently writes "value" sentences designed to produce dissonance—especially when states of embodiment and love cause the dissonance.

All these lost relationships to an inhabited value are aligned with the loss of ground and balance throughout this relentlessly axiological novel— where LaVache's leglessness has become epidemic. With imagery of bodies rendered more grotesquely than anywhere else in Wallace, this balancing book reads as a collective search for ground and a stable relationship to it; a good subtitle would be "Philosophical Groundlessness and the Unbalanced Male." The Incandenza brothers are all unbalanced. An iteration of the vulnerable Achilles, Hal has an injured ankle that requires him to do daily "therapy" (a multivalent noun here) in which he stands on one foot: the "balance" "worked muscles and ligaments in the ankle that were therapeutically unreachable any other way" (*IJ* 851). He plays at times "terribly ankle-conscious"—a phrase suggesting a root, inbuilt fragility that most repress to get through the game of life (*IJ* 454). Middle brother Mario needs a police lock to lean on, especially when he saddles his head with a Bolex camera (*IJ* 315). His "block feet" are "too short to be conventionally employed," a state that, together with his delicate spine, makes Mario, no addict, walk like "a vaudeville inebriate, body tilted way forward" (*IJ* 313). The eldest, Orin, abandons tennis and its asymmetrical arms but ends up with an oversized right leg; he is off balance and vulnerable when he raises the leg as high as possible to punt (the metaphorical meaning of which—deferring responsibility and action—is crucial). These three imbalanced sons descend from a tall man nicknamed "the Stork," a top-heavy animal with long, thin legs (*IJ* 238). The discovery with which he in effect dooms North American ecology, annular fusion, arises from an abstracted vision of connecting to the ground: a spinning door knob "perfectly schematized what it would look like for someone to try to turn somersaults with one hand nailed to the floor" (*IJ* 502).

Infinite Jest is also the story of murderous men who have played a "nihilistic" game leading to the loss of the use of their legs (*IJ* 1058n304). Containing meditations on "ground-rule[s]" (*IJ* 338) and nightmares about a "face in the floor" (*IJ* 252), this novel constructs highly physical versions of the terror of philosophical groundlessness, depicting bodies with absorbing precision. The claim of one young player about stressful rankings—"I know just where I stand at all times"—embodies a naïveté that makes the E.T.A. scenes tragic: none of these children really know where they stand, or how (*IJ* 112). Freudenthal's ("Anti-Interiority," 192) claim that *Infinite Jest* insists on "anti-interiority" as the path to psychological health (that is, "a subjectivity generated by the material world" and "divested from an essentialist notion of inner . . . life") misses the way Wallace's expressionist idiom, inspired by Kafka, uses bodily deformity to vivify inward states: imbalance and leglessness are not realistic symptoms of psychology so much as a cultivated language for the psyche all its own.[15] For Wallace, the metaphysical again resides in the physical, where it can be exposed to absurdist fictional examination.

The Field-inspired sense of personal value determines as well the sad weightlessness the addict endures, as though she has ceded the felt value of her own substance to the drug itself (often called, with a telling capital, the "Substance" [*IJ* 201, 273, etc.]). One resonance of Gately's DG initials is the decigram, a common measure for drug sales, the "tenth of a gram" cocaine customers beg for (*IJ* 561) (though for a much more salutary DG, see below). "Weight" is also street slang for drugs in general, as when "yr-struly" speaks of "who else is holding weight in Enfield or Allston" (*IJ* 130). In moments of extremity, characters assert their own weightiness according to mathematical measure, as though they seek assurance of their solidity. Joelle, on the verge of attempted overdose, resorts to quantifiable values: "I am 1.7 meters tall and weigh 48 kilograms. I occupy space and have mass" (*IJ* 234). The dyne is a unit of force in physics, and with the surname van Dyne, Joelle, like Lenore, struggles to inhabit her identity and feel her own weight.

Thus when Hal says in the book's stark, one-line second paragraph, "I am in here" (*IJ* 3), rather than a statement of location, it is the cry "I EXIST," familiar from Wallace's Markson review (*BF* 83).[16] I hear in this remark "I . . . in-here" or "I inhere," meaning there is a substantialness to Hal's valueless self, to his "Empty Plenum" (the title of the Markson review). Note, too, that Hal's opening revisits Lenore's crisis of leglessness through subtle effects of word choice and grammar. "I am seated in an office," he begins, turning a statement of ontology—"I am"—into a passive verb form, with "office" (as in bureaucratic role or function) reinforcing his distance from agency (*IJ* 3). Wallace, in Hal's review of his sitting poses, travesties verbs that the rest of the novel will show to be bereft of their traditional ardor: "I *believe* I appear neutral"; "I have *committed* to crossing my legs I *hope* carefully" (*IJ* 3; italics mine). How to stand and bear weight in such a world? How to believe, commit, and hope? How to avoid "feeling as though . . . every axiom of your life turned out to be false"?[17] When Hal tries to "rise" from his chair and incites "horror" in the administrators with his voice before one makes him "taste floor" (*IJ* 12), we see that this encyclopedia of axiology, working back in time from this mysterious breakdown, will occur within that "agonizing interval between something falling off and its hitting the ground" discussed in the introduction (*GCH* 165). In lieu of a traditional *agon* of novelistic conflict, this agonizing interval is where we do interpretive work, identifying the opportunities Hal and others have to find ground and value. Can they do so by working? Can they do so by exchanging value for value? The next two sections address these questions in turn.

ECONOMIES OF SELF: THE PROTESTANT DRUG ETHIC

With all its troubled illustrations of internality, *Infinite Jest* depicts a quest not just to consume but to *contain*, to store up and accumulate, as though a concavity might be permanently filled. Bombardinis abound. But such quests for containment are often explored, ironically, through the well-managed appetites of the Protestant work ethic—a language applied, surprisingly, to the "discipline" of drug and alcohol use. Erdedy sets the pattern with his approach to (quitting) marijuana: he will "smoke the whole 200 grams . . . in four days . . . all in tight heavy economical one-hitters off a quality virgin bong." Like a good worker he will "start[] the moment he [wakes] up" and proceed with "discipline and persistence and will" (*IJ* 22).

Timothy Aubry also recognizes Erdedy's "injection of a Protestant ethic" into his addictive behavior (calling it "a dubious proposition"), but the reach of this thinking in the novel is tremendous, extending well beyond this early section.[18] In another scene of secret smoking, Hal's one-hitter has "the advantage of efficiency: every particle of ignited pot gets inhaled." The principle is even set off as a balanced economic equation: "Total utilization of available resources = lack of publicly detectable waste" (*IJ* 49). This is a family trait: James's alcoholic father tells his future alcoholic son in 1960 that his flask has "never had an errant drop, not drop *one*, spilled out of it" (except, of course, into him) (*IJ* 161). This patriarch speaks highly of economy in all things, from the "gentle and cunning economy behind" (*IJ* 158) Marlon Brando's actions to "maximum economy and minimum effort" in tennis (*IJ* 165).

The journalistic piece Wallace wrote with *Infinite Jest* in press, "A Supposedly Fun Thing I'll Never Do Again," is sometimes used (for example,
by Holland)[19] as an encapsulation of the novel's satire of pleasure industries. But the essay also contains less overt evidence of Wallace's belief in
the Protestant work ethic as a counterforce. His persona expresses faux-
humble anxiety over his assignment's cost to *Harper's*, and he keeps fum-
blingly trying to connect with workers—his diligent housekeeper and Ti-
bor the waiter, for whom Wallace has "an almost reverent respect" (*SFT*
259). But the ship erases and distorts labor. Again proving he is in dialogue with Pynchon, Wallace sees an unearned Election everywhere, with
the hard-working "preterite staff liv[ing] in mortal terror" of their bosses
(*SFT* 266n13). "A Supposedly Fun Thing" views life under capitalism as
innately eviscerating of workers' emotional states, as in the relentless "Professional Smile" Wallace laments (*SFT* 289n40). He understands, in his
constant attention to the selling of the self, what Hardt and Negri call the
"immaterial labor" of manipulated affects that neoliberalism demands.[20] In
this environment, the Protestant work ethic serves superficial maintenance
of a capitalist dream: "It's not an accident [cruise ships are] all so white and
clean, for they're clearly meant to represent the Calvinist triumph of capital and industry over the primal decay-action of the sea" (*SFT* 263). Those
on board the *Nadir* need awakening to the reality of work like Gately's at
Shattuck.

Work at E.T.A. is really working out, that ritual of postmodern gym
culture and body perfection that defined the 1980s–2000s U.S. zeitgeist
in which Wallace wrote. Mark Bresnan, studying the novel under the title "The Work of Play," argues persuasively that tennis at E.T.A., far from
"liberating," becomes "surprisingly predictable" and leads to "anxiety and
paranoia."[21] Bresnan does not tie such tendencies with play to the broader
depiction of work in the book, however. Seen as a place of work, E.T.A. is
obsessed only with potential, its name suggesting a flight not yet landed—
still showing its Estimated Time of Arrival—and thus more states of Heideggerian thrownness. E.T.A. defines the youngsters' economic agency
primarily as practice repetitions in service of an extended, all-or-nothing
gamble on making "the Show" (*IJ* 53). Ted Schacht, suffering from Crohn's

disease, is a telling comparison for Hal and others on this point: Schacht disturbs classmates because his disease forces a confrontation with the body's porousness (and with feet: Hal broods on Schacht's "enormous purple shower thongs under the door of the [bathroom] stall" [*IJ* 103]). More importantly, though, Schacht's resignation to steady work as a dentist (this text's version of accounting) shadows Hal and others as they strive for a more glamorous adulthood—and Hal would do well to attend to the health of his teeth too (*IJ* 117).[22]

As the analogies between tennis and capitalist striving mount, we imagine the E.T.A. players as young workers who have difficulties—and who are systematically kept from—balancing their massive physical exertions with mental labor on the question of what all this body-work is for, the "question[] of *why*" (*IJ* 900). From this perspective, the weight-room guru Lyle becomes a sinister and parasitic figure. Associated with the underground and foundational, Lyle speaks pithy truths, among them a formula on work, lifting, and respecting embodied limits: "Let not the weight thou wouldst pull to thyself exceed thine own weight" (*IJ* 128). A floating listener and therapist, Lyle anticipates Shane Drinion in *The Pale King* and is, Holland writes, a "spokesperson for positive self-forgetting" ("'The Art's Heart's Purpose,'" 240n11). Yet note that Lyle's weight room is a scene for Himself's continued drinking (*IJ* 379), and compared to the mentors of AA, Lyle, his tongue out, is an invasive and suspect figure. His licking practice underscores the strange economy that keeps E.T.A. running: he upends the cliché of living off the sweat of one's brow; he in a sense lives off the sweat of *others'* brows, children's, a byproduct of their difficult thinking, however sauna induced the sweat seems. For while he does help the youngsters think, their capacities for it are underdeveloped compared to the outsized anxieties their obsessions produce. Lyle is an heir to Zusatz's hewing and has as a namesake the also levitating Lyle Bland of *Gravity's Rainbow* (290–291), Slothrop's Freemason uncle, responsible for selling his nephew for Pavlovian experimentation. Are the children of E.T.A., many essentially orphaned by negligent parents, new kinds of test subjects, expressive of their own culture's dark excesses? In Wallace's world, it seems so.

ECONOMIES OF NATIONS: "FREE TRADE,"
NEOLIBERALISM, AND UTILITARIANISM

Work is undermined in *Infinite Jest*; so too is trade, whether with other persons or other nations. Living transactions seem difficult or impossible to achieve. Individuals' frantic attempts to enclose the self are reflected in the fates of countries and vice versa: the geography of annular fusion—with borders Concave or Convex—takes on the vocabulary of the mirror in which the individual regards herself and finds the internal externalized, distorted, and seemingly manipulable. Examining this motif, Paul Quinn, in a Jamesonian reading, sees in O.N.A.N. "a society that, subsumed under capital" and exchange value, "cannot relate to anything outside itself," and Heather Houser, focusing on environmental terrorism and border manipulation, argues that the novel urges "not detachment from but attachment to other people and our surroundings."[23]

Reconfiguration also shows Wallace again refracting economic history close at hand. If 1980s economic crises are a backdrop against which to judge his first two books, in *Infinite Jest* he parodies NAFTA, major news in that 1991–1992 period in which the novel came "alive" again—including in the 1992 presidential campaign, the moment when the Democrat Bill Clinton's acceptance of the pact proved that neoliberalism would hardly be limited to Republican presidencies. Wallace gestures toward his own use of NAFTA headlines when he comments on fellow quasi-historian Mario's "parodic device of mixing real and fake [articles and] historical headers" in the service of "exposition" (*IJ* 391). Continuing in the wariness of a consumption-driven economy, Wallace essentially claims that the contemporary United States has no national product to export in a trade agreement but its own massive amounts of waste, the side effect of (and, in a recursive structure, fuel for) Himself's annular fusion.

Bradley J. Fest and Daniel Grausam historicize *Infinite Jest* as a product of the early 1990s and the confusions of the immediate post–Cold War period (thus, both discuss Eschaton and Himself's military work).[24] But while it seems a stretch to call this inwardly drawn novel a true follow-up to *Gravity's Rainbow* or forerunner of *Underworld* as a nuclear text, the free trade promised in NAFTA's name cuts to philosophical and metafictional cores of Wallace's book, which coheres as an encyclopedia of coercive and death-oriented transactions and exchanges, from Erdedy's thwarted opening marijuana deal to "yrstruly's" trip to Hung Toy's, Pemulis's acquisition of the DMZ, and larger-scale developments. "Westward" stripped away the conventional buffering of money in order to confront grain, credit, and persons themselves as media of exchange. A focus on trade in *Infinite Jest*, not just commodification, allows Wallace similar liberties in assessing what can return in an exchange (always, it seems, some version of Freud's repressed). And making the reader probe networks of complicated exchange and return militates against the subliminal "messages" Wallace says he hears in TV: "'relax, we're going to give to you, you don't have to give anything back, all you need to do is every so often go and buy this product.'"[25]

The Entertainment, despite being an extreme embodiment of the consumer product, is notably never bought or sold for money or treated as a normal commodity as it circulates through the book; rather it is always unwittingly stolen, given freely (and sadistically), or "barter[ed]" (*IJ* 481). Someone (probably a vengeful Orin) sends it to the Middle Eastern medical attaché from Phoenix with the message "*HAPPY ANNIVERSARY!*" ("the medical attaché knows quite well that the English word *anniversary* does not mean the same as *birthday*," underlining the moment as a "gift"-giving occasion [*IJ* 36]). Elsewhere what we presume is the film becomes "barter" and, in a further link to annular waste, garbage: in a well-hidden transaction, Sixties Bob gets from Bertrand Antitoi a lava lamp and apothecary's mirror for the DMZ and a "waste bag" of cartridges (*IJ* 482).

NAFTA, negotiated throughout the late 1980s and ratified in December 1992, is widely seen as a signature extension of the logic of neoliberalism from the Reagan-Bush years into the Clinton era. As James McCarthy writes regarding the deregulatory and antistate logic behind such agreements, "These common neoliberal prescriptions [are] contributions to an overarching goal of increasing the flexibility and profitability of capital." McCarthy also notes the dire effects of such agreements for environmental regulation and health,[26] which Wallace toys with in depicting the Great

Concavity. NAFTA has been in place for several years already in the future setting of *Infinite Jest*; getting Canada to agree to be part of O.N.A.N. required a threat to make NAFTA "NULL," suggesting that the trade treaty's market success has overtaken decisions of sovereignty—a neoliberal effect (*IJ* 391). Domestically, the administration of Gentle, a Reagan figure who brings entertainment principles to bear in his presidency, is neoliberal to the core, with the government aiming to get a "'PIECE OF THE ACTION'" by nationalizing InterLace and selling the commonwealth value of the calendar itself through Subsidized Time (*IJ* 392). Freedom in such an environment is reduced to consumer decision making and made dependent on "appeals to an American ideology committed to the *appearance of freedom*" (*IJ* 1031n164). Reconfiguration, another historical pastiche, makes numerous allusions to past political flashpoints that have now all been subsumed by market logic: Nazi imperialism ("O.N.A.N.ite Anschluss" [*IJ* 421]); the Civil War (Lincoln's "Greater-Good-of-the-Union" decisions [*IJ* 402]); George H. W. Bush's broken 1988 "Read my lips" antitax pledge (Gentle: "Look into my eyes: no new [revenue] enhancements" [*IJ* 441]); and, with this last, even an uncanny prophecy of a future political meme ("Tea-party," the Secretary of Defense says of fears of a "tax revolt" over high-cost waste disposal [*IJ* 441]). The only question left for Gentle is how dubious governmental schemes "can be sold to the public": political persuasion has bowed to market principles (*IJ* 403).

Wallace excels at finding the longstanding philosophical values beneath topical contemporary expressions (consider his ability to read so much civic history through a single year's debate about tax policy). As I noted in the introduction, in *Infinite Jest* his object of intense and merciless scrutiny is the American religion of utilitarianism underlying the neoliberal. In debating Marathe, Steeply consistently advocates utilitarianism, whether the subject is indivisible soup or not. In the A.F.R.'s "malice" Steeply can see "no agenda or story," a metafictional point about Americans' antinarrative reduction of intentionality to sheer profit motives, not ardor, political, religious, or otherwise. Thus he wants from the A.F.R. "some set of ends we can make sense of . . . Then it's just business . . . We know which end is up when it's business" (*IJ* 422). Wallace appears to have considered the names

Inge (= ingot? or the start of "ingest"?) and Slott (as in what coins go in, at casinos in particular) before settling on Steeply, a name suggesting a steeple and thus the American church of economic utility.[27] A novel fundamentally "about belief" (Burn, *Reader's Guide*, 63), *Infinite Jest* is especially interested in those quasi-religions that go unacknowledged because to explore their worshipful stances, as Marathe does in discussing the etymology of "fanatic" (*IJ* 106–107), would disturb the notions of free will that undergird definitions of the sovereign liberal subject.

Steeply's name also suggests the steeply sloped yield curve of returns on investments, which are often rendered in terms of mathematical function as $Y(t)$, or yield over time—hence a "steep Y" (= Steeply?). Thus does the Field-driven logic of abstracted curves produce dissonance with actual ground, seen clearly as well in the "cardioid" building curves that have replaced real hearts at E.T.A. (*IJ* 983n3). Steeply's difficult ascent in his high heels to the "outcropping or shelf about halfway up" (*IJ* 88) the incline in his first scene tells us that at stake in his dialogue with Marathe is the American response to a leveling of economic yields, a reconciliation with the impossibility of endless boom, perhaps keenly on Wallace's mind as he wrote in the recession years of the early 1990s that would lead Clinton to campaign against Bush on the slogan "It's the economy, stupid." The specter of diminishing returns looms everywhere in the novel, from drugs to tennis. From the "shaved[-]flat" hilltop perch of E.T.A., another plateau (and one ironically reminiscent of Winthrop's city on a hill), these players, as representative Americans, have nowhere to go but down (*IJ* 79).

"A STRANGE KIND OF SLAVERY"

It must be noted, though, that the novel spurns identification of Marathe with antiutilitarianism, giving us, for instance, his gruesomely sadistic murder of Lucien Antitoi, punctuated by the multivalent word "*In-U-Tile*" (*IJ* 488). A keen understanding of U.S. economic values does not necessarily lead Marathe ("basically a fascist," Wallace says [Wallace and Lipsky, *Although of Course*, 157]) to see utility as a moral dead end. So too, given his wheelchair-bound state, Marathe is far from immune to his own criticism when he indicts the "fanatic of desire" as "a slave to your individual subjective narrow self's sentiments; a citizen of nothing . . . You stand on nothing. Nothing of ground or rock beneath your feet. You fall; you blow here and there"—all riffs on the leglessness and, ultimately, valuelessness the A.F.R. encapsulate (*IJ* 108).[28] Describing the many variations on this "lost" state takes Wallace hundreds of pages, so let me focus, in the context of work and economic subjectivity, on slaves: "the slave who believes he is free," as Marathe says. "The most pathetic of bondage" (*IJ* 108). Wallace again seeks idiosyncratic variations on Hegelian bondage, a difficult state to transcend in the course of self-making. Marathe's comments reflect Wallace's own in a 2003 interview: "systems that work very well in terms of selling people products . . . do not work as well when it comes to educating children or helping us help each other know how to live," says Wallace. The "feeling of having to obey every impulse and gratify every desire" is "not happiness"—it is, rather, "a strange kind of slavery."[29]

While *Infinite Jest* obviously develops around analogies between addict and consumer, less obvious is the role played by slavery in defining the interface between the two. Wallace portrays the addict as one who lacks true economic agency to the point of being a slave—to being, in my terms, one who receives no value at all in return for his work. In a climactic realization, Hal notes, "The original sense of addiction involved being bound over, dedicated, either legally or spiritually. To devote one's life, plunge in" (*IJ* 900). These definitions were once the novel's starting point: an early typescript begins, in a Melvillean mode, with a set of dictionary entries for "Addict" and "Addiction." With spaces left for the phonetic pronunciations (to be filled in later by hand), the first entry reads:

'Addict—(   ) tr.v., To devote or give (oneself) habitually or compulsively. Used with to.—n. (   ) One who is addicted, especially to narcotics[Latin <u>addictus</u>, "given over," one awarded to another as votary or slave, past participle of <u>addicere</u>, to award to.' <u>American Heritage Dictionary of the English Language, New College Edition</u>[30]

Here, the slave meaning, which merely shadows Hal's rendition in the published text, is explicit. At the etymological roots from which Wallace built his axiological narratives, his addicts, whatever their drug, are slaves, unable to secure value and subject to transactions in which it is they who are bought and sold (the *OED* has as meanings of the Latin *addicere* "to deliver, award, yield; . . . make over, sell").[31] This dependence of drug culture (and, by the book's logic, consumer capitalism) on transacting a person's body calls forth Wallace's renewed efforts to propose the human as currency for transacting in a different, salutary sense, as we will see with Gately.

Wallace provides no shortage of masters to underscore the general sense that many here are enslaved: the "Master" (*IJ* 489) copy of the Entertainment so many seek, generations of Eschaton "game-master[s]" (*IJ* 171), and the grim meanings derivable from Himself's former title of "Headmaster" (*IJ* 79)—the suggestion that he embedded the Entertainment in his own head, his enslavement to his mind, and so on. Add to these the numerous images of prisons (Orin under a bell jar, Gately in Billerica, many iterations of spiderweb and cage), and our sense grows that the fundamental state for Wallace's subjects is to be "bound over," in bondage.

A hallmark of historical typologies of slavery is the denial of the slave's right "to form contracts" and make legally meaningful promises.[32] Wallace thus registers the infuriating effects of the addicts' lack of agency in their desperate appeals to contract language, now rendered with greater emotional texture than in *Broom*'s use of the trope. One Ennet House resident raises the contractual to avoid the accepted meaning of AA's key identifier, also echoing the language of being "bound": "I'm simply asking you to define 'alcoholic'. . . . Is it *denial* to delay signature until the vocabulary of the contract is clear to all parties to be bound?" (*IJ* 177). Gately, by contrast, expresses skepticism that contracts work at all for recovering addicts: "The idea of a person in the grip of *It* being bound by a 'Suicide Contract' . . . is simply absurd," he thinks of Kate Gompert, because it "will constrain such a person only until the exact psychic circumstances that made the contract necessary in the first place assert themselves" (*IJ* 697).[33] The addicts and some of their caretakers cling to the contractual because it seems to allow for a set of principles that might prove manipulable because they are less than grounded, less than axiomatic. Geoffrey Day recognizes this: "AA's response to a question about its axioms, then, is to invoke an axiom about the inadvisability of all such questions" (*IJ* 1002n90). At the same time, Wallace sees a general deracination of the liberal subject in these failures of contract, part of the novel's general anatomy of degraded freedom and other gateways to the soft fascism that first emerged in "Westward," emblematized here by the Gentle administration's reliance on the *"Totalitarian's Guide to Iron-Fisted Spin"* (*IJ* 404).[34]

The decline of all those crucial capacities that the enslaved addict shows in negative—capacities for contract, consent, devotion, and giving (of) oneself—might be traced along many paths in the novel: the unraveling of the verb *commit*, for instance, in Hal's worries over posture and Erdedy's repeated claim that he has "committed himself" (*IJ* 21) to his smoke-out, an early trend that the extended description of AA speaking "Commitments" tries to reverse (*IJ* 343). Hal also summarizes another aspect of slavery in climactic ruminations that occur, appropriately, on the floor: "We are all dying to give our lives away to something, maybe. God or Satan, politics or grammar, topology or philately—the object seemed incidental to this will to give oneself away, utterly" (*IJ* 900). We might fill in "for free" after his obliterative "giving our lives away," linking his formulations back to slavery and lack of value. On the list of "object[s]" of this summative transaction—this so-called giving—from the diseased postmodern self, a human being ("some other person" [*IJ* 900]) enters only as an afterthought. What other forms of commerce for the self are possible? Enter Don Gately—and with him new forms of currency, work, and giving with which to make such transactions living, rather than compulsive erasures of life.

COINS OF GRACE

What's in your wallet? In *Infinite Jest*, more than that credit-card slogan suggests. Replying to the desperate quest to accumulate and building on tropes pioneered by Gaddis, the novel depicts uncanny wallets and purses that follow on Lenore's lottery-ticket-laden one, in most cases displacing the presumed contents—money—with materials that have life-or-death value. Early on, a news article describes someone later revealed to be cross-dressing Poor Tony snatching a purse that holds a woman's artificial heart, which "ferried life-giving blood" to "her living, active body"—a living transaction indeed. The woman gives chase, yelling out "She stole my heart!", and passersby smile (*IJ* 143). Along these same lines, in portraying drugs' self-destructive pleasures and death by entertainment, Wallace registers an undoing of rational-choice theory and of the supposed appeal to self-interest and enhanced pleasure in new products. For instance, discussing videophony, he notes a "queer kind of self-obliterating logic in the microeconomics of consumer high-tech" (*IJ* 145). "Self-obliterating" has a double meaning here, like the one Wallace recognizes in "self-denial" in his Kafka essay: the self is the real casualty in the clash of narcissism and high-tech that obliterates videophony (*CL* 63).

Human consciousness, no embodiment of *homo economicus*, often resists so-called rational value, and in a novel making Menippean satiric use of quasi-scholarly essays (on TV heroes [*IJ* 140–142], on the roots of the A.F.R. [*IJ* 1055–62n304]), the analyses of videophony and the end of broadcast advertising (411–418) become Wallace's body-centered replies to the case studies of his undergraduate economics training (the account of tongue scrapers on TV arises as a memory of a "mammoth research paper" by Hal [*IJ* 411]). We might even regard the central conceit of the Entertainment, regarded in less fantastical terms, as an essay in economic theory, with the film an example of "inelasticity of demand," the concept Wallace defines in a 2006 interview: "the ideal piece of entertainment would be something that people would want to see over and over and over again and pay for each time. The analogy for me is . . . narcotics or addictive drugs."[35]

But monetary value itself, not just the products it purchases, is where the radical instability truly lies. Throughout his career, Wallace sought those seams within systems of externalized value where seemingly iron-clad rules of quantification and accumulation broke down. Having written of people as pounds, kopeks, and marks, in notes for *Infinite Jest* he pens intriguing paragraphs about yet another minimum unit of currency: the penny. As its materiality eclipses its role in exchange, the penny undoes many assumptions about value, coming to stand for the abject human. Again, Wallace dwells in the axiological realm of assessing objects' glow rather than the abstract system that asserts their value:

> Pennies are about the most interesting unit of currency. They buy nothing, really, so they're less like a medium of exchange than just dun red objects. Other monies are so pregnant with possibility the physical aspect of bill and coin is lambent. Other money flickers, physically. Pennies sit there. They are metal lozenges and have weight. They fill dresser-top jars that become tough to lift. Banks disdain them, even, unless rolled and encased like sausage.
>
> Pennies are most interesting however because their primary value is that they keep you from getting more pennies. You either get rid of them or you get more. Woe bedite [*sic*] the penniless at point of purchase? Totals are always like $16.01 or $1.17. Darn, says the customer, I have no pennies. The cashier grins, happy to get rid of some pennies.
>
> Pennies and their weird inverse value are a powerful metaphor for something about human beings. It's not like pennies are like love, or little bits of your soul. They're a little like a kind of aggression, right?—Direct it outward lest it come your way but not exactly. Can you think what pennies are like? I'll pay you . . .[36]

This remarkable fragment defines a twisted "aggression" of giving away that structures much of *Infinite Jest*, in particular the "U.S.A.'s Experialistic 'gift'" to Canada (the whole pennies passage might be read, alongside Reconfiguration and the giving of the Entertainment, as an allegory of the sadistic generosity that besets those with low conceptions—just one cent—of self-worth) (*IJ* 58). At the base of the monetary system, its smallest constituent unit is not a stable building block but an inversion of the accumulation the system supposedly codifies, a "weird inverse value." In its suggestion that "giving" money leads to antivalue and that humans use small change to mask deeper issues, these paragraphs also form a foundation for the spiritual parable of Barry Loach begging "Touch me, please" but finding that people "substitute[] abstract loose change for genuine fleshly contact" (*IJ* 970).

While the pennies passage does not appear in the published novel, its spirit—and its reduction of a "medium of exchange" to "dun red objects"—often seems present. *Infinite Jest* periodically underscores currency as simply material signifier, subject to a displacement by the organic transactions—the shared human value—it ideally represents. Regarding Pemulis's relationships with Mario and Hal, for instance, the text warns, "friendship at E.T.A. is nonnegotiable currency" (*IJ* 155). An unidentified Ennet House voice says in a story that seems related to the pennies writing, "Our cult burned money for fuel. . . . We used Ones," with the cult leader, the "Semi Divine One," feeding a stove (*IJ* 729). James sees drops of his father's sweat as "small dark coins" (*IJ* 499), and Bruce Green's punched nose emits "coins of blood" (*IJ* 618)—both associations of coinage with the porous body and reminiscent of the "coins of water" that resemble "cancres" in "John Billy."

Wallace questions, in *Infinite Jest* more than ever, the value inhering in wealth. Throughout, a person's value and his social status are severed in favor of an understanding of self-value that must be built metaphysically, from the ground up. Poor Tony, for instance, is a homeless thief who wears a feather boa and heels and, never receiving help, ends up drying out from heroin addiction in a bathroom. Decoded as poor/toney, his name says much about this world: beneath signifiers of glamour, an inner poverty abides. The name of Aubrey deLint echoes the Boston street slang (presumably invented by Wallace) for having no money in your pockets, *"sporting lint"* (*IJ* 202). But deLint's deficiency is not of money but of three-dimensional standing and spine, that rarest of Wallace commodities: Hal "sometimes cannot quite believe [deLint] is even real, and tries to get to the other side of [him], to see whether [he] has a true z coordinate or is just a cutout or projection" (*IJ* 460). To exist in this world is to lie somewhere on an external scale of valuation, often monetary. The question becomes how to take the self's coin and express with it some other form of value.

D.G.

To answer that question, I return to Gately. Throughout, coins point to his search for value. In the earliest passage about him, Wallace begins a pattern of rare-coin collections, rare-coin shops, and flipped coins in all his subsequent fictional works, portraying Gately the thief unconsciously hunting out not just any commodities but the one that mediates exchange. Gately's burglary of the ADA's house nets (notwithstanding the opportunity to pull the tainted-toothbrush gag) "a coin collection and two antique shotguns" (*IJ* 56), and before being gagged, Guillaume DuPlessis, the Quebecois leader, tries to tell Gately in French of "some antique pre-British-takeover Quebecois gold coins" hidden behind a painting (*IJ* 58). Late in the novel Gately will express "hate[]" for a drug-dispensing South Asian doctor who has "a weirdly classically white-type face you could easily imagine profiling on a coin" (*IJ* 885). But Gately must mature in relationship to value to gain the right to reinscribe the faces of coins; through such growth Wallace mediates the person-centered currency his books, in effect, issue to readers.

The passages describing Gately's indoctrination into AA (*IJ* 343–367 and, with some interruptions, 367–379) have been frequently mined by critics, especially those tackling irony and sincerity.[37] This montage is subliminally concerned with AA's displacement of typical economic relationships in favor of an absolute value that cannot be accounted for in human ledgers—as if Wallace again proposes that eschewing irony is intertwined with adopting, with honoring, an unacknowledged kind of human currency and semantic value. As the AA scenes begin, in contrast with Hal's meditation on "giv[ing] our lives away," Wallace writes of the twelfth step of "Giving It Away," engaging in the network of speaking Commitments, as "a cardinal Boston AA principle. The term's derived from an epigrammatic description of recovery in Boston AA: 'You give it up to get it back to give it away,'" with sobriety itself "less a gift than sort of a cosmic loan" to be paid "forward" (*IJ* 344). Wallace draws together his images of the ritual of shared nourishment, the divine, and the fiduciary by locating these moments of sincere speech in "the Provident's cafeteria" (*IJ* 344). Provident here names a nursing home, but it is more often a name for a bank. As Aubry argues, in Wallace's AA "every act spreads its value in all directions," making "self-interest and generosity . . . symbiotic partners" (*IJ* 108).

These grand terms of rewritten value also find reflection in micromotifs, centered on Gately's wallet, that prove more practical, buffers against what could become an unreachable AA imperative to generosity. Building on the image of a heart in a purse, Wallace has AA veterans "give [Gately] their phone numbers on the back of their little raffle tickets," which he carries "in his wallet" (*IJ* 353). The image, hearkening back to Lenore's lottery tickets, combines communication (phone numbers) with luck (the raffle). The numbers amount to a physical instantiation of "The Gift of Desperation," since if you are a new initiate who has it, you "carry [these] numbers talismanically in your wallet" (*IJ* 354). Wallace (ever metafictional) aligns the creation of his huge, decentered act of communication—*Infinite Jest* itself—with such contingencies by making the raffle prize a copy of "the Big Book," *Alcoholics Anonymous: The Story of How Many Thousands of Men and Women Have Recovered from Alcoholism* (which, appropriately, the winner gives away to someone newer) (*IJ* 360). If Wallace links artistic success with winning the lottery, getting sober seems to work in the same contingent way, not entirely under agential control—as does the writing of the "Big Book" that emerges from the experience.

Less ennobling displacements of value are afoot in the pivotal AA passage as well. A hefty Irishman at an AA meeting says of "his first solid bowel movement in adult life," after getting sober, "'Twas a sone so wonefamiliar at t'first ay tought ay'd droped me wallet in t'loo" (*IJ* 351). Working with abject materials, Wallace often pursues the implications of Freud's famous claim that the seeming antitheses of gold and feces are united in the unconscious through the pleasure the child takes in both excreting and retaining a "precious" substance; "gold," Freud writes, "is seen in the most unambiguous way to be a symbol of faeces."[38] In Wallace's hands this conjunction militates against seeing money as a cold object or abstraction. In this AA speech, the wallet in the toilet not only denigrates the monetary but gestures toward the liberation of repressed, unconscious material occurring throughout these AA stories of traumatic origins.

Initials continue generating meaning for Wallace here. The joke meaning of Hal's HI initials is that he is high all the time, but there is also a sacred meaning available to him, an eastern variation on his incandescence: in Japanese Buddhism, the character transliterated as "ka" or "hi" means fire, one of five elements and associated physically with body heat and mentally with passion.[39] Gately's DG has sacred possibilities as well, for the letters point to his most important coin association, an abbreviation seen, among other places, on the obverse of the British pound: along the edge it reads, "ELIZABETH II DG REG FD." The Latin phrase abbreviated here is "*Dei Gratia Regina Fidei Defensor*"—"By the grace of god, Queen and defender of the faith." A more common shortening (on the Canadian quarter, for instance) is simply the monarch's name and "DG," *Dei Gratia*. Wallace also gets meaning out of the initials' reversal, the GD signifying the opposite of divine grace, "God-damned": thus Gately encounters doppelgängers to overcome in the AA resister Geoffrey Day (*IJ* 1000–1003n90) and Guillaume DuPlessis (whose death from asphyxiation is both a kind of self-murder for Gately and a foreshadowing of his hospital muteness). These initial-based readings might seem mere coincidences, except that *Infinite Jest* makes much of the meaning of the phrase *Dei Gratia*, "by the grace of God," which, removed from the context of a sovereign's divine right, is used liberally in AA-speak—but to note the general *deprivation* of grace. As they get to know each other at AA, Joelle complains to Don about "these earnest ravaged folks at the lectern say[ing] they're 'Here But For the Grace of God'"—objecting not, as Gately expects, because of religious language but because the phrase, transposing a subjunctive as an indicative, is "literally senseless" (*IJ* 366).

Gately's reaction indicates his awe of Joelle's intelligence and connects him to the deadly Entertainment, with her veil seeming like "a screen on which might well be projected" a "smily-face," sign of both the film and his nightmare of being removed from AA (*IJ* 366–367). As Gately, in part because lovestruck, struggles to respond and as "his own heart grips him like an infant rattling the bars of his playpen" (*IJ* 366), Wallace continues paralleling Joelle and the "Militant Grammarian" Avril (*IJ* 288), making Gately's attraction a species of mother-love (in an attempt to repair a horrific childhood) and foreshadowing Joelle's role as the apologizing mother figure in the Entertainment. The challenge, for Gately, is to avert his panicked feeling that it is "inevitable" he is "going to get high again and be back in the cage all over again"; he must overcome fear and reach out for Joelle's love, rather than compensating for his vulnerability through relapse to addiction (*IJ* 366). In this moment, Gately demonstrates, unconsciously, a means of resisting the Entertainment's deadly siren's call: remaining attached to, and not intimidated by, a love object, thereby not reverting to the narcissism of playpen/addiction-cage. In the context of the "Grace of God" conversation, Gately is also modeling a way, without overintellectualizing it, of accepting grace—for Joelle is a Mother Mary figure here, as opposed to in the film (note too that in Hebrew Joelle means "Jehovah is God"). This is also a moment of challenging (and deeply Lacanian) self-identification for Gately because, if my DG association is correct, he recognizes a version of "himself" (i.e., his initials) in the "Here But for the Grace of God" discussion—and recognizes as well his potential cancellation, according to Joelle's technical reading of the phrase.[40]

Several critics have illuminated the limited and pragmatic religious faith *Infinite Jest* endorses: Konstantinou claims that Wallace offers "not so much a religious correction to secular skepticism" as a "religious vocabulary (God, prayer, etc.) emptied out of specific content,"[41] and David H. Evans finds Wallace agreeing with William James's notion that "faith 'becomes' true by its results."[42] Burn argues that while *Infinite Jest* has a "religious subtext [that] is not explicitly articulated," the quasi-religious meanings that gather around Gately nonetheless "provide[] an enriching texture to the otherwise desolate narrative of Hal" (*Reader's Guide*, 63–64). In support Burn quotes Wallace saying that his interest in religious subjects often dissolves when the claims take on any specificity and shape: "the stuff that's truly interesting about religion is inarticulable."[43]

All these critics are persuasive, but I take from Wallace's comment on the inarticulable a more particular mechanism in *Infinite Jest*'s creation of muted or indirect religious meaning around grace—and the points of pressure are the Gately/coin nexus, the possibility of self-cancellation, and the intuitive approach to language the AA scenes endorse. Shortly after Gately's talk with Joelle, in a horrific account of incest, "It," and the Raquel Welch mask, the unnamed speaker remarks on her father remaining "oblivious (But for the Grace of God, in a way) to the fetally curled skinny form of the adopted daughter lying perfectly still in the next bed," i.e., the speaker (*IJ* 372). The phrase is inserted parenthetically, as though it comes not from speaker or listeners but the all-important zone of shared identification between them. The phrase also comes with "here" or "there" shorn from the front and the doubt-inducing "in a way" added to the back. This grace formula or prayer thus functions ambivalently, freed from the solecism that enraged Joelle but nonetheless entangled in another of the text's many double binds. For, on the one hand, the father ignoring this woman *is* a moment of grace, since the speaker knows that, in her sister's absence, she would "get promoted to the role of Raquel" (*IJ* 372), but on the other hand, how can one find *any* sort of grace in this family, even the speaker, if—as suggested by many moments here—the speaker is herself implicated in the family's denial?

"But for the Grace of God" can thus refer to a moment being both infused with grace and utterly lacking it; there is a contingency to it that makes the original "correct" phrase seem presumptuous, full of that American arrogance about Election that Pynchon sees: "There but for the grace of God go I," the proper formulation, assumes one is chosen *not* to go "there." The strategic inarticulateness and ambiguity Wallace arranges around this prayerful formula, then, mesh with both Gately's contingencies and the many inversions he senses in AA's definition of freedom. The "smily-faced Sergeant-at-Arms[]" of his AA dream takes people *out* rather than keeping them in, with the seeming prison of the "Boston AA 'In Here' . . . protect[ing] against a return to 'Out There'" and its seeming freedom (*IJ* 374).

GATELY WORKING JUST FINE

We might say, echoing Evans's understanding of the importance of human will in religion, that in this atmosphere Gately must make his own grace—must enact it, regardless of theological arguments and without expectation of reward. Such a challenge for Gately mirrors the one faced by Wallace as he carves out for his writing an unorthodox spiritual and intellectual space on the subject of grace, all the while dwelling in ambiguities and inarticulateness and wondering whether the Protestant work ethic can survive the ceding of its language to drug users. Wallace shares Gaddis's drive to "redeem" the Protestant ethic but operates in a less polemical and sardonic mode, more permissive of a range of possible religious ecstasies: tennis, for instance, as played by Roger Federer, could be an unexpected vehicle of bodily "grace" for Wallace (*BF* 8), "a 'bloody near-religious experience'" (*BF* 7), possibilities glimpsed too in the "animal grace" and "liquid grace" of *Infinite Jest* players (*IJ* 158, 652). In Weber's account of the origins of capitalist accumulation in Calvinist predestination, "it is solely by the grace of God"—that phrase Wallace plays with—that some are chosen for salvation.[44] The solution seems to lie not in redoubling the efforts of the will to work hard and earn money but in being able to redefine the monetary reward that—Gaddis, Pynchon, Weber, and Wallace all essentially agree—overwrote the spiritual at some point in American history. At the same time, there can still be no presumptions about grace or any other sort of redemption: in the context of an addict's recovery that Wallace has in mind, a secular embrace of existential contingency suffuses all.

Finding his position on this issue, Wallace laces scenes of Gately at his "humility" work with a human-centered, etymological link to divine *Gratia*, an action Gately *can* control: the often pointedly capitalized "Gratitude" (*IJ* 443, 446, 596) and "Grateful" (*IJ* 369–370, 468). Hal describes early on, via Hegel, a "belie[f]" that "transcendence is absorption," but an unexpectant Gately may find such a state in his janitorial work for Stavros, in terms Hal would probably regard as philosophically inauspicious (*IJ* 12). Often cited in *Infinite Jest* criticism is the scene of Gately having "nothing in the way of a like God-concept" but praying anyway "to the ceiling," yet rarely attended to are the less momentous means of transformation limned in the same sentence—and with Wallace we should always be on the lookout for unremarked elements of abiding, waiting, and working. Gately pretends "his sneakers were like way under the bed" in order to cover the appearance of praying,

> but he did it, and beseeched the ceiling and thanked the ceiling, and after maybe five months Gately was riding the Greenie at 0430 to go clean human turds out of the Shattuck shower and all of a sudden realized that quite

a few days had gone by since he'd even thought about Demerol or Talwin or even weed.

(IJ 467)

Wallace describes in this moment of absorption the unearned and even un- thought nature of grace according to an ideal Protestant understanding of immersion in work. Here lies AA's real defeat of the rationalizing mind that counsels relapse. Gately, after his extremely early shift, "rides the Greenie back up the hill with his Gratitude-battery totally recharged" (*IJ* 435). "Greenie," meaning Boston's Green Line subway, suggests cash and is also street lingo for amphetamines, playing on the sources of value and energy in Gately's previous life (once addicted to downers, he now has a salutary daily upper). So too does a "Gratitude-battery"—in need of gradual reen- ergizing, ironically, by exertion—contrast with the "motherboard" under- standing of the self that defines pleasure among the addicts: the declines of the latter are catastrophic, "the whole system" subject to being "shut . . . down," "all the circuits" "blow[n] out" (*IJ* 20, 53).

With gratitude thus underscored, it becomes important that *Infinite Jest* essentially twice erases Thanksgiving, the American holiday of thanks: the WhataBurger tournament (named for a grim fast-food feast) occurs just before Thanksgiving break (*IJ* 52), and thus the narrative "ends" right before that holiday in both the Year of Glad and the Y.D.A.U. The one Thanksgiving we do witness is a prime date in the disintegration of the Incandenza family. In a parallel move, Steeply and Marathe dialogue while May 1 dawns, but the "young persons" gathered around a bonfire "ring" (*IJ* 423) below are celebrating not International Workers' Day but *Walpurgis- nacht*, the witches' revels of April 30 associated with the German Brocken (see the "*Bröckengespenst*-shadow," Wallace's reference to Goethe by way of Pynchon [*IJ* 89]) and symbolic of a consumerist apocalypse, like J.D.'s party.

Wallace also uses the semiopaque, intransitive verb "work" to oppose AA's powerful pragmatism to forces of "congenital skepticism" (*CL* 272). If "you ask the scary old guys How AA Works," "they smile their chilly smiles and say Just Fine. It just works, is all; end of story" (*IJ* 350). In still more koan-like terms, in one of the clichés Wallace prizes, an AA slogan says, "It works if you work it" (*IJ* 270). This is another Wittgensteinian placement of a word in context, so that meaning may not go on "holiday." Note, especially in the "Just Fine" example, the short-circuiting of the calculating, observing mind by pragmatist action—whatever works, as that philosophy is sometimes summarized.[45] We might even read the name of Ennet House itself as a cue to the addicts to take up this felt or intuitive relationship to truth value, what eluded Karrier in "Crash of '69" and will here elude Fackelmann (who says "That's a goddamn lie" to the most obviously true assertions [*IJ* 935]). That is, for Ennet, read "Innit," slang for "isn't it" (often associated with a lower-class British context). The word gestures toward a constant, minute-to-minute elaboration of tiny truth values rather than any singular Truth. Notably, too, "innit"—heard as "ain't that the truth"—seeks communal validation and "Identification" with others, in the oral form AA prizes (*IJ* 345). But some of AA's authoritarian resistance to newcomers' backtalk inheres in the pun too: "innit," as in "isn't it so?", is a rhetorical question that shuts down further queries, much as the Crocodiles do with Gately and Gately does, in turn, with others.[46]

Yet in spite of their importance, work and will are never enough for redemption in Wallace; as with the lottery in *Broom*, one needs that secular aspect of grace that goes under the name luck, a force that can cut in both positive and negative directions. Gately may begin the novel as a thief and manslaughterer and end it having sacrificed himself to protect Ennet House, along the way serving Ennet House as a Frank Furillo–like "hero of *re*action" (*IJ* 141). But before anointing Gately as redeemed hero or saint, we should note that, in this book's networked complexity, he is often linked with the accidental, with bad luck and gracelessness. This DG is often without *Dei Gratia*. For whatever the virtues of his recovery, Gately is in a sense responsible for the threat that looms over the whole narrative: he unwittingly puts the Entertainment into circulation in Boston ("this alleged Master copy from the DuPlessis burglary" [*IJ* 489]), as Michael North's tracking confirms.[47] His deep affection for Pat Montesian's 1964 Ford Aventura (a car model made up by Wallace) is a sign of his association with adventure and the adventitious, and his Aventura scene ends as he zooms past Lucien Antitoi, about to become a brutal victim of the quest for the Entertainment that Gately set in motion (*IJ* 480).

In this context, Wallace insinuates that finding a limited grace means combining hard work with an essentially aleatory view of the self that is reminiscent of existentialism. Gately adopts the language of the sports streak for his sobriety but does so with luck and the inadequacy of will alone in full view: he "still feels like he has no access to the Big spiritual Picture. He feels about the ritualistic daily *Please* and *Thank You* prayers rather like like [*sic*] a hitter that's on a hitting streak and doesn't change his jock or socks or pre-game routine" (*IJ* 443). Gately is thus a counterweight in a narrative of planning, ritual, and endless repetitions of tennis serves; far more than any E.T.A. player, Gately enacts Schtitt's joyful embrace of the "chance to play," which rings as well with a resignation to the *play of chance* (*IJ* 84). In this way Gately also overcomes the "*Analysis-Paralysis*" of addicts who try "to prepare for all the contingencies and consequences" of every action (*IJ* 203). Wallace, still stressing the lotteries of life and inspired by Sartre's *Nausea* as much as Pynchon's schlemihls, vacillates between endorsements of strong will and extreme contingency, placing *Infinite Jest* on that "fault line[]" in the national character described by Jackson Lears in his history of gambling in America, where "an impulse toward risk" and "the longing for the lucky strike have been counterbalanced by a secular Protestant ethic that has questioned the very existence of luck."[48]

We should see Gately as, like Nunn in "John Billy," a "goodluck badluck man," a gambler in the Dostoevskian mold.[49] No wonder, then, that Wallace chooses certain images in the Pamela Hoffman-Jeep shaggy-dog story that ends this novel with so many key questions unanswered: in his evil past, Gately served as a creator of fake ID's and a murderous enforcer for Whitey Sorkin, who (like his namesake Whitey Bulger) fixes bets and, with "MA-Statehouse bagmen-cronies," the state lottery (*IJ* 927). For Wallace, in both of his first two novels, there can be no fixing of the lottery of art, communication, and life. There is only the chance to play.

In addition to grace and gratitude, *gratia* has a connection to the gift: the Latin means "favor," and the *gratis* is literally done "for thanks" (i.e., no payment). Kelly, pessimistic about a trope I have invoked positively several times already, makes a powerful argument aligning Wallace's understanding of the impossibility of sincerity with Derrida's claim that the true gift is impossible—the gift as, inevitably, an aporia, since it necessarily produces an expectation of return or reimbursement. As Derrida writes in *Given Time*, "If the gift appears or signifies itself, if it exists or if it is presently *as gift*, as what it is, then it is not, it annuls itself."[50] Describing *Infinite Jest* and parts of *Brief Interviews* in the language of double binds that populates both texts, Kelly finds Wallace's fiction agreeing with Derrida that the true gift giver's necessary lack of calculation regarding return cannot be separated "from conditionality, from the self-conscious anticipation of how the other will understand the gift"; these "two poles thus become interminably entangled in any action, and we can never know for certain . . . if any single event of giving or receiving is the genuine article or not," just as avowals of sincerity are no guarantee of the thing itself. Beyond the aggressions of pennies, the ample evidence of this suspicion of giving in *Infinite Jest* would include the United States' sadistic "gift" to Canada, the failure of Barry Loach's experiment, and Hal's use of "giving . . . away" to define a solipsistic compulsion toward oblivion. Especially in moments when givers wrap themselves in the mantle of generosity or "do a service for somebody's gratitude" (*IJ* 286), the gift in *Infinite Jest* does have an inverted meaning exemplary of what Kelly calls Wallace's "impatience with rhetorical innocence."[51]

Again, though, we should acknowledge Wallace's continuing urge to stage conflicts with poststructuralism rather than wholly embrace its destabilizing drive. There are parallels here to the existentialist language of action with which Wallace complicates his overview of poststructuralist sureties about the death of the author in the final sentence of "Greatly Exaggerated": "critics can try to erase or over-define the author into anonymity for all sorts of . . . reasons, and"—in a quote from William Gass making an AA-esque assertion—that "'anonymity may mean many things, but one thing which it cannot mean is that *no one did it*'" (*SFT* 144–145). Likewise, untenable rhetorical avowals of the gift do not exhaust all the instances of generosity a reader can glimpse in *Infinite Jest*: people do it, people give, and one path to being sincere and generous for Wallace seems to lie in remaining absorbed in work and not recognizing a need to avow an intention at all.

A parallel with Lenore's LB is relevant here: Lenore, in the displacements of *Broom*'s many nesting stories, had to say "See, she weighs about one pound" rather than "I am one pound," a position of balance-scale authority from which she might have wielded a transcendent moral authority (or—such is the sinuous ambiguity of Wallace's construction—seen herself as weightless, ontologically cancelled). Neither can Don recognize his own name's ancient meaning (limned in this chapter's epigraph) and say, "I am the gift," or even "I am generous"; that path remains suspect for Wallace on into *The Pale King*, which depicts the "pathological generosity" of Leonard Stecyk (*PK* 544). Such pathological people are, to decode Stecyk's emblematic name (Ste.-cyk?), sick saints. But these extreme characters also expose a domain of existential generosity that, while difficult to occupy, may be said to slip from linguistic purview rather than fall necessarily into aporetic impossibility. Harris, a friend and teaching colleague of Wallace at Illinois State, describes this domain in a biographical mode when he says the "ethical imperative" of Wallace consisted in "other-directed acts of unostentatious empathy."[52] Max describes further extratextual evidence: when awarded his MacArthur, "no sooner did [Wallace] have the funds than he tried to get rid of them," paying for the college tuition of friends in his recovery group and funding others' projects (*Every Love Story*, 239). Novelistic language can still be marshaled in the representation of this sort of empathetic humility. In fact, the intricacy with which Wallace hides the *Dei Gratia* meaning of Don's initials functions as something like a bulwark against too easily accepting an orthodox set of Christian motives, against failing to see, as Dostoevsky did, the radical uncertainties of being a true Christian (many of them laid out in the question-laden interludes of "Joseph Frank's Dostoevsky").

Another effective approach to the gift and Gately can be found in labor, will, and absorption as defined by Hyde's *The Gift*, in which Wallace underlines and marks the majority of a passage on the "labor of gratitude," even circling the page number (something he reserved, his library shows, for pages especially important to him). Hyde writes,

> In speaking of gratitude as a "labor" I mean to distinguish it from "work" . . . Work is what we do by the hour. It begins and ends at a specific time and, if possible, we do it for money. . . . Washing dishes, computing taxes, walking the rounds in a psychiatric ward, picking asparagus—these are work. Labor, on the other hand, sets its own pace. We may get paid for it, but it's harder to quantify. "Getting the program" in AA is a labor. . . . Writing a poem, raising a child, developing a new calculus, resolving a neurosis, invention in all forms—these are labors.
>
> Work is an intended activity that is accomplished through the will. A labor can be intended but only to the extent of doing groundwork, or of *not* doing things that would clearly prevent the labor.[53]

Amid annotations in many different pens suggesting multiple re-readings of *The Gift* (common in Wallace's beloved books), the red fleer-tip with which he marks this passage is the same one that he used for later marginal notes that say "IJ" and make explicit connections to the novel's characters.[54] Even without the allusion to AA, the passage above reads as a set of clues to the construction of Gately (or Wallace's later reflection on that construction). The passage seems to apply particularly to Don after he graduates from custodial work and takes on the truly humbling job of managing Ennet House. The passivity of the laborer in gratitude that Hyde describes also bears some connection to Mark's transformation in "Westward," which depended on passive verb forms—"Only that can be only given," "You are loved"—rather than allowing free rein to the overbearing "I." For Don, one more dimension of his name is the French *donné*, meaning, in addition to gift or endowment, the given of a system. In finding Don's labor of gratitude, we should look anew to those unassuming, more passive moments of *Infinite Jest* that usually escape critical notice—

but where Wallace again explores the axiological overlap of giving of the self and becoming a given.

For instance, at Ennet House, Wallace makes comedy of Don's cooking, a scene of caritas underwritten by eros, a warmth and incandescence that is not wasted by a supposedly efficient marijuana pipe. Here, again, the *oikos* of home and hearth is renewed in the economics of the close-at-hand. Don's terrible food arrives

> with [his] big face hovering lunarly above it, flushed and beaded under the floppy chef's hat . . . his eyes full of anxiety and hopes for everyone's full enjoyment, basically looking like a nervous bride serving her first conjugal dish, except this bride's hands are the same size as the House's dinner plates and have jailhouse tats on them, and this bride seems to need no oven-mitts as he sets down massive pans . . .
>
> (*IJ* 469)

In Gately's flush lies another path to that Luddite electricity of "interfacing" that *Infinite Jest* valorizes (*IJ* 190): the "voltage or energy . . . hanging between you" that Lenz fears when saying he likes someone (*IJ* 554). These are the kinds of heat that Wallace associates with the physics of work and opposes to capitalist greenhouses. The natural contrasts to Ennet meals are Avril's macrobiotic dietary restrictions (and her bad parenting) and all the weightless addicts. Later, Hal has a vision of a food room that, indebted to *Nausea*, recaps the pathology of hoarding and opposes Gately's second-by-second Abiding: "Day after day after day. Experiencing this food in toto" (*IJ* 897).

Don's immensity puts Wallace back in the "John Billy" and "Westward" realm of the tall tale, the epic hero, and archetypes of sacrifice, but now with a mature realism. One Wallace strategy against mere avowals of generosity is to enforce the physicality of the "Big Indestructible Moron['s]" donation to Ennet House (*IJ* 448): "Gately'd bled all over" Ennet House and in Pat's Aventura (*IJ* 821). "How much does Don fucking *weigh*, anyway," as Thrust asks (*IJ* 821), for Gately gains yet more metaphorical solidity here, just as Wallace hopes his reader will from feeding on this text: "The reader walks away from real art heavier than when she came to it" (*CW* 50). What was a momentary, heavy-handed effect in Lenore's sudden ontological nosebleed has now, a novel later, a boldly tragic texture.

Burn links the hulking Gately to Heracles, while Max sees him "taking on, in a Christlike way, the sins of his flock" (*Every Love Story*, 215). The latter association allows Wallace to offer one more doppelgänger for Don in Tiny Ewell, whose name combines meanings of Christ as sacrificial lamb (ewe), an object of ritual incandescence and the hearth (the Yule log), and this world's diminishment of both. The idea that Don has been in search of home and a steady log in the hearth—a strong *oikos*—will solidify further in the grim scenes of his cooking binge with Fackelmann, where a film of "shots of small flames" (*IJ* 974) (probably Himself's looping *Various Small Flames*) plays over their drug-felled forms. At Don's bedside, Ewell begins the book's late turn to deeply situated memories for both protagonists, fulfilling Wallace's axiological wish for a structure that moves not toward the future but back toward foundations. Ewell takes us back to where Don began—thieving—by telling of his "Money Stealers Club," the boys he led in a false charity scheme leading up to the Christmas holiday his name travesties (*IJ* 810). Ewell speaks, in line with the perversion of gift language, of his "gift for bullshit," his "gift for it, the emotional appeal of adult rhetoric," that distrusted opposite of sincerity (*IJ* 811). Ewell "revel[s] in the fraud of it, the discovery of the gift," "the verbal manipulation of human hearts" (*IJ* 811). The Money-Stealers Club thus serves, in the transactional logic of the text, as an early-life allegory of insincere economics that the "Provident" world of AA has fought against for both Ewell and his sacrificial redeemer, the bloody lamb and restored gift: big, indestructible Don.

To complete this consideration of gift aesthetics in a central contemporary novel, let me turn for a few pages to a writer who, responding to Wallace's influence, embraces many of his values but also trenchantly criticizes him. Jonathan Lethem, who calls Hyde's 2007 reissue of *The Gift* "epiphany, in sculpted prose," has been far more radical than Wallace in interpreting the book's implications, particularly on the idea of a shared artistic commonwealth.[55] In "The Ecstasy of Influence," Lethem offers a daringly performative defense of artistic plagiarism constructed entirely from stolen sentences, in which "E Unibus Pluram" is twice a source.[56] Hyde gets credit (in the notes at the end) for Lethem's vision: "Above any other book I've here plagiarized, I commend *The Gift* to your attention" (*Ecstasy of Influence*, 114). The theme of generosity and gift in Wallace, from *Broom*'s bedesmen to Barry Loach, almost always comes tied to a suggestion of a spiritual ethic, often Christian. By contrast, Lethem takes his gift in secular terms, the force of magic clinging to it that of comic books and fantasy. Lethem's ecstasy is aesthetic, and his models of community are intense friendships, bands, virtual communities, and likeminded cadres built around shared art, not Wallace's groups of solipsists brought awkwardly together by work, common suffering, or halfway-house living rooms.

Burn has already recognized the references Lethem makes to Wallace in *Chronic City* (2009): Ralph Warden Meeker's giant novel *Obstinate Dust* and the marijuana supplier Foster Watt, who shares one name with Wallace and one with an actor in Incandenza's films (*Reader's Guide*, 4). But what is the full significance of these allusions? First, the intricate renaming: it begins (Ralph Wa——) to identify Wallace as our twenty-first-century Ralph Waldo Emerson, a view with which Giles would agree.[57] But the name resolves into a suggestion of imprisonment by meekness, resonating with Lethem's suggestion, in a direct written analysis of his work, that Wallace's power derived not from his "philosophical speculation" but from his "master[y]" of an etiolated "self-conscious remorse *at the fact of* self-consciousness" (*Ecstasy of Influence*, xv). On the question of how to inhabit a public persona as novelist, it would be hard to imagine a figure more opposed to the self-conscious Wallace than Norman Mailer, one of the "Great Male Narcissists" (*CL* 51). But in fact, with two M——er names, Lethem implies a Mailer/Meeker (and thus Mailer/Wallace) binary, one bold, the other meek. Lethem's allegiance is with Mailer, a quite rare position in contemporary U.S. letters: he takes Mailer's *Advertisements for Myself* as his model for the structure of *Ecstasy of Influence* (xx), and a sign of Mailer's pervasive presence in *Chronic City* comes in a summary of Perkus Tooth's rants: "Norman Mailer on Muhammad Ali, Norman Mailer on graffiti and the space program . . . Mailer, again and again."[58]

With *Obstinate Dust*, though, this equally complex allusion demonstrates that Lethem's contentious relationship to Wallace finds partial resolution in their bond as fellow exponents of *The Gift*. Lethem largely denigrates *Obstinate Dust*, from the abject name forward: the "gigantic" (*Chronic City*, 43) book goes unread (a bookmark never advances beyond "a quarter or a fifth of the way through" [*Chronic City*, 100]), and the parts we see are warmed-over Joycean lyricism (though not close enough to Wallace to be considered a parody of him). Lethem, when asked about his intent, overcompensates for what are fairly clear digs at Wallace's unreadness: Lethem says *Obstinate Dust* is part of his interest in "endlessness and inapproachability in art" but "also a joke about the way unread books can become cultural tokens." When Wallace died during the composition of *Chronic City*, the references "became strange," and Lethem considered cutting them altogether. "It seems possible to think I'm dishonoring *Infinite Jest*," Lethem says, but he protests that what may seem like "attack[s]" are just the "scuff marks" of his engagement with a work he finds has "tremendous value and interest."[59]

Lethem says he salvaged the allusions by "putting [*Obstinate Dust*] in again at the end to make it mean a little more" (Clarke, *Conversations*, 174), but he actually turns dishonor into respect earlier by calling on Hyde, in a scene that inters both *Obstinate Dust* and, symbolically, Wallace himself. *Chronic City* in general critiques memorial practices, skewering the abuse of 9/11 memory by public institutions and examining remembrance on many scales, from a hollow funeral for an iconic science-fiction writer to Chase's book-long commemoration of Perkus. The official response to 9/11, the death of a writer, and improvisatory gestures all commingle when Chase and his girlfriend visit the artist Laird Noteless's *Urban Fjord*, a giant crevasse cut into the Bronx and a clear parody of the 9/11 Memorial at Ground Zero. The neighborhood African American boys who lead them from the subway to the dispiriting site ask, "What you gonna give?" as they gesture toward the trash visitors have thrown into the so-called artwork (*Chronic City*, 110). Chase hurls in *Obstinate Dust*, seemingly in one last jab at Wallace. But the verb the boys choose, "give," is important: Noteless, commissioned by wealthy Manhattanites, is alien to this poor African American community, and he violates the maxim from which Hyde builds his vision of artwork as gift: the idea that "a circulation of gifts creates community"

(Hyde, *The Gift*, 194). Unlike these trashed commodities for which neighbors think this artwork an appropriate home, "the gift is not used up in use," Hyde writes (189). It is thus the common bond to Hyde's sense of artwork as gift that makes *Chronic City* a muted Wallace tribute—no trashing or dishonor intended. Both novelists are keen to expose the untapped potential of ideas of (another of Hyde's subjects) a cultural commons or commonwealth. I now close this chapter by examining *Infinite Jest*'s coded use of that word.

WAYS OF LIVING ON COMMONWEALTH

In creating Enfield, seeking to hint at how this degraded world might make its way back from deracinated gifts and *"Low-Temperature Civics"* to real communal bonds (*IJ* 687), Wallace does not disturb one feature of existing Brighton-Allston geography: the long spine of Commonwealth Avenue. Enfield Marine is "just off" it (*IJ* 87); E.T.A. students jog along it "in a pack" (*IJ* 173); its length and variety provide Gately with mental stimuli (*IJ* 476–477). Wallace intends a cumulative force from all the mentions of both this street and the state name it follows from, the Commonwealth of Massachusetts. "Comm.-Ad." (*IJ* 51, 80, 95, etc.), recurrently used for E.T.A.'s "Community and Administration Bldg." (*IJ* 52), doubles the frequent use of the abbreviation "Comm. Ave." (*IJ* 53, 83, 152, etc.) but also points toward a deficit of community at E.T.A., which is administered so as to increase isolation and competition. In these shortened uses, connections between community, commonwealth, and another "com," communication, also arise. As I claimed in the introduction using Hardt and Negri, for Wallace, language is the ultimate commonwealth, and he uses the awareness of complex networking and causality that economic understanding calls for to offer a metaphor for the human sharing of language while still honoring the Wittgensteinian edict against attempting to see to the edges of our all-encompassing medium.

With that claim in mind, and surveying the perspectives on many types of economy gathered in this chapter, I present a final contrast between Hal and Gately. Whereas Wallace critiques the idea of language as property or fantasized incorporation into the self, Hal treats words as consumable objects. Indeed, from his childhood mold-eating forward, his instinctual response to the world is to eat it, regardless of whether something can be actually assimilated. Hal raises Bombardini's specter of cannibalism when he exclaims about finding his father dead, *"something smelled delicious!"* (*IJ* 256). Avoiding that trauma, Hal "chew[s] through" books on grieving in order to perform sadness for his therapist (*IJ* 254). "The boy reads like a vacuum," an E.T.A. staffer says. *"Digests* things" (*IJ* 15). As with the lines about *"value"* being part of "rarified equations" (*IJ* 964), in his dictionary digestion Hal experiences no felt incorporation of words' meaning, nor is he always correct with his definitions.

Consider an error Wallace slips into Hal's dictionary research, leading into a chain of codes filled with commonwealth meanings. As he travels to what he thinks is a Narcotics Anonymous meeting, Hal muses on a reversal of spelling in the history of "anonymous": the word "was joined way back somewhere at the Saxonic taproot to the Olde English *on-ane*, which supposedly meant All as One or As One Body and became Cynewulf's eventual standard inversion to the classic *anon*." The etymological change from *on-ane* to *anon* only "maybe" occurred (*IJ* 797), Hal says, and in fact Wallace is giving a bogus etymology. But he does so wanting the close reader to recognize in this false history the hope for a possible cultural shift from O.N.A.N. (*"on-ane"*) to Alcoholics Anonymous (*"anon"*)—from masturbatory solipsism to an idea of "All as One" and "One Body," those commonwealth practices of paying it forward that mark AA's economy. Hal's adherence to onanistic principles of ownership is reinforced by the location of his meeting, "Quabbin Recovery Systems," a vaguely corporate setting that plays on the Quabbin Reservoir, the primary water source for metro Boston. The Quabbin Reservoir lies hundreds of miles farther west than Natick, where this passage locates it; in fact the reservoir is just eighteen miles from Northampton, home of Amherst College. As Burn notes in his *Reader's Guide* (50) while detailing this geography, Wallace hopes to invoke the role played by the historical Enfield, Massachusetts, in the creation of the reservoir. Quabbin, a public utility, thus partakes in *Infinite Jest*'s subtle communication of commonwealth values: the reservoir was created in 1938 when, over objections from residents, the Swift River was dammed and the valley inundated, leading to the submersion of four towns, including the historical Enfield, Massachusetts. The majority of Enfield's town center rests today, Atlantis-like, underwater. In transporting Enfield east to Boston, Wallace resurrects a moment of municipal sacrifice and the sharing of public resources and offers a counter to the In-Field meanings of value I discussed earlier in this chapter.

Hal gets the kind of value he expects from his Quabbin: he enters ready to pay for membership and with an "appraising" eye, carrying a money-filled wallet contrasting with the ones seen at AA (*IJ* 799). This increasingly salivaless boy, having just eaten two bran muffins without "tonic," could use some of the Commonwealth's drinking water (*IJ* 796). In more emotionally straightforward terms, Hal's chosen pseudonym suggests who needs to accompany him: "'My name's Mike,'" Hal practices in the rearview mirror (*IJ* 797). Pemulis, despite having suffered horrific parental abuse, never submits to therapies at all—though he has a symbolic double in the novel's final AA scene, a monologue by a "Mikey" (*IJ* 958). This may be Wallace's elliptical way of turning Hal's friendship with Pemulis into negotiable currency, through the power of AA's idealized economy. As with Poor Tony's unaided drying out and its contrasts with Gately's recovery, Wallace—attending to various kinds of value in his epic, at least elliptically—includes class differences and those excluded from even the free AA economy.[60]

In earlier developments around the idea of language as currency, the E.T.A. boys reflect Hal's misrecognition of value and collectively claim that there is such a thing as "word-inflation" (*IJ* 100). But language's value does not operate like money's, Wallace again implies. Implicitly responding to Barth's idea of "the felt exhaustion of certain [literary] possibilities,"[61] Wallace has the tired boys begin trading synonyms after practice. "'Tard tard tard,'" says Stice:

> Group empathy is expressed via sighs, further slumping, small gestures of exhaustion, the soft clanks of skulls' backs against the lockers' thin steel.
>
> . . . . .

'So tired it's out of tired's word-range,' Pemulis says. 'Tired just doesn't do it.'

'Exhausted, shot, depleted,' says Jim Struck . . . 'Cashed. Totalled.'

. . . . .

'Beat. Worn the heck out.'

'Worn the *fuck*-all out is more like.'

'Wrung dry. Whacked. Tuckered out. More dead than alive.'

'None even come close, the words.'

'Word-inflation,' Stice says . . . 'Bigger and better. Good greater greatest totally great. Hyperbolic and hyperbolicker. Like grade-inflation.'

(IJ 100)

This scene portrays a "group empathy" subtly different from the "Identification" (*IJ* 345) of AA meetings, for shared language here, even as the boys collectively define their state, complicates the mute agreement of "sighs" and "shared gestures." Stice's "word-inflation" both ends the group's language game and gets its rules wrong: Stice expands language not through synonym proliferation but (like Karrier in "Crash of '69," who said "It's great" rather than "It's good") through comparative valuation, proposing superlatives. Lurking in this scene is the inflated language of advertising, and grades signify yet another model of external valuation.

But while the players think their words for exhaustion are, like them, exhausted, the accumulating words actually testify to the vitality of language's immense (infinite?) variety. Wallace Stevens writes, "Yet the absence of the imagination had / Itself to be imagined";[62] Wallace suggests that even the exhaustion of language has to be spoken of in (voluminous) language. Reflecting the novel's detail-rich, maximalist aesthetic, the scene as a whole belies any idea of words' inflation in the economic sense (i.e., devaluation) by using the same method of paratactic synonym variation to describe the environment. For instance, Hal—reflecting on human waste, a parallel to exhaustion that calls out for language's fullness—muses on the spiritual implications of Schacht on the toilet (and in the process Hal proves himself a footwear-minded descendant of Lenore):

Luther's shoes on the floor beneath the chamber pot, placid . . . Luther's 16th-century shoes, awaiting epiphany. The mute quiescent suffering of generations of salesmen in the stalls of train-station johns, heads down, fingers laced, shined shoes inert, awaiting the acid gush. Women's slippers, centurions' dusty sandals, dock-workers' hobnailed boots, Popes' slippers. All waiting . . .

(*IJ* 103)

The toilet, grounding us all each day, is universal, and language's plenitude here is a palpable extension of the sharing of human experience across centuries and social positions, something the novel's multithread structure suggests on a larger scale. Moving in an opposing logical direction, Troeltsch later adds to Stice's thought, regarding Avril's prescriptive-grammar exam, "Phrases and clauses and models and structures. . . . We need an inflation-generative grammar" (*IJ* 100). The hyphenation here produces ambiguity: Troeltsch calls for a grammar that *itself* generates inflation, but his phrase ends up invoking Noam Chomsky's well-known idea of a generative grammar. Generative grammar inflates the language *not* in the sense of monetary valuation, though; rather, it offers grounds for a never-ending expansion in the mind of possible word combinations—language is indeed infinitely expandable.[63] Language's value is inflation proof (says the encyclopedic novelist) because it arises from a naturally inflatable grammar.

Gately's wraith scenes work toward correcting these E.T.A. ideas about language, value, and possession by proposing a radical openness with words. Gately's hospital experience with the wraith would "belong" to Hal in a more psychologically conventional novel (the kind of workshop product Wallace acidly says contains "no character without Freudian trauma in accessible past" [*BF* 40]). But the great twist on *Hamlet* here is that the ghost of Hamlet Senior appears only at the end and to the wrong man, for Wallace wants the reader to reassess her own involvement in making the text "communicate": while she readily recognizes the wraith as Himself, Gately cannot. Here is another turn on Gately as contingent agent and, potentially, full of grace, if he proves a keen listener and is able to interpret the wraith's story and explain Himself's intentions to his son. At the same time, what makes Don human and compelling is the extreme volatility of his agency and intention: in the perplexing scene fleetingly co-created by his dream (*IJ* 934) and Hal's mention during his breakdown of "John N.R. Wayne . . . standing watch in a mask as Donald Gately and I dig up my father's head" in the Great Concavity (*IJ* 16–17), we should note the echo of Don in a clown mask unwittingly sending the Entertainment into circulation by first stealing it from DuPlessis. In the exhumation, presumably a search for the masters that, according to Joelle, "were buried with him" (*IJ* 940), Don, perhaps trying to do good, risks releasing the Entertainment in an even more deadly—because copyable—form (though Don's premonition, if trustworthy, says they arrive *"Too Late,"* maybe a sign Orin beats them there [*IJ* 934]). With Don's readerlike task thus left ambiguously fulfilled and, in essence, up to the *actual* reader, the wraith scenes corroborate Boswell's recurrent claim that Wallace's structures push readers into "the world of the real, the world outside the text."[64]

Moreover, Gately's experience of "lexical rape" by the wraith acts as a foil to Hal's eidetic dictionary consumption: Hal possesses words, while Gately is possessed *by* them. "Terms and words Gately knows he doesn't know from a divot in the sod come crashing through his head with . . . ghastly intrusive force" (*IJ* 832). Aubry claims that this scene indicates Wallace's chagrin about his own mind (so much more knowledgeable) "usurping [characters'] status as the primary actors in the drama," but such a reading undermines that respect for unintellectual intuition that Wallace urges on us (Aubry, *Reading as Therapy*, 116). Wallace is trying to get us to wonder not about characters' minds but about ours as readers, about what happens when we encounter words—words we know, words we think we know. With Wittgenstein's maxim of contextual use as meaning in mind, we read novels like *Infinite Jest* looking to "acquire" language all over again—a task no drug can accelerate, a task for which metaphors of ownership are radically insufficient.

"So yo then man what's *your* story?" (*IJ* 17). The fact that 1,000+ pages containing hundreds of different people's stories follow this question shows this italicized *"your"* to be another of Wallace's implicitly foreign terms, about to be translated, over countless joined narratives, for the reader's consciousness. *Your* story is not your property and not singular; language escapes us, decenters us, connects us. Stories, like the language they are made of, belong to everyone, participating in an economy that resists quantification even as the bound book goes to market under a single artist's name. Language is commonwealth, and *Infinite Jest* is an example of the novel as "a node in a network" (Burn, *Reader's Guide*, 6). Even before the text-proper begins, *Infinite Jest* is "about" Gratitude for the stories it treats as common property, in Wallace's canny use of the copyright page's acknowledgments: there, he effaces the autobiographical aspects of the novel by implying that his material was gleaned from "Open Meetings, where pretty much anybody who's interested can come and listen . . . A lot of people at these Open Meetings spoke with me and were extremely patient and garrulous and generous and helpful," the acknowledgments continue. "The best way I can think of to show my appreciation of these men and women is to decline to thank them by name." We know now what the interviewers of the 1990s to whom Wallace repeated variations on this background (see, e.g., *CW* 59, 79–80) did not: Max's biography reveals that Wallace, a member, attended AA meetings from the late 1980s onward; he was, though, contra the copyright page, distrusted by some, with Big Craig telling Max he suspected his roommate "was looking for material for a book" (*Every Love Story*, 317n5).

I wish not to impose any autobiographical reading but to show the interrelationship of Gately's openness to words, his education in Gratitude, and Wallace's reflections on the novel's composition. In the top margin of many of the looseleaf pages on which he drafted *Infinite Jest*, Wallace writes in block capitals "NOBODY." Was this reassurance, undone now by Ransom Center visitors, that nobody would see these drafts, where he was striving for "CLARITY," a word he often wrote alongside "NOBODY"?[65] Was he reminding himself *he* was a nobody, under no pressure to produce a great work? We cannot know. But I have argued in this chapter for a way of reading "NOBODY" as the signature of the anonymous collective—the "One Body"—that coauthors this commonwealth text.

Many interlocking stories, rather than one Hideous Man's, will still be on Wallace's mind as he turns back to the short form. In "Octet," at the center of *Brief Interviews*, Wallace returns to Marathe's economic problem of the undividable good, now in tragic terms that echo biblical parables: the story opens outside "the Commonwealth Aluminum Can Redemption Center" as two "terminal drug addicts" spend the night under a single coat, setting up a question of moral calculus that has no answer and hence no question mark, "Which one lived" (*BI* 131). "Octet" imagines an attempted merger between these bodies, "pressed right up against" each other, at the base of commonwealth redemption (*BI* 131)—an exchange of heat that cannot be assimilated to mathematical or monetary division. Depicting exchanges that produce neither a scarcity for one side nor a balance of divided value, Wallace seeks in language a sharing of wealth that transcends accounting and money's privations. Only in that transcendent state can we achieve redemption and truly meet the other, the task that is the next chapter's major subject.

4

OTHER MATH

HUMAN COSTS, FRACTIONAL SELVES, AND NEOLIBERAL CRISIS IN *BRIEF INTERVIEWS WITH HIDEOUS MEN*

math, n. 1: Now *arch.* and *Brit. regional.* A mowing; the action or work of mowing; that which may be or has been mowed; the portion of a crop that has been mowed. See also aftermath *n.*, day's math *n.*, lattermath *n.*, undermath *n.*
—*OED*

LOVE IS no set theory or math equation, but we might understand it better if we imagined it so—or acknowledged the ways, such as referring to a spouse as "my other half," we already do. This chapter shares a title with an uncollected 1987 story Wallace included in a draft table of contents for the book that became *Brief Interviews with Hideous Men* (before the "Brief Interview" sequences existed).[1] Three pages long, "Other Math" concerns a boy named Joseph, a sincere naïf in the mold of Mario and Stecyk. Joseph declares to his grandfather that he is "in love with" him in an opening section; he asks his grandmother about romantic love in the second section while dealing with his grandfather's death ("Other Math," 287). Finally, in the third section, which moves back in time to continue the first, the grandfather tells a chilling story of a medical-school classmate of Joseph's father who carried around a cadaver in public, claiming to be in love with it. Like many Wallace narratives, "Other Math" invests in a Lynchian gothicism played for uneasy laughs, meanwhile asking intense questions about love, as in Joseph's query of his grandmother about couples holding hands, "Do they feel something, when they do it?" Her answer is sobering: "It's unclear whether things are felt, or whether it's just a demonstration" ("Other Math," 289).

The mysterious title, never mentioned in the story, plays on "higher math" and suggests both an alternative mathematics and, perhaps, a method of combining self and other in love: is love two values added together? Or two values hopelessly divided, as Joseph's grandparents seem to be? Perhaps, given the story's pairing of a romanced cadaver with the grandmother's chilling claim that "Grampa's hand was a dead thing . . . an extension I never recognized and certainly never held," the title means that there is an absolute alterity to the love object—even though so much of the discourse of romantic love promises attachment, merger, or, as Joseph hopes, "feel[ing] something" ("Other Math," 289). Indeed, the title, run together as "othermath," echoes the obsolete meaning of "math" as mowing shown in this chapter's epigraph. For Wallace, this story is about the Grim Reaper's mowing and, by analogy, the human tendency to kill off the other even in the midst of life.

The death of the other, a topic throughout Wallace, is especially meaningful for *Brief Interviews* because of the permanent silence of the book's mysterious "Q," the female interviewer of the Hideous Men, who more than once threaten her with violence. In parallel terms, the horrific encounter of the final subject's beloved with a serial rapist-killer—the "Granola-Cruncher" story, "B.I. #20"—is an in-interview version of the death of another (miraculously, combated and survived on the literal level). Wallace himself confirms we are to imagine "Q" as a singular being: "Something bad happens to her over the course of the book . . . something *really* bad," he says (*CW* 90). Tom LeClair's review persuasively suggests that arranging the scattered interviews chronologically reveals "a unified though episodic story of a woman . . . who, after being abandoned by her lover, travels America trying to understand" men,[2] before apparently being attacked in "B.I. #72 08-98," the chronologically final interview. It abruptly ends "oh no not again behind you *look out*!" (*BI* 226). Wallace keeps Q's fate elliptical, though, expecting readers again to fashion an ending for themselves, just "outside the right-frame of the picture," as he said of *Infinite Jest* (*CW* 145).

In this chapter, demonstrating the interlocking nature of several meanings of Other Math, I explore its varied operations in *Brief Interviews*, a volume suggestive, often, of certain mathlike relationships at the heart of the experience of reading Wallace's texts: investigating the "addition" of one character to another in love and sex (or, more often, their "division"), actively converting "random" variables into a more determinate structure, balancing one value against another, assessing fractional selves, and recognizing that the numbers represented in the text become crucial to its linguistic meanings, rather than merely serving as typical page and section numbers. Though atomized into twenty-three stories, with most further divided into multiple and incongruous parts, *Brief Interviews* is more unified than it appears—and this unity of disparate, "random" parts, as it is attained by the curious calculations of the reader, becomes a central thematic concern tied to the book's critique of neoliberal political economy and financialization.

If "Westward" proposed as its starting point that we "could love only what we valued" (*GCH* 234), *Brief Interviews* investigates the perils of conceiving of love *in terms of* mathematical value, especially when those terms align with contemporary methods of monetary accumulation—all the ways erotic expectations receive distorted reflection in the mirror provided by modes of value accrual. Such accrual, Wallace asserts, is the sort of Other Math that does reign in contemporary U.S. culture, without the eerie disturbances rampant in his fiction. These dominant forces turn the traditional romantic meaning of "date" into abstract "datum," for example, as explored in "*Datum Centurio*" (*BI* 125). *Brief Interviews* exposes the unthought assumptions behind such valuation of persons—and even its inherent insanity. Building from the foundation I discussed in chapter 2, this collection refocuses Wallace's interest in accumulation by pointing to the intimate consequences of a phase of capitalist expansion dominated by financialization, a development begun in the 1980s that Giovanni Arrighi identified in 1994 not as a sign of robust value creation but as the "signal crisis of the

US regime[] of accumulation" (a prediction confirmed by 2008).[3] Citing the massive growth of securitization, derivatives, and futures trading, Harvey agrees with Arrighi, drawing on the ideas of Randy Martin to state that "neoliberalization has meant, in short, the financialization of everything," on Wall Street and in everyday life.[4]

Wallace saw this story collection as a unified whole; indeed, mathematically minded, he seemed—as O'Donnell suggests in reading the part-whole relationships of *Broom*[5]—always attentive to the "sets" that his various narrative parts formed, whether microfictions and longer stories here or the many small, recursive stories making up his novels. Fractions—signifying a part's relationship to a whole, the ratios at the heart of the rational— mattered deeply to Wallace, particularly when such relationships found reflection in notions of human wholeness and unwholeness. Max quotes him writing to Costello about the integrity of *Brief Interviews*: "I like the way [the manuscript's parts] play off one another and the way certain leitmotifs weave through them," "the child-perspective-self-pity of 'The Depressed Person' vs. the parent-perspective-self-pity of 'On his Deathbed . . . Begs a Boon' vs. the more quote-unquote objective intrafamily pain of 'Signifying Nothing' and 'Suicide . . . Present.'"[6] Thus throughout this chapter I read *Brief Interviews* (not just the clearly linked "Brief Interviews") as an integral, if unwieldy, whole.[7]

Working without a strict sequence in my readings, I first draw together the book's parts in porous groupings based on value-related subtopics: randomness, work, cost accounting, gifts, coinage, and contracts. I then turn, in a climactic reading, to what in the book's structure is illuminated by the battle between randomness and financial returns in the computerized stochastic mathematics of currency markets portrayed in "Adult World." In this diptych story, Wallace aligns the pursuit of financial capital with the image of fractional, incomplete selves, culminating in his rereading, laced with images of finance's hegemony, of Plato's famous image of the lover's soul seeking out completion by its "better half." As a social-historical corollary to such themes, "Adult World" also extends Wallace's use of financial crises as fictional backdrops into the late 1990s. His subject now is the threat of devaluation and economic ripple effects brought about by the "Asian Flu," a phenomenon I examine in light of the neoliberal economics that reinforces many of the suspect valuations of human bonds that *Brief Interviews* stands against. These critiques of the late-1990s moment lead to a coda for this chapter in which I examine two other writers—Teddy Wayne and Zadie Smith—mounting homages to Wallace that expand his visions of value into realms of post-9/11 global history and gender difference, areas he does not extensively examine.

My ultimate aim in this chapter, focused anew on the calculation of moral values, is to reveal the dynamic interaction between balanced simplicity and chaotic complexity at the heart of Wallace's postmodern moral art. I thus describe another version of the career-long challenges Wallace set for himself: first, using "postmodern technique" but "to discuss very old traditional human verities" of moral and communal life; and second, tackling the job of "mak[ing] . . . up" "meaningful moral values." How exactly does one make up moral values and involve the reader in the process in the late twentieth century, especially amid so much technological computation in work and social life? *Brief Interviews*, bridging *Infinite Jest* to the later work, affords an opportunity to see forms of moral computation under formation in Wallace's imagination, where highly technical knowledge and systems necessarily intermingled with the direct, "old-fashioned" relationship he cultivated with readers.

RANDOM VALUES IN A POSTINDUSTRIAL WORLD

Wallace, more than any other contemporary experimenter outside of perhaps Mark Z. Danielewski, submits readily to analysis in terms of what Gerard Genette calls paratexts and, in a homophone registering their place on books' edges, peritexts: footnotes and endnotes, the dedication "For L—" in *Girl*, the acknowledgments of *Infinite Jest*, and (as we will see in *The Pale King*) the copyright page's legal disclaimers.[8] The table of contents of *Brief*

Interviews, with its mysterious use of numbers, is another such strange peri-text. How to account for the many values on display, before diving into the stories? The numbering of anything in Wallace's work is never an innocent or mechanical endeavor. The collection as a whole seems to present only parts of larger series. Each of the "B.I.'s" is numbered, though not consecutively or in any easily discernible order. Three stories appear under the title "Yet Another Example of the Porousness of Certain Borders" and a different form of numeric notation, Roman numerals—XI, VI, XXIV. Both numbers and title suggest we are seeing only the tip of an iceberg. Seemingly in parallel with the shifts between minimalist and maximalist forms throughout, Wallace will use some of the shortest stories to imply a potentially infinite accumulation: the title and the numbering imply a list without end. Also implied is the discarding of other Examples in producing the book.

"Octet" has a numerical title, but contains, we see, abortive, unconsecutive "Pop Quizzes" that do not add up to eight. Various other oddities of numbering and valuation crop up: the pages start from 0 rather than 1, and surrounding the page numbers in the lower corners of each page are distinctive brackets that, with small bumps on their sides, appear curly. These brackets are also used around the name of the book on the title page and, throughout the text, in place of what would usually be square brackets. These special brackets appear within nesting parentheses, but also, for example, in "Someone once told me of an Australian profession known as [flexion of upraised fingers] *chicken-sexing*" (*BI* 100). Wallace was known to be meticulously involved in the look of his pages, and curly brackets are used in designating numerical sets. The reader wonders whether to regard verbal information in the text as she would numbers, something also suggested by the names for characters in "Octet," X and Y. The idea of a pattern—a key to all *Brief Interviews'* mythologies—is naturally enticing, but it is the *impression* of random values given by this summative view of the text (and not a "solution") that is important to Wallace's ultimate game, which concerns stochastic math, financial modeling, and the reader's discomfort with randomness. LeClair's review ("Non-Silence of the Un-Lamblike") wittily suggests the collection "could have an intricate design, perhaps generated by a 'stochastic' mathematics" but in ways that can only be revealed by Wallace "or someone who has read the collection thirty times." After only four or five readings, I argue that the book is indeed stochastic, implicating even the first-time reader in taming its randomness by giving it design.

Much ink has been and will continue to be spilled over whether Wallace is a postmodernist (and exactly what sort of nonpostmodernist he might be). But *Brief Interviews* locates his work in cultural history under the sign of the "Postindustrial." The first story, "A Radically Condensed History of Postindustrial Life," provides an overall heading of sorts. "Postindustrial" is a term that emerged in the 1960s, according to Howard Brick, and fully flowered in the 1970s. Explicating David Riesman's work, Brick writes of the postindustrial era, "Work no longer seemed central to people's lives, but consumption alone provided no meaningful replacement."[9] For Wallace, the kinds of ironic social values on display in this opening story are attributable not to the dominance of media or a cultural style held together under the always unwieldy category of postmodernism but, as with the leisure-cultivating figures of *Broom* and *Infinite Jest*, an attenuation of the work impulse and its production of value. "Radically Condensed" tells this story through the mathematical and pronominal. Starting on page 0, it describes potential romance followed by actual disconnection and concludes, "One never knew, after all, now did one now did one now did one"—as though the story, and perhaps the whole collection, is stuck in an initial accumulation of value, too "condensed" to count beyond "one," both the number of solipsism and the pronoun of ironic self-distancing. Wallace also generalizes the absence of meaningful work in a postindustrial culture into a widespread zerohood, notably marked down at the bottom, or on the "ground," of the initiating page. In confirmation, "Death Is Not the End," a meditation on Wallace's 1997 MacArthur "genius" grant, follows "Radically" with a portrait of the writer idling—here not in a beret or leisure suit but swim trunks.

Seemingly in sublimated compensation for such worries over accolades, work, and self-worth, Wallace in *Brief Interviews* begins to pursue the melancholy accountant identity for his characters that will prove so complexly powerful in *The Pale King*. In "Forever Overhead," for instance, the bite of the title is like that of the joke transcendence and *memento mori* lurking in *Infinite Jest*, since we recognize in the seemingly eternal suspension

into which the "You" "disappear[s]" both existential thrownness and a term
of accounting (*BI* 16): "forever overhead" means that there is always the
cost of doing business, of being alive and submitting to entropy's debit
on the order that makes life possible. The thirteen-year-old of this story,
Tennyson-like, is prematurely preoccupied with old age and death; he sees
in the adulthood he is approaching a decay and death, the fat older woman's
body in front of him already implicit in the teenage girls he has begun to
notice. Barefoot on rough surfaces, he is Wallace's clearest portrait of the
consciousness of feet and embodied weight since Lenore, though here in a
tone that makes far more visceral sadness manifest: "The rungs hurt your
feet. They are thin and let you know just how much you weigh. You have
real weight on the ladder. The ground wants you back" (*BI* 12). The story
awakens this young Dasein to Being-toward-death, as experienced not by
the thinking end of the human but its sensitive opposite, its "tender and
dented" feet (*BI* 14). The poolside poet of "Death," having forgotten these
truths, wears "simulated-rubber thongs" (*BI* 2).

The challenge of "Forever Overhead" is a Kierkegaardian one familiar
from *Infinite Jest*: decide to leap anyway, lift the weight that will someday
be a corpse (but not yet), and receive the final line's echo of the beginning
"Hello." For it is only in this moment of authenticating decision in spite
of fear that the second birth(day) Cavell discusses can occur. Only then,
perhaps, can this "You" become an "I." The "little bits of soft tender feet" at
the end of the diving board (*BI* 14) thus offer a dark double for the brand-
new feet of "You[r]" newborn sister (*BI* 7). A redeeming value like Gately's
may be possible, in this pre–*Infinite Jest* story: a sun "full of hard coins of
light that shimmer red as they stretch away into a mist that is your own
sweet salt" suggests a natural money the self might absorb—though with
the color red and the dissolution into mist, we are reminded again of the
debit side of the ledger (*BI* 15). Such images point subtly to the cost accountant Wallace compared himself to in his 1997 interview with Rose:
Wallace's addiction and troubles in his twenties were not "substantively
different from the sort of thing where somebody who wants to be a really
successful cost accountant [and] achieves that at fifty and goes into something like a depression. . . . 'The brass ring I've been chasing does not make

everything okay.'" Importantly, a cost accountant's job is not to balance books on the present or past but to forecast areas of future loss for a firm—operating like this boy and like an actuary in health insurance, a field I show Wallace metaphorizing in chapter 5.

"Cost" is where the central sequence begins conceptually. In moving from the "Brief Interviews" published in the October 1998 *Harper's* to the book version, Wallace dropped a short opener, such that the first line of the collection's "B.I.'s" became "It's cost me every sexual relationship I ever had" (*BI* 17). "Cost" makes *Brief Interviews* cohere; as we read we learn distinctions between the monetary terms many write onto themselves (especially in dealing with deficiencies—for instance, a shriveled arm as "the Asset" [*BI* 82]) and cost conceived in a more human, possibly unquantifiable sense. In "Octet," for instance, the "writer" attempts to define this human price that many of these stories drive toward, in a passage Zadie Smith aptly seizes on as definitive.[10] In a very long sentence that requires excerpting to be critically manageable, Wallace writes that the pieces of "Octet" (and, I suggest, those of *Brief Interviews*)

> all seem to be trying to demonstrate some weird ambient *sameness* in different kinds of human relationships, some nameless but inescapable '*price*' that all human beings are faced with having to pay at some point if they ever want truly 'to be with' another person instead of just using that person somehow . . . a weird and nameless but apparently unavoidable 'price' that can actually sometimes equal death itself, or at least usually equals your giving up something (either a thing or person or a precious long-held 'feeling' or some certain idea of yourself and your own virtue/worth/identity) whose loss will feel, in a true and urgent way, like a kind of death . . .
>
> (*BI* 155–156)

Another word whose italics signal not just emphasis but foreignness, this "nameless" "'*price*'" can only be evoked through experience of these uncanny fictions. The word "weird" and the repeated use of "*sameness*"—also italicized—nod to Freud's *unheimlich*, which arises out of a feeling of resemblance between experiences and phenomena that ought not to exist, according to the conscious mind. To return to this chapter's title, "Other Math," this passage both claims that an alternative form of math (not determined by numerical or monetary values) structures human relationships. Such new math points us toward an ineluctable mowing/math/"death" of the ("use[d]") other, of the self, or, in more uncanny developments, of both. In this unavoidable cost on every transaction between persons, Wallace also moves tentatively toward an image system built around tax.

At the same time, in a more hopeful turn, "your giving up something"—a refashioning of Hal's oblivion-oriented "giving our lives away to something"—can also become the site of bonding with the other. While the title "Octet" seems to refer to the projected number of quizzes, Wallace, always seeing microscopic heat transfers as the ultimate arbiter of connection, also points to the Octet Rule of chemistry. According to it, atoms of a low atomic number tend to combine in such a way that they have eight electrons in their valence shells. The carbon and oxygen atoms in the carbon dioxide we breathe out each have eight electrons surrounding them, with the central carbon "giving up" electrons to share two covalent bonds with the oxygen atoms. Such electron sharing suggests that the reader's responses to the story's Quizzes might help it add up to the desired eight (a number that might be taken for infinity, as Orin's date proves [*IJ* 47]). More concretely, the Octet Rule is the basis for the body heat one addict offers to another in the opening Quiz, possibly giving up his own life in the process. Thus when Wallace (in a written interview) describes feelings of loneliness and inferiority as "the great valent bond between us all," he understands the shared etymology—the Latin *valere*, "be worth"—between electrons' bonds of valence and the values we often assume to be merely abstract (*LI* 58). In "Octet," his economic atavism and refusal of conventional value transfers—with money stripped away and only a single coat to share between two dying people—show us value as shared energy, as (co)valence.[11]

Wallace's stories often remind us of what Wendy Brown says about neoliberalism "not presum[ing] the ontological givenness of a thoroughgoing economic rationality for all domains of society" but actively seeking to construct and disseminate such rationality.[12] Indeed, *Brief Interviews* relies at times on a quasi-folkloric idiom that resonates with the work of Hyde, Campbell, and anthropologists of value such as Graeber and Michael Taussig, who question contemporary Western capitalism by attending to the rejection of money's rationality by more "primitive" societies. In the first "The Devil Is a Busy Man," for instance, a wise farmer (a figure almost entirely silent at the Avis counter in "Westward") provides a punchline on the slavish devotion to allegedly rational price when his son asks for the "lesson" to draw from their inability to give away a tiller: the father "said he figured it's you don't try and teach a pig to sing" (*BI* 71). The line may be a throwaway, but what might a pig ("like a reader . . . down here quivering in the mud," in the words of "Octet" [*BI* 160]) know about use value that these tiller-skeptics do not? This father is selling an implement for the working of the ground, and in the brief tale lie traces of the decline of a farming economy Wallace often uses to index the maddening departure into price as value. The "devil" of this story, never mentioned, is not some all-purpose evil figure but, perhaps, the one that Taussig, in *The Devil and Commodity Fetishism*, hears invoked by Bolivian miners who, upon first confronting capitalism, understand the "fabulations that the commodity engenders" as inherently satanic.[13] In what sense is the devil a "busy man"? This twice-used title (both times for stories in which gifts are thwarted) is Wallace's reply to the folk wisdom "Idle hands are the devil's playthings," for his devil's busy-ness is the world of business the utilitarian Steeply adored, not productive labor. The narrator's father is giving away the tiller presumably because it is now useless to the family, the potential buyers of his food in the thrall of (the devilish possession of?) negotiating prices and being microfinanciers.

FLIPPING COINS AND SIGNING CONTRACTS

With these markers of value in place, let me knit together more of *Brief Interviews* through, again, coins, which in *Brief Interviews* (as with the pennies of chapter 3) become associated with low self-worth, with abject and morose states. The executive washroom attendant of "B.I. #42" is a good example: sacrificing himself over decades to a humility job that Gately could hardly fathom, this man works, his son ruefully says, "for coins" (*BI* 89). His father's "effacement cannot be too complete or they forget he is there when it comes time to tip. The trick of his demeanor is to appear only provisionally there, to exist all and only if needed" (*BI* 89). Small currency thus underscores yet another radical attenuation of a self's ontology. Here, though, Wallace's allegory of small change and work gains important social contexts: he returns to the topos of slavery in the Hegelian sense, granted new dimension by the fact that the speaker is African American, meditating on a history of subjection by white wealth along with his father's particular suffering.[14] "Effluence. Emission. Orduration, micturition, transudation, emiction, feculence, catharsis—so many synonyms: why? what are we trying to say to ourselves in so many ways?" (*BI* 88). For Wallace, as in the *Infinite Jest* word-inflation scene to which this paratactic bathroom moment is kin, the generation of so many synonyms for seemingly valueless waste points to a redemptive wealth in language's plenitude. His source here is *End Zone*, where Gary finds in the Texas desert a pile of waste and muses on its names: "defecation, as of old women in nursing homes fouling their beds; feces, as of specimen, sample, analysis, diagnosis, bleak assessments of disease in the bowels" (the list extends for eight more lines).[15] Like DeLillo, Wallace formally undermines the perspective that sees "nullity in the very word, shit" (*End Zone*, 88).

For Wallace, the point of placing coins alongside waste and this lowly man among the uncaring wealthy is to agitate interviewee and reader to the point that an attunement to the uncertainty of one's foundational values (in Freudian terms, the liberated unconscious and an Oedipal drama) becomes possible. For how can the interviewee reconcile the support of his upbringing those coins represented with the seeming total evacuation of dignity in the work, that sense the speaker has that the job compromised his father's personhood, that "he brought his work home," in "the face he wore in the men's room," which his "skull conformed to fit" (*BI* 90)? Is this work that exacts more human cost from a person than can ever be balanced by money? In this general atmosphere of value agitation the speaker of "B.I. #42" wonders what moral values his father's work held: "do I admire the fortitude of this humblest of working men? The stoicism? The Old World grit? . . . Or do I despise him[?]" (*BI* 90–91). This is a version of the ur-memory the narrator of "Signifying Nothing" has of his father "waggling his dick," though here with the power dynamic inverted (*BI* 75). In his last line, after notably reemphasizing that the father worked "for coins," the interviewee seems to abandon the stark duality of choice he has just laid out: "What were the two choices again?" (*BI* 91). This deluded man has *already* made his choice of how to regard his origins, not having seen his father "since 1978" in an interview set in 1997 (*BI* 89). This speaker's hideousness is hard to discern compared to that of many others, but it must lie in what Kierkegaard means in *Either/Or* when he calls the delaying of fundamental choice impossible, since the choice effectively gets made in spite of what the delayer (dwelling in "aesthetic irony") may say.[16]

Wallace returns to images of existentialist contingency and thrownness and connects them with the coin in the very brief "Yet Another Example of the Porousness of Certain Borders (VI)," about "Mr. Walter D. ('Walt') DeLasandro Jr.'s Parents' Marriage's End" (*BI* 211). Young Walt's thrownness is literalized in the form of a coin toss: dividing up property in a divorce, with one offering to trade Walt for ownership of a truck, his parents decide to flip for him. There may be no greater caricature of a living transaction in all of Wallace, no greater instance of an undividable good (for this story inverts the scene of wise Solomon suggesting a child's division). Does Walt hear them, or is the scene "reconstructed" in a different sense? The ambiguity speaks to *Brief Interviews'* motif of primal scenes so traumatic they almost *must* be consigned to an oblivion (to anticipate a later title) for the subject to survive, even if pain necessarily remains, ready to erupt.

We do see the parents' coin, in both its dilution of tough decision making and its troubling commodification of the human, as it marks Walt into adult professional pursuits—as though he continues to be paid in the trauma that coin signifies. His first appearance in the collection is as an older man in "The Depressed Person," where, a "professional arbitrator" and "highly respected Conflict-Resolution Specialist," he charges the title character's parents $130 an hour to resolve not an emotional question but a financial one: who will pay for her orthodonture (*BI* 46). Walt's job titles emblematize legalism papering over the essential existential drama, and given the valorization of choice in Wallace, "professional arbitrator" is particularly offensive—while "arbiter" would be correct, this form sounds a "-trator"/"traitor" pun. Appropriately, given his shadowy relationship to his parents' separation, through monetary structures (and the porous borders between these stories) Walt becomes an absent presence in "The Depressed Person," seen only in the form of "his business card" and essentially returning psychically to the arbitrary fate of his child self by mediating his clients' lives (*BI* 46).

The depressed person herself, reliving childhood as a grownup, has tried to convert her radical uncertainty about love into the surety of a paid relationship, encountering another instance of Other Math and marking Wallace's return to the deforming effects of the contractual. The "contracted hourly $90" she pays the therapist makes the "relationship's simulacrum of friendship . . . [an] ideally one-sided" arena for sharing her neediness (*BI* 56n5). Yet those exact conditions of an imbalance "purchase[d]" with money produce in her emotional ledger feelings of patheticness over being allowed to fulfill her "narcissistic fantasies" of not having to "reciprocally meet" or "give" to an other—an other who might as well be dead and ends up literally so (*BI* 57n5). With a name that echoes the legal category of Displaced Persons of World War II, who were stateless and stripped of identity (her childhood is "a battlefield or theater of conflict" [*BI* 39]), the depressed person is yet another Wallace character who seems to be denied existence. The name the story gives her both identifies her completely with her illness and seems to require continual reassertion, lest she slip into insignificance (read: nonsignification). Many times, to Kafkaesque comic effect, the story adds "(i.e., the depressed person)" after pronouns that already clearly identify her (i.e., the depressed person—you get the gag) (*BI* 50, e.g.). Expanding on the ineffectuality of contracts for those who feel worthless (recall the Suicide Contracts of *Infinite Jest*), Wallace parodies legal specificity here in a prose that ends up otiose. The abbreviated *id est*, usually translated "that is," increases the sense of abstraction: *est*, meaning "is," makes this a highly indirect version of Wallace's "I EXIST" refrain, but *id*, meaning "that," is a word assigned to objects—*id* in another grammatical context would be "it." The invertebrate girl of *Infinite Jest* lurks in the margins.

Contract terminology and the bracketing of meaning also warp human relationships in "B.I. #48," the story of a "chicken-sexer" describing his sadomasochistic game playing (*BI* 101). From LaVache to J.D., Wallace frequently made contracts' mastery the province of sadists, characters who inflict pain and call it pleasure under the cover provided by what this interviewee calls the "*rules*, as it were, of the game" (*BI* 106). This character has the odious distinction of being Wallace's most annoyingly ironic speaker (at least up through *Brief Interviews*): he constantly uses the "[flexion of upraised fingers to signify tone quotes]," abbreviated as "[finger flexion]" and eventually, as they pile up, "[f.f.]" (*BI* 102–103). Here "Q" seems to respond in ways a therapist might—though, true to the Hideous Men's logic of hermetically sealed language, the speaker outdoes her with psychological explanations: "The purpose of the contractual nature of masochistic or [f.f.] *bonded* play . . . is to formalize the power structure" (*BI* 106). His constant scare quotes, especially around the terms of the women's alleged consent, make him scary, Wallace knows, but also an exaggeration of the plausibly human: the bracketing speaks to a common impulse for any speaker to make language's transactions "ideally one-sided." This interview exposes the allegiance of contract writing not with law but with a sadism that makes decisions for the other—all in a monologue spoken not to a person but into a void, the other mown down.

Across almost all these stories, as the discourses of psychoanalysis and self-esteem are crosscut with those of school, contract, and finance, those who become deeply identified with the terms of external valuation—especially of money and market—suffer the same functional dementia and debilitation that the Fed Chairman, beset by gold-standard questions, did in "Crash of '69." His brain injury has spread outward: in "Adult World (I)," Jeni's "Former Lover" works for the aptly named "Mad Mike's" auto dealer, whose salesmen, under great pressure to sell, are each made to wear a "hospital gown and arrow-through-head-prosthesis" (*BI* 182). The ranting, hospitalized father of "On His Deathbed . . .", who reduces his child's life to a matter of accounting, is the Chairman's second coming, now shifted from philosophical to familial skepticism, in keeping with Wallace's general move toward personalizing abstract themes. Through her "inner fund of loathing," the mother of "Suicide as a Sort of Present" leads her child to perversely "repay the perfect love" with his death, a sadistic gift recalling those in *Infinite Jest* (*BI* 286). "N.B.: hammer home fiduciary pun," Wallace writes in "Adult World (II)," identifying a method of character construction he follows throughout this collection—and, indeed, his whole career (*BI* 187).

MY OTHER HALF

When tasked with characterizing that whole career, critics have most often turned to the primer of "Octet," a potent summary of sincerity as call to arms that has a relationship to Wallace's oeuvre (especially *Infinite Jest*) similar to the one Pynchon's compact *The Crying of Lot 49* has to his much longer novels.[17] Let me loosen critical homogeneity by instead giving my most sustained reading to "Adult World," where Wallace was forging ahead rather than staying in what Boswell in 2003, even without knowledge of the new Wallaces to come, called *Brief Interviews'* mode of "consolidation[]."[18] As Pietsch reveals,[19] Wallace began "Adult World" as part of *The Pale King*, probably within what Max reveals was an intended pornography business subplot (*Every Love Story*, 321). Anticipating insertion into the interstices of private and public economies in the tax novel, "Adult World" shows Wallace attuning his abiding question of value and the moral to the complexities of economic causation, captured in the stochastic fluctuations of currency trading, a prime example of the proliferation of tenuous financial value that Arrighi and Harvey criticize.

"Adult World" concerns the Other Math—the presumed combination of selves—known as marital love. Sadly, for married couples, one does not equal two, and two will never truly become one. On such distinctions the fundamental order of numbers depends, we learn when the collection climaxes on the psychopath of "B.I. #20," Wallace's most horrifying nihilist and his refashioning of figures from horror novels by Thomas Harris and Stephen King that he surprisingly listed among his favorite books (and sometimes also taught).[20] The rapist-murderer's "forehead's [bloody] mark" in "B.I. #20" "was not a rune or glyph at all . . . but a simple circle, the Ur-void, the zero, that axiom of Romance we call also mathematics, pure logic, whereby one does not equal two and cannot" (*BI* 314). Here is a grim summation of the essential distance between one and an-other: the page o that connoted an ironist's value in the opening story (where two people also fail to become one) has, more than three hundred pages later, the direst implications (the finger-flexing sadist is an intermediate step in this progression). Madame Psychosis made an equally pessimistic claim in *Infinite Jest*: there were "two really distinct individual people walking around back there in history's mist," and "all difference descends from this difference. . . . No Zen-type One, always rather Two" (*IJ* 220).

But we subscribe all the time, *Brief Interviews* knows, to a mythology of love relationships that shows two magically becoming one—Other Math as the addition of one to an-other. This insidious philosophical story regarding love and value arises from Plato, with whose images Wallace plays throughout. The time-stopping sexual fantasies of the Soviet boy in "B.I. #59" recast the *Republic*'s discussion of the ring of Gyges (and the moral dilemmas of invisibility). This and other Socratic dialogues are a distant precedent for the Brief Interviews, with the Hideous Men often playing sophists, no Socratic questioning in sight (except from the reader, filling in Q's). In a revision of Plato's cave, the depressed person feels a "life-or-death need to describe the sun in the sky and yet [is] able or permitted only to point to shadows on the ground" (*BI* 59n5). That state resonates with the entrappedness of "Yet Another Example . . . (XXIV)," which replies to the cave allegory with a silent battle between twin brothers: one has his hair cut while the other, reflected in the pantry door, "cop[ies]" his expressions, making them "distended and obscene" (*BI* 319–320). With the stove "scorching" behind the shorn boy (i.e., the fires that throw shadows onto the cave wall), he operates with the maddening awareness of the images' irreality that Plato's figures do not have (*BI* 320). In a final Platonic example, "Octet" turns upon a distinction between two locations: "down here quivering in the mud of the trench with the rest of us"—the domain of "a reader"—and "some gleaming abstract Olympian HQ," the presumed place of "a *Writer*" (*BI* 160). In Plato's terms, the latter godly space is the heaven from which ideal forms emanate, the world of "mud" the plane of the thingly. Wallace wants that distinction undone.

Let me illuminate this Wallace critique of Platonism through a brief interlude on a pointed homage in Tom McCarthy's remarkable experimental novel *Remainder*. About a fifth of the way into *Remainder* the amnesiac narrator—seeking a purpose after winning a huge legal settlement for an accident he does not recall—attends a party given by a man who never actually appears, David Simpson. A David with a Scottish surname: code for David Wallace, who, from Bruce in "Here and There" to Barry Loach, used many Scottish self-references. The connection is sealed when the narrator replays Joelle's freebasing in the bathroom at Molly Notkin's party, about a fifth of the way into *Infinite Jest*. In Simpson's bathroom, though, the narrator meditates not on crack cocaine but on a crack running down the wall. Simpson "had stripped the walls, so there was only plaster on them, plus some daubs of different types of paint where David had been experimenting to see how the room would look in various colours. I was . . . looking at this crack in the plaster when I had a sudden sense of déjà vu"[21]—in plot terms, the conjuring of an uncannily similar scene that launches his first of several elaborate reenactments of half-remembered events. But in metafictional terms, the description points to McCarthy's memory of David experimenting in *Infinite Jest*, now regarded as a blank canvas on which to try new colors.

Simpson's party is a housewarming for a flat he "has just bought . . . on Plato Road" (*Remainder*, 35). A crack in a new apartment equates to a crack in the metaphysical edifice. McCarthy suggests many things here (the nonviability of Platonism, Henry James's bowl . . .) and also challenges my reading of Wallace as a seeker of ground. McCarthy, emphasizing more his deconstructive habits, sees Wallace as a writer who continually observes the cracks in metaphysical systems, identifying persistent lack. In conversation with Max, challenging the biographer's account of a writer who decided he could not be a postmodernist, McCarthy characterizes Wallace as a Derridean mind who argues consistently that "a metaphysical belief system does

not work" and seeks "an aesthetics of commitment that would not subscribe to a notion of authenticity on one hand or pat irony on the other."[22]

McCarthy uses his Wallace and Plato references to launch a descent into
extreme solipsism and simulacral life—more ultrapostmodernism than
postpostmodernism. But in *Brief Interviews* it is the Plato of love and idealized union that draws Wallace's most acid parodies. "Adult World" toys
with the famous *Symposium* imagery of Zeus slicing humans' ancestors in
half. In a metaphor with tremendous staying power in the Western tradition, Plato's Aristophanes observes that love "draws the two halves of our
original nature back together and makes one out of two . . . Each of us
[has] been cut in half like flatfish, making two out of one, and each of us is
looking for his own matching half."[23] "My other half" or "my better half":
many millions in history have cited this maxim, having no clue about its
Platonic provenance or the visceralness and narcissism the metaphor entails, and as many have lost sleep over the myth of finding a "soul mate."
Wallace, always interested in why certain clichés take hold, probes the limits of the self interpreted in these mathematical terms in "Adult World,"
which is full of "flatfish," half-people with "inner deficits" (*BI* 184) alienated from each other but without the Platonic happy ending. The schizoid
self-division Burn sees throughout *Infinite Jest*[24] has a renewed persistence
in *Brief Interviews*, which uses the "B.I." abbreviation to signify "bi-" and
thus bivalency, split identities. In "Adult World," the imbalanced halves
range from the "slight asymmetry" (*BI* 173) of Jeni's breasts to her former
lover's "facial asymmetry" (*BI* 179–180) and the "emotional asymmetry" of
rampant "misconnection" (*BI* 184). Jeni's husband has "insecurities about
his right profile" and prefers being seen from the left (his sinister side); his
"turn[ing] his face toward Jeni" as he drives an ambulance in her dream
becomes a moment of "obscene" horror (*BI* 179). These figures are "ideally
one-sided" in the sense that they live in realms of abstraction inspired by
the logic of money and contract.

Even the story is riven—I/II or ½—and the choice of parenthetical Roman numerals, "(I)" and "(II)," makes a visual joke about the attempted
addition of one solipsistic self to a second, forming two separate *I*s, rather
than the promised "ONE FLESH," the subtitle of "(II)" (*BI* 183). Wallace
also loads the split story's ending with many ironic suggestions that Plato's

vision of combined halves has been thoroughly subverted. "Binding them now," the end of "(II)" says, "is that deep & unspoken complicity that is adult marriage is covenant/love → 'They were now truly married, cleaved,'" a word meaning both unity and division (*BI* 188–189). The equally ironic last line suggests they "'. . . were ready to begin, in a calm and mutually respectful way, to discuss having children [together]'" (*BI* 189; ellipsis in the original). The joke is that the "together" part may be optional for these atomized individuals, probably headed for divorce. But in the context of Other Math as the possible combination of self and other, the near-curly brackets become especially meaningful, both here and in the earlier mention of "one flesh, [a union . . .]": in set theory, which the term "union" brings up, curly brackets with no numbers between them—{}—would signify the empty set, and thus this couple, the chicken sexer and the heavily bracketed Depressed Person (who is "frightened for herself, for as it were '[her]*self*'" [*BI* 68]), are subject to an utter negation or erasure. Naturally, market value accompanies this ironic Other Math: the marriage, so fraught before, now "afforded Jeni O. Roberts a cool, steady joy" (*BI* 189)—an image of reliable cash flow, product of the revelation that she has not only resigned herself to masturbation but secured a "separate investment portfolio" (*BI* 187).

STOCHASTIC VALUE: FITTING NARRATIVE POINTS TO A LINE

Global capital in the neoliberal age—both in their investment portfolios and everywhere in their lifeworlds—is the warping force flowing through these characters. From its opening paragraph "Adult World" evokes the sensory confusion of attempts to "feel" eros alongside value in a market-obsessed and fetishistic society: the protagonist Jeni, presaging the overwriting of the body by currency throughout (the Japanese currency as primary referent for yen, for instance), notes the "vague hot-penny taste of rawness when she took [her husband's] thingie in her mouth" (*BI* 161). Wallace's coin returns here as an object of ingestion, penis reduced to "thingie," to fetish (in both the sexual and commodity senses—well-marketed dildos will later appear). The "vague[ness]" arises from taking a penny as an arbiter of "taste" and heat. In related developments, Wallace also strategically gives Jeni's language a vagueness in the parody of linear stories in "(I)" and their too-obvious Joycean telos—"Amazingly (she realized only later, after she had had an epiphany and rapidly matured) . . ."—and that vagueness seems to follow from this first confusion of value categories, of money taken for food (*BI* 163).

Jeni's currency trader husband is referred to throughout as "the stochastic husband," a name that both repeats the nonidentity trope of "The Depressed Person" and juxtaposes contrasting moments in economic history: "stochastic" describes a form of probability making possible postmodern, lightning-fast financial accumulation of the sort that Arrighi analyzes (and that I mentioned in chapter 2), while "to husband" means to grow land and animals, or to use economic resources conservatively, steadily accruing value. Like the poet of "Death Is Not the End" and Rick Vigorous, this onanistic husband is postindustriousness, his so-called work space a fraud. "Sometimes the husband would arise at night and use the master bathroom and then go out to his workshop off the garage" to pursue "his hobby of furniture refinishing" (*BI* 168): the sophomoric joke is that sanding furniture covers for his compulsively—my finger flexions—"worked wood" (note too the trace of "masturbate" in "*master bat*hroom"). Part of Wallace's effort to write "poorly" in "Adult World (I)" is not only to belabor the implausibility of Jeni's singular epiphany but to indulge in transparently Freudian metaphors, from this woodshop to its denizen's embodiment of Bluebeard. The husband's fake artisanship points toward the sterility of his job in the immaterial finance economy of monitoring the yen. In a traditional version of "Adult World," the story might resolve itself by forcing the husband's yens back from masturbation and market contingencies to more stable husbanding. But instead Wallace pushes the Roberts couple onto the global financial stage, turning his eye for economic apocalypse to the Asian currency crisis that began in July 1997.

Spreading from major devaluation of the Thai baht brought on by rumors that it lacked sufficient backing in dollars, the "Asian Flu" raised fears of a worldwide economic crash and, in one year, led to $600 billion vanishing from Asian stock markets.[25] The global effects of this crisis in the "rupiah and the won and the baht" ripple through "Adult World" (*BI* 163): Mad Mike's "pressure" to move Hyundais on the last three banking days of each month stems from the dealership's South Korean affiliation (*BI* 181), and Jeni's "hi-tech mastrbtory [*sic*] appliances" are industrially "manufactured in Asia" (*BI* 188). Naomi Klein argues that there was potential in the Asian Flu for "a crisis of 1930s proportions"—though Clinton, confirming his neoliberal credentials, blithely called it "a few little glitches in the road" (*Shock Doctrine*, 320). The crisis proved a case study for the neoliberal principle of viewing collapse as endemic to capitalist systems and occasion not for repair but exploitation. Klein, anatomizing "disaster capitalism," which extracts value and rewritten laws from "shock," argues that the Friedmanite economists in charge of U.S. policy, who called for market correction over bailout loans, saw the misery as "an opportunity in disguise" to demand deregulation as the price for bailout offers (*Shock Doctrine*, 320). Harvey says the 1997–1998 crisis "exacerbated" the already "declining ability of the state to discipline capital during the 1990s" (*Brief History of Neoliberalism*, 110). The global economic impact was dire, but—in a premonition of 2008 outcomes—social losses produced large private gains.

Expanding on his image of an entire life determined by a coin flip, Wallace uses the currency crisis to globalize his portrayal of the subject as contingent, especially when pegged to the "Ever-Changing Status" of monetary values (*BI* 161). "*Stochastic* meant random or conjectural or containing numerous variables that all had to be monitored closely"—much like, we notice, the reading of characters' fates in Wallace's fiction. The husband, in another association of financial value with dementia, jokingly adds that his job "really meant getting paid to drive yourself crazy" (*BI* 167). Stochastic mathematics, based on early 1900s work on French bond prices by Louis Bachelier but not fully implemented until the mid–twentieth century, makes the risk taking and massive value accruals of contemporary markets possible by reducing uncertainty in predicting prices (often called their "random walk") within a continuous timeframe.[26] Stochastic math, in essence, enables financial capital by increasing assurance of "Return on Investment" or "ROI" (*BF* 183n11). But so too do stochastic models enable the stark opposite of cost-accounting's conservatism: "casino capitalism," a description of finance that has grown increasingly common since 2008's gambles were revealed. The Sierpinski gasket, which Wallace revealed had structured *Infinite Jest*, is based in stochastic math,[27] and Wallace is also building on Pynchon's example of human moral agency in the thrall of, and anterior to, systems: *Gravity's Rainbow*'s Roger Mexico grows frustrated trying to explain why his stochastic charts confirm a pattern of probability for V 2 hits but cannot predict a spot for the next one.

In my terms, the stochastic provides a metaphor for being an active reader of Wallace in the neoliberal age. The important maneuver of the stochastic predictor involves fitting random points on a graph to a line or a smooth curve, approximating what a reader does in moving from page 1 through to 981 and trying to order even the most disparate events into a causal chronology. These are maneuvers that long, important endnotes turn into a difficult and self-conscious affair, requiring "random" movement from, for example, "point" (page) 23 to 983 or 64 to 985 (for a nine-page filmography), as well as decisions about when to follow intraendnote references. Chronologically reordering the Brief Interviews to determine Q's fate is another such move. Stochastic math reminds us that straight lines, like narratives, are always constructions, products of "fit" and imposed, after the fact, on a flux of points (which offer no clear path to the telos of an epiphany). We might also consider the complexities of stochastic narrative as Wallace's rewriting, outside the idiom of analytical philosophy, of his undergraduate refutation of fatalism in *Fate, Time, and Language*.[28]

Wallace has played with such meanings often in previous short fiction, without explicitly naming the field. *Stochas*, the Greek root, literally means a pointed stick at which archers aim their arrows in target practice, and thus when he riffs in "Westward" on a writer like himself aiming an "off-angled target arrow that will stab the center, right in the heart," Wallace refashions a common illustration in probability textbooks and calls fiction innately conjectural and stochastic (*GCH* 294). "Little Expressionless Animals," at the other end of *Girl with Curious Hair*, scatters events across time, expecting the reader to order them. Reflecting that act, Julie claims of her childhood habit of playing with the "straightedge" that her abusive mother locks her away with, "I could make worlds out of lines. A sort of jagged magic"—and thus the often acute angles at the head of each section must be hers (*GCH* 10). We should see the suicide's razor hinted at in this language and in the angles' sharpness, though, along with a *Tractatus*-inspired approach to "worlds" as line-drawn pictures (or cases) that Wallace hopes this story will transcend. With her straightedge Julie mimics the action of the stochastic mathematician who, faced with a random array of points, follows the method of linear regression to find the least jagged line to connect them. When the final drawing, three pages from the end, violates the "rules" of linearity and forms a triangle, graphed abstractions (and *Jeopardy!* data) meet the flux of living, with the triangle's three lines gesturing toward connection and even three-dimensionality (*GCH* 39).[29] Finally, the uncollected "Order and Flux in Northampton" names the poles between which stochastic stories cause readers to vacillate: underscoring the fallacy in Barry Dingle's plan for falling in love, this story dissolves into a log of loosely connected events occurring worldwide—fittingly random precursors to Barry's final moment, which ends up being a dog bite to the genitals instead of a kiss.

Likewise, "Adult World" dissolves into a set of "points" that asks the reader to take the active role Wallace usually demands to a higher level. "Adult World (I)" may seem on the surface a well-ordered, realistic representation of mind and event, while "(II)" smacks of robotic, computer-program-like directives, what the narrative calls "schematic/ordered" (*BI* 183). Yet that is only because of the reader's conditioning by "Workshop Hermeticism," with its "epiphan[ies] whose approach can be charted by any Freitag on any Macintosh" (another set of lines undone by Julie's odd angles) (*BF* 40).[30] "Adult World" makes us think anew about what we mean when we call an ending predictable. "(I)" is indeed "dramatic/stochastic" (*BI* 183) because drama tends to turn random flux into predictability, a familiar line that—as underscored by the metacommentaries on when Jeni's realizations occurred in relation to "lived experience"—simplifies the Beckettian eventlessness that Wallace's anticonfluential plots record (*BI* 177). With spellings like "mastrbtory" and "hmn race" (*BI* 187) in "(II)," the reader fills in blanks in the same way she must on the level of narrative. In the same way, the many graphic arrows nod to *stochas* and signify not obvious causation but narrative construed as an arc of events dependent on a reader's sense of the probable. In "(II)," the reader—looking through the restaurant's window frame as though at a TV, reading through a "Schema" that sparks associations with screenplays—must acknowledge his complicity in shaping the mechanistic, soap-opera-like plot of secret sex and melodrama (*BI* 183). In "(I)" a reader can get away with disdain for Jeni and her shallowness, but "(II)" makes palpable what Smith observes: "If one is used to the consolation of 'character,' . . . Wallace is truly a dead end. His stories [are] turned outward, toward us. It's *our* character that's being investigated" (*Changing My Mind*, 273).

Armed with the stochastic, we can finally return full circle to the table of contents, which begins to make greater sense as an investigation of *our* character, our expectations of being guided toward order, and our related ways of defining moral values in the era of financialization. Wallace gives the reader at the outset, in the various noncontinuous numbers and systems, an array of random data, suggesting that the stochastic method of fitting a line to certain data points and necessarily discarding others (such as all those apparently left out of the "Yet Another Example" and "Brief Interviews" series) might characterize both the writing of this book and its reception by the involved reader. Yet such valuation of many variables, once the reader gains intimacy with the people behind those titles and numbers, should also give way to a moral calculus that reduces to simpler choices, often starkly binarized: in "Octet," this is the rhythm of the Quizzes' conclusions, "Which one lived," "Is she a good mother," and "So decide" (*BI* 131, 135, 160). That last imperative tellingly appears at the midpoint of this balancing book, its exact center (160.5 pages—remember to count page 0—is half of 321). It is as though a balance scale is constructed by the materiality of the book as well as its themes, the fulcrum of "decid[ing]" always at the center.

In the introduction I claimed Wallace's work tries to extract a balance scale from a world dominated by not only market principles but computerized systems of decision making, which according to Wallace inevitably have a distancing effect on the close-up work of human valuation and moral living. *Brief Interviews*, conceived as an interweaving of computerized stochastic valuation and balance-scale valuation, proposes that achieving a fiction of moral values in postmodernity involves working simultaneously through *both* types. The title "Octet" contains a faint trace of this dual task: in computing, an octet is another term for a byte, a unit of digital information consisting of eight bits, a state of systematic completeness this human, fallible story aspires to but fails to reach—while hoping that "the $2 + (2(1))$ pieces add up to something urgent and human" (*BI* 154). With the ending "So decide"—decide about the sincerity and thus, essentially, the humanity of the narrating voice—Wallace also obliquely evokes the Turing test, in which a computer may be regarded as a human being if its auditor decides it is based on its language use.

As he combines postmodern technique with old verities and values, Wallace knows that the writer who continued penning didactic tales of moral mimesis in 1999 without acknowledging the dominance of computerized systems would be like the Arizona teacher in "E Unibus Pluram" who, numb to historical changes to consciousness, insists on fiction of a "Platonic Always" and refuses to admit how technologies like TV are now "part of reality" (*SFT* 43). Wallace hopes, in this dialectic, to combine valuation old and new through what "Octet," after portraying a quasi-stochastic process of discarding quizzes, describes with the more fundamental mathematical operation of reduction, that means of simplifying fractions or clarifying the two balanced sides of an equation: "these apparently different and formally (admit it) kind of stilted and coy-looking 'Pop Quizzes' could all reduce finally to the same question (whatever exactly that question is)" (*BI* 156). The desired effect—the goal of a postmodern moralist—is for the reader, oscillating between complexity and simplicity, to ask not what "exact[]" moral question a text didactically poses or answers but how a text, through the accumulation of its provocations, sharpens her ability to define moral values herself. The exact moral questions are personal to the reader, to what she puts in the blanks left by Q. All this occurs within a world that hardly ever thinks about value outside the market's terms, and the values discovered undercut neoliberalism's assumptions that bonds to others, on personal and communal levels, can always be subjected to the market's math.

In what may be his clearest refutation of Pynchon's legacy, then, Wallace tends ultimately toward embracing reduced complexity and the balancing effects of binarisms, led by his sense that a renovation of moral decision making now takes priority over Pynchon's 1960s mission of upsetting rigid, technologized thought—those "matrices of a great digital computer, the zeroes and ones . . . hanging like balanced mobiles right and left," that Oedipa sensed in San Narciso.[31] "It seems to me that the intellectualization and aestheticizing of principles and values in this country is one of the things that's gutted our generation," Wallace says in 1993 (CW 60). Finding greater verbal complexity beneath the apparent order of a numbering system, the reader of Brief Interviews moves toward a decision making and sense of "values" that employ the precision of the intellect but do not allow for the calcifying of "intellectualization." Likewise, by falling short of the symmetry the numbered parts imply in "Octet" and the "Yet Another Example . . ." series, Wallace also undermines the reader who might try to avoid values by admiring a distanced aesthetic perfection. Moral art, in postmodernity, must be ugly, asymmetrical art, down in the mud of the trench, if it hopes to keep the other alive and unmown.

FICTIONAL FUTURES, STOCHASTIC ART, AND DIFFICULT GIFTS

For all its merits, the moral project of Brief Interviews remains, admittedly, rather esoteric and difficult to extract, especially for the reader seeking direct indictments of the fictions underlying finance and neoliberal value. As a coda to this chapter, let me examine two writers who, like McCarthy, both pay homage to Wallace and take his examples in newly productive and bracingly vivid directions, extending concepts of value from this chapter (and previous ones). The first, Teddy Wayne (born 1979), represents a rising generation of writers that encountered Wallace at college age and is likely to have taken him as a gateway to the postmodernist predecessors he challenges. Wayne was a Wallace scholar first: his 2001 undergraduate thesis at Harvard, a Wittgensteinian reading of *Infinite Jest*, is quoted in a few later articles.[32]

Wayne's first novel, *Kapitoil*, pays tribute to its inspiration while also, in its story of immigrant striving, adding dimensions of racialism, globalism, and realpolitik lacking in Wallace's vision. Its protagonist, Karim Issar, is a prodigious mathematical mind and programmer just arrived in the United States from Qatar in the fall of 1999 to work on the Y2K bug in the World Trade Center offices of Schrub Equities, for which he develops a lucrative oil-futures algorithm he names Kapitoil—combining *capital*, *oil*, and his initial K but also, with the ending "toil," unconsciously questioning the ambivalent status of work, class, and even slavery within this world. Wayne invites us to read his novel as an allegory of the United States and Middle East before and after 9/11: the villainous boss Derek Schrub (i.e., Shrub) is George W. Bush, and Karim, taken as a son by Schrub as long as he promises to give up the assets of his financial model, represents the site of Bush's post-9/11, oil-focused imperial project (not to mention the elder Bush's). All this occurs in such a way that (as will be the case in Wallace's "The Suffering Channel") we read with the dramatic irony of 9/11 in mind for those Karim leaves behind in late 1999, when he returns to Qatar and the novel ends.

En route there are numerous allusions to Wallace, particularly to the pitfalls of technical mastery and logical coldness. "My mathematical brain makes me very skilled at racquetball," says Karim as he plays Schrub,[33] sounding much like the Wallace of "Derivative Sport." Earlier, in a *Tractatus*esque list of points, Karim calculates that he could fit 3.5 million racquetballs inside the court, if he could get rid of the space between the spheres—but this "ideal cannot exist, because then they would not truly be balls anymore" (*Kapitoil*, 85). Like Hal, Karim has thoroughly repressed the traumatizing death of a parent: Wayne doles out the story of Karim's mother's death from breast cancer when he was thirteen (Hal's age when Himself commits suicide [*IJ* 248]). Wayne mines Nabokov's controlling, nonnative English speakers for Karim's hilariously awkward voice, but it is Hal and Bruce of "Here and There" (of which Wayne is a devotee)[34] who form the template for Karim's robotic attempts to treat English as a mathematical system. Speaking often of language as "deciphering" (*Kapitoil*, 4, 120) and taping his daily life on microrecorder, Karim ends each chapter with a list of words he has learned, with each definition involving an equal sign—thus often pointing, unintentionally, to Wittgensteinian precepts regarding contextualization.

A late chapter featuring Karim making out with his girlfriend to Bob Dylan ends with a lyric they discuss that shows the limits of the linguistic mathematicization that *Brief Interviews* also courts: "warehouse eyes = an example of a metaphor that may not have a directly logical meaning" (*Kapitoil*, 232). Remembering lyrics to a Beatles song will prove integral to Karim's true grieving of his mother's death. Such emotional and aesthetic learning for Karim necessarily coincides with the unraveling of Kapitoil, since its algorithm converts language into data, making oil trades based on word frequency in news coverage. As a child Karim discovers his abilities by observing "parallels between the cracks and the arrangement of glass on the ground" (*Kapitoil*, 18) when he breaks a window; later he compares an algorithm's exclusions of certain data in reading the market to sorting through the "layers and colors and patterns of paint" in a Jackson Pollock exhibit he attends (*Kapitoil*, 24). Wayne thus finds new ways to work in Wallace's realm of the stochastic, the fractal, and the Sierpinski gasket, where certain forms of complex postmodern art innately dialogue with financial markets' models of data evaluation.[35]

Karim = generous, in Arabic, and Wayne, again following Wallace's lead, resolves his difficult allegory of global tensions in part by dissolving the political and offering Karim the emotional gold standard of Rebecca Goldman, who grows from officemate to Dylan makeout partner. The arc of generous Karim may not be that of Don the gift, but *Kapitoil* does push back against market and mathematical values with those of generosity. Wayne makes much of Karim awkwardly saying "It is my gift" when paying for his and Rebecca's first coffee date (*Kapitoil*, 31), and Pollock-inspired art reclaims stochastic beauty when Karim gives Rebecca the "gift" of his "algorithmic drawing" remapping the colors of a watermelon

(*Kapitoil*, 221). At Thanksgiving, Karim gains a new set of black friends who contrast with his white-dominated workplace (and add further texture to the Islam/Judaism fusion he and Rebecca represent). Free of equal signs, Karim coins a verb phrase at the feast: "I would like to thanks-give to you and your family for inviting me" (*Kapitoil*, 203). "Possibly I should learn not to view my values as a series of binaries and instead find a compromise," he later says to Rebecca—that is what "relationships are about," she confirms (*Kapitoil*, 242). Wallace would nod as well, perhaps while noting that his disciple has found a new avenue of globalism and post-9/11 politics down which to pursue his techniques.

Another globalizer of Wallace is Zadie Smith, whose brilliant reading of *Brief Interviews*, "The Difficult Gifts of David Foster Wallace," I have cited in this chapter. In a memorial tribute Smith says Wallace had no "equal amongst living writers,"[36] and she too shares his love of Hyde's *The Gift* (*Changing My Mind*, 290). Her novel *NW* (2012) pays several tributes to Wallace: a section titled "Host," references to "oblivion" at key moments,[37] and a system of numbering for the contents of the book's first part, "Visitation," that seems indebted to *Brief Interviews*' table of contents and theme of contingent values. Four sections numbered "37" are randomly interspersed amid twenty-three other sequentially numbered sections. The sections numbered 37 unearth the secret and unconscious: one concerns white co-protagonist Leah's abortions; another, set in her lesbian past, explains that the number 37 has a "magic about it"—"watch for it . . . in our lotteries, our game shows, our dreams and jokes" (*NW*, 42). Such remarks speak to *NW*'s intense scrutiny of the luck of class position, the randomness with which one is granted privilege: "Could things have been differently arranged, in a different order, in a different place?" as another 37 section asks, questions resonating with the divergent fates of white Leah and her black best friend, Natalie, who becomes a successful lawyer (*NW*, 74). In a book titled for a postal code and exploring the unexpected (but also seemingly fated) encounters that take place within it, Smith wants to wed Wallace-inspired, postmodern contingencies to the tradition of urban tumult in the English novel (Dickens is always on Smith's mind, and in this book of many daytime affairs and city wandering, *Ulysses* is a primary reference point).

In the final section 37, Leah repeats her name to a store clerk who cannot find her photos, only to be given pictures of Shar (read: share), the downtrodden woman who starts the text by knocking on Leah's door with a plea for money. A novel about the distribution of lottery funds (Leah's office job), *NW* is a commonwealth text too, evoking elements of *The Broom of the System*.[38] Those contrasts evolve through juxtapositions of charity in Leah's office and neighborhood existences; in the latter, she is haunted by the initial request from Shar, which will not sit within the lottery office's institutional framework. Leah's surname, Hanwell, has the title's postal designation at its heart, for the random others in one's city actually constitute the self, points that resonate with Smith's multicultural themes and her own interracial background.

Smith proves on the whole more incisive than Wallace in describing issues of social welfare and charity, without so many of the allegorical abstractions and moral fables he brings to bear. She argues most thoroughly with the examples of Wallace and Hyde on the issue of gender and gifts. *NW* is about the suffering of women who turn down the rewards their culture insists they should be grateful for, from a stable relationship (Natalie does not bank on boring Rodney Banks and later jeopardizes her marriage to the more exciting Frank with Internet hookups) to motherhood (Leah struggles to tell her mate she does not want children). Having recognized Wallace's circumspection regarding artistic gifts (she says he viewed his own "as a suspicious facility to be interrogated"), Smith in *NW* focuses on the particular ways women negotiate giving, talent, and gratitude (*Changing My Mind*, 256). After Natalie muses about a pop singer from their neighborhood who says she does not "own" her beautiful voice, Smith writes an "Aphorism" that echoes the title of her essay on Wallace, but in a register that nuances the gendered affect surrounding gifts: "What a difficult thing a gift is for a woman! She'll punish herself for receiving it" (*NW* 346).

A shift in the estranged friends' interpersonal economy might alleviate some of these pressures—but a balance of minds is elusive. In the final pages, in scenes indebted to Toni Morrison, Natalie feeds Leah "proverbs" about love, "the truth content of which [Leah] could only assume from their common circulation, the way one puts faith in the face value of paper money" (*NW* 398). Natalie, we see a page later, interprets Leah's motherhood story "as a sublime sort of gift" and wants "to give her friend something of equal value in return." But, perhaps because she sees her professional achievements as hard won, not gifts at all, Natalie falls here into "self-preservation" mode, failing to see that "the perfect gift at this moment was an honest account of her own difficulties and ambivalences" (*NW* 399). The connection of "difficulties" and "gifts," forged in her analysis of Wallace, leads Smith to a feminist idiom of exchange and layers of psychological realism and specificity missing in her influence's texts.

Wallace's own efforts to add layers of realism to his subjects would lead him to refine not so much his understanding of gifts as of another central motif: work. He had written and compiled *Brief Interviews* at a time, Max recounts, when he thought he should be working on *The Pale King*, his novel on the crushing effects of tax accounting (*Every Love Story*, 255). Despite throwing his fiction efforts again in the direction of the novel, Wallace would end up with another story collection, *Oblivion*. In these new narratives, positions such as professional arbitrator and currency trader—jobs with allegorical import—would give way to newly mundane kinds of work, transformative for Wallace's preoccupation with occupations.

5

HIS CAPITAL FLUSH

DESPAIRING OVER WORK
AND VALUE IN *OBLIVION*

Think of the letters given over to flames and garbage dumps, the unsorted boxes of
papers lying in attics and basements, the notebooks scrawled in drunken, half-
legible squiggles and codes, kept in fading ink, never to be deciphered. What
glories, what banalities, what secrets!
—DONALD JUSTICE, "OBLIVION: VARIATIONS ON A THEME"

WHY DOES work often feel futile in a postmodern and neoliberal society? Why do even many highly rewarding jobs seem dehumanizing
and attenuating amid superabundant wealth and leisure? Philip Mirowski
argues, "Not only does neoliberalism deconstruct any special status for human labor, but"—in terms resonant with my readings throughout—"it lays
waste to older distinctions between production and consumption rooted in
the labor theory of value, and reduces the human being to an arbitrary bun-
dle of 'investments,' skill sets, temporary alliances."[1] These are some of the
areas of a fully ascendant neoliberal culture that Wallace probes in *Oblivion*. "Probably all jobs are . . . filled with horrible boredom and despair and
quiet little bits of fulfillment that are very hard to tell anybody else about,"
Wallace said in an interview about *Oblivion* in 2004 (*CW* 129). As he read
the post-9/11 American economy, Wallace was willing to extrapolate his
own work conditions into another of his hoped-for universalisms, the notion

that all jobs led to the despair that increasingly characterized the position in the office of literary art he had decided to take in 1985.

In this story collection Wallace begins mediating his observations on work and value through a system he had come to know well: being a relatively well-known novelist in the age of celebrity. Repeatedly, *Oblivion* describes what Wallace thought had happened to him upon reaching "the Show." While only parts of *Brief Interviews* were first published after *Infinite Jest* and the fame it granted, all of *Oblivion* was; all of it postdates his 1997 MacArthur as well. Terry Schmidt, the murderous advertising man in "Mister Squishy," is thirty-four, the age Wallace turned a few weeks after *Infinite Jest* was published (*O* 17). For Schmidt's despair over his "*small-ness* within a grinding professional machine you can't believe you once had the temerity to think you could help change" (*O* 31–32) and his desire to be "superior, more . . . central, meaningful" (*O* 30), read Wallace's worries about the place of *Infinite Jest* in the literary canon and his inability to transcend the commercialism in which Schmidt is enveloped. Wallace did not sign the story initially, using the pseudonym Elizabeth Klemm, his new attempt to write as a "NOBODY."[2] The opening of "Philosophy and the Mirror of Nature" commingles spider, convict, and book "releases": "Then just as I was being released in late 1996"—about the midpoint between Wallace's *Infinite Jest* and *Supposedly Fun Thing* reading tours?—"Mother won a small product liability settlement and used the money" to get botched plastic surgery (*O* 182). The main result of a monetary influx here is vanity—and then worse consequences.[3]

One of Wallace's typescript drafts of *Oblivion*'s title story included as its epigraph, "What glories, what banalities, what secrets!"—part of Justice's examination of three poets who faded in their forties and were forgotten.[4] Wallace turned forty in 2002, as some of *Oblivion*'s stories were first being published. "Forever Overhead" had taken entering the teenage years as a moment to contemplate death; now Wallace was in actual midlife. The Justice quotation points to an easily overlooked dimension of *Oblivion*'s title: its self-*un*canonizing gesture, the state of forgottenness that Wallace let shadow him, whether as a chastening of his fame or an expression of fear that he could no longer produce top work (or both). *Oblivion* is united by this despair over aesthetic value, particularly as that value withers in a commodity culture. The final story begins "But they're shit" (O 238) and ends with an artist of fecal matter tricked into appearing on a stage that obscures his creations. "Good Old Neon" suggests that "the infinitely dense and shifting worlds" inside oneself are "fully open and expressible" only after death (O 178). The title "The Soul Is Not a Smithy" rejects Joyce's clarion call to the heroic modernist artist. However we ultimately judge these stories, they suggest we think twice (or more) about calling their creator an artistic "genius." Writing pseudonymously, refusing to rest on his laurels (the cliché behind the satirical name of Laurel, a bad writer in "The Suffering Channel"), Wallace has found new ways to make us start at zero in assessing his (work's) value.

Much of *Oblivion* also comes into being in a 1999–2004 period in which the country's massive economic growth met with downturns, news to which Wallace had proven himself consistently sensitive: the dot-com bubble burst between 1999 and 2001, and after 9/11 the Dow Jones average lost more than 14 percent and a poor U.S. economy weakened further. At either end of *Oblivion*, Wallace catches office cultures suffused with optimism but on the brink of these downfalls: the newly formed Team Δy in "Mister Squishy" (set in 1995, published in 2000) wants to use web-based advertising methods to appeal to the "promising market" of Internet start-ups (O 61); in a far grimmer turn, the *Style* staffers of "The Suffering Channel," housed in the World Trade Center, face not just potential downsizing because of media consolidation but 9/11, ten weeks after the story ends.

Oblivion signals that Wallace, while still holding work to be sacred, has largely given up his faith in the powers of the Protestant call to work that echoed throughout his writing up through *Infinite Jest*. Less prominent in *Oblivion* and after is the writer who allegorizes work in terms of Lenore's switchboard and foot-pounds, while newly emergent are dull, long-term workplaces, rendered in detail and at length: advertising agencies, insurance offices, demographic systems. Jobs themselves now spread out to form characters' mental ground, and work no longer really works for one's well-being. As Walter Kirn writes in his review of *Oblivion*, "Often the jobs we do end up doing us."[5] If, in *Infinite Jest*'s Hegelian code, transcendence potentially lay in absorption, in *Oblivion* all is distraction; no one really forgets himself, except perhaps the narrator of "Smithy" (to his peril).

Such despair about work derived primarily from Wallace's writing desk, where jobs had always functioned as avenues for considering the creative process—and Wallace was struggling still with the dynamic he had described to DeLillo in May 1997 after news of his MacArthur: "If past experience holds true again I'll lay stupid neurotic paralyzing trips on myself for several months, starting work and then getting scared/depressed and tearing the work up," before getting so exhausted and scared he "can really . . . start working."[6] At the same time, having examined a postindustrious society in *Broom* and *Brief Interviews* and reconceived the cliché about the "sweat of one's brow" in *Infinite Jest*, Wallace will move tentatively in *Oblivion* toward a ruddy-faced mental laborer, Skip Atwater, whose Kafkaesque depiction in "The Suffering Channel" mediates anxiety about (artistic) work and serves as a guardedly optimistic climax to this chapter's readings.

Anticipating *The Pale King* at a few points, I judge *Oblivion* to be a difficult, transitional text in which, in no coincidence given these changed relationships to work, Wallace (with a few notable exceptions) largely abandons the portrayals of grounding in axiom and worth that had signaled the desired destination for the self throughout the previous seventeen years. No barefoot boys or supine men in this weightless world; that vocabulary is placed on hold until it reemerges transformed in *The Pale King*. The languages of workplaces and bureaucracies, often amoral or meaninglessly mathematicized, colonize the minds on display and thus Wallace's prose. At the same time, key motifs return with new accents: coins (with their inscriptions read in greater detail, part of Wallace's expanded attention to civics), the glow of energy producers, and indictments of minimalist aesthetics, all of which structure my linked readings. I attend also to Wallace's intensified interest in what McHale calls the "ecologies of institutions"[7] by extending chapter 2's history of 1930s social welfare into a new area of contingencies: the U.S. health insurance and health-care industries. Lastly, I situate Skip as a figure reminiscent of Lenore, a counterforce to the workless and weightless image economy of "The Suffering Channel." But first I must unpack the essay in which Wallace, a few years after *Oblivion*, retrospectively rationalized his new style while shifting his definition of a reader's mental labor and the accompanying creation of values.

"DECIDERIZATION" AND QUESTIONS
OF WORK AND VALUE

Mocking aggrandizing news mechanisms as well as George W. Bush (who proclaimed in April 2006 regarding Donald Rumsfeld's post–Abu Ghraib fate, "I'm the decider, and I decide what's best"),[8] Wallace gives the title "Deciderization 2007—a Special Report" to his introduction to *The Best American Essays* 2007. Ostensibly an account of Wallace's selection process, the introduction expansively describes a method of excluding information that I showed ruling *Brief Interviews*' stochastic moves toward reduced randomness and ordered lines: in a condition of "Total Noise," seen from the "perspective of Information Theory," Wallace writes, "the bulk of [his] labor actually consists of excluding nominees from the final prize collection" (*BF* 303–304n3). In typical Wallace metareflections of observer by system and vice versa, this same quality of careful exclusion marks the essays he chooses as best: the way they "handle and respond to the tsunami of available fact" (*BF* 312). The key maneuver is "deleting/discarding/resetting"— here and throughout, we are invited to think of humans as posthuman, as not entirely dissimilar from the "98.6° calculating machine" Wallace once feared he was (*CW* 41). We are again in the realm I defined in chapter 4, where human decision making can no longer disentangle itself from computing's complexity. Wallace seems to have been led to this point by Tor Nørretranders's *The User Illusion: Cutting Consciousness Down to Size*, a book he heavily annotated and source of an idea central to his style in the last two books of fiction: "Every single second," Nørretranders writes, "every one of us discards millions of bits [of sensory information] in order to arrive at the special state known as consciousness."[9]

"Deciderization" justifies the creation of entropic minds like Schmidt's, Randy Napier's, and (in *The Pale King* to come) Claude Sylvanshine's. They all try to think clearly within complex bureaucratic systems, resulting in prose that exponentially expands the task faced by the reader of *The Broom of the System*, that of having to "place" tagless phone calls along with Lenore. "Deciderization" should be seen in a lineage of Wallace statements on readers' and writer's symbiotic work going back to the 1993 interview comments from which I began chapter 1. While more dry than its predecessor, "Deciderization" could be critically mined in illuminating the more difficult later work in the way "E Unibus Pluram" has been for Wallace's midcareer growth. Some have begun this process: Boswell regards the essay as the basis for the detail-rich style of *Oblivion* and the sermon of Fogle's tax teacher in *The Pale King*, noting that "the pleasures that once emerged from the completion of the 'hard work'" Wallace asks for are "abandoned in favor of a persistent confrontation with pain and suffering."[10] David Letzler applies "Deciderization" to the superfluity of *Infinite Jest*'s endnotes, arguing that they resemble "cruft," excess programming code that forces readers to separate the necessary from the contingent.[11]

But in defining Wallace's strange prose machinery we should also question his ultimate *moral* purpose in invoking information sorting; we should ask how learning to value certain details over others leads to aesthetic value and, indirectly, to a strengthening of a reader's moral values and civic responsiveness in an information-glutted world. In "Deciderization" the postmodern moralist comes to an impasse and tries to resolve it the Wittgensteinian way by testing out his central term in different contexts. Illustrating again the tug of war between tradition and innovation that defined him, Wallace lets his postmodern tendencies arise first in the way the essay keeps deferring the definition of aesthetic value (elaborate evasions seen as well in another take on prescribing standards, "Authority and American Usage"). Wallace says he tried "to use overall value" to sort the essays, but this "entitles you to ask what 'value' means here" (*BF* 311). His answer is indirect: as a term of adjudication, "'value' sidesteps some of the metaphysics that makes pure aesthetics such a headache" and admits to being dependent on "some limited, subjective human doing the valuing" (*BF* 311–312). Yet "there's still the question of just what this limited human actually means by 'value' as a criterion" (*BF* 312). Thus does Wallace, in a display of postmodern technique, defer the question of aesthetic definition, instead describing value by considering certain criteria for it and then *excluding* them for not being all-encompassing: most of the essays "show a masterly awareness of craft," but "others . . . don't"—"but they have other virtues that make them valuable" (*BF* 312). About a page later, Wallace reminds himself, "The point is to try to explain part of what I mean by 'valuable'" (*BF* 313). But I have been suggesting throughout that Wallace knew that the labyrinth of his fiction, with its permission to play associatively with different types of value, had long been the only place he could work out the problem of saying all that he meant by "value." "Deciderization" makes vivid Wallace's commitment to making this search for value a performative process for a reader—in fact, one in which differentiating one detail's importance from another's and being the "human doing the valuing" *are*, in effect, aesthetic value itself. No definition of it exists aside from the dynamic one that readers, with expert guidance, decide on for themselves.

Such is the implied ground of not just aesthetically pleasing writing but moral writing as well. In a multipage footnote, Wallace throws in a portentous postscript adding more layers to the value question, these arising from his "traditional human verities" side: "What exactly are the connections between literary aesthetics and moral value supposed to be? Whose moral values ought to get used in determining what those connections should be? Does anyone even read Tolstoy's 'What Is Art?' anymore?" (*BF* 311n7). Despite his admiration for the Russian, Wallace in 2007 cannot be Tolstoy and cannot make any stabilizing proposal that (as he paraphrased from "What Is Art?" in a 1993 interview) the "purpose of art [is] to communicate the idea of Christian brotherhood from man to man" (*CW* 18). Wallace instead makes vivid for his reader postmodernism's inexorable intertwining of moral values with the kind of information sorting that makes up these essays' aesthetic contributions. The outcome here is a democratic deciding (not Deciderization) that previews the title of the novel he was working on: these essays are the best for 2007 America because they oppose the propagandistic writing that works "like the silky courtier's manipulations of an enfeebled king," also presumably pale (*BF* 316).

LUMINOUS GUYS AND LOW-VALUE COINS

"Deciderization" adds complexity to the role of the accountant of human costs that structured *Brief Interviews*, but in all cases, as Wallace thinks through models of moral computation, he does not lose sight of the central axiological act of keeping the glow of human worth visible, safe from wrongheaded valuations. He continues to seek in *Oblivion* a fiction that "reconciles," that balance-book verb, the markers of external valuation with those senses of self-worth and health that may remain internal and hidden (*O* 181). This is the logic behind the volume's most celebrated story, "Good Old Neon," which brings to mind the hidden narrator of "Westward" and his quest for the terms in which to value Mark. In "Neon," Neal is the new Mark, and the story climaxes with hidden narrator "David Wallace trying, if only in the second his lids are down, to somehow reconcile what this luminous guy seemed like from the outside with whatever on the interior must have driven him to kill himself" (*O* 181). As with other mise-en-abyme endings (like that of "Octet"), "Neon" is ultimately hard-pressed to assert fully a sense of unnumbered internal worth that emanates from a sincere core, "the realer, more enduring and sentimental part of" David: that internal voice's oracular command, "Not another word," draws the story into a sublime, silent closure that is then undercut by the number that is the real ending, a ".418" batting average—a statistic of athletic valuation, one thing Dave remembers about Neal (*O* 181). The story's title, too, seems caught in nostalgia for the "good old" days and "the seemingly almost neon aura around [Neal] all the time of scholastic and athletic excellence and popularity and success with the ladies" (*O* 180). Neon, while known for producing a glow useful to ads, is itself colorless and odorless and has only two-thirds the density of air—insubstantial in the terms of weight Wallace uses to signify ontological stability.

Wallace ascends to a higher level of value analysis in "Another Pioneer," an echo of Gaddis's *The Recognitions* and Kafka's "Josephine the Singer" that makes an important point about the relationship between language and economy as Wallace perceives it: through our language and our treatment of human potential, we make choices about what kind of economic exchange we have. In other words, while language may be exchange, Wallace must strip away the trappings of modern economies so that we see language as the foregrounded term in that analogy, not a mere servant to money. In parallel with the growth of an economy around a stationary woman in "Westward," "Pioneer" places a boy on a dais and has economy grow up around him, beginning with gifts exchanged for his wisdom. Villagers come with a yam, for example, and leave with an answer, and in the "mythopoeic cycle" the story supposedly draws on, "this arrangement is represented as the origin of something like modern trade in the villagers' culture. . . . [T]here was evidently nothing like actual barter or trade until the advent of this child" (*O* 122). Wallace again employs quasi-anthropological language to illustrate language as commonwealth, as an edenic, peaceful sharing of wisdom that persists beneath economic striving.

The villagers, though, instrumentalize the boy: a *"consultant caste"* arises, easily read as a parody of the contemporary financial-information industry as well as Arrighi's regime of accumulation (*O* 123). The shamanic consultants' "rhetorical skill" and self-consciousness in language focus on converting the boy's words from their truth value to another system of valuation, as a second order of trade develops, not in goods but information: the consultants structure "a monthly question in such a way as to receive a maximally valuable answer from the extraordinary child," selling "these interrogatory skills to ordinary villagers who wished to extract maximum value for their monthly question" (*O* 123). The villagers seek a guarantee on the utility of language, when Wallace wants to expose contingency and inutility. "Pioneer" thus recasts "Crash of '69": the words of another gifted but vulnerable young man exist at the nexus of truth value and economic value, and as with Karrier, the clear statements of logical proofs, with 1 (true) or 0 (false) to be assigned to them, are again put to the test of a complex narrative context.

The coin image Wallace has used so often before also helps synthesize parts of *Oblivion*, though now Wallace remakes the motif along lines of rarity, inscription, and poison. In "Philosophy," where money has led to paralysis, the narrator's repeated mentions of poisonous spider "species" (*O* 191, 192, etc.) quietly pun on "specie," or coins, an association made, as Shell points out, in "The Gold-Bug" by Poe, whose horror fiction is an animating force throughout *Oblivion*.[12] The narrator's briefcase, often a carrier of cash in literature and film but here a home for deadly spiders, suggests this connection to money while recalling many previous uncanny wallets and purses. In "Mister Squishy," currency is also linked to poison: Schmidt, a focus-group expert conversant in ultimately meaningless statistical values, has turned to rare-coin collecting and a subscription to *"Numismatic News"* in search, it seems, of values with some weight (*O* 51). What results, though, is moral valuelessness—the great Wallace enemy of nihilism—and a revisiting of *Infinite Jest*'s killer pleasures. For Wallace the rare coin represents not just money but money hoarded, removed from circulation in pursuit of greater value. In a link between numismatics and terror, Schmidt finds that injecting the poison into *Felonies!* snack cakes "turned an area the size of a 1916 Flowing Liberty Quarter" into "sludge" (*O* 57). The castor beans needed for ricin he weighs down in their soaking pan using "low-value coins combined and tied in an ordinary Trojan condom" (*O* 52)—an image of awful weight and the sterility Schmidt represents. These coin metaphors reflect the subversion of civic responsibility's (and flowing liberty's) language throughout: an ad focus group treated as jury duty, for instance, with "voir dire" procedure (*O* 14).

The "coin" of "Smithy," even more hidden, extends *Oblivion*'s subjects from derangement by monetary value to the unexpected means by which counteracting moral values are inscribed on consciousness. Throughout "Smithy," an Oedipal drama set in 1960, patriarchs fall: in addition to the narrator's father there is Ruthie's dad (his arm's dismembering a symbol of castration) and the deranged civics teacher—a "substitute[]" in Freudian terms, he is shot through the eyes, a nod to Oedipus's fate (*O* 75). An extension of Wallace's indictments in "E Unibus Pluram" and his Updike essay of the 1960s' "brave new individualism" (*CL* 54), "Smithy" laments the passing of a 1950s family-values-driven *Lassie* episode (a clear analogue for the enframed windows tale) and a future of destroyed communal bonds in the Vietnam War, deadly for some of the students. Wallace summarizes this fall of treasured icons by having the narrator recall his abbreviated adult viewing of *The Exorcist*, a 1973 film rife with Vietnam-era anxieties. He remembers "a lengthy, slow motion view of a Roman Catholic medal falling through the air, as if from a great height, with its thin silver chain undulating in complex shapes as the *coin* rotates as it slowly falls" (my italics), intercut with "a brief flash of Father Karras' face, terribly transformed," "the face of evil" (*O* 96–97). Karras's horrifying visage signifies the toppling of religious values in *The Exorcist* and, in "Smithy," the unraveling of the U.S. Constitution in the insertions of "KILL THEM ALL" by the psychotic Richard Johnson (named for the U.S. presidents from 1963 to 1973, leaders of the Vietnam War) (*O* 91). In this compressed social history in symbols, the fragility of all values arises in the way this falling "coin" slides from associations with divine control to the arbitrariness of a coin flip—"rotat[ing] as it slowly falls."

Both medallions and coins are imbued with religious or monetary values through a process of stamping, engraving, or embossing. But in this passage Wallace—in accord with the "peripheral" and "incongruous" nature of the most powerful memories in *Oblivion* (94, 97)—inverts associations of stamping with permanence, saying instead of the subliminal film frame, "its very brevity serves to stamp it on the viewer's consciousness" (*O* 97). Evil, this image suggests, writes itself on the mind more readily than the ego's more noble values. In addition to prescriptivism in many spheres, Wallace took interest in the often comic ways the engraved wisdom of cultural mores failed to transmit to the minds it targeted (for more on his made-up Latin mottos, see chapter 6). The idea that a split-second's horror-film frame could "stamp" itself upon the mind, when more didactic wisdom seems easily sloughed off (especially by post-1960 culture), vindicates Wallace's mining of popular culture for deep meanings as well as his embrace of Wittgenstein, Kafka, and Lynch as models of apothegmatic representation. They shock us into recognition, rather than being didactic.

Etymological links are always worth pursuing with the dictionary-reading Wallace, and "coin" is no exception: it derives from the Old French (twelfth-century) *coing* meaning wedge, stamp, or the money made with such tools (the Latin *cuneus* means wedge, as in cuneiform writing), but also corner, angle, or nook—a sense preserved in the modern French *coin* and the English "quoin," both for cornerstone (a meaning used in *Infinite Jest*, where a building has "granite quoins" [*IJ* 797]).[13] A principle for the construction of *Oblivion*—and almost all of Wallace's multiperspectival, multistranded books—presents itself here: Burn, drawing on archival evidence that Wallace placed importance on the abbreviations he used for his titles, suggests that the initials of "Good Old Neon", G.O.N., connote "gone,"[14] but the more direct invocation is of -*gon* from the Greek *gonia*, meaning angle. *Oblivion*, giving minute proof for its major claims about the "peripheral" nature of perception, contains many shifting angles: "Mister Squishy" has "blinding pockets of reflected sun that changed angle as one's own angle . . . changed" (*O* 15), the boy of "Smithy" is deeply sensitive to the squares and rectangles overlaying any view, Neal tries to describe himself "from several different angles" (*O* 167), and the list could go on. I discussed in chapter 4 the "off-angled" and stochastic methods of "Little Expressionless Animals," "Westward," and "Order and Flux," which gives a pithy motto for this method: "Look from just one angle: things seem aimless, disordered. Flux reigns. Change the angle: illumination. Pattern. Order."[15] Knowing the angle-based etymology, Wallace gets us to see the values that various coins instantiate as products of particular inscriptions, particular angles, particular "subjective human[s] doing the valuing." In other words, values are the contingent products of human writing, as poststructuralist theory teaches us. But that does not mean values can be dismissed or eluded.

WALLACE AND THE INSURANCE INDUSTRY

If value is fundamentally contingent for Wallace, then he was bound to become interested, especially as *Oblivion* sifts through various institutions, in the systematic means by which people build up shared value *against* contingency and risk, such as the governmental insurance detailed in chapter 2. Two stories in *Oblivion* with links to *The Pale King* explore insurance anew, now on the more difficult terrain of the private U.S. insurance industry, a field Wallace knew well. He worked for the longest continuous stretch of his writing career (1993–2002) in Normal, Illinois, twin municipality to Bloomington. Bloomington-Normal's largest employer by far is State Farm Insurance, specialists in home, auto, fire, and health. In his 9/11 essay, "The View from Mrs. Thompson's," Wallace writes of Bloomington as "the national HQ for State Farm, which is the great dark god of US consumer insurance and for all practical purposes owns the town" (*CL* 133). The corporation's influence on the area mirrors what the essay as a whole registers in the local response to 9/11, the community-building effects but also a sense of division—with Wallace as an alien, unable to find an American flag to buy and separated from his "innocent" neighbors by his politics and knowledge of New York (*CL* 139). State Farm has over many years written versions of such schisms onto Bloomington, in "smoked-glass complexes and Build to Suit developments," the "beltway of malls and franchises that's killing off the old downtown," "plus an ever-wider split between the town's two basic classes and cultures," emblematized by SUVs and pickup trucks (*CL* 133). State Farm has the opposite of the local bonding effects its history as an alliance of Illinois farmers seeking better car-insurance prices in 1922 would suggest. Saying State Farm "owns" this small town (while possessed of profits from consumers in thousands of other locales) suggests there is irony for Wallace in a corporation with a public mission of sorts failing to integrate itself into the community from which it grew eighty years earlier.[16] Such tensions are especially important, this background implies, as the nation enters a postdisaster period of repair and self-redefinition.

Insurance has been overlooked as one of the several boring and antidramatic institutional structures through which Wallace marks out his distinct path within postmodernism. His insurance narratives—focused on intimate and melancholy effects and expressing a nostalgia for older social orders—provide an alternative to the bracing, sometimes thriller-oriented views of risk in writers such as DeLillo and Richard Powers, whose novels of environmental anxiety are the prime examples of postmodern literature in Ursula K. Heise's influential discussion of risk perception and narrative form.[17] Wallace also operates in *Oblivion* with awareness of how the risk-management models of contemporary insurers come freighted with ideology and resist valorization as embodiments of the communal interest that he sought through governmental insurance in chapter 2. Building on Ulrich Beck's concepts of risk communities and a reflexive modernity, Heise writes of risk perception as culturally determined, not objective; risk perceptions become intertwined with the "self-perpetuation of certain social structures" and, of course, corporate profit structures (*Sense of Place*, 127).[18]

An insurance-based view of life proves to be crucial to "Smithy." Among the falls of patriarchs in the story, the most pathos laden is the early heart attack of a father the narrator never really knew, an actuary. In climactic ruminations on that fact, we come to see the boy's comic-book vision of a noble dog, child, and father as a prodigious lie when compared to the inherently antidramatic nature of adult life, which plays out in an insurance office. Of his father's work, the narrator says,

> I knew that insurance was protection that adults applied for in case of risk, and I knew it had numbers in it because of the documents that were visible in his briefcase when I got to pop its latches and open it for him, and my brother and I had had the building that housed the insurance company's HQ and my father's tiny window in its face pointed out to us by our mother from the car, but the actual specifics of his job were always vague. . . . Looking back, I suspect that there was something of a cover-your-eyes and stop-your-ears quality to my lack of curiosity about just what my father had to do all day.
>
> (O 105)

Using the same "HQ" language that described State Farm in "Mrs. Thompson's," Wallace has the narrator, though a retrospecting adult, maintain his boyish naïveté of his father's insurance work, as though the pathos of the disconnection between father and son includes in its weight a neglect of certain social principles. We have just heard at remarkable length of the narrator's "cover-your-eyes and stop-your-ears" response to the classroom trauma, but in the oblique way in which "Smithy" and almost all the stories in *Oblivion* expose life's real traumas through seemingly tangential remembered events, it is the daily challenges of the adult world that this narrative evokes—a realm in which the unnoticed risks of everyday life take precedence and instill a lasting terror.

"Smithy" thus presents Wallace's highly intimate approach to the theoretical categories of risk perception and risk management. It is not the classroom hostage crisis, the window daydream, or the movies that bring the narrator to a psychic bottom; rather, he cannot handle the notion of insurance and remaining systematically vigilant about a grim view of the future. His chronic "nightmare" from childhood is not a recurrence of the classroom scene but an anticipatory vision of the insurance-office desk order that awaits him—a room the size of a soccer field, "utterly silent" and with "a large clock on each wall," counting out an unbearable time (O 103). This insurance office is not just a workplace but an existential landscape, complete with a bygone sense of ethical duty.

As I argued in chapter 2, Wallace showed how the alignment of irony and advertising in the 1960s had left his 1980s generation without access to the values of FDR's New Deal. Roosevelt is subtly present in "Smithy" as well. It ends with a memory of the class President's Day presentation, in which one of the four hostages, Chris DeMatteis, plays FDR at the 1933 inauguration (occasion for announcing many parts of the New Deal agenda) but fails to remember his lines and, "thrust[ing] his lower jaw . . . out further," simply repeats "'Fear itself, fear itself,' over and over" (O 113). This forgetful Chris, who often sleeps in class and has no time to study because he is a child laborer on his father's paper route, is Wallace's nod to the deep background from earlier in American history and his own career that informs "Smithy": a forgetting of (an obliviousness to) the communal confidence and New Deal programs needed to overcome economic disaster and child labor.[19]

Pietsch reveals that Wallace began "Smithy" as part of *The Pale King*,[20] and Burn uses the archive to show that much of *Oblivion* emerged in symbiosis with the tax novel.[21] Indeed, the father's dreamt-of workplace, containing ordered rows of actuaries, strongly resembles Peoria, and Fogle will also be given the "Smithy" narrator's word-counting ability. Moreover, this 1960 moment would have set the narrator of "Smithy" up to join the many tax examiners who have been recruited to the Regional Examination Center (Sylvanshine speculates in Wallace's notes) because childhood "trauma or abandonment" somehow grants them the concentration tax work requires (PK 545). Did Wallace see this insurance job as complementary to the tax accountancy that the narrator of "Smithy" (had he gone into *The Pale King*) presumably would take up after his trauma and daydreaming, potentially remedying the violent undoing of civics class? Or did Wallace shift from tax to insurance once "Smithy" became a separate fictional world? Regardless of the unknowable answers, I have reached a point in my account where the last two books bleed together, and some of their pieces benefit from simultaneous interpretation—the case, too, with insurance in "Oblivion," which brings Wallace's treatment of the actuarial into the twenty-first century of neoliberalism and financialization.

In the neoliberal economic order that gives the lie to any nostalgia for a sharing of value, State Farm's ownership of Bloomington and larger swaths of the nation has been an increasingly normative practice, aligned with the general dismantling of the U.S. welfare state in favor of free-market principles in social services. Harvey argues that neoliberalism's touting of personal responsibility and choice is exposed, in the case of health insurance, as an "authoritarianism in market enforcement," resulting in "exorbitant premiums to inefficient . . . but also highly profitable insurance companies."[22] Mirowski describes a life-insurance industry that "has become 'securitized' in much the same way as most other personal income streams have been financialized" (*Serious Crisis*, 125).

Sensitive to such trends and set in the present, "Oblivion" transforms the positive (even awe-inspiring) insurance-associated elder of "Smithy" into a grotesquely powerful figure of the for-profit insurance industry—changes in Wallace's idiom that seem appropriate to the particular cruelties of U.S. health insurance. "Oblivion" narrates the attempted repair of a deeply troubled marriage in a surreal sleep-clinic setting that is revealed, in the final page's dialogue, to be the dream creation of Hope, a woman who is in fact dreaming in the parodic voice of a projected version of her husband, Randy. Dream logic and dream fears suffuse the narrative, which Wallace so loads with psychoanalytic tropes that he seems intent on capsizing any Freud-inspired method of interpretation. For instance, Hope projects a Randy who has pedophilic desires for his stepdaughter Audrey, Hope's child from a previous marriage. Is Randy his actual name or Hope's dream-pun for an excessively sex-minded husband? Hope is also mediating an attitude toward her own stepfather, Dr. Sipe, referred to throughout, in a remaking of "Crash of '69," as "Father," even by Randy (or, to play the story's own game of attenuated signification, "Randy") (*O* 191). Does

Randy's desire for Audrey recapitulate the implied incestuous rape of Hope as a child by Dr. Sipe? Does Audrey even exist? Doubling, sexual innuendo, and disintegrating identities abound. "Sipe," the family name, means to seep—which is what happens to every identity and self-sameness here, from Hope's voicing of her husband to the endless bleeding of words into multiple near-synonyms and recontextualizations.

In its hall of mirrors "Oblivion" also narrates a version of contemporary health care and insurance that, while horrifically surreal, seems (like all well-interpreted dreams) to hold deeper truths about these institutions. "Father" is a physician but makes his living in "something called 'Demographic Medicine,'" which involved his evidently not ever once, during his entire career, physically touching a patient" (*O* 211). Demographic Medicine may not actually be a field, but we readily recognize in it an only slightly exaggerated version of the profit-oriented practices of health-insurance conglomerates. Randy (in dream terms, an inadequate substitute for Hope's powerful Father) exists farther down insurance's long bureaucratic chain, an "Assistant Systems Supervisor" (read: A.S.S.) for a company called "Advanced Data Capture," "which provided out-sourced data and document storage facilities and systems for a number of small- and mid-sized insurance providers in the Mid-Atlantic region" (*O* 194). Randy encapsulates Wallace's new vision of the subject determined by work. Exemplary of what Boswell calls *Oblivion*'s preference for narrators "controlled, sometimes to the point of madness, by . . . layered, nested, entropic" idioms ("Constant Monologue," 151), Randy seems to have no thought truly free of his employer's systems: he speaks of a decision made with Hope as "a compromise or [in the language of insurance regulation] 'Technical compliance' with this priority" (*O* 203; brackets in the original). Upon seeing his own brain activity represented on an EEG machine, he describes his very consciousness in terms of the money pried from a larger demographic body: the lines seem "trended with dramatic troughs and spikes or 'nodes' suggestive in appearance of an arrhythmic heart or financially troubled or erratic 'Cash flow' graph" (*O* 228). "Oblivion" depicts neoliberal health care's version of the posthumanism Giles finds across Wallace's works, this story included.[23] Such posthumanism, though, Giles argues, is balanced by a sentimental traditional value system—which, in my reading, correlates with Wallace's idealized, antineoliberal vision, beneath all the absurdity, of what collective militating against risks might become in a less market-oriented world ("Sentimental Posthumanism," 330).

That view of for-profit insurance's very different tradition emerges in traces Wallace leaves in the story of the history of Dr. Sipe's employer, Prudential Insurance, which played a more decisive role in earlier drafts. Dr. Sipe makes "a point of referring to a draft Feigenspan lager as '[a] P.O.N.'" (*O* 191) because he knows its Newark, New Jersey, origins:

> A career Medical executive for Prudential Insurance, Inc.—or, 'The Rock,' as it is often popularly known—as his own father before him evidently was, as well, as well as being a 'Fourth Ward' historical district native born and bred, [Sipe] knew Feigenspan lager by its original trademark, 'Pride of Newark' (or, 'P.O.N.'), and made rather a point of referring to it in no other way.
>
> (*O* 194–195)

In a note in a handwritten draft of "Oblivion," Wallace directly attributes the "P.O.N." detail to Kurt Eichenwald's *Serpent on the Rock*, which Randy brings to the sleep clinic as (appropriately disturbing) bedtime reading, reinforcing the sense that the true nightmare is that of corporate insurance's degradations.[24] Eichenwald's book exposes 1980s securities fraud at a subsidiary of Prudential-Bache (the name of the new company after Prudential expanded into investments) that cheated 340,000 investors of eight billion dollars, resulting in fines but no jail time for the perpetrators. Eichenwald shows the fraud to have been a result of Bache Securities, seeking a merger partner in 1981, trying to wrap itself in the "blanket of respectability" provided by Prudential's "unwavering integrity" as an insurance provider.[25] Prudential was more than a century old, founded by John Fairfield Dryden in 1875 in Newark on the basis of his "Widows and Orphans Friendly Society, a nonprofit [group] that would sell insurance [primarily burial insurance] to its members" and pave the way for a for-profit business. This description comes from the same page of Eichenwald's book on which the "P.O.N." beer detail Wallace exported appears (Eichenwald, *Serpent on the*

Rock, 95).[26] Another of Wallace's handwritten drafts of "Oblivion" even begins with a sentence referring to Dryden and Prudential Insurance's 1875 origins—as though Wallace considered making the perversion of the insurance company's mission more explicit in the story (Wallace, "'Oblivion': handwritten draft, undated"). In a tale of suburban New Jersey luxury built on Demographic Medicine, Wallace also implicitly links the transformation of Prudential from a civically proud insurance company into a financialized moneymaker with the concomitant decline of Newark (long ago fled by "Father") into one of the U.S.'s poorest cities.

Let me look "ahead," again briefly, to *The Pale King*. Prudential-Bache's fraud, as Eichenwald details, emerged from the expanded selling of investments known as tax shelters, the demand for which exploded with 1970s inflation, facts Wallace may have been intending to add to the complex matrix of economic history in which *The Pale King*'s fictional 1985–1986 is situated. One Sylvanshine goal is "to enhance Peoria 047's ability to distinguish legitimate investment partnerships from tax shelters whose entire purpose was to avoid taxes" (*PK* 13). Later, the young David Wallace learns that the "Immersives" he witnesses at work are "shelter specialists" "engaged with anti-shelter protocols" (337–338). The Tax Reform Act of 1986 eliminated the advantages of tax shelters, "gut[ted]" the business, and led to Prudential-Bache's eventual prosecution (Eichenwald, *Serpent on the Rock*, 279). *The Pale King* mentions the 1986 TRA once, claiming that the profit-based logic of the Spackman Initiative (a Wallace invention) was "ostensibly" a product of this 1986 Act, though in development long before that (*PK* 71). Does Spackman, though, amount to the government's reflection of Prudential's shift from the insurance business to nefarious finance that in effect undermined the tax code's moral purpose? Would Prudential-Bache have played a central role had Wallace completed the puzzle that was *The Pale King*? He must have sensed an alignment between, on the one hand, the market-based logic of Spackman and, on the other, Prudential-Bache's financialized expansion, at the expense of tax returns, into investment capitalism (away from its core business of consumer insurance and far away from nonprofit services for widows and orphans). While these conjectures may be unconfirmable, it seems clear that the complexity of economic causation examined in chapter 4 was to be followed in *The Pale King* by an investigation of the networking of taxation, government interest, and private maneuvers in a just and prosperous society—and that the mixing of insurance's social mission and investment capital represented for Wallace a sharp ideological conflict.[27]

But to return to the more tractable domain of "Oblivion," the healthcare institution toward which Dr. Sipe leads Hope and Randy in the story's resolution is a travesty of care that seems not to serve patients at all. The "Darling Memorial Sleep Clinic" (*O* 215)—its name suggesting a loved one's death—is a dystopian scene of surveillance. This nightmare of a sleep clinic inexplicably has the cacophony of Prudential's capital at work in the near background: a blender makes frozen drinks, and "some type of construction, maintenance or related activity," with loud power tools, is also "under way" (*O* 227). No quiet rest, no space free of capitalist relations, is to be had. While the Darling Clinic is affiliated with a university and devoted to research, the profit motive shadows the staff as well, and Wallace may indirectly criticize the interaction of research and the pharmaceutical industry: Dr. Paphian, "the Sleep specialist's cognomen or sur-name," later slides into lowercase with mention of "the young, forbiddingly nubile or 'paphian' technician[]" (*O* 230). While "paphian" primarily pertains to illicit love in general, a secondary meaning is prostitute.

Finally, in the saddest angle on a satiric tale, "Oblivion" reads as Wallace's surreal allegory of his *own* journeys through the U.S. mental-healthcare system and its treatments—most, unlike AA, not free. Max details Wallace's course of electroconvulsive therapy in 1988, his 1989 breakdown in Boston (spent at Harvard's McLean Hospital, "ensconced within the teaching hospital" of a university, like the Darling Clinic at Rutgers),[28] and his ongoing relationships with therapists he sometimes paid in cash, lacking health insurance (*Every Love Story*, 117, 134–137, 169). In 1989, Max writes, Wallace was twenty-seven and still dependent on his parents: his "encounters with the mental health system had cost his insurance company a lot of money, and when the insurance ran out, his family had had to foot the bill, filling Wallace with guilt" (*Every Love Story*, 118). He went to graduate school at Harvard in part for the health insurance and viewed some of his teaching jobs in similar terms (*Every Love Story*, 50, 118–119). "Oblivion" seems to be coded revenge against a system that treated him like a point on a demographic cash-flow graph rather than part of a commonwealth of individual/universal stories.

Wallace's baroque recastings of his life caution against any naïve transposition of biography into fiction, but "Oblivion" calls out for some associative interpretations. "Snoring," along with the obsessive insistence that one is not doing it and does not need treatment for it, is a grotesque, expressionist form through which to explore the spirals of mental illness as well as, more broadly, the problem of limited, solipsistic minds, a problem that always moved Wallace to metaphor. "Oblivion" thus describes through sleep and snoring two intimates' ultimately opaque relationship to each other, mediated by language or unconscious, incommunicative noises, somewhat like Hal's in the opening of *Infinite Jest*. Perhaps Wallace's ECT experiences are limned in the story's EEG leads and wires (*O* 222). In general, in its recursive and intersubjective intricacies, "Oblivion" points toward something U.S. health care as Wallace experienced it does not foster: he opposes an ethic of reader attention to the technologized "brain 'reading'" of data-dependent health care and those who speak its language for valuing the human (*O* 225).

NEW BRAT PACK (STILL CAN'T WRITE)

Wired, graphed, and made demographic object in "Oblivion," the posthuman body is made more subtle in "The Suffering Channel," which, in another exploration of metastasizing institutions, documents media consolidation under the invented German conglomerate Eckleschafft-Böd Medien A.G., owners of "three of the six major" big soft glossy magazines (*O* 296). A "-schafft-Böd" evokes a dystopian "shaft bod(y)" suggestive of posthumanism and the widespread anorexia and body disgust among the characters. This is a vision of the social body, too—*schaft* is German for "society," perhaps here with an ironic echo of Weber's *Gemeinschaft* (community). Wallace is skewering the German conglomerate Bertelsmann A.G., the world's second-largest media company and owners of Knopf, Random House, and many other houses. But when Wallace writes of the Suffering Channel being "in the late stages of acquisition by AOL Time Warner . . . involved in talks with Eckleschafft-Böd over a putative merger" (*O* 290), he puts under scrutiny his own literary product. "The Suffering Channel" is indeed an "acquisition" of AOL Time Warner, a media giant that eclipses Bertelsmann in size and includes among its holdings Little, Brown, Wallace's publisher since *Infinite Jest*. The story thus meditates on what distinguishes artistic fiction like Wallace's from the products of a massive entertainment-and-data corporation, much like the title *Infinite Jest* forced us to separate novel and film.

While more words are published at *Style* than at *The Frequent Review*, "The Suffering Channel" still marks Wallace's return to the specter of writers idling and failing to free themselves of corporate frames. Rather than editing or composition, the New York scenes portray ambidextrous typing, lunch, looking at photos, and workouts, as though *Style*'s writing work is stuck within the consumerist and image-driven economy it covers. Like any Wallace investigation of workers, this one evokes slavery in the Hegelian sense: the *Style* scenes portray unpaid interns, most of whom "traditionally come from Seven Sisters colleges" (which include Mount Holyoke and Smith, consortium partners of Amherst) (*O* 261). Wallace is documenting class immobility (Mirowski laments the alliance of neoliberal practices and many forms of unpaid labor, especially internships [*Serious Crisis*, 142–144]) but also again drawing a boundary between his Midwestern work ethic and the poseurs of his college years. Titles like "executive intern" make this story another philosophical allegory of action, agency, and the *intern*al, troublingly unstable here: the interns are disgusted when Brint Moltke's shit sculptures provoke thoughts of their insides becoming external (*O* 323). Laurel, who assimilates many of the body lessons for the reader, wonders why one's own saliva, when placed in a glass for drinking, becomes automatically "disgusting": "But why? When it's in your mouth it's not gross, but the minute it's outside of your mouth and you consider putting it back in, it becomes gross" (*O* 307).[29] In this metafiction, Wallace tries to reclaim style from *Style* by drawing on the puncturing force of the

Latin etymology: *stilus* means a "stake or pale" (an image to be seen again) or a "pointed instrument for writing," analogues to the *cuneus* glimpsed in "coin" ("Style"). Wary of the "upbeat angle" *Style* prefers, Wallace is again on the lookout for unexpected, cutting angles (*O* 245).

These unpaid workers living on parental funds struggle, naturally, in the discernment of value, here probed in monetary, aesthetic, and bodily senses. Laurel is another Wallace anorexic, denying herself and evoking a spiritual scarcity. She is one of many: Skip Atwater complains of the "sucking cheeks and starved eyes of Manhattan's women" and of seeing, in a perversion of Wallace's favorite motif, "interns weighing their food on small pharmaceutical scales" (*O* 250). A mature Wallace can now find the sadness and suffering within his allegorical characters, and thus with Laurel he portrays not John Beadsman or Kopek Spasova but a person in denial, the creator of a personal economy of work for food: she is "slender almost to the point of clinical intervention," and her "caloric regimen," recalling the addicts' perversions of the Protestant ethic, "included very precise rules on what parts of her Nicoise salad she was allowed to eat and what she had to do to earn them" (*O* 264). While the interns eat at a restaurant named "Tutta Mangia," they hardly eat it all (*O* 260).

Musing on Kafka's "The Hunger Artist," Wallace examines "tropes like *starved for attention* or *love-starved*" and the "innocent . . . factoid" (or not so innocent) "that the etymological root of *anorexia* happens to be the Greek word for longing" (*CL* 63). In "The Suffering Channel" Wallace pursues these implications, generalizing states of vacuity among characters of both genders, interested (as he was with disabled bodies in earlier works) in the metaphysics the physical states express. Skip, who experiences lightheadedness at the sight of his blood, frequently has "the queer sense that he was in fact not a body that occupied space but rather just a bodyshaped area of space itself . . . with a certain vacuous roaring sensation we tend to associate with empty space" (*O* 313). Laurel recalls an associate editor in the WTC elevator who, during her orientation, put "his arms up over his head and made his hands sharp like a diver's and said: 'Up, up, and away'" (*O* 286). Describing these rapid rides, Wallace returns to Doony Glynn's bricks, aligning characters' lack of value-creating work with reliance on technological lifting and an ignorance of weight: through "some principle of physics she didn't understand, the box in [Laurel's] arms felt slightly heavier when the elevator was in motion. Its total weight was only a few pounds at most" (*O* 286). In the context of 9/11, the elevator scenes (especially that upward dive) become more ominous, evocative of those who leapt rather than being burned to death—and, notably, were kept out of media averse to showing certain gruesome forms of suffering.[30]

Like Lenore, Laurel is often seen handling office communications, but Wallace makes her a terrible writer ("She was . . . all but incapable of writing a simple declarative sentence") and shows her staring at her computer screen, much like an oblivious TV watcher (*O* 252). While her first name suggests the false fulfillments of the American winning streak Wallace often describes, Laurel's surname, Manderley, is a mangled form of the mandala, an ancient eastern symbol of balance and a parallel with the yin-yang symbol. *Mandala* literally means "circle," and it is Brint Moltke who (with an echo of the Zen archer imagery in "Westward") projects circularity: in "the arrangement of the artist's hands . . . thumbs and forefingers formed a perfect lap level circle, which Moltke held or rather somehow directed before him like an aperture or target"—signals that the Keatsian living hand resides in Indiana, away from Wall Street and global capital's invisible one (*O* 248). Wallace's prose also subtly registers Laurel's insubstantialness, echoing "The Depressed Person" by referring repeatedly to "Laurel Manderley" (*O* 239, 243, 244, etc.). One of five interns "named either Laurel or Tara," she is an interchangeable part (*O* 261).

Wallace fights an old battle through these young women, one he probably ought by this point to have sensed he had won, in cultural standing if not in sales (though how early in his career he began "The Suffering Channel" is an unanswerable question). Boswell finds the early Wallace satirizing the "thin, anemic work" of "Brat Pack" writers,[31] led by Bret Easton Ellis and Jay McInerney. Here, the dull narcissism of the *Style* scenes stirs up associations with the low-level magazine work of "you" in *Bright Lights, Big City* and with the meals in *American Psycho* at which Wall Streeters compare assets. At his lunch, Wallace's satire of minimalist style through *Style* comes into focus: "The *Style* interns all still possessed the lilting inflections and vaguely outraged facial expressions of adolescence," contrasting with "their extraordinary table manners and . . . the brisk clipped manner of their gestures and speech." Meanwhile, "their outfits' elements were nearly always members of the same color family, a very adult type of coordination that worked to convey a formal and businesslike tone to each ensemble" (*O* 261). As the vocabulary of voice, "manners," "color," and "ensemble" hints, these are, symbolically, immature artists, authors of "brisk, clipped," minimalist sentences, monochrome in form. They descend from the narrator of "Westward," who promised to "get economically to business." These rule followers, were they actual artists, would produce a "*careful, accomplished* national literature, mistake-free, seamless as fine linoleum" (*BF* 61). The staffer most focused on, Ellen Bactrian, who has initials mirroring E-Böd's, facilitates media capitalism's conversion of text into image, coming up with the Suffering Channel idea with a mind that (in a narrative of mysterious arrows) constructs "flow charts" with "actual boxes" and "Roman numerals" (*O* 334). No ragged, "Host"-like flowcharts for these folks (*CL* 275ff.).

The deeper question behind this veiled sniping concerns literary art's ability to propose alternatives to commodity value. Consider the description of a jacket meant to contrast with the molting (the shedding of an outer skin) suggested by Moltke's name and art:

> There was also something just perfect about the editorial intern's jacket's asymmetrical cut, both incongruous and yet somehow inevitable, which was why Yamamoto was generally felt to be worth every penny. At the same time, it was common knowledge that there was something in the process or chemicals used in commercial dry cleaning that was unfriendly to Yamamotos' particular fabrics, and that they never lay or hung or felt quite so perfect after they'd been dry cleaned a couple times; so there was always a kernel of tragedy to the pleasure of wearing Yamamoto, which may have been a deeper part of its value.
>
> (*O* 262–263)

Parodying minimalism in the first sentence, Wallace loads in the vagueness of "something just perfect," "somehow inevitable," and "generally felt"

—all leading up to the implicit claim that minimalism, with no "deeper" sense of value, can only affirm the "worth" of the brand-name jacket dictated by its inflated price in the luxury marketplace. Wallace wants fiction to follow the jacket into its entropic decline, focusing on the true "tragedy" in consumption's aftermath, something beyond the "sense of tragedy" Atwater has sought since being told by an editor that he lacks it. Titling his two big novels after *Hamlet* and a waning king, Wallace locates his "kernel of tragedy" in art objects and unmasked bodies that are truly "incongruous" and "asymmetrical."

SKIP'S CAPITAL FLUSH

Finally, at the center of "The Suffering Channel" are Brint and Skip. Having shown the fallout of attempting to turn waste into productive energy with annular fusion in *Infinite Jest*, Wallace returns to miraculous but dangerous value and energy creation in Brint. Central to this story's mythos is artwork that symbolizes the United States as readily as the stars and stripes: "The Moltkes' side's front door had had a US flag in an angled holder and an anodized cameo of perhaps a huge black ladybug or some kind of beetle attached to the storm door's frame" (O 247). Next to the official flag Wallace places a signifier of national fantasy. In a story of "miraculous poo" (O 262), this ambiguous insect must be the scarab beetle worshiped in ancient Egyptian mythology, a dung beetle that rolls its own waste into a ball, hides it underground, and either eats the ball itself or, laying an egg on it, leaves it for larva to feed on. The Egyptians thought the beetle a manifestation of the sun god Ra, and Wallace sees in it a model of energy replenishment and the overcoming of waste's disorder that Moltke's art embodies—that second pun in his name, on the "molten," the source of the "steam from a fresh new piece" (O 273). Again, we are led by Wallace to reassess what we regard as glowing and warm, what contains energy and value. Moltke as scarab beetle offers audiences a miraculous vision—one the interns reject even as they remain drawn to, and awed by, the great dream of limitless energy, reminiscent of capitalism's promises, that the sculptures suggest. "The Suffering Channel" is thus yet another attempt to expose unacknowledged, contradictory objects of American worship.

Wallace once called the voice for his mock-epic of mythological figures in a TV age "the fuzzy Hensonian epiclete Ovid the Obtuse," accompanied by the "tragic historian Dirk of Fresno" (*BI* 235, 237). But here there is greater seriousness in the storytelling of Virgil Skip Atwater, whose real first name and initials (VSA—that is, USA as it would be rendered on a monument) evoke antiquity and its epic poetry. Setting the action over the few days before July 4 and playing again at being Joseph Campbell, Wallace confronts the mythic origins of America—and poses Moltke's metamorphosis (to nod to the Ovidian as well) as a possible epic rebirth or reconstitution of the nation and its definitions of value and beauty.

But Wallace also portrays in Moltke's "strange and ambivalent gift" (*O* 255) a myth closer to home, one he knows himself to have shared in at times: a romanticized version of the effortless modern artist, founded in the philosophy of Kant. Consider Kant's formulations on the ideal of effortlessness in fine arts such as sculpture in *Critique of Judgment*:

> The purposiveness in the product of fine art, intentional though it must be, must not have the appearance of being intentional; i.e. we must be able to *look upon* fine art as nature, although we recognize it to be art. But the way in which a product of art seems like nature, is by the presence of perfect *exactness* in the agreement with rules prescribing how alone the product can be what it is intended to be, but with an absence of *laboured effect* (without academic form betraying itself), i.e. without a trace appearing of the artist having always had the rule present to him and of its having fettered his mental powers.[32]

As Kai Hammermeister explains, Kant's analysis is affiliated with the Renaissance ideal of *sprezzatura*, "the seemingly effortless production of works of art" that appear "uncontrived, natural."[33] Consider the seeming consonance between such descriptions and the miraculous traits Wallace grants to Moltke: his art is an effortless product of "nature," and he suffers not at all from "academic form," as "a person with maybe like a year or two of community college" who is highly unlikely to "know Boccioni's *Unique Forms of Continuity in Space*" (*O* 319). Brint thus seems to have overcome that debilitating self-consciousness that made Himself's films so cold. Yet Moltke the untutored genius also produces art that is wholly imitative, always of known figures, if in absolutely precise detail (*O* 328). What Wallace ultimately questions here is the paradoxical role of will in the production of art.

But he explores that question most thoroughly, and surprisingly, through nonartistic Skip. The story's allegiances rest not with either of its clearly juxtaposed locales of Indiana or New York but with this "salaryman" (*O* 239), a Hermes figure who shuttles between the two, much like Wallace bringing Midwestern scenes to New York–centered magazines. Let me close this chapter by examining Skip as an ingenious attempt to resurrect aspects of the ethos of work, especially cognitive labor, that Wallace does not wholly give up on despite the despairs of *Oblivion*. A dorky, overweight exception at *Style*, Skip marks a partial return to the balancing and information-sorting efforts of Lenore. He has mastered a version of the writing that "Deciderization" calls for, constructing pieces by "pouring into his notebooks and word processor an enormous waterfall of prose which was then filtered . . . down to 400 words of commercial sediment"—more images of stochastic exclusion to find dirty ground. While Skip may not have Lenore's penchant for clarity, "The Suffering Channel," much of it narrated through him, balances with relatively straightforward prose the mental frenzies of Schmidt, Napier, and the spider collector of "Philosophy." The "salaryman" appellation, used ten times, even places Skip outside American labor altogether: the term refers to the stereotypically boring, white-collar Japanese worker willing to pull long hours, showing Wallace has not entirely left behind the imagery of Reagan-era east-west competition that influenced "Westward" (and there are more U.S. salarymen to come, in the 1980s of *The Pale King*).

In Skip, the agential hand of work meets symbolic frustration: his tic is to make "a waist level fist and move[] it up and down in time to his stressed syllables" (*O* 239). He is awed by the Buddha-like Moltke in part because the latter's "digital mudra" offers a contrasting vision of calm, free of striving and fists (*O* 305). Counting in time with syllables, Skip's is a metafictive writer's hand as well, and Wallace may be meditating on lines he marked in Hyde's *The Gift*, follow-ups to the passive labor of gratitude and grace I quoted in chapter 3 and, in a sense, a more practical form of Kant's aesthetic standards: Hyde writes, "When the will dominates, there is no gap through which grace may enter . . . and for an artist, no moment of receptiveness when the engendering images may come forward."[34]

In one other embarrassing feature of Skip, Wallace finds a solution of sorts to the impasse at which he found himself and his society with work: since childhood, "a deep perfusive flush to Atwater's ears and surrounding tissues was the chief outward sign that his mind was working to process disparate thoughts and impressions much faster than its normal rate," producing "heat coming off [his] ear itself" (*O* 286–287). Here is a mind hard at work; he seems to be a model of willed attention, literally uncool when attentive and engaged. Wallace puns here and throughout "The Suffering Channel" on "flush," juxtaposing its toilet-bowl meaning and blood meaning (other links include the card player's winning hand—heir to Lenore's lottery metaphor—and the idea of being "flush with cash"). Moltke's art offends most people because it goes public with what is made "in a special private place, and flushed," Laurel insists. "People flush so it will go away" (*O* 244). Blood is like waste, meant to remain inside: "We don't . . . want to see our blood" (*O* 308). Skip, no pale king, is thus a more palatable, flexible Moltke: Skip makes abject bodily material public, moving around in the world with a kind of MRI on display, occasion for a "'brain' reading" different from Napier's. His flush presages David Cusk's sweating in *The Pale King* but marks a manageable grotesqueness, the working mind not overwhelmed by self-consciousness.

We see in Skip's blood too a retreat from the Christ-figure dramatics that marked Gately's bloody sacrifice; the red head is an image more in line with being able "to sacrifice for [people] over and over, in myriad petty little unsexy ways, day after day" (*TW* 120). That blood rushes to Skip's ears as well as his "forehead," the site of the frontal cortex that has damned so many in Wallace's work, is especially important: listening must support rational thought (*O* 241).

Wallace may not have been politically minded enough in *Oblivion* to offer a coordinated solution to the degradation of work under neoliberal capitalism, unpaid internships, and minds drowning in an information economy, but he does suggest that Skip's form of hard-won attention has broad implications for the social world. Wallace caps his series of flush puns by tying them to large-scale economic terms: he refers to Skip's red head as his "capital flush" (*O* 323). Art is a capital flush in interlocking senses: a product of labor that is irrational in its expensiveness to the producer, Wallace's art denies capitalism's pervasive logic of accumulation and profit and replaces that value with the savory warmth of thought that remains in the bodily plain, away from "coldly cerebral" abstraction (*CW* 41). "The Suffering Channel" thus finds a contained, more work-oriented means of achieving the arrow through the heart that "Westward" so melodramatically called for: Skip's head, working hard, grants Wallace a sustainable symbol of "being willing to sort of die in order to move the reader" (*CW* 50). Consider Skip's flushed head as one more version of Keats's living hand that wants the reader's blood to fill it: if Wallace's text succeeds in getting us to think so hard that our brains must receive more blood, we all become red-headed Skips, "process[ing] disparate thoughts." Another pithy formulation of Wallace's postpostmodern ambition—to "mak[e] heads throb heartlike"—is symbolized here as well (*BF* 74).

Skip's "quite large or protrusive" ears also pay homage to Kafka, the writer who, as Toon Staes demonstrates, defines the artist in "The Suffering Channel."[35] But Wallace pays tribute to Kafka's body (rather than simply his texts) because he seeks to exploit a particular element of Kafka's expressionism that will carry forward into *The Pale King* and mark a victory in a longstanding philosophical battle. Wallace's interest in mental labor, from *Broom* to "Deciderization," has always been about finding a partial solution to the problem of minds' opacity to each other, the lack of physical proof that the other is thinking and remains unknown, just like oneself. As Wallace writes regarding the refutation of Descartes' *Cogito* argument in his Markson essay, "the truth of 'I think' entails only the existence of *thinking*, as the truth of 'I write' yields only the existence of text. To posit an 'I' that's *doing* the thinking/writing is to beg the very question Descartes had started out impaled on" (*BF* 84). In response, Markson chose portraying the malign consequences of a "*Tractatus*ized world" occupied by a solipsist, as many earlier Wallace texts also would (*BF* 77). But in "The Suffering

Channel," building on the grotesques of *Infinite Jest*, Wallace chooses a protagonist who seems to be trying to embody mental states that usually remain opaque to others. Skip offers a proof of thinking that uses the undeniable materiality of blood to sound those old Wallace refrains of good writing: "I am in here," "I EXIST."

Skip's red head, likely sign of high blood pressure, also foreshadows a novel, *The Pale King*, where hard, perhaps pointless (and even deadly) work will abound. Blood's circulation will also often be at issue (particularly in the hypertensive flush of the man most valorized for his civic values, Fogle's father), and the pale of the title will serve as both sign of poor circulation and its counter, the pricking, aggressively wielded stylus, a "hatchet with which we chop at the frozen seas inside us," as Kafka defined good literature (*CL* 61). Might the blood released by a hatchet-pen's cuts, in addition to further images of waste, be an unexpected form of abject American value that literary writing can show us how to exchange, a new form of commonwealth connection and living transaction? Wallace spent his final years asking that question in grand, tornadic fashion.

6

E PLURIBUS UNUM

RITUAL, CURRENCY, AND THE EMBODIED
VALUES OF *THE PALE KING*

Even tax collectors came to be baptized. "Teacher,"
[the disciples] asked, "what should we do?"
—LUKE 3:12

And there is no trade or employment but that the young man following it may
become a hero.
—WALT WHITMAN, "SONG OF MYSELF" (QUOTED
IN CAMPBELL'S *MYTHS TO LIVE BY* AND CIRCLED BY WALLACE)

value, n.: . . . 3b. . . . a fair or satisfactory equivalent or return
—*OED*

ATTENDING TO the foundations of value in monetary, moral, and civic
senses and devising idiosyncratic rituals through which a shared sense
of these values might be restored: these are the aligned objectives of Wallace's final fiction, *The Pale King*. This chapter shows value circulating
through the unfinished novel in many forms, from Lane Dean's "terrible
lack of values" (*PK* 42) in his encounter with his girlfriend's stolid Christian ones, to (in an extension of "Deciderization") the examiners' efforts to
"process and reduce the information in [a] file to just the information that

has value" (*PK* 344). Wallace turns to the unlikely novelistic subject of taxes for a flexible vocabulary of value, reconciliation, and transaction, the million acts of book balancing occurring constantly at the IRS, regardless of most Americans' notice of or stance on them. Consider this book a dilation on the *"price"* that Americans pay "truly 'to be with'" one another, to quote "Octet," though now being with others is not an intimate concern but a civic one. The IRS examiners must decide repeatedly whether Americans have sent in "fair . . . return[s]," to play with the *OED* definition of value in my epigraph; in doing so they continually compute value conceived in a monetary sense while necessarily invoking a set of moral values, a concept of fairness. This tension in the definition of value was to structure the novel, the "big Q" of which, Wallace's notes say, "is whether [the] IRS is to be essentially a corporate entity or a *moral* one" (*PK* 545). Wallace agrees with Whitman: the IRS's "moral warrior[s]" (*PK* 548) *can* be heroes—of "ordering and deployment of . . . facts" and of the strange antinovel Wallace wanted to write (*PK* 234).

In answering his big Q, the practicality of "real-world accounting" appeals to Wallace, who so often found math a gateway to the unfeeling, the merely ingenious over the morally viable (*PK* 233). The constant reference to the IRS agents as "examiner[s]" (*PK* 25, 29, 70, etc.) marks them as pursuers of Socrates' examined life, just as frequenting the bar "The Unexamined Life" marked E.T.A. students as the opposite (*IJ* 50). This novel maintains Wallace's view of philosophy as a grounded art form—based in the accountant's practical "books" rather than the scholar's citations. But balance must be actually sought in the world, too; for while devotion to ascetic tasks—"real courage" as "enduring tedium"—is clearly prized, this novel also becomes another Wallace chronicle of the spine, of standing up to become part of the three-dimensional world, of the need to move away from the torturous office desk (an image of Wallace's own writing desk) (*PK* 231). Note how many of the "syndromes/symptoms associated with Examinations postings" are exacerbated by contorted spines like Sylvanshine's, from "lordosis" to "lumbago" (*PK* 89–90).[1]

Extremes of work are a tonic in parts of *The Pale King* (Fogle's narrative most prominently), but Wallace seems to have been intent on using this ensemble of surveilled and manipulated accountants to explore further the ambivalence over work, will, and their potential futility that I documented in chapter 5—the kinds of feelings that led Wallace late in life to consider giving up fiction altogether and opening a dog shelter (Max, *Every Love Story*, 296). A reprisal of the father from "Smithy," Frederick Blumquist— an examiner dead at his desk of a heart attack at fifty-three, undiscovered for four days—haunts this novel in more ways than one. "He was always absorbed in his work" (*PK* 30), a supervisor says, in an ominous echo of Hal's belief in transcendence as absorption. For blooms like Blumquist (from the Swedish for flower branch), there is not necessarily any cultivation in tax work, and the sense that Wallace might salvage a Weberian calling for himself or for postmodern America seems again suspect here, with Fogle's conversion to a work ethic ending on another ominous note: the recruiter gives him the "smile of someone who, on Christmas morning, has just unwrapped an expensive present he already owns" (*PK* 254).

The predicament of Wallace's workers has, as usual, both personal and large-scale implications. For example, in the bleak outlook of the numismatically named Stu Nichols, a stewing man of low self-esteem who offers his "two cents," issues of self-making are once again tied to political economy (*PK* 144). In the stalled elevator of §19, Nichols steers a conversation about American civic history toward the topics of "metaphysics"— "existential" feelings of "smallness," "insignificance," and "mortality" (*PK* 145)—and, as another voice succinctly summarizes for him, a reading of the service-consumer economy and neoliberalism's effects similar to that offered in my foregoing chapters: "the move from the production-model of American democracy to something like a consumption-model, where corporate production depends on a team approach whereas being a customer is a solo venture," has led to "consuming citizens" who feel metaphysically small and weightless (*PK* 148).[2] In one of many signs that his draft remained temporally ununified, Wallace sets this scene in 1980, with the characters predicting "a Bush-Reagan ticket" (not the other way around) that will push Jimmy Carter from office, and Nichols's combined approaches of metaphysics, politics, and economics in effect theorize the rewriting of subjectivity and political choice under an atomizing neoliberal regime often taken to have been crystallized in Reagan's 1980 election (*PK* 150). As Nichols says, "the post-production capitalist," focused on ways to free up capital, increase consumption, and reduce taxes, "has something to do with the death of civics" (*PK* 146). As I argue in this chapter's most extensive reading, Wallace evokes an antineoliberal currency that might have the kind of simultaneous civic value and consumer value that Nichols/Nickels calls for here: a coinage that truly reads *E Pluribus Unum* and supports civic identification rather than solipsistic citizenship via consumption.

Several critics have already recognized, in §19 and elsewhere, tensions between civic and economic values, underscored by the conversion of the IRS's moral mission into a profit-based principle in the invented Spackman Initiative. Ralph Clare sees the novel "bring[ing] together economic, political, cultural, and social explanations as to why the neoliberal revolution came to be" in the 1970s and 1980s,[3] and Godden and Szalay call *The Pale King* a "study in the neoliberal transformation of American governance," focusing especially on rampant financial speculation as the main agenda of neoliberalism.[4] Boswell hears in DeWitt Glendenning's criticism of Vietnam War protesters echoes of Wallace's lament of the commodification of rebellion.[5] Like Boswell (and Shapiro), Kelly focuses on the civics dialogue in §19, examining Wallace's ongoing effort to transcend "traditional liberal/conservative or left/right binaries" in search of democratic values.[6] Turning to many untouched scenes for evidence and continuing in the vein (pun intended) of Skip's capital flush, I reach down to the level of less rhetorical directness the novel also exposes in the challenges of everyday, embodied life. For through attention to waste, blood, wounds, and dirt, we see Wallace's fusion of dark, psychoanalytic tropes with the novel's many captivating rhetorical statements about public affairs and social duty, adding grotesque dimensions to Burn's claim, based in Wallace's research in neuroscience, that entering this IRS means probing the unconscious mind.[7] My readings dialogue frequently with those of Godden and Szalay, who also find value to be the frequent subtext of the novel's abject materials.

Confronting the unconscious and the bodily in *The Pale King* means seeing the self once more as fundamentally porous and unarmored, unable to engage in the fantasy of accumulation capitalism inspires. Wallace recapitulates a trope I have tracked throughout by locating the Peoria Regional Examination Center on "Self-Storage Parkway," suggesting that, despite a focus on ascetics rather than hedonists, the logic here remains one of the self (and, more prominently than before, the mind) as storage receptacle (*PK* 29). Some treat the self and its senses as a canvas for totalizing feats, whether in the unnamed boy's desire to kiss every inch of himself in §36 or, in a scene added to the paperback, the goal of Hovatter (mad as a hatter?) to watch every second of television for an entire month (*PK* 12–25). Such scenes extend the motif of living within Schtitt's "second world inside the lines," though now without the ecstasies of athletic achievement to leaven the pain (*IJ* 459).

From title on, *The Pale King* punctures personal enclosures, undoing dreams, like the self-kissing boy's, of being "self-contained and -sufficient" (*PK* 403). Building on the *stilus* motif of "The Suffering Channel," this late Wallace recommits himself to an art of making holes—to signifying absence. The pale of the title can mean a border, as in "beyond the pale" —appropriate for a book beginning in "the place beyond the windbreak" (*PK* 5), with "tilted posts" and wire "more a symbol of restraint than a fence per se" (*PK* 6). But the Latin *palus* also means stake, that which digs a hole in making a border. There is aggression in the image: another meaning of *palus* is the staff or stave used for fighting in ancient Rome, a meaning Wallace plays on in Sylvanshine's *memento mori* description of an older plane passenger's "staved-in face" (*PK* 12). In an example of the many great concavities of being, Dean has the "sensation of a great type of hole or emptiness falling through him and continuing to fall and never hitting the floor" (again, Wallace's "agonizing interval" between fall and grounding) (*PK* 380). Dean realizes that "*boring* also meant something that drilled in and made a hole" (*PK* 380). The pale king, in one sense, would be the holder of the dangerous stylus, Wallace himself, called "the living human holding the pencil" (*PK* 68)—though in a book of odd bites (Dean realizes that the "strange indentations in rows on [his] blotter's front edge were . . . the prints of teeth" [*PK* 382]), we should emphasize the moment David Wallace is seen "holding a ballpoint pen in my teeth" (*PK* 304). As Derrida writes in *Spurs*, illuminating some of Wallace's assumptions about writing,

"In the question of style there is always the weight . . . of some pointed object," which "might be only a quill or a stylus" but "could just as easily be a stiletto, or even a rapier."[8] Abject materials, from feces to blood, come pouring out in this puncturing novel, and Wallace challenges us to find the glow of value in these flows.

As in "John Billy," then, which I claimed in chapter 2 anticipated this novel, characters must get "stuck" to "g[e]t valuable." For Wallace there is no other way. In the three main sections of this chapter, I attend to three subjects circulating around the issue of value and its relationship to Wallace's porous and intersubjective bodies. First, in one last rendition, work: Wallace interprets work in ritual terms here, seemingly trying to restore the spiritual potency it once had for him and, in a newer development, illustrate work's potential for codifying shared values. I conclude this section with a final comparison case, Dave Eggers, who expands Wallace's critiques of neoliberalism into the age of social media and entrepreneurs' displacement of the state. Second, forms of capitalist value: in the culminations of two obsessions I have examined throughout, Wallace places both the contracts that undergird his published books and the money that circulates through them on a human, often quite grotesque footing. Solemn versions of the AA wallet in the toilet come to dominate the Peoria landscape. Third, attention, the means by which a reader participates from afar in the uncanny forms of value production suggested by these first two sections: having intertwined bodies and money, Wallace constructs a final model of cognitive labor based on the attention our minds pay, our comparative valuation of the novel's thousands of details. In all three sections I also portray this final axiological novel as a summation and rereading of the Wallace themes of value, ground, and balance—especially since the book revisits his mid-1980s acceptance of the vocation of fiction writing.

RITUALS IN NEED OF PRIESTS

Among many other identities, *The Pale King*, as a "vocational memoir," is Wallace's metafictional elegy for a lost relationship to a magical labor

(*PK* 72). By portraying 1985, the novel toys with what Wallace knows had become, through the literary celebrity system, well-known facts for his core readership. To avoid confusion, I refer here to the author-persona as David Wallace, with just Wallace reserved for the writer himself. The 1985 leave of absence David Wallace must take from college because of his paper-writing business postdates the leave Wallace took in the fall of 1983 for mental-health reasons (the business may be true to life but was not the reason for a leave).[9] The 1983 leave, his second from Amherst, was a time during which he suddenly "found [him]self writing fiction" (*CW* 35). As for the actual May 1985, it must have been a moment of both celebration and resignation for Wallace: he had become a serious writer over the previous year by drafting *Broom*, but now revision awaited (*CW* 35). Like so many of his characters, he had come to his own end-as-true-beginning, his Cavellian second birth. David Wallace's arrival at the REC occurs "sometime in mid-May" and "quite probably on or very near Wednesday, May 15," dates that place the novel in the midst of Wallace's final days at Amherst (*PK* 258–259).[10] Such renderings of Wallace's mid-1980s life, even if interpreted without this precision, create a peripheral zone in which the novel can, freed from but still linked to autobiography, metaphorize mental-health problems (by exploring inauthentic paper writing and the boredom of many depressives) as well as salutary old work habits (by exploring superpowers of concentration and self-forgetting).[11]

Wallace consistently recalled the mid-1980s as a period when he naturally achieved a seemingly effortless relationship to writing work, time passing without his notice. "Writing fiction takes me out of time," he says in 1987 (*CW* 7). In 1990, recovering at Granada House, he recalls "times in 1984, 85, 86, 87 when I'd sit down and look up and it would be hours later and there'd be this mess of filled up notebook paper," leaving him feeling "well fucked and well blessed."[12] Now struggling again, Wallace devised a metafiction that reimagined his early writing days through the lens of an alien profession, one in which time's slow passage could be transfigured by miraculous concentration, as it had been in the real 1985. The hole bored in Dean, one of Wallace's numerous alter egos, is in effect the destruction of that magical temporality, record of a writer who could no longer fathom "doing this day after day": Dean does a return, "then another one, then a plummeting inside of him as the wall clock showed that what he'd thought was another hour had not been. Not even close" (*PK* 378–379). A relapsing Lenz had no embodied relation to a time he always asked for in exact numbers, a personified "Time spread [Poor Tony] and entered him roughly and had its way" (*IJ* 303), and Gately only beat drugs' temptation by somehow living within each second's passage. Fraught relationships to time are what bind Wallace's disparate narrative worlds together.

TURN IN CIRCLES, TURNING PAGES

How to regain a magical relationship to time? The answer seems to be attending to ritual, "a structured interval of communion with both neighbor and space," as the state-fair essay says it (*SFT* 92). Ritual, a natural extension of his interest in games and work, has been a subject for Wallace since Sykes's travesty of religious speech and J.D.'s plans for a Dionysian "altar" rigged to "shower U.S.D.A. Grade A blood" (*GCH* 310). *Infinite Jest* may be marked by what Greg Carlisle calls the "obsessive rituals" of addicts, scenes of secrecy and shame,[13] but daily or near-daily AA sessions become a therapeutic social ritual that comforts the addicts. The ritual aspects of both *Infinite Jest* and *The Pale King* owe the most, though, to a story I did not discuss in chapter 4, "Church Not Made with Hands," a favorite of Smith[14] and an example of what George Saunders registers when he describes reading *Brief Interviews* as a "ritual stripping away of the habitual."[15] In "Church," a Joycean account of an art therapist named Day, Wallace writes a first draft of Fogle's riveting tax teacher (in "Church" it is an actual Jesuit rather than a presumed "Jesuit" in "'mufti'" [*PK* 217]), and mental superpowers form an analogue to the reader's experience of the text (Day's colleague Yang, who may need a Yin to balance him out, can mentally rotate any object). With Day's name suggesting that his godliness (*dei*) depends on his embodied relationship to time's passage (one day at a time), "Church" ends with the command to "Rotate" (*BI* 210). In Wallace's symbolism, the lost are those debilitatingly fearful of time's cyclical passage; see Rick inexplicably "in the edge of the Erieview shadow, moving gradually with it," at the end of

The Broom of the System (451). The imperative to rotate is also prevalent in *The Pale King*, where inner narratives of ritual redemption are joined by external depictions of bodies performing the gestures of Wallace's quirky civic religion.

"The thing to do, I thought, is to walk in circles. This is demanded by the mythology of all deserts and wasted places," Gary says in *End Zone*.[16] Wallace's sense of how to write ritualism in the postmodern context is hugely indebted to DeLillo, who, Amy Hungerford argues, "imagines the ritual aspects of language—of conversation, especially—in sacramental terms modeled by the Latin mass."[17] For Wallace, who lacks grounding in any specific tradition like DeLillo's childhood Catholicism (see Neal sifting through spiritual alternatives in "Good Old Neon"), ritualism is often signaled by a generic, unremarked turning in a circle, a shape Burn sees recapitulated on numerous scales in *The Pale King* ("Paradigm for the Life of Consciousness," 155). The contrast is with nihilists who reject ritual turning by saying J.D.'s panning "big No" to the cornfields.

The opening of *The Pale King*, also on farmland, asks readers to make a very different kind of rotation, an atavistic sort that seems designed, like the rain ritual of "John Billy," to give life to a dry, "untilled" field (*PK* 5). This "very old land" (*PK* 5) is "the imaginative geography," says Burn, "of ancient Greek myth" ("Paradigm for the Life of Consciousness," 161). The reader is invited to describe a circle with her gaze: "Look around you. The horizon trembling, shapeless. We are all of us brothers" (*PK* 5). With the reiterated "past" of the novel's first sentence connoting deeply embedded memory, like that of "a mother's soft hand on your cheek," we enter, if not the unconscious per se, a psychically vulnerable space (*PK* 5). The way the arresting claim that "We are all of us brothers" arises without rhetorical lead-in suggests that it too, liberated in the ritual air of bodily motion, exists as an instinctual ("innit") feeling more than a reasoned claim. There are echoes of Emerson's essay "Circles," a text emblematic of the "sentiment of 'union' and fellow-feeling" that Giles finds Wallace's earlier work adapting.[18] Here that reading complements the general Transcendentalist vibe and the Whitmanian associations, stylistic and thematic, of a catalog of grasses. As the narrative eye descends to inspect the ground and cow patties, like Lynch's camera finding bugs or a severed ear in *Blue Velvet*, we are reminded of humans' humble standing and prepared for characters who will find the ground unstable or in upheaval, such as Toni Ware. Her childhood traumas in §8 will be coupled with Wallace's newly realistic turn on ecological exploitation, gypsum mining that blows up trees and makes "it rain[] fine ash" (*PK* 56), transforming place, or "where," into commodity, or "ware."[19]

In §1 Wallace juxtaposes primitive relationships to the ground's natural plenitude with the modern system of bureaucratic valuation that will be the book's subject, playing Campbell and Eliot again and getting us to see April 15 as an annual American ritual of return(s) and sacrifice. Having rewritten Veterans Day in *Infinite Jest* as a celebration of American solipsism, in *The Pale King* (featuring several actual war veterans and always allowing for misprision in the meaning of being recruited into "the Service" [*PK* 73]) Wallace orbits a day of national sacrifice that seems, as the title suggests, to have been bled nearly dry. Examining sacrifice in a 2000 review of bad novels about math, Wallace, unpacking a metaphor for a mathematician refusing to publish his findings, underscores a reference to Ovid's story of King Minos's refusal to "return . . . via religious sacrifice" the bull Poseidon captured for him (*BF* 234). Wallace glosses this "alienated selfishness" (*BF* 234) through a quotation of Campbell, who writes, "By the sacrilege of the refusal of the rite [of sacrifice]," Minos "cuts himself as a unit off from the larger whole of the community. . . . He is the hoarder of the general benefit."[20] While Minos is far from the only analogue for the pale king of the title, his refusal to "return" reflects the reluctance of many twentieth-century Americans (little kingly solipsists) to send in a fair tax return. They too "hoard[] . . . the general benefit."

Idiosyncratic rites require a cast of unorthodox priests, *The Pale King*'s Christian subtext repeatedly suggests—not the Priethts, heartless Harts, or even bedesmen a less mature Wallace created in the actual 1985. The Jesuit tax teacher who may not be a Jesuit is a treatment of tax examining as holy office, as are the "Immersives" (a religious term) that David Wallace glimpses, each working, monklike, "in a small tight circle of light at what appeared to be the bottom of a one-sided hole," one of many moments suggesting transcendence through immanence (*PK* 292). I noted in chapter 3 the translation of Stecyk into sick saint; also unstably righteous is the Christian examiner Lane Dean, whose name reads as street-cleric, suggesting the profane commingled with the sacred. Father Karras, the movie exorcist who is challenged in his faith, would have found himself at home here had "Smithy" become part of *The Pale King*. A surprising reading recommendation Wallace once made to Franzen—Brian Moore's *Catholics*, about a remotely located Irish priest continuing to celebrate the Latin mass after Vatican II—further suggests that unorthodox priests and reinvigorated ritual were important subjects for Wallace (Max, *Every Love Story*, 164).

In fact, *The Pale King* seems like a direct response to a passage from Kierkegaard's *Fear and Trembling*, so closely does it track with the novel's search for spiritual power among tax collectors. Kierkegaard writes about seeing the knight of faith and "instantly push[ing] him" away:

> [I] say half aloud, "Good Lord, is this the man? Is it really he? Why, he looks like a tax collector!" However, it is the man after all. I draw closer to him, watching his least movements to see whether there might not be visible a little heterogeneous fractional telegraphic message from the infinite . . . No! He is solid through and through. His tread? It is vigorous, belonging entirely to finiteness . . . He belongs entirely to the world . . . He tends to his work. So when one looks at him one might suppose that he was a clerk who had lost his soul in an intricate system of bookkeeping, so precise is he.[21]

With his sturdy footing in finitude, Kierkegaard's knight of faith may be the ideal of grounding that Wallace has been trying to describe, often in negative form, throughout his balancing books, especially given his affinity for Kierkegaard's teachings.[22] Add to this connection the mention of the deeply ordinary tax collector, and many of *The Pale King*'s spiritual and existential principles seem foretold.

By invoking the tax collector, Kierkegaard brings Christ's challenges into modernity; for "truly, I tell you, the tax collectors and the prostitutes are entering the kingdom of God ahead of you."[23] So too does *The Pale*

King, a book about recruitment, rework the Gospels by the light of Wallace's coupling of materialism and belief. Several of the examiners live at an apartment complex called "Angler's Cove," marking them as fishermen, a profession leading to disciplehood (*PK* 24): "I will send you out to fish for people" (Matt. 4:19). Just as Wallace was leery of using religious language with any piousness or certainty in *Infinite Jest*, though, *The Pale King*, while more forthright in its portrayal of a postmodern charisma and asceticism, refrains from associating these workers unequivocally with the holy. With apostolic recruitment and infusions of energy under scrutiny, Wallace's plan for the plot to be a "series of set-ups" where "nothing actually happens" may reprise the pointed exclusion of Thanksgiving from *Infinite Jest*: the mid-May day of arrival in which action is concentrated places the novel (as we have it) short of May 26, 1985, the date of Pentecost on the Christian liturgical calendar, when the Holy Spirit descended upon the apostles.[24] As Evans suggested about *Infinite Jest*, Peoria's religious meaning, whatever it is, will be made by individuals on the ground, not forces from above.

And made too by readers—for reading, the mystery Wallace so often probes in portrayals of work, is the ritual action under scrutiny from the moment "Look around you" couples with "Read these" in §1 (*PK* 6). While still always writing metafiction, Wallace also fashions a meta*reading* in describing the examiners continually scanning and turning over papers. He seeks new ways to escape the traps of self-consciousness that beset metafiction by attempting a form of *other*-consciousness—that is, consciousness of the eyes that will stare down at the page once his work is through, forming a community of their own, making the rote into ritual, and potentially sharing values as well. In the strangely structured §25, which, in two columns, mimics the accountant's ledger, "'Irrelevant' Chris Fogle turns a page. Howard Cardwell turns a page. Ken Wax turns a page," and so on (*PK* 312). A return to the themes of coauthorship and the commonwealth of anonymous stories that concluded chapter 3, this section holds a mirror up to its reader, who also repeatedly "turns a page." Pietsch reveals that Wallace at one point considered this section as the novel's opening;[25] in that position, shortly after the title page, these names (and, by implication, the reader's own) might have registered as coauthors to David Foster

Wallace. "Jay Landauer and Ann Williams turn a page almost precisely in sync though they are in different rows and cannot see each other" (*PK* 313): causing intimates and strangers to be "precisely in sync"—whether in a church chant or a dance formation—is what rituals do, including the quite individuated task of silent reading. For you and Jay Landauer may be turning the same page of *The Pale King* in sync—and thinking similar silent thoughts about it—right at this moment.[26] With the book incomplete it is impossible to know, but it seems likely Wallace would have included names in this section that he focused on or used nowhere else, to reinforce the sense that the anonymous many (the figurants?) who made up his audience had a place in his text. In this way he hoped to show readers once again the stakes and necessity of their work—and how they too might be operating "in sync" and "unalone" (*CW* 62), overcoming solipsism through reading.

"THE NIHILISTIC RITUAL OF THE FOOT"

Those are readings of Wallace's utopian vision of ritual participation, which seems to promote sharing and common values, but most often we are among hoarders of the general benefit. The prevailing negative definition of ritual arises in Fogle's §22, where the potential for grace is enfolded into what reads as a spiritual conversion narrative, one clearer in import than Gately's search for *Dei Gratia*. Fogle's tale, its trauma centered in the subway, is a series of ground-based signs: the foot, the base, and the shoe structure this axiological narrative of values being fitfully born and the personal becoming political.

(Dis)identifications with value strongly assert themselves at §22's beginning. Fogle's name suggests "fog" or perhaps a corruption of "focal" (hazy on details, he lacks focus); "fogle hunter" is nineteenth-century slang for a pickpocket—a fogle is a silk handkerchief, but we should draw links to purses, wallets, and Gately the thief.[27] Fogle calls his younger self "the worst kind of nihilist—the kind who isn't even aware he's a nihilist" (*PK* 156). He is the character in the corpus most clearly under what Wallace, describing contemporary writing's lack of Dostoevskyan moral engagement, calls a "type of Nihilist spell" (*CL* 271n28). Fogle's preferred drug of abuse is Obetrol, an anorexiant or weight-loss pill (recall Laurel and the interns). Before his conversion, he stops his accounting studies at "depreciation," which he calls "fatal" (*PK* 157)—as though he cannot handle the entropic implications of cost accounting and the eternal overhead of his "wastoid" ways (*PK* 160).

These associations are far from simply personal, though. Part of Fogle's narrative occurs in 1977, and here Wallace plays one last time with presidential rhetoric on commonwealth themes. In one scene, Fogle's father returns home unexpectedly to find his son and friends stoned and with the heat turned up, creating another hothouse, perverting the *oikos* and hoarding the general benefit. Fogle scrambles "to turn the thermostat back down to sixty-eight," feeling "like a spoiled little selfish child" (*PK* 173). The reference is to the "energy conservation" (*PK* 172) policies of not just Fogle's father—who Wallace of course notes "grew up during the Depression" (*PK* 169)—but the United States as a whole. In one of the most enduring memes associated with his presidency (and with 1977 in particular), Jimmy Carter gave his "sweater speech" on February 2, 1977, shortly after his inauguration. In it he called for "cooperation," "mutual effort," and "modest sacrifices" from the American people, who by keeping thermostats at 65 in the daytime and 55 at night could "save half the current shortage of natural gas."[28] The nationally televised speech (a latter-day version of FDR's fireside chats, in spirit and setting, with Carter appearing next to a roaring fire) is remembered for the president's sartorial choice: he wore a cardigan, implying it was the clothing of civic caring (especially for those without big fireplaces?). Appropriately, Fogle at the beginning of his memoir vaguely recalls "Jimmy Carter addressing the nation in a cardigan," a memory that slides in the same sentence into apathetic gossip about Carter's brother (*PK* 166). In a finished *Pale King*, revisiting 1970s energy politics might have developed into a captivating dialogue with the Iraq War, tense U.S./Middle East relations, and climate-change denial amid which Wallace worked on the novel—which Pietsch says "came alive" again for him in spring of 2005,[29] the period of the "Author's Foreword" and a time with no shortage of chicanery from "the Decider" and his cabinet in the news. With Spackman's changes proving "attractive[] . . . to the free-market conservatives of the current administration" looking to "deregulate" the IRS like any other business, Wallace may associate sweater-clad Carter with a last gasp of commonwealth values before neoliberalism took command (*PK* 115).

In the central images of his college years, Fogle describes devising an antiritual: rather than structure time and solidify values, he destroys them. In the "nihilistic ritual of the foot," exercising none of the choice Wallace's heroes must move toward, Fogle lets a podiatrist's rotating sign determine his fate, looking to it every night to determine whether he and his room-mate study or drink at a bar called the Hat (*PK* 187). Rather than center-ing the rotating self, Fogle's ritual replays *Infinite Jest*'s externalized organs, from Lung to Brain, and substantiates the belief in a second, virtual exis-tence outside embodied reality. Lit by good old "neon," the imposing foot is another instance of weightless gas masquerading as solidity. And in another image of imperceptible entropic depletion and a malignant relationship to time, the "sign's rotation didn't stop all at once. It more like slowly wound down, with almost a wheel-of-fortune quality about where it would finally stop" (*PK* 163). Fogle thus accepts an externalized and mechanical tempo-rality, a system of the arbitrary. Chance must be acknowledged in Wallace's world, but not like this. The foot is a gigantic idol, an example of the "wor-ship" that "everybody" engages in, most often mindlessly (*TW* 100).

To move Fogle toward the transformative ritualism of the REC, Wal-lace creates a mythical space in the Chicago subway system—importantly, a publicly funded resource. Fogle follows his father into the underworld and emerges from this journey to serve his nation: Wallace is revising Ae-neas's famous encounter with his dead father in the underworld, part of the hero's journey toward founding Rome. With early scenes of taxation's breakdown set in Rome, New York, *The Pale King* portrays the decline of a decadent American empire for lack of social cohesion—and, potentially, the refounding (the regrounding) of a better nation. In the gruesome death of Fogle's father, Wallace returns as well to his mythos of the founding of Collision, Illinois, but now with less hope for a "settlement way beyond le-gal." At stake once more are the foundations of community financial value, emblematized by an invented 1977 moment of threatened commonwealth: the Illinois progressive sales tax "disaster" (*PK* 197), based on a policy that, while attempting to increase revenue and discourage inflation-causing overconsumption, leads Nichols's "consuming citizens" (consumers first, citizens second) to divide up retail transactions into values lower than $5.00. The absurd retailers' slogan of "Subdividable!" retools Marathe's tale of the undividable good and exposes consumption as an inevitably atomizing force (*PK* 198). In the postproduction age of Spackman and manipulable financial data, the IRS has the same logic: Fogle's teacher says, in an image that slides from homey to violent, "The pie has been made— the contest is now in the slicing," and "you aspire to hold the knife" (*PK* 234). "Subdividable!" becomes the book's dark countercredo to "We are all of us brothers," upsetting the footing, or base, of Illinois society. For as Fogle ruefully notes after reviewing the equation T[ax] = B[ase] x R[ate], the "base, B, of a progressive tax cannot be something which can be easily subdivided" (*PK* 195).

In tragic illustration of the relationship of two "bases," personal and social, the desperate run of Fogle's father before he is dragged along by the accelerating subway train creates a "widening gap or fissure" in the platform crowd (read: a break in the social order). Never before has Wallace so compellingly rendered the life-or-death stakes of achieving groundedness. The gift is a victim here too: Christmas shoppers holding "numerous, small subdivided packages" drop them and flee, leading to "the illusion that it was somehow spurting or raining consumer goods" (*PK* 204). The falling packages echo the chaotic Rome office's discarded sacks of returns, another failure of taxation's order. With the death of the father—a dedicated civil servant in the "cost systems" with which Wallace identifies his own art (*PK* 177)—civic values are allegorically sacrificed.

The nihilism of Fogle's tawdry foot ritual continues resonating in the demise of his father's value system, with Wallace finding in feet a peripheral locus for unendurably traumatic memories. Among "vivid but fragmentary details," Fogle remembers a man being "interviewed while holding my father's right shoe, a tasseled Florsheim loafer, of which the toe portion and welt were so abraded by the platform's cement that the sole's front portion had detached" (*PK* 205).[30] We are witnessing the building of Fogle's sharpened memory and attention from the ground up, even as the anonymous man's attachment to the shoe's totemic pathos allows Wallace to inject emotions of trauma into the scene without betraying Fogle's glazedness, so essential to the voice of this section. A parallel muted encounter with the father's shoes occurs after the accident, though earlier in the section, when Fogle recounts cleaning his father's closet and finding shoe trees, "some of them . . . inherited from his own father": Fogle does not "know what they were for, since I never took care of any of my shoes, or valued them" (*PK* 176). Here, the doubled image of rootedness (shoes and trees) combines with the discovery of shoe-value, forming an axiological counter to Fogle's unthought Oedipal struggles against elders' authority. Later preparing for employment under the "man of style" and civic idealist Glendenning (*PK* 436), Fogle buys suits, shirts, and "Nunn Bush leather wing tips" after turning to tax, an act of redemptive consumption attaching him to his father's legacy (*PK* 236). These shoes redeem the nihilistic foot, and "prepar[ing] to wear the hat" the tax teacher holds "aloft" (a new object of worship) remakes the bar where Fogle wasted time (*PK* 235).

DePaul is Fogle's college because he finds there a Pauline moment of "'put[ting] away childish things,'" as he quotes from 1 Corinthians (*PK* 174). Footwear is again our expressionist guide to the internal transformations of spirit and axiology: Fogle, not yet having taken up his father's attention to shoes, wears fashionable Timberland boots in "dogshit yellow," "with laces untied and dragging" (*PK* 192), in contrast with the "neatly tied" leather business shoes of the accounting students and the "dazzling" "shine" of the teacher's dress shoes (*PK* 217). The "dogshit" boots allow Wallace to align multiple moments of unorthodox ritual and spiritual transformation: like the reader in §1 who rotates before looking to the cow patties at her feet, Fogle, through the tax sermon's imperatives, can get in touch with the values at the base of a strong social order and the waste (Wallace's general emblem for trauma) on which he stands. In a way that recalls Gately's unassuming spiritual path, the chanced-upon classroom ritual and dogshit boots displace the parallel story of a Christian woman who suddenly turns into a church parking lot and is "'born again,'" supposedly saved (Fogle sneeringly recounts) from "barely clinging to any kind of interior sense of value" (*PK* 213). Her cowboy boots have on them "a rich, detailed, photorealist scene of some kind of meadow or garden," making them look "like a . . . greeting card" (*PK* 213). While "greeting card" broadens the satire, note that the "photorealist" has always signified the abstractions of "*Tractatus*ized" picture theory for Wallace, and here he signifies Fogle's departure into the more personalized and existential values this novel attempts to realize—away from prefabricated rituals and pretty pictures of completed, unchallenging Christian cultivation.[31]

During the teacher's rousing speech about becoming "cowboys" of information (*PK* 235), reminiscent of Ahab's incitements on the quarter-deck, Wallace reconfigures the American call to work by drawing on one of the greatest scenes of communal labor in the nation's literature, also from *Moby-Dick*: "A Squeeze of the Hands," chapter 94, on which Wallace wrote a three-page close-reading essay his first year at Amherst.[32] Echoing Melville's homoerotic language, Wallace writes,

> A sudden kind of shudder went through the room, or maybe an ecstatic spasm, communicating itself from senior accounting major or graduate business student to senior accounting major or grad business student so rapidly that the whole collective seemed for an instant to heave—although, again, I am not a hundred percent sure this was real, that it took place outside of me, in the actual classroom, and the (possible) collective spasm's moment was too brief to be more than sort of fleetingly aware of it.
>
> (232–233)

Fogle's uncertainty about internal and external is the state an attentive communicator lives in, and in expressing uncertainty he honors Wittgensteinian laws, operative everywhere in this novel, that the ground of linguistic togetherness can be sensed but not pointed to directly (note that "possible" modifies both "collective" and "spasm" here). One sentence later, Fogle has "a strong urge" to tie his boot laces—though he does not do it, he instinctively senses this is an axiological moment (*PK* 233). His fleeting awareness of being in sync across rows of seats is also endemic to ritual, a foreshadowing of the Immersives room, David Wallace's view of which will "last[] only a moment" (*PK* 291).

If this moment contains hopes for the American workplace in the 1970s and 1980s, what of work in the 2010s? Fogle's insights into work mark an occasion for a final interlude on another key Wallace follower, Eggers, who, as Konstantinou suggests, has through *McSweeney's* and associated activist ventures fashioned from Wallace's anti-irony an "optimistic ethos that mixes an offbeat aesthetic with . . . philanthropy and . . . alternative institutional structures."[33] Eggers's writing has also been marked everywhere by Wallace's approach to value: the early work, for example, arises from stories of wealth, expenditure, and gifts, themes uniting *A Heartbreaking Work of Staggering Genius*, in part about spending his parents' life-insurance settlement, and the round-the-world giveaway of *You Shall Know Our Velocity!*. It is in *The Circle*, though, that Eggers finally writes his *Infinite Jest*, the book he had the honor of introducing in its 2006 edition. *The Circle*, set in a near-future world, is a "campus" novel where an E.T.A.-like structure at a huge social-networking company keeps employees, constantly likened to children, unquestioningly competing with one another and charting their status and plateaux. *The Circle* also expands Wallace's videophony into an era of body cameras and the cloud-ing of everything. Eggers reveals his source when a character with a history of abuse inexplicably has "a papier-mache mask he'd made as a child" hanging above his bed; moments later, he takes video of sex play that is uploaded, irrevocably, to Circle servers.[34] Meanwhile, the intricacies of The Circle's data-gathering procedures owe something to "Mister Squishy," which Eggers edited for *McSweeney's*. And an unlikely shark-feeding scene that reflects on Web ecologies and predation pays further homage to Wallace when a lobster is gruesomely eaten alive (*PK* 317) (Wallace's shark fears—revealed in Max's biography, which Eggers blurbed—add another layer to the scene [*Every Love Story*, 5–6, 53]).

In a country that builds endless opportunities for "connection" but no longer makes anything, *The Circle*'s endorsement of essentially Thoreauvian economic values comes through Mercer Medeiros, the protagonist Mae's Luddite ex-boyfriend, who stands for inefficient artisanship (he makes antler chandeliers) and rants about what The Circle does to in-person interactions. Mercer is Eggers's tribute (as Alan Clay was in *A Hologram for the King*) to the American small businessman standing against the huge corporation: for "*Mer*cer," read merchant in the old, face-to-face sense. With his "Me—— Me——" name, Mercer signifies Eggers the small publisher, obsessing over a low-profit venture in beautiful artifacts. But in his hulking, "Sasquatch"-like appearance, Mercer also resembles the physical Wallace, with whom he shares several opinions about media's sacrifice of the interpersonal (*The Circle*, 370). Mercer is in effect driven to suicide by the constant visibility that Wallace lamented in "E Unibus Pluram" and that Eggers shows expanding a hundred-fold in the age of live-streaming video.

The Circle is among the first *Pale King*–influenced novels as well, applying Wallace's insights into mechanized labor to the fully digital era. While there are no "Tingle tables" here (*PK* 276), Eggers satirizes the endless streams of stressful, pointless, and self-obliterating work in a supposedly hyperefficient age: Mae's desk goes from one screen of customer help requests, to two screens bursting with emails and fake intimacies, to a computerized bracelet and wearable camera that make her every reaction and perception an object of worldwide surveillance and profit. Eggers projects a near-future enslavement to a system of "likes," customer surveys, and data generation that makes Mae's purchases and online image the seat of her value creation, all plausible extensions of current Facebook saturation. *The Circle* can seem *im*plausible much of the time, too, but that quality arises from the credulousness and willing acceptance of every Circle incursion by its protagonist, whom Eggers pointedly names after a word of permission. A feckless and Fogle-like character, Mae-as-May embodies the perverse new liberty implied by the word neoliberal: applied to technological formations, liberal now essentially refers not to citizens' rights but to the freedom they grant corporate systems to instrumentalize their tastes and habits. Crime prevention and many other civic domains are soon to fall as well under The Circle's corporate control. If *Infinite Jest* told us in 1996 where digital entertainment "choices" would lead us, *The Circle* predicts the neoliberal dystopia to which today's wave of (social) media saturation is headed. It also offers a far more detailed account of the technocorporate methods by which the American social contract is being sundered, a subject *The Pale King* addresses in much more mysterious terms.

PAINFUL CONTRACTS, UNSPOKEN CODES, AND STRANGE CURRENCY

While the design of *The Pale King* will remain forever indeterminate, Wallace was clearly developing a tension between its two first-person narrators: Fogle and David Wallace, who no doubt surprises readers by disparaging Fogle as his "logorrheic colleague[]" in a section Pietsch places soon after the rather moving §22 (*PK* 261).[35] Their differences on valuing "Irrelevant" (*PK* 261) details will be the concern of this chapter's final section, but here I draw attention to the legal-economic term that divides them: the contract, fetish object of a neoliberal society that purports to reduce every relationship to monetary balance and legal consent. Fogle endures a legal imbroglio after his father's death that shows the severance of contractual reciprocity from justice: the family's lawyers try to use "some ambiguity in the legal language" to nullify an obligation, while loopholes in the very sort of contracts the father helped broker for the city complicate assigning ethical responsibility for the train doors' malfunction (*PK* 206). Fogle senses, too, that, in the late-twentieth-century United States, any notion of a social contract that arises from Locke or Rousseau figures as an afterthought, overshadowed by a more readily understood quid pro quo: Americans are only really "free" in a contract-based society in relation to "strangers," and "buying or selling something doesn't obligate you to anything except what's written in the contract—although there's also the social contract, which is where the obligation to pay one's fair share of taxes comes in" (*PK* 194–195).

David Wallace, by contrast, becomes not just a "creature of the system" (*PK* 548) but a creature of contract—with individual words omitted from his account if they are not allowed by the corporate lawyers said to be hovering over the text. In the "Author's Foreword" of §9, which takes metafictional self-consciousness to a new extreme in order to evoke realms beyond it, Wallace brings to bear on his agitated persona all the malign effects of language taken as contractual object and authorship taken as an avenue to sales figures, on which §9 provides much hard data. David Wallace even lets contracts intrude directly on the writer-reader relationship that is Wallace's holy ground, as the "Foreword" finally turns Wallace's longstanding critique of contracts on his own products, expanding the satire of Little, Brown's ownership in "The Suffering Channel." As Godden and Szalay argue, §9 represents the general American ceding of personhood to the "imperatives of corporate finance" ("The Bodies in the Bubble," 1279). But Wallace also mediates here a more idiosyncratic neurosis over signing a contract and taking *any* money before a book was complete. In 1996 he said he only reluctantly signed a contract and took an advance partway through *Infinite Jest* because he needed time for research: "It would have been a lot more fun if I hadn't taken any money" (Lipsky and Wallace, *Although of Course*, 2). Of a potential contract for his next book he said, "It would just be pain. And I'd be being paid to undergo pain, which I don't want to do"—another suggestion that somatic costs and monetary compensation do not balance (Lipsky and Wallace, *Although of Course*, 124). Wallace maintained this anticontract stance until his death. Pietsch describes the heartbreaking note he left on the disk containing 250 pages of *The Pale King*: "For LB advance?"—a sign that Wallace was still uncertain about Bonnie Nadell's encouragement to send her chapters so that she could negotiate a contract (*PK* x). Reflecting principles visible since *Broom*, Wallace was reluctant to convert his words into money too soon.

In §9, David Wallace, sounding like the frustrated axiom-seeking Day in *Infinite Jest*, tries to go back to the text's unnoticed grounding in legal disclaimer, setting up the entire novel as a liar's paradox—"if you believe one you can't believe the other, & c., & c." (*PK* 69)—or what Wallace calls in *Everything and More* a "Vicious Infinite Regress," an unhealthy circling that contrasts with ritual repetition (*EM* 49). Wallace has played before, though never so daringly, with publisher boilerplate and its implicit statements about the mimetic effects of his figurations. As in "Philosophy and the Mirror of Nature," the story this section resembles, Wallace is reacting to his drama as legal subject when he writes, "Like many Americans, I've been sued—twice, in fact, though both suits were meritless" (*PK* 73n5). Boswell documents the connections between *Girl's* legal troubles, its rewritten disclaimer, and §9[36] but omits *Infinite Jest*, where Wallace went further, and with real-world legal consequences: "Any apparent similarity [of characters] to real persons is not intended by the author and is either a coincidence or the product of your own troubled imagination," that book's disclaimer reads. None of the satirized corporations or celebrities objected, but the real Kate Gompert, who played junior tennis with Wallace, claimed defamation and brought a suit that was dismissed before going to trial.[37]

Inspiring the writing in §9 is, again, Gaddis, named as one of the sort of "immortally great fiction writer[s]" David Wallace wanted to become (*PK* 75). This section builds upon both Gaddis's entropic style and Oscar Crease's lawsuits in *A Frolic of His Own* and may even offer Wallace's response to his best friend's controversial rejection of their mutual influence. Demonstrating that he saw conjunctions between Gaddis's fiction and the Gompert case (and thus §9 as well), Wallace complains to DeLillo in 1998 of "having to get deposed for a lawsuit filed by some loon with the same name as a book-character who alleges an entire 1000-page novel was written to harm her (the EGO in people's sense of injury—I thought Gaddis's *Frolic* was kind of nasty-spirited when I read it [recently], but now I'm starting to see what he was talking about . . .)."[38] In *The Pale King's* "Foreword," Wallace, imitating Gaddis's legalisms, is also responding to Franzen's argument for a novel of "Contract" over one of "Status" in his infamous 2002 criticism of Gaddis, "Mr. Difficult": Franzen prefers "Contract" books that "sustain a sense of connectedness" and reader "pleasure," whereas "Status" works like Gaddis's, sure of their "art-historical importance," do not worry about the "average reader."[39] Wallace argues the inverse, disdaining Contract models of reading; he aligns himself again with Gaddis, who in *J R* (in words Franzen has in mind but never directly cites) writes repeatedly that "the whole God damned problem's the decline from status to contract."[40]

Among Wallace's purposes in his "Foreword" is to juxtapose controlling contracts with what David Wallace calls, in reference to the rules of memoir reading, "unspoken codes" (*PK* 75). "Code" is a word of simultaneous regimentation and mysticism that applies to much in the novel, from unspoken civic bonds that transcend the legal to code in the computer programmer's sense, retail's "Charleston code" (*PK* 393n2), and, most importantly, the "tax code"—an emblem of novelistic language itself that, "once you get to know it, embodies all the essence of [human] life: greed, politics, power, goodness, charity" (*PK* 84; brackets in the original). David Wallace's attempts to define human relationships through contract rather than code become, in the terms from Wittgenstein I quoted in chapter 1, misbegotten efforts to name language's "operations and boundaries." For David Wallace is trying to redraw the borders of a text in which readers have already become immersed, have already taken as immanence. Consider his description of the "codes and gestures" (both words with connections to ritualism) that make up the "unspoken contract" defining memoirs as "true":

> What I'm trying to do right here, within the protective range of the copyright page's disclaimer, is to override the unspoken codes and to be 100 percent overt and forthright about the present contract's terms . . . Our mutual contract [of memoir] here is based on the presumptions of (a) my veracity, and (b) your understanding that any features or semions that might appear to undercut that veracity are in fact protective legal devices, not unlike the boilerplate that accompanies sweepstakes and civil contracts, and thus are not meant to be decoded or 'read' so much as merely acquiesced to as part of the cost of doing business together, so to speak, in today's commercial climate.
>
> (*PK* 75)

From needless tics like "so to speak" to the totalizing "100 percent" and invocations of "cost" and "business" anathema to previous metafictional tropes, this is decidedly *not* the voice of the "real author" (*PK* 68). It echoes instead the "business"-minded narrator of "Westward." We hear in this overbearing voice a preference for mechanism (the computer-like sound of "semions" and "override the . . . codes") mixed with outright power plays—the prohibition on reading and decoding, the need to "acquiesce[]." Stonecipher, LaVache, J.D., and the chicken-sexer were all legalistic tyrants, even fascists; here, the tyrant is David Wallace, whose constant identification as "author" inspires questioning of the connections between authorship and authority, especially when he claims that his methods have "yielded" (in more of Wallace's strategically bad phrasing) "scenes of immense authority and realism" (*PK* 74).

As chapter 1 argued, writing contracts to govern human relationships violates Wittgenstein's maxim on (dis)agreements that is worth repeating here: "It is what human beings *say* that is true and false; and they agree in the *language* they use. That is not agreement in opinions but in form of life."[41] With that edict in mind, Wallace, quite surprisingly, undermines a well-worn and seemingly democratic trope for reading: the author-reader relationship is too enigmatic to be reduced to a business contract. At his most ambitious, in the ecstatic, quasi-religious mystery with which he treats civic bonds, Wallace sought a path from the articulated philosophy of social contract to something like an unspoken code of democracy. That would be the biggest bounty he could hope for from years of treating all the unspoken values and bonds—from weights and measures to common experiences of embodiment, illness, and waste—that each gestured toward a broad, lived agreement, toward the social contract as a form of life.

David Wallace does find peace, though, by the end of the "Foreword," which subtly transforms into a calm meditation—and comes to rest on another image of grounded value. The section's last long footnote, on David Wallace's reading of the IRS's archives, pays homage to DeLillo's *Libra*, where the historian Nicholas Branch, reading through the massive Warren Report that prefigures Wallace's metafictional tax code, calls the government analysis "the megaton novel James Joyce would have written if he'd moved to Iowa City and lived to be a hundred."[42] Wallace's echoing moment is, characteristically, oriented toward empathic acknowledgment of how much reading effort is shared by reader and writer—coworkers, always—and an implied promise of the sacred satisfaction that reading his own Joycean Warren Report can produce:

> I'm reasonably sure that I am the only living American who's actually read all these archives all the way through. I'm not sure I can explain how I did it. Mr. Chris Acquistipace, one of the GS-11 Chalk Leaders . . . and a man of no small intuition and sensitivity, proposed an analogy between the public

records surrounding the Initiative and the giant solid-gold Buddhas that flanked certain temples in ancient Khmer. These priceless statues, never guarded or secured, were safe from theft not despite but because of their value—they were too huge and heavy to move. Something about this sustained me.

(PK 86N25)

Here is the immovable base of common value that 1977 Illinois needed, an astonishing image of great weight in which Wallace shows the portable monetary value of gold giving way to the (moral) values that make up the golden Buddhas' religious significance. Recalling "Crash of '69," the image points to the commonwealth of the U.S. Treasury, where gold is stored, but David Wallace is finding metaphorical illustration here for the value not of gold but of a vast amount of paper and text—it is American sign systems and usage that have so much weight and value that they can never be stolen, hoarded, or spent. In similar phrasing, Glendenning calls the Constitution and *Federalist Papers*, two other repositories of civic value, "utterly priceless" (*PK* 135).

Nowhere else in Wallace does a footnote seem like such a "foot" for a balancing book, with the placement at the bottom of the page visually enacting the Buddhas' grounding and opposing Fogle's nihilistic foot. The peculiar name of this counter-Fogle—Chris Acquistipace, a man of "innit" "intuition"—reads as the *acqui*sition not of market goods but of peace (from the Latin *pace*), or perhaps of a pace, the measure of a single foot as it interfaces with ground. The "silence" surrounding boredom at §9's end—common ground that is also huge, "hidden by virtue of its size"—has the power to move David Wallace, creature of contract, toward unspoken code (*PK* 87).

TRANSLATING VALUES: FROM "E UNIBUS PLURAM" TO *E PLURIBUS UNUM*

The greatest of *The Pale King*'s unspoken democratic codes lies in Wallace's follow-up to the Latin *Dei Gratia*. This chapter's title, "*E Pluribus Unum*," seen on the Great Seal of the United States, reorients a Wallace essay title that has received little commentary amid much on the essay it-self: "E Unibus Pluram" comes from Michael Sorkin's writing on the par-adox of aloneness in TV watching, which Wallace summarizes, "We are the audience, megametrically many, though most often we watch alone: E Unibus Pluram" (*SFT* 23). Wallace liked the phrase; in *Infinite Jest*, Evan Ingersoll utters it (*IJ* 112). The civic ideal "From many, one" now reads as "From one, many," meaning, as Ingersoll's scene says, individuals paradoxi-cally have only their "aloneness" in common (*IJ* 112). Clear too is the new motto's connection to advertising's atomizing influence: ads of the 1970s and 1980s began proposing to help the American consumer "'stand out from the crowd,'" repressing the obvious fact that "products billed as dis-tinguishing individuals from crowds sell to huge crowds of individuals" (*SFT* 55, 56).

Surely Wallace, though, a militant grammarian, knows the inversion, in capturing this new logic, mangles the Latin: "E Unibus Pluram," simply switching the endings of the last two words, makes little sense in proper Latin, joining other awkwardly rendered Latin maxims that Wallace wrote, such as James Incandenza's E.T.A. motto about being killed but not eaten (*IJ* 81, 994n32). "From one, many" should read *Ex Uno Plures*. Solecisms are always meaningful in Wallace, and this Latin one registers the aged formula's failure to "translate" logically to postmodernity, particularly on the currency through which the Latin phrase most often enters everyday American life. Using coin to buy uniform means of supposed individua-tion, citizens may think they can effect a market-based polity of free indi-viduals. But while it sits alongside a number of monetary value, the unity-minded civic value on the coin—a vision of society as "one," the ultimate undividable good—proves not so manipulable.

Wallace has long seen the rewriting of Latin on U.S. currency as a way of undermining neoliberal views of cash as a neutral medium unaffected by what is exchanged or who profits. In "Westward," J.D. has a complex scheme in which, giving money away in exchange for word of a person's greatest fear, he surveils subsequent purchases with a silicon transmitter embedded in the bills, "what looks vaguely like a monocle over the eye that separates *Annuit* from *Coeptis* on The Great Seal" (*GCH* 283). To the right of the pyramid is the seal's obverse, an eagle holding in its beak a banner with *E Pluribus Unum*. *Annuit Coeptis* means "He nods at the undertaking," a claim of divine approval of the United States, now broken up by J.D., god of mammon and a new iteration of the Freemason conspiracy associated with the pyramid's eye. Thus do the fears that Wallace thought bonded his readers become, in the birth of the neoliberal age "Westward" documents, a way of turning a community medium into an exploitable form. Pynchon remade stamps; Wallace rewrites currency.

In *The Pale King* Wallace mediates his analysis of *E Pluribus Unum* through the invented, varyingly legible seal and motto of the IRS, parts of the text's effort to alienate us from automatic practice and teach us (from the ending of §1 forward) to "read" language anew (*PK* 6). In §14, the orientation film ends with the "incised seal and motto that flank the REC's north façade. 'Just like the nation's *E pluribus unum*, our Service's founding motto, *Alicui tamen faciendum est*, says it all—this difficult, complex task must be performed, and it is your IRS who roll up their sleeves and do it,'" yet another encounter with the clichéd signifiers of hard work (*PK* 104).[43] Examiners joke about the "failure to translate the motto" for average tax-payers, who are "presumed to know classical Latin" (*PK* 104). The narrative voice suggests that the Director of Personnel may be "testing whether the prebriefed examiners catch this error"—apparently referring to leaving the Latin untranslated (*PK* 104). But what error and nontranslation really occur here? The film's translation of the Latin *is* embellished—a strict word-for-word translation might read, "Still, someone has to do it"—and Wallace is setting up his string of different, subjective readings of the seal's statement about work. But the examiners engage in a productive misreading in a different sense: the film *does* paraphrase the IRS motto but *not* the national-unity motto—assumed to be well known but, Wallace implies, actually unknown in American civic practice. He wants both the country's and the tax agency's foundational values to remain untranslated, alien, and in a process of making. Here he thus reinvests in the tension between fleeting consciousness and "stamped" coin values discussed in chapter 5.

Despite not having Wallace's choices as to the novel's sequence (as Pietsch's preface explains [*PK* x–xi]), we can see that a game is afoot with this IRS seal. In §22 Fogle studies it at a recruiting center and gets a closer look and a new translation: a print of the seal, hanging "askew" above the recruiter's desk, shows "the mythic hero Bellerophon slaying the Chimera, as well as the Latin motto on a long unfurling banner along the bottom"; the IRS motto "essentially means '*He is the one doing a difficult, unpopular job*'" (*PK* 246). The italics that usually set off foreign phrases are intentionally given to both the Latin and its English rendition, for Wallace wants to keep the English of the civic value foreign to us as well (recall here *value* being a foreign word for Hal). Bellerophon is the IRS's "official symbol," "rather the way the bald eagle is the United States as a whole's" (*PK* 246). Bellerophon and the Chimera were also subjects inscribed on coins in ancient Greece, like many mythical figures, and Wallace works once more with "mediated myths" in contemporary settings (*CW* 41). Bellerophon's story, also a subject in Barth's *Chimera*, is told in the *Iliad*, and it speaks to *The Pale King*'s theme of chastened heroism and remaining grounded: Bellerophon is born of humans and, upon riding the Pegasus and slaying the Chimera, tries to ascend to Mount Olympus and become a god, but he falls to earth. In more of his signature groundward movement—away from "some gleaming abstract Olympian HQ" (*BI* 160)—Wallace's IRS heroes hew toward transcendence through immanence, down in their holes.

David Wallace, in §24, shows us the IRS seal in context, as part of an entrance baroquely made to look like a giant tax form, but here the seal shifts shape again, as though, like the doubloon of *Moby-Dick*, it is a metatextual sign that admits only the varied interpretations of individuals, part of a mirrored building reflecting the viewer back at himself. Like a group coming into uneasy alignment on an important sign's meaning, the reader and the diegetic viewers of the seal work toward synchrony on an object that seems (like all political representations) quite striated, rife with characteristics Wallace has given the text: "shifting p.o.v.s, structural fragmentation, willed incongruities" (*PK* 74). Enacting multivalent meaning and suggesting the mirrored IRS building admits of many views (for is the edifice another attempt to represent language itself?), David Wallace in a passing car "had to move and twist my own neck awkwardly to make out the Exam Center's various features" (*PK* 277). The associations with the unconscious that Burn senses elsewhere present themselves forcefully at the REC's entrance, in "coded signs" (another association of the IRS with codes), "complex and disorienting" shifts of appearance, and the fact that "the REC's ostensible rear was really the front" (*PK* 283)—with "rear" here connoting both a repressed anality (an association Godden and Szalay make as well ["The Bodies in the Bubble," 1302]) and the more primitive parts of the brain behind the lately evolved frontal cortex.

The seal appears twice—appropriate to a novel of doubles and incongruities—within an incredibly "stylized" "façade" (a further suggestion we should look beyond, to unconscious meanings): "It was some kind of tile or mosaic representation of a blank IRS 1978 Form 1040, both pages of it, complete in all detail" (*PK* 283). The tax form is "flanked" (further suggestions of embodiment and anality) at either end "by a large, round inset intaglio or glyph of some kind of chimerical combat and a Latin phrase, indecipherable in the right-hand side's deep shadow, which turned out to be the Service's official seal and motto" (*PK* 284). We may think we already know that the seal depicts Bellerophon's victory, but the phrasing "chimerical combat," alongside "deep shadow," seems to make Bellerophon's struggle itself into the illusion, while also further unraveling the heroism and righteousness of the IRS's hard work. David Wallace complains that he did not know about the seal when he first saw it, and we see again here the interstitial nature of almost all perception and interpretation in *The Pale King*, the suspension ("faithful to the memory of that experience itself" [*PK* 285]) in which Wallace asks us to hold the IRS's meaning. Developing this idea, David Wallace uses Latin often in the footnotes of his sections but finds the seal's Latin "indecipherable"—whether because of the light or because he learned the language later (or just phrases?) is itself indecipherable. As with the "errors" of the orientation film, the scene keeps readers in a tense relationship with the real meaning of foundational values, lest they slip into the oblivion that *E Pluribus Unum* has in the national consciousness.

BLOOD/MONEY (AND WASTE/MONEY)

In discussing Wallace's searches for new currency and value, I have referred to Freud's demonstration of the buried psychic associations between feces and money; such conjunctions are ascendant as never before in *The Pale*

King. Freud could well be describing the atavistic atmosphere this novel creates when he writes that "wherever archaic modes of thought have predominated or persist—in ancient civilizations, in myths, fairy tales and superstitions, in unconscious thinking, in dreams and in neuroses—money is brought into the most intimate relationship with dirt."[44] Let me return here to the incredible richness of §1, set on the "very old land" Freud's words almost perfectly describe. The passage's many value associations begin with the "coins of sunlight" glinting on the river in the first sentence, pointing to the elemental economy of the nitrogen cycle preceding the monetary. This is not just typical nature symbolism but nature in direct contestation of money economies. In this zone, insects, not companies, are "all business all the time" (*PK* 5). While Wouters says §1 "suggests that our technologically-driven, human-organized present has . . . superimposed itself on an eternal environment," Wallace allows us to see nature strongly asserting itself in this scene of competing economies.[45]

Unearthed as the narrative eye zooms in on the axiological ground are wholly unexpected, waste-based versions of the U.S. and IRS seals, as well as coinage. The "shapes of . . . worms [are] incised in the overturned dung and baked by the sun all day until hardened, there to stay, tiny vacant lines in rows and inset curls that do not close because head never quite touches tail" (*PK* 6). "Incised" is used multiple times to describe the IRS seal. In this opening section, which Wallace published as a separate story,[46] there is no rough-draft mistake in his use of the word twice in quick succession to link readers to the dung: "Your shoes' brand incised in the dew," a few lines before the worms, suggests a loss of dewy innocence while also hinting that it is grounded human beings—you, reader—who are the pale or stylus that make the cuts of civic seals (and must do so repeatedly, perhaps every workday, since this incision in the dew is sure to be quickly erased). The nontouching "head" and "tail" of the worm connote the two sides of a coin and, once again, contingency: flip a coin, heads or tails. But in the syncretic ritual context this cow patty also brings to mind the baked-in designs of the oracle bones of ancient China (heated until they cracked, with the cracks read for prophecy). The near head-to-tail of the worm points to the yin-yang symbol as well. These images are still not done with us: the "lines in rows" (*PK* 6) foreshadow the examiners in their desks and the tax forms they examine, telling us that accounting's abstractions, too, will be put in touch with the direct energy cycles of fertilization. So rich are the associations here that the reader is almost inevitably already "[r]ead[ing] these" in many senses before reaching that potent last sentence (*PK* 6). Rather than imitating Pynchon's or Coover's use of similar materials to repulse the reader and indict society, Wallace tones down the gross-out factor, as he did with Moltke's sculptures, hoping we will look closely at the glow of value in this waste.

Sylvanshine, a failed Emersonian at the end of §2, weakly repeats §1's ritual, "turning 360° several times and trying to merge his own awareness with the panoramic vista, which except for airport-related items was uniformly featureless and old-coin gray and so remarkably flat that it was as if the earth here had been stamped with some cosmic boot" (*PK* 26). Here again is the nuance-obliterating sign of the monetary, "old-coin gray" (no vivifying coins of sunlight here), while a distant, impersonal force, parallel to Fogle's nihilistic foot, substitutes for "your shoes' brand." This boot-stamping has no potential for instilling collective value. Sylvanshine has the "impression of being at the center of some huge and stagnant body of water": fertility, flow, and ritual cyclicality have fled with his systems' arrival (*PK* 26).

As Wallace moves throughout *The Pale King* from the level of civic doctrine to more intimate views of his characters' minds, he enforces an approach to the beauty and preciousness of art and money through the subterranean routes of the childhood traumas emblematized by waste and other abject body products. Godden and Szalay offer a riveting (if at moments dense and rigidly Marxist) reading of many similar alignments of waste, blood, and semen with money in *The Pale King*, extending a reading of Marx's doubled body of the commodity throughout the book to argue that Stecyk, Bondurant, Cusk, Drinion, and others, in their resemblance to money, comment on "the failure of financial liquidity" and on "the unstable relation between corporeality and the forms of abstraction inherent in finance capital" ("The Bodies in the Bubble," 1274, 1276). For Godden and Szalay, money, in the period of financialization that bridges *The Pale*

King to the present, is always "derivative money," money made from money rather than production, money no longer guaranteed by the state and fundamentally based in debt ("The Bodies in the Bubble," 1275). Wallace's IRS in this period is thus "best understood as a factory for debt processing," and the IRS agents are preoccupied with waste because "shit" invariably represents deficit, debt, and the "money emptied of value" they spend their days examining ("The Bodies in the Bubble," 1286, 1289). Even *The Pale King* itself becomes in their interpretation expressive of financialization's dominance, "a literary version of derivative money" ("The Bodies in the Bubble," 1275). Yet as my reading of §1's waste (unexamined by Godden and Szalay) has suggested, I find Wallace's embodied money fundamentally more hopeful, drawing on broader domains of social and psychic life and expressive of an axiological invitation to the reader to recognize a new ground for commonwealth, the living transaction of communication, and elements of infrastructure that Godden and Szalay do not countenance.

Such are the ideas that structure my reading of §16, Dean's break (which Godden and Szalay also leave unexamined). There, Wallace asks us to think of value alongside a wound, returning to the claim in "Mister Squishy" that there is madness in rare-coin collecting. Like "Mister Squishy," §16 is one of Wallace's many multitrack narratives in which an oral discourse describes one thing while a wandering mind (despite being engaged by the external talk) explores something else entirely; our mission as readers—reconciling incompatible ideas, as in Freud's unconscious—is to ferret out the connection between the two tracks. Here, an unnamed examiner tells the other of a dinner at Hank Bodnar's. The talk is of barbecued salmon and the satisfactions of food—use value—but also the hoarding of exchange value: Bodnar is "a serious coin collector," a "hobby" Dean, a Christian, perhaps invoking biblical maxims about God and mammon, finds "debased and distorted" (*PK* 126). That is a description a normative view would apply to his keen interest in the listening man's "benign cyst or growth on the inside of his wrist," which the listening man openly contemplates (*PK* 124). "Composed of what looks almost like horn or hard, outgrowthy material," the cyst "appears reddened and slightly inflamed" (*PK* 126). With Dean's Christianity in mind, the cyst raises associations with Christ's stigmata, but this is everyday martyrdom, appropriate to the empathy for low-level suffering that Wallace points to in *This Is Water*: Dean imagines the man's shirt "cuff's movement back and forth over the growth throughout the day might . . . hurt in a tiny, sickening way each time" (*PK* 127).

The connection between the cyst and coins lies in Dean's desire somehow to "hoard" the cyst against the boredom he struggles with (*PK* 126), activating the text's broad association of value with human attention. Thus does Dean demonstrate a type of living transaction, an embodied and empathic alternative to hoarding rare coins. Dean "almost envies" the person who works close to the man's cyst, for which he imagines "a career as an object of distraction and attention, something to hoard the way a crow hoards shiny useless things it happens to find, even strips of aluminum foil or little bits of a locket's broken chain" (*PK* 126). Recall that pecking crows turned up the cow-patty coins of §1; here Wallace is having Dean override a disgust mechanism to make of this cyst, like the cow waste, a shiny, beautiful object, again disturbing our sense of what counts as valuable or as abject or worthless—much as the Bodnar feast, the desireableness of which would have been obvious to ancient humans long before monetary valuation became ascendant, conflicts with exchange value's abstraction. Empathy for the wounded is the true value at stake. Wallace has in mind, too, the eagle holding the thin *E Pluribus Unum* banner in its beak. Dean is tapping into his primitive bird-nature, seen earlier when he "feels like running out into the fields . . . and running in circles and flapping his arms" (note the invocation of ritual circles) (*PK* 125).

"Inflamed" (*PK* 126) and possessing a "penumbra" (*PK* 127), the cyst is like the sun, or perhaps a coin of sunlight. In this same vein, the "horn" of the cyst is (*PK* 126), like the bird instincts on display here, part of the book's interest in humans' animal history, the "tail" that might touch the "head." This horn, in the context of value, stigmata, and a plentiful dinner, also connotes the horn of plenty, which Shell shows is associated in Arthurian legend with the Holy Grail and Christ's body.[47] Shell also notes that the communion wafer was historically "understood as the coin that is Christ."[48] The cyst, then—"something to hoard," possessed of a "career"— is quite the source of ecstatic value; it is indeed "benign," as Wallace inscribes his idiosyncratic sense of the sacred potential in everyday suffering and empathy (*PK* 124). Given this conjunction of flesh, food, and psychic disturbance, no wonder Dean asks "What do you mean?" at the mention of "get[ting] eaten alive" by mosquitoes at the barbecue, "hysteria in his voice" (*PK* 128).

Blood escaping the body and being eaten—being taken as valuable energy—is what accounts for Dean's alarm and conjoins mosquitoes and the glowing "penumbra" he sees in this cyst, an outer ring of blood welling under the skin's surface. Mythologizing bodily fluids, Wallace tropes again, as with Skip's head, on the circulation of blood (particularly blood's nourishing quality) and the circulation of unexpected forms of value. This motif also partly explains a traumatic scene of an arm's incision that, like many in *The Pale King*, seems tangential until we see Wallace's allegory of embodied value at work. Stecyk in §5 may be the sick saint, but he grows up some in §39, administering heroic first aid to his teacher, Mr. Ingle, a pale king "gray with shock" who has sliced off his thumb with the circular saw and bleeds in great spurts (*PK* 421). An ingle is a fireplace: Wallace is exploring another character who embodies the heat of the hearth and *oikos*. But Ingle's warm blood is also trumping money, in this contest of economic forms: Wallace's Ing- names—Inge (Steeply's discarded name), Ingersoll (commenter on "E Unibus Pluram"), Ingle—frequently suggest juxtaposing humans with ingots, synonymous with money but technically the blank metal discs from which coins are struck.

This scene makes the connection when classmate torturers of nerdy Stecyk ask him to fetch "an ingot of cast iron [secretly heated] red-hot with an acetylene torch" (*PK* 418). Stecyk's swift, precise saving of the blood of a living hand (like Keats's) is clearly a premonition of his tax work keeping the nation's "lifeblood" pulsing through the "body politic" (*PK* 103). Stecyk relies on the attention to protocols that will "transform[]" him into a "brilliant and able Service administrator[]" (*PK* 418). That is why the scene comments on Stecyk's value, leaving the word somewhat vague, to indicate the deep rethinking going on (for onlookers and readers): Stecyk reveals "the distinctions between one's essential character and value and people's perception of that character/value" (*PK* 419) and upsets expected "relations between coolness and actual value" (*PK* 423). To have value(s), as with Skip, is to be *un*cool. So too does Stecyk, like the examiners/writers throughout, embody what Wallace describes as "art that locates and applies CPR to those elements of what's human and magical that still live and glow despite the times' darkness" (*CW* 26). Luckily, this future accountant knows CPR, and a completed novel might have shown Stecyk finding still more alternatives to "pathological generosity," as Wallace continued wrestling with the possibility of gifts.

Wallace returns to the motif of Dean's break—placing rare coins in the manifest content and following the mind's wandering to more grotesque content—in §29, where, in a subplot that remains undeveloped, CID agents stake out "Peoria Hobby 'n' Coin," doing another extremely boring job, where conversation drifts to distant points (*PK* 350). Having associated coin collecting with moral valuelessness in "Mister Squishy," Wallace chooses a rare-coin shop and its symbolism of hoarded exchange value for an investigation of what we presume to be criminal tax fraud. This is one of several moments in which Wallace makes boredom—itself an object of repression that "living people do not speak much of" (*PK* 87)—lead to wandering conversation in which other repressed content is exposed. Moreover, following Freud's cues, a scene in which characters are ostensibly staring long and hard at money becomes a talk about waste and one's "earliest memory" (*PK* 349) of it. Such scenes are, in the leveling act of this novel, just as analytically incisive and important as the stalled-elevator discussion of Tocqueville and civic theories in §19 that has already drawn much critical attention—for political questions must be explored in embodied terms.

The coin-shop-surveillance team tells three stories in the car, all infantile and scatological narratives of "seared-in memories" (*PK* 351). The first, reprising §1's footprint of dewy innocence lost, recounts stepping in dog feces as a crisis of existential guilt, such that it is "embedded in the sole," an obvious pun on "soul" (*PK* 349). The stories move up a bodily ladder from here, with the next rung being the hands, which are "especially close to your idea of your identity of who you are" (*PK* 351–352). This storyteller, having fallen hands-first into a pile of dog waste, remembers playing the "horrible shit-monster" (*PK* 351) and chasing his friends, the kind of base horror that makes Lynch's movies so unnerving for Wallace; so too does Wallace tie back into his gothic uses of "This living hand" by underscoring how the waste-covered hands reach out, "as far out away from [the story-teller] as was humanly possible," adding "to the monster-aspect" (*PK* 352).

From the hands, finally, Wallace goes to the face, the real seat of identity, and also returns to money. The third story, Bondurant's, is of "Fat Marcus the Moneylender" (*PK* 352), his pants down, sitting on unsuspecting sleep-ers in Bradley dorm rooms as they are held down, until "Diablo the Left-Handed Surrealist" (adding to the motif of strange bites) sinks his teeth in and gets the perpetrators, including Bondurant, expelled and sent to serve in Vietnam (*PK* 355). While §1 led us to get closer to the ground and read waste without disgust, Fat Marcus is the travesty of that delicately con-structed moment, pressing down unbearably from above, like the "cosmic boot" Sylvanshine imagined. Fat Marcus does this just for kicks, not in the collection of debts, but his behavior and recurring epithet ("Fat Marcus the Moneylender") suggest a fascism and nihilism within money logic, usury specifically. David Wallace is a figure of debt, worried over repayment of his student loans after his own expulsion from school, and in a completed novel we might have seen still more attention to the Fat Marcuses of the debt system squashing American lives in the neoliberal age.[49]

FACE VALUE

Interpreting Fat Marcus leads naturally to a figure who contrasts with his, well, asshole behavior: the examiner who levitates rather than sitting on people, Shane Drinion, intense listener to Meredith Rand's suffering and an avatar of the type of extraordinary shared value *The Pale King* urges us to contemplate. For Drinion Wallace invents the job title "UTEX" or "utility examiner[]" (*PK* 460)—a traveling agent who goes where needed—to sug-gest an association with public utilities, those elements of commonwealth infrastructure evoked by the Quabbin Reservoir in chapter 3. As he listens, Drinion builds up a miraculous energy able to lift him out of his chair in defiance of physics' laws. Such power is associated with both a direct relationship to "you" the reader and a public utility: "having [Drinion's] eyes and attention on you . . . is intense, a little bit like standing near the high-voltage transformer park south of Joliet Street" (*PK* 504). Drinion resembles the flushed, heated Skip and another character associated with infrastructure, Fogle's father, who "seems to give off a slight hum when at rest" (*PK* 176). But Drinion's SD initials also point to a more abject public utility: they are a common U.S. city abbreviation for Sewer District, the waste system that annular fusion and giant catapults sought to replace in *Infinite Jest*. Drinion shifts the associations with the horrors of waste I have developed here by accepting and "process[ing]" (*PK* 452) Rand's "shit," the trauma of her mental illness beneath a cosmetic perfection. With Brint Moltke's BM a clever shorthand for bowel movement, Wallace has played before with initials and waste.

Waste is another "return" to a central handling facility, a flush that Americans wish not to think about in psychic or civic terms, making it a good site for considering dreaded taxes and what they pay for. While Drinion is the public-waste figure in the novel, Lane Dean's name suggests not just grounded priesthood but a sacred command over public road-ways and traffic, topics David Wallace considers at appropriately boring length in §24. Wallace gave his characters new names "constantly," writes Pietsch (*PK* xiii), but other REC names—the forest (*sylvan*) in Sylvanshine, the land and river valleys (*glen*) in Glendenning, the *bloom* in Blumquist, the *fish* in Fisher, the deer (*hind*) in Hindle, the *bus* in Bussy, and the *bond* (to pay for public works) in Bondurant—suggest that a finished *Pale King* might have had much to say about many different public resources, natural and infrastructural. After a novel featuring names of deletion and death (Blott, Struck, Schacht [i.e., shocked], Axford), Wallace was writing a story with glimpses, amid the paleness, of a glowing plenitude.

Given Drinion's public-works associations, it seems telling that Rand is the name of both a conservative think tank usually dedicated to private-sector solutions (to problems like waste management) and of the objectivist Ayn who inspires many of them.[50] While he appears robotic to Rand (like "an optical reader scanning a stack of cards" [*PK* 455]), Drinion represents a key synthesis in the novel's man/machine dialectic: he connotes an objective, detached but involved empathy that models not only good therapy but the reading of a stack of cards/pages we ourselves are doing. He is another example of metareading eclipsing metafiction.

In §23 an unnamed narrator has a nightmare of the two-dimensional existence tax examining might produce: in the "rows of foreshortened faces," "one or two, the most alive, looked better in an objectless way," but "many others looked blank as the faces on coins" (*PK* 255). Many examiners also see blankness in themselves or (often more horrifying) in others, including Dean's fear that Sheri is "blank and hidden" (*PK* 42), Ware's eerily "blank eyes" when playing dead (*PK* 66), and the fear of David Wallace (who wants to present himself in Keatsian terms as "the living author") that corporate legal strictures may render his memoir of Peoria "some enormous, unexplained, and unmotivated blank" (*PK* 80n16). All these instances resonate with both the blank stares of boredom (e.g., the "blank absent" look of an agent on the stakeout [*PK* 354]) and the compensatory drive to—in the Frank Bidart quotation of the epigraph—"fill" the blank tax forms that make up the examiners' work (*PK* 3).

Yet with Drinion, who excels at recognition of the other and resisting the mowing of Other Math, Wallace works against associations of a coin's blankness with coldness and distance, finding one last way to make coinage human and based in sharing rather than privation. Having begun his career with an idealized reader-analogue named LB for the British pound, Wallace ends it with an idealized SD, named for shillings and pence (thus completing the abbreviation £.s.d., for *librae, solidi, denarii*—Wallace's guide here may be Joyce's *L*eopold *B*loom and *S*tephen *D*edalus, central characters in a novel with much to teach about human expenditure). The *Pale King*'s bar scene offers multiple replies to the blank dream sequence, suggesting Drinion's listening risks an erasure of ego that holds great value in this (communicative) exchange: his face "isn't blank, but it's bland and neutral in a way that might as well be blank for all it tells you"; "his face isn't very defined or structured" (*PK* 457–458, 453). His nickname, "Mr. X" (*PK* 448), links him to the impressionable nature of the mirror-inspecting ghost Garrity, whom Dean calls "Mr. Wax." Garrity's body makes "X-shaped rotations" in repeating an inspection routine that, while deforming for him, provides so many others with unwarped mirrors in which to find a clear identity, much as tax examiners are thanklessly charged with wielding common standards to support a well-run community (*PK* 386). Moreover, Drinion's blank but "intense" face, as it stares at "you," is Wallace imagining the staring eyes of readers taking in his text (*PK* 504).

Godden and Szalay read Drinion as money as well, but by highly indirect means ("The Bodies in the Bubble," 1299) that miss some of Wallace's direct associations with the numismatic. In coin production, "blanks" refer to ingots before they are stamped with an image. Such blankness is connected, as well, with other rhetorical signs of Drinion's willingness to hold his own ego back and thus be stamped or "impressed" with Rand's story—and here, on a microlevel, is a justification of Wallace's refusal to engage with the expressive realism that dominates so much contemporary fiction. "When I was imagining it, my impression was that he'd be frightened," Drinion says of Rand's husband, before repeating the key word, "My impression is that he's frightened of you. This is just my impression" (*PK* 453). Rand, while she "usually interprets expressionlessness as inattention, the way someone's face blanks out when you're talking," comes to see that "this is not the way Drinion's expressionlessness seems" (*PK* 487). In all these suggestions of what appears on Drinion's facial coin, this expressionless animal has the potential to reinscribe *E Pluribus Unum*: he is one who, by listening, is able to unite many, a position that the numismatic DG was forced into in the hospital. As Wallace notes, the IRS is a branch of the U.S. Treasury, a fact one examiner uses to try to hide his taxman identity from potential dates (*PK* 107). In all the ways I have documented, Wallace hopes we see the IRS as a site for an embodied minting of coinage, that job of another branch of Treasury. Being such a coin and embodying such value, though, Drinion demonstrates, is processual and of the communicative moment— more than a mint that stamps a metal blank once to inscribe value, the attentive self is a sewer plant or power plant, always working, always open.

VALUING DETAILS AND MAKING UP MORAL VALUES

In all these parallels between humans and money, Wallace is telling us what we mean by the clichéd expression "pay attention"—what kind of currency

attention *is*, how it can serve as our means of "sensuous trade." In the terms
I have developed, we should note how attention as a subject refashions Wallace's central metaphor for returning work to its basic meaning: the weight-
lifting pulley. Consider David Cusk, the compulsively sweaty accountant:
as he seeks release from self-obsession through what is essentially an inner
thermostat to regulate his temperature, he replies to all those solipsistic
hoarders of energy who have preceded him, from Lenore Sr. (who lacks such
an inner thermostat) to Fogle (who keeps an external one on high). Cusk
knows that paying attention to things outside him, things other than his
fear of an "attack," can stem his sweat's flow but also that such outward attention is heavy lifting: "Paying attention to anything but the fear was like
hoisting something heavy with a pulley and rope—you could do it, but it
took effort, and you got tired, and the minute you slipped you were back
paying attention to the last thing you wanted to" (*PK* 320). Cusk is learning here the concluding lesson of *This Is Water*: the willed choice to pay attention is the "job of a lifetime, and it commences—now," taking up every
minute of every day, the call to real American work (*TW* 136).

The simple machines Cusk's metaphors suggest contrast with the type
of technology the systems camp favors, just as Gately's "Gratitude battery"
contrasted with the addict's "motherboard" understanding of self. Cusk's
metaphor thus turns a treasured Wallace motif—the physical illustration
of metaphysical processes through manual labor—toward the social world.
The Pale King was to be Wallace's most social novel yet, in which themes
of commonwealth and shared values that I have often had to extract from
hiding places in earlier work had become manifest. An extensive group discussion of democratic political philosophy takes place in a stalled elevator
(*PK* §19)—also readable as a failed act of weight lifting by pulleys—and
here too Wallace retunes Lenore's, Laurel's, and others' individual explorations of how to rise, making the quest for fulfilling ontology an even
more difficult collective venture. But such widespread rising seems at least
possible: a short section (§10) suggests that the outward ripples of hundreds of small acts of inner pulleys like Cusk's are key to understanding the
special "physics and imperatives of cause" in bureaucracy, a form of workplace organization that Wallace—searching for charismatics at the IRS and

again working against the grain of *Gravity's Rainbow*—wants not only to understand but even lionize, defending it from being defined as a "parasite" larger than the body from which it feeds. Instead, bureaucracy may be "a large and intricately branching system of jointed rods, pulleys, gears, and levers radiating out from a central operator such that tiny movements of that operator's finger are transmitted through that system to become the gross kinetic changes . . . at the periphery" (*PK* 88). The Pynchon school would surely see this operator as cause for paranoia, but the postparanoid Wallace instead explores authority figures like Glendenning—who, a figure of "balance" (*PK* 436) rather than a "tyrant" or "fake friend" (*PK* 435), treats his employees "both as human beings and as parts of a larger mechanism" he governs (*PK* 436).[51] There is definitely hope for a democratic, humane bureaucracy pulling the levers of society in *The Pale King*.

Attention has the potential to become, like sincerity for an earlier moment in Wallace studies, a concept that closes off arguments rather than opening his images up to more minute scrutiny. Let me conclude this chapter, then, by suggesting that we can open up attention in *The Pale King*, as both ethical imperative and antidote for depressed solipsism, by regarding it as synonymous with the act of comparative valuation, the mental act I have been tracking since Karrier in chapter 2. Boswell gives a brief glimpse of one of these themes: "Whereas for a tax examiner in the new, machine-driven, for-profit IRS . . . value will be fiduciary—that is, which data will yield the most tax revenue?—for Wallace's readers, . . . value will be the human element that the data have obliterated and replaced" ("Author Here," 35). Relevance, as Boswell shows, is the relevant category here, and that word provides a means of expanding his claim and another way into the rivalry between Fogle and David Wallace.

When he returns in §24, David Wallace expresses his disdain for the other narrator by nicknaming him "Irrelevant" Chris Fogle (*PK* 261). A submerged definition for Fogle's nickname may lie in a 2004 review of Edwin Williamson's *Borges: A Life*, which Wallace criticizes for reducing mystical complexities to autobiographical exposition. That Borges's model of the self's multiple consciousnesses is important to *The Pale King* is apparent from its epigraph, which adds another layer to the bifurcation of the writer in "Borges and I" by quoting not Borges's story with that title but Frank Bidart's prose poem about it (*PK* 3). Wallace ends his book review, "Even if Williamson's [biographical readings] are true, the stories so completely transcend their motive cause that the biographical facts become, in the deepest and most literal way, irrelevant" (*BF* 294). In transmuting his own autobiography through David Wallace and calling the emotional life-story of Fogle "Irrelevant," Wallace allows for the kind of daring reading Williamson avoids, leaving open peripheral paths by which the reader might identify and thus transcending the strictures authors of autobiographical fictions or straight memoirs unconsciously impose. In this way Wallace imitates Borges, who "collapses reader and writer into a new kind of aesthetic agent, one who makes stories out of stories, one for whom reading is essentially—consciously—a creative act" (*BF* 293–294).[52]

Inviting the reader into that act, David Wallace dilates on Fogle's nickname in a claim about the "value" of details:

> What logorrheic colleagues like Fogle failed to understand is that there are vastly different kinds of truth, some of which are incompatible with one another. Example: A 100 percent accurate, comprehensive list of the exact size and shape of every blade of grass in my front lawn is 'true,' but it is not a truth that anyone will have any interest in. What renders a truth meaningful, worthwhile, & c. is its relevance, which in turn requires extraordinary discernment and sensitivity to context, questions of value, and overall point—otherwise we might as well all just be computers downloading raw data to one another.
>
> (*PK* 261)

As always, talk about value must turn groundward: this axiological passage compares truths about grass, effectively pointing to *The Pale King* itself, which catalogs grass types in its first sentence: "shattercane, lamb's-quarter, cutgrass," and so forth—perhaps not a "comprehensive" list but long enough (especially when added to, for example, Sylvanshine's sections) to indicate where the novel's sympathies lie on the question of how many details to include (*PK* 5). Indeed, as with his remarks on the "true" in terms of contracts and codes in his first appearance, we are led here to read against the insistent David Wallace, who seems (ironically, given his own verbosity) to believe in, if not minimalism, at least the danger of word inflation. As Wallace knows, a reader will probably have found Fogle's narration well wrought (and Wallace was pleased enough with it to consider publishing it as a novella [Max, *Every Love Story*, 294]).[53] That anticipated reader must define an aesthetic value against the "author's" here, though. Likewise, by remarking on "discernment" and "sensitivity," David Wallace, while he thinks he is describing his own job, activates a reader's awareness of her involvement.

Wallace chooses those words—"discernment" and "sensitivity"—because they are used to describe both aesthetic and moral judgments and values. Taking a cue from the continual deferral of a definition of value in "Deciderization," we should draw lines from David Wallace's information theories to more conventionally mimetic scenes of moral values in action, such as Dean's moment with Sheri. As he worries over what to say to her, the abstraction of "values" seems to assume for him a solidity they previously lacked: faced with the abortion decision, Dean feels "some terrible weakness or lack of values," as though they are "a muscle he just did not have" (*PK* 42). With the fallen tree dominating the scene, Dean is trying to figure out what can root solid values—and where his own shoe tree might lie.

In a final instance of metareading, Wallace transfers his discourse on value and relevance to the consumer context. Mentioning a progressive sales tax, an IRS trainer's metaphor describes a method of consumer computation that might have saved the civic values of Fogle's father.

> There you are at the market while your items are being tallied. There's an individual price for each item, obviously. . . . At checkout, the cashier enters the price of each grocery, adds them up, appends relevant sales taxes—not progressive, this is a current example—and arrives at a total, which you then pay. The point—which has more information, the total amount or the calculation of ten individual items . . . The obvious answer is that the set of all the individual prices has much more information than the single number

that's the total. It's just that most of the information is irrelevant. If you paid for each item individually, that would be one thing. But you don't. The individual information of the individual price has value only in the context of the total; what the cashier is really doing is discarding information. What you arrive at the cash register with is a whole lot of information, which the cashier runs through a procedure in order to arrive at the one piece of information that's valuable—the total, plus tax.

(PK 343–334)

Wallace drew this grocery passage, changing the wording only slightly, from Nørretranders' *The User Illusion*, where it serves as a general illustration of information sorting.[54] But imported into *The Pale King* the metaphor serves as a meditation on an archetypal commercial transaction that Wallace once again wants us to compare to the "living" one of art, ideally beyond the marketplace but never, Wallace knew, wholly separated from its mechanics. The reader is the cashier, making her way through a range of "individual items" (read: the multifarious stories of *The Pale King*). The reader is, like this cashier, working toward "the one piece of information that's valuable—the total, plus tax." Wider discourse communities and critical schools are acknowledged: "Different groups and teams within groups are given slightly different criteria that help inform what to look for" (PK 342). But all focus on the total, which becomes a symbol for a calming view that can combat "Total Noise" as well as for the universal meanings and experiences Wallace so often sought: "the individual price" (read: individual person) "has value only in the context of the total." This total, like the "B" for base in Fogle's equation, ought not to be subdivided into "individual items."

How thoroughly unpostmodern all this is, even as it employs "postmodern techniques"! There are parallels here, in the invitation to see calculation as discarding of information, to the stochastic math of *Brief Interviews*: while a computer keeps many shifting variables under control, human minds must find stopping points at which they reduce complexity to the binary choice of the balance scale. In Dean's abortion choice, that binarism, a Kierkegaardian either/or, arises in the bracing (and, again, quite solid) image for his hypocrisy: "two great and terrible armies within himself, opposed and facing each other, silent," remaining "motionless" and "uncomprehending" of each other "for all human time." Being halved is a "hell" throughout Wallace, yet this fraction, expressive of an essential humanity, seems his moral matrix's bulwark against forms of (in)decision that lack vividness and urgency (*PK* 43).

As Wallace worked for so many years on his final novel, the question occurred to him of just how great his fiction's "total" had to be. Having struggled for so long to produce another novel, would he really have to write five thousand pages and "then winnow it by 90%," as he suggested in a 2006 letter to Franzen (Max, *Every Love Story*, 289)? Even as he spun off its constituent parts into stories over his last decade, Wallace was convinced that his narrative had indeed to be a "long thing" (*PK* v), the phrase Boswell uses to unite three disparate novels in an edited essay collection. This was something other than the tortured Flaubertian artist searching again and again, over years, for *le mot juste*: since Wallace knew he in fact preselected all the details in a novel, thereby essentially making them relevant, including only a minimal amount might disempower the reader, make her a passive spectator. To bond truly with his reader he had to make her share in the imperative Pietsch plucks from the margins of the *Pale King* manuscripts: "Cut by 50% in next draft" (*PK* xiii). Our common ground, Wallace's twenty-first-century turn on Whitman suggests, is less the lyrically described grass than it is the cutting-room floor.

CONCLUSION

IN LINE FOR THE CASH
REGISTER WITH WALLACE

"THERE YOU are at the market while your items are being tallied" (*PK* 343). To conclude, I leave Wallace there, where he has in a certain sense been his entire career, waiting for value to resolve itself into something other than the price tag on a commodity. His work is often quite Beckettian, but there is no blasted landscape, no Godot—one waits instead for reconciliation at the cash register. From the voice of Mindy saying "Total: seventeen-fifty" (*B* 380), to the Avis counter in "Westward" with a credit transaction stalled, from the notes on pennies for *Infinite Jest* and their sadistically generous cashier, to the supermarket queue of *This Is Water* and the atomized Illinoisans of *The Pale King* willing to wait in multiple lines rather than pay a bit more sales tax, Wallace places his characters often on the frustrating verge of purchases that seem more existential than incidental, more hidden opportunities for innate growth than external accumulation. He updates the Sartrean trope of endless tarrying in hell by moving it to the marketplace (with stops at the diving-board ladder and Tavis's waiting room). In the cash register he sees the modern form of a device that would have been, in the ancient agora he has often hearkened back to, a balance scale, weighing goods and ensuring fair trades. In a long footnote the last novel even zooms in on grocery-store price tags to suggest an allegory for much of Wallace's writing and its exploration of the difference between words and numbers: the letters (language) of the "Charleston code" tell the IRS-trained reader what the retailer paid for it and thus help reconcile the item's value with the stated numerical price (*PK* 393n2).

Wallace's supermarket scenes also respond to *White Noise*, perhaps particularly on his mind at Kenyon, since the novel appeared when he was a college senior. Wondering often what ancient mysteries of death the supermarket holds, *White Noise* ends in a "slowly moving line" at the checkout, "where we wait together . . . our carts stocked with brightly colored goods."[1] But while he shares DeLillo's sense of a spiritual hunger going unmet ("Everything we need that is not food or love is here in the tabloid racks" [*White Noise*, 326]), Wallace shifts the focus of DeLillo's paradigmatic 1980s postmodern scenes away from the goods and their luster. Neither is Wallace exceedingly interested in commodities' production, the class structure that leads to them, and all the elements of the Marxist critique underlying so much of U.S. postmodernism. His bounty is different.

In addition to being suitably boring, his checkout line has the advantage of being emptied of moral content: the clerk at the till totaling the sale is neither an industrialist nor the advertiser who carries, inside the project of "selling" the goods, an entire ideology. Taking the checkout line as a default mechanism of the culture, Wallace had a clear and original space in which to create for his reader a hidden realm not of capitalist oppression but of thwarted affect, of potential living transactions of real communication. The pennies passage for *Infinite Jest* that I quoted in chapter 3 ends, "Can you remember the last time a whole day went by without your buying something? No matter how small. Something. Is this a bit weird?"[2] With passages like the one in "Octet" on a "weird" "*price*" for the self in interaction with another, Wallace strove to insert into the mindless, everyday functioning of the market the uncanny, attention-arresting materials of the human, from Don's graceful coin to the waste-based currency of *The Pale King*. There was conscious strategy in the distrust his oeuvre evinces for monetary forms of value but also, it seems, a sincere insecurity, an obsessive anxiety: in anecdotes that seem powerful in light of all the preceding analysis, his sister says that for some portion of adulthood he would not use

ATMs,[3] and Max describes Wallace's girlfriend, when he was twenty-three, "help[ing] him to take the money he routinely kept in his sock drawer and open a bank account with it."[4] Wallace once analyzed his compulsive cleanliness by creating "hygiene anxiety research" (*B* 120), but an intricate value-anxiety theory, equally concerned with porousness, was an ongoing construction in his career, reflecting a culture often on the financialized brink, from 1929 to 2008.

By redescribing the cash register, Wallace made a counterinvestment in a low-level "market" free of neoliberal financial vagary, where Lenore's grounding work-for-food equation was unimpeded and the Other Math of adding oneself to another could more readily assert itself. Revising the scene of endless consumer choice into one of what to "*choose* to pay attention to," Wallace transformed computerized accounting into face-to-face encounters between persons who need sustenance and value not from products but each other, from sharing personal accounts (*TW* 54). They discover in the long line of his Dantean "consumer-hell" that, in paying with attention rather than despairing over the wait to pay with money, they can access the energy underlying all of Wallace's explorations of commonwealth infrastructure: they tap into the "sacred," "on fire with the same force that lit the stars—compassion, love, the subsurface unity of all things" (*TW* 93), an allusion to the other end of Dante's cosmology, *Paradiso*, as Hubert Dreyfus and Sean Kelly show.[5] Whitman's iconic "Crossing Brooklyn Ferry" seems another reference point. The possibility of such ecstatic or charismatic transfers of value I have documented throughout: the heat of physical touch, the communal effects of insurance, the plenitude of the gift, farmland, and even a coworker's cyst. But these are, admittedly, exceptions: what rules instead is an unfulfilled desire for products, fetishes, and privative possession.

Every value-earning adult has to figure his taxes (or sign and take responsibility for the amounts, if an accountant is hired). At the grocery store checkout *everyone* is instinctually an accountant, using their math to get good value on purchases that become energy with some immediacy. In such contexts, Wallace could play the clear-headed, witty high-school math teacher—our "Dr. Goris"—whom he clearly relishes ventriloquizing in *Everything and More* (23n10). Grocery-store math maintained the "interesting context" that college math had "stripped away" from a problem like Zeno's dichotomy: "you don't walk away bathed in relief at the resolution to the paradox" when you are shown the abstract solution, Wallace complains (*CW* 123). Relief, resolution, and paradox are terms suited to the catharsis of art, and in a sense his preoccupation with fictions of value, balance, and numerical characters emerges from the college notebooks he describes to McCaffery, with their "gnarly attempted solutions" to logical proofs: hoping to pass on the sublime "click" of a suddenly clear proof to his readers, Wallace created incongruous, gnarly aesthetic structures in which unexpected solutions might present themselves, outside of modern realism's well-worn epiphany mechanism (*CW* 35). He remained confident that logical positivism's cold project could be made warm and affective if value were allowed to bleed across the fact/value divide—bleeding that led him to compare human value transfers to the circulation of blood, that everyday sacred fire rising to the surface and reddening the skin.

As he embraces moral precision but diverges from utilitarianism, as he advocates prescriptivism but recognizes the problems with enacting it, and as he wonders what allows various weights-and-measures experts to calibrate the pound and the dollar, Wallace sees that the only viable kind of postmodern moralism is ultimately what he defines in "Authority and American Usage" as a technocratic authority. This is the sort of authority a competent human cashier or accountant embodies, if we take him as a symbol of the adjudication of moral transactions always occurring in human life and language. The grammarian Bryan Garner in his dictionary, Wallace concludes, "casts himself as an authority not in an *autocratic* sense but in a *technocratic* sense." The technocrat "is not only a thoroughly modern and palatable image of authority but also immune to the charges of elitism/ classism that have hobbled traditional Prescriptivism" (*CL* 122). Garner's work is distinguished by "passionate devotion, reason and accountability," "experience," "exhaustive and tech-savvy research," "an even and judicious temperament," and "the sort of humble integrity" that not only makes him "likable but transmits the kind of reverence for English that good jurists have for the law, both of which are bigger and more important than any one person" (*CL* 123–124). This portrait will sound, to the long-term reader of Wallace, like a description of his *own* voice and thorough research, for it is intended to be that. In Garner's "passionate devotion" there is an echo, too, of the call for "morally passionate, passionately moral" fiction in the mold of Dostoevsky. Among the professionals whom we do not label "elite" when they prescribe a course of action, Wallace includes doctors, lawyers, and those who tell us "how we should do our taxes" (*CL* 122). Here lies a real-life version of what Fogle, describing the tax teacher, is surprised to find: an "authority relation" that, while "not a 'democratic' or equal one," still "could have value for both sides, both people in the relation" (*PK* 229). There *are* worthy, democratic moral authorities, as Wallace has been telling us since at least "E Unibus Pluram," and the real move against political cynicism in a neoliberal age is to believe that they can lead effective governmental organizations, even huge and bureaucratic ones. Wallace the New Deal liberal could not see it otherwise.

Unlike "E Unibus Pluram," "Authority and American Usage" names no literary predecessors to rebel against, but the high postmodernists' minds would reel, Wallace knows, at the idea of advocating technocrats, much less calling their authority democratic. While his devotion to a punned-upon value leads Wallace to find great hope in the service of the moral by the technical mind, Pynchon, Coover, Burroughs, and DeLillo would almost certainly see technology as the primary referent for the "techno-" in "technocrat." Wallace, by contrast, seems to see in that prefix the possibility, in postmodernity, of the ancient Greek virtue of *techne*, which he defines in his Tracy Austin essay as "that state in which . . . mastery of craft facilitate[s] a communion with the gods themselves," a sublime version of the rewarding work I have examined throughout (*CL* 150).

In less momentous terms, across Wallace's texts, the technician—kin of the technocrat but with a different sort of authority—is simply a trustworthy and grounding figure, one who lets us see how intricate work leads to the culture's products. Franzen says aptly of the journalism that Wallace "did his best work when he was able to find a technician—a cameraman following John McCain, a board operator on a radio show—who was thrilled to meet somebody genuinely interested in the arcana of his job."[6] These are people, as Wallace says of a producer in "Host," with "all-business competence and technical savvy" (*CL* 340). This tic of his journalism, perhaps born of a reluctance to interview the center of attention (as in the Lynch article), was connected to a larger philosophy: remaining peripheral could valorize the worker's perspective and follow up on *Infinite Jest*'s theory of figurants, showing us how much of our mediated reality is framed and staged. The writer was fundamentally a technician too: Wallace's admiration of Tom Clancy thrillers (Max, *Every Love Story*, 198) seems explainable if we think of Clancy as a good board-op, getting a thousand details right. And through his technicians, technocrats, bureaucrats, and mechanisms like the cash register, Wallace hoped to build up gradually a description of contemporary life showing readers that the romantic template of the moral artist as a "solitary, heroic figure wrestling with his own soul"—as he described it to Michael Silverblatt in 2006—could no longer be affirmed. Moral authority was now possible for fiction and essays only if they proved they had worked through some of the many calculations of the information age—proved they had gone to school in the boring balancing of books, wedding whatever objectivity was available in postmodernity to an empathic set of personal standards. In a time of Total Noise, these are the voices that need hearing.

WRITING THE UNWRITTEN WALLACE

Wallace's work teaches us at every turn to be its co-creators, and so even as I have looked throughout to Lethem, Wayne, Smith, and others, perhaps the greatest example of Wallace's legacy is Wallace himself—or his many dedicated readers, imagining the books he did not live to write. Over many pages I have resisted the urge, which occurs to anyone writing about him since September 2008, to consider his suicide as a text itself to be read or as the personal telos he was evoking in narratives like "Good Old Neon."[7] But eschewing readings of his work as an extended suicide note does not eliminate the aching sense of literature lost—the desire to speculate about what *The Pale King* would have become, as well as what fictions and essays might have followed it, had Wallace won this battle (and future battles) with mental illness. To identify writers who dialogue with his work is admittedly to seek surrogates for the books we wish we could look forward to from him—which is not to reinscribe the singular "genius" model Wallace rejected at every turn but to see what in his work was, if not prophetic in the sense De-Lillo is often credited with being, still tuned to tremors occurring beneath the surface of the culture. The demise of videophony can teach us about the strange discomforts of Skype, and we can and should ask how well Wallace's TV-centric understanding of media culture will hold up in the age of smartphones, Web 2.0, and children kept quiet in restaurants with tablet computers. But throughout I have shown him responding as well to the big movements of political economy—productivity anxieties, NAFTA, the Asian currency crisis, and more—and we would expect a finished *Pale King* and other hypothetical works to have given insights into, say, the 2013 scandal of the IRS targeting conservative nonprofits or the huge impact of the Tea Party and tax resistance on U.S. electoral politics. Likewise, David Wallace's claim in *The Pale King* that his authorial "persona" is "mainly a pro-forma statutory construct," "like a corporation," would have set Wallace up for moral opposition to the U.S. Supreme Court's 2010 *Citizens United* decision, which defines corporations as people and—in an equation everything in Wallace and this book argues vehemently against—money as speech (*PK* 68).

In the weeks before he committed suicide, Wallace cancelled plans to attend the Democratic National Convention to profile Barack Obama for *GQ* (Max, *Every Love Story*, 299). What might Wallace's account of the candidate have looked like? Universal health insurance would almost certainly have figured. But how would Wallace have positioned single-payer versus the private-insurer-friendly model that has prevailed with Obamacare? On September 12, 2008, when Wallace hanged himself, the federal government had taken over Fannie Mae and Freddie Mac four days earlier, and Lehman Brothers would file for bankruptcy four days later, one in a string of bank failures in the ensuing months. While his suffering and death are no national allegory, it does seem uncanny that, just as Wallace left the world with his critique of value unfinished, his society began to undergo one of the greatest crises in the meaning and stability of value it has ever endured. Moreover, some of the attractiveness of Wallace's difficult works to an Occupy generation should be attributed to his understanding of the dire emotional consequences of a cultural environment in which value has been emptied out and financialization made ascendant, a world in which the most plentiful riches ever somehow produce dissatisfaction and perceived scarcity, not to mention unconscionable class stratification. Has Bernie Sanders's presidential candidacy marked a resurgence of New Deal values for a new generation of liberalism? Wallace might have shown us the answer.

With his canonization increasingly secure, where will the legacy of Wallace take literature, in the United States and among his many disciples around the globe? Certainly away from irony and toward earnestness and sincerity, areas critics will continue to use his bold claims to define. He is likely to figure in the future of American literary studies as an example of fiction writing turned essentially inward, away from the transnational and the global, for even when he attends obliquely to the forces leading up to 9/11, as Konstantinou argues, Wallace proves exemplary of a "postmodern parochialism," sequestered in middle America.[8] Yet as I have shown here, he always sought the symmetries between impoverished inner economies and the world with which they were symbiotic. By resolving on value as his major subject he tied the processes of metaphysical and moral development to the fluctuating fates of global currencies and prices. The language of sincerity was just one aspect of his quest to find true coinage in which the relationships of a moral society could be transacted. To let values remain unresolved and attention unfortified was to take the human coin and flip it into the air, waiting for a fall beyond our control, whether into unnourishing aesthetics or civic dissolution. Grounding in the axiomatic was possible, Wallace showed, but only as a collective venture of readers, who might build from silent synchrony to conversations that acknowledge the agreements on which the very possibility of those conversations is based. A balance of mouth and ears, head and heart, upper and lower, must rule. None of this work is easy, it is all heavy lifting, and to do it we will need, as he once wished his audience, way more than luck.

NOTES

INTRODUCTION. A LIVING TRANSACTION: VALUE, GROUND, AND BALANCING BOOKS

1. Mary Poovey demonstrates the importance of the balance book to modern episte-mology, locating in double-entry bookkeeping "a prototype of the modern fact." *History of the Modern Fact* (Chicago: University of Chicago Press, 1998), 11. Wal-lace's resurrection of the image is one example of his break with certain postmod-ern methodologies—this introduction notes several other examples.

2. Ludwig Wittgenstein, *Philosophical Investigations: The English Text of the Third Edition*, trans. G. E. M. Anscombe (Englewood Cliffs, N.J.: Prentice Hall, 1958), §107.

3. Pankaj Mishra, "The Postmodern Moralist," review of *Consider the Lobster*, by Da-vid Foster Wallace, *New York Times*, March 12, 2006.

4. David Foster Wallace, "Le Conversazioni 2006," YouTube video, 1:17, posted by "Dazzle Communication," May 26, 2007, https://www.youtube.com/watch?v=MsziSppMUS4.

5. Adam Kelly, "David Foster Wallace and the New Sincerity in American Fiction," in *Consider David Foster Wallace: Critical Essays*, ed. David Hering (Los Angeles: Sideshow Media Group, 2010), 133.

6. Stephen J. Burn, "'Webs of Nerves Pulsing and Firing': *Infinite Jest* and the Sci-ence of Mind," in *A Companion to David Foster Wallace Studies*, ed. Marshall Bos-well and Stephen J. Burn (New York: Palgrave Macmillan, 2013), 71; Stephen J.

Burn, "Toward a General Theory of Vision in Wallace's Fiction," *English Studies* 95, no. 1 (2014): 88.

7. These ambitious efforts at defining a new cultural phase, led by Wallace's break with Barth, Pynchon, and others, bear similarity to a few more focused claims: Marshall Boswell on Wallace's relentless efforts to reach out to readers and, bucking poststructuralist theories of all-encompassing textuality, "create a space outside his work where direct, 'single-entendre' principles can breathe and live" (*Understanding David Foster Wallace* [2003; repr., Columbia: University of South Carolina Press, 2009], 207); and Allard den Dulk's reading of Wallace's anti-irony through the lens of Kierkegaard ("Boredom, Irony, and Anxiety: Wallace and the Kierkegaardian View of the Self," in *David Foster Wallace and "The Long Thing": New Essays on the Novels*, ed. Marshall Boswell [New York: Bloomsbury, 2014], 43–60). Lee Konstantinou has expanded his postirony argument in *Cool Characters: Irony and American Fiction* (Cambridge, Mass.: Harvard University Press, 2016), which appeared while this book was in press.

8. D. T. Max, *Every Love Story Is a Ghost Story: A Life of David Foster Wallace* (New York: Viking, 2012), 255.

9. Mary K. Holland, explaining the phase after postmodernism as a reinvigoration of humanism, swims against the anti-irony tide, arguing that *Infinite Jest* is unable "to overcome the irony of which it is conscious" because of its "failure to recognize and address the cultural drive toward narcissism that fuels and is fueled by that irony." *Succeeding Postmodernism: Language and Humanism in Contemporary American Literature* (New York: Bloomsbury, 2013), 57. David P. Rando argues for "collaps[ing] . . . the sentiment-irony opposition" too many Wallace critics have accepted. "David Foster Wallace and Lovelessness," *Twentieth Century Literature* 59, no. 4 (2013): 576.

10. Bruce Weber, "Wallace, Influential Writer, Dies at 46," *New York Times*, September 14, 2008.

11. Stephen J. Burn, review of *Consider David Foster Wallace: Critical Essays*, by David Hering, *Modernism/modernity* 18, no. 2 (2011): 467.

12. Lucas Thompson, "Programming Literary Influence: David Foster Wallace's 'B.I. #59,'" *Texas Studies in Literature and Language* 56, no. 2 (2014): 116.

13. Tore Rye Andersen, "Pay Attention! David Foster Wallace and His Real Enemies," *English Studies* 95, no. 1 (2014): 8.

14. Richard Godden and Michael Szalay, "The Bodies in the Bubble: David Foster Wallace's *The Pale King*," *Textual Practice* 28, no. 7 (2014): 1311.

15. Stephen Shapiro, "From Capitalist to Communist Abstraction: *The Pale King's* Cultural Fix," *Textual Practice* 28, no. 7 (2014): 1258. A scholar of the fictions undergirding finance, Leigh Claire La Berge concludes her 2014 study of 1980s

U.S. banking narratives by suggesting that it could be extended to "our own present" through *The Pale King*'s evocation of "the relationship between financial and literary form." *Scandals and Abstraction: Financial Fiction of the Long 1980s* (New York: Oxford University Press, 2015), 193. Two books with contributions to the discussion of Wallace and neoliberalism were published while this book was in press: Clare Hayes-Brady, *The Unspeakable Failures of David Foster Wallace: Language, Identity, and Resistance* (New York: Bloomsbury, 2016); and Mitchum Huehls, *After Critique: Twenty-First-Century Fiction in a Neoliberal Age* (New York: Oxford University Press, 2016).

16. Maria Bustillos, "Inside David Foster Wallace's Private Self-Help Library," *The Awl*, April 5, 2011, http://www.theawl.com/2011/04/inside-david-foster-wallaces -private-self-help-library.

17. Wallace took a film seminar with Cavell while enrolled in Harvard's philosophy Ph.D. program in 1989. David Lipsky and David Foster Wallace, *Although of Course You End Up Becoming Yourself: A Road Trip with David Foster Wallace* (New York: Broadway Books, 2010), 236. Wallace did not finish that fall semester, checking himself into McLean Hospital over suicidal thoughts. Max, *Every Love Story*, 143.

18. Stanley Cavell, *Disowning Knowledge in Six Plays of Shakespeare* (1987; repr., Cambridge: Cambridge University Press, 2003), 187.

19. While he limits his readings of it to *The Broom of the System*, Boswell (*Understanding*, 50, 54) was first to note Wallace's yin-yang symbolism.

20. David Foster Wallace, "The Jester Holds Court: An Interview with David Foster Wallace," by Valerie Stivers, *Stim.com* 1, no. 1 (May 15, 1996), http://www.stim .com/Stim-x/0596May/Verbal/dfwmain.html.

21. Brian McHale, *Postmodernist Fiction* (1987; repr., New York: Routledge, 2003), 3–25.

22. The idea that literature ideally communicated a culture's values arises early in his archive: in a paper from his first year at Amherst on the French medieval *Tristan and Iseult* (a legend that stayed with him: see its use in *Infinite Jest* [105] and "Tri-Stan: I Sold Sissee Nar Ecko"), Wallace states that the narrative "was a product of the same age as The Song of Roland . . . and thus should reflect . . . Romanesque 'values.'" Wallace discusses "the value of honor" and the differences between "internalizing" plots and an "'externalizing' story in which values and priorities came out in actions and deeds." His *Song of Roland* paper calls the poem a "tapestry, in which different values and priorities and personalities blend and clash as the characters . . . conflict," "reveal[ing] a lot about what the society depicted in the [*Song*] really values." This sounds like the tapestry a big novel weaves as well. For a writer who would incorporate mock student essays into his work, a literary

ethic of "very old traditional human verities" seems to be brewing here, tellingly not in contemporary writing but in centuries-old narratives. Other freshman-year writing stayed with him, too: another paper in the archive is on Prince Hal in *Henry IV, Part One*. See David Foster Wallace, "Amherst College: essays and exams, 1980–1981, undated," box 31, folder 6, David Foster Wallace Papers, Harry Ransom Center, Austin.

23. David Foster Wallace, "*The Gift: Comments and Reviews*," blurb, http://www.lewis hyde.com/publications/the-gift/comments-reviews/.

24. Paul Giles, "All Swallowed Up: David Foster Wallace and American Literature," in *The Legacy of David Foster Wallace*, ed. Samuel Cohen and Lee Konstantinou (Iowa City: University of Iowa Press, 2012), 4.

25. Conley Wouters, "'What Am I, a Machine?': Humans and Information in *The Pale King*," in *David Foster Wallace and "The Long Thing": New Essays on the Novels*, ed. Marshall Boswell (New York: Bloomsbury, 2014), 175.

26. Nathan Ballantyne and Justin Tosi, "David Foster Wallace and the Good Life," in *Freedom and the Self: Essays on the Philosophy of David Foster Wallace*, ed. Steven M. Cahn and Maureen Eckert (New York: Columbia University Press, 2015), 138.

27. Jean-François Lyotard, *The Postmodern Condition: A Report on Knowledge*, trans. Geoff Bennington and Brian Massumi (Minneapolis: University of Minnesota Press, 1984), 30.

28. John Barth, *The Floating Opera and The End of the Road* (1967; repr., New York: Anchor, 1988), 295.

29. Michael LeMahieu, *Fictions of Fact and Value: The Erasure of Logical Positivism in American Literature, 1940–1975* (New York: Oxford University Press, 2013), 5.

30. Charles B. Harris, "David Foster Wallace: 'That Distinctive Singular Stamp of Himself,'" *Critique* 51, no. 2 (2010): 174.

31. Robert C. Jones, "The Lobster Considered," in *Gesturing Toward Reality: David Foster Wallace and Philosophy*, ed. Robert K. Bolger and Scott Korb (New York: Bloomsbury, 2014), 183. For Wallace's opposition to Benthamite "*value hedonism*," see Ballantyne and Tosi, "David Foster Wallace and the Good Life," 141.

32. John D. Caputo, *The Mystical Element in Heidegger's Thought* (New York: Fordham University Press, 1986), 53.

33. Wallace underlines his effort to reach back deeper into philosophical tradition than many postmodern novelists and critics had done when he complains to his former teacher about students who "pretend to 'understand' Derrida without having read Heidegger and Husserl" (unpublished letter, quoted in Boswell and Burn, preface to *A Companion to David Foster Wallace Studies*, ed. Boswell and Burn, ix). For other Wallace references to Heidegger, see "Greatly Exaggerated" (*SFT* 140–141), the McCaffery interview (*CW* 45), "The Empty Plenum" (*BF* 63,

66), and the use of "dasein" to refer to the infantile self in the cruise-ship essay (*SFT* 317).

34. "All That" was left at Wallace's death as a possible part of the *Pale King* manuscript, but the editor Michael Pietsch opted to publish the story separately. "Everything and More: *The Pale King* by David Foster Wallace," panel discussion with Laura Miller, Michael Pietsch, Rick Moody, and Sandro Veronesi, PEN World Voices Festival video, April 26, 2011, http://www.pen.org/video /everything-and-more-pale-king-david-foster-wallace.

35. "The world is all that is the case" is the common translation of Wittgenstein's "Die Welt ist alles, was der Fall ist." Ludwig Wittgenstein, *Tractatus Logico-Philosophicus*, trans. D. F. Pears and B. F. McGuinness, rev. ed. (New York: Routledge, 1974), §1.

36. Paul Giles, "Sentimental Posthumanism: David Foster Wallace," *Twentieth Century Literature* 53, no. 3 (Fall 2007): 327–344.

37. Mary K. Holland, "Mediated Immediacy in *Brief Interviews with Hideous Men*," in *A Companion to David Foster Wallace Studies*, ed. Boswell and Burn, 111.

38. Jean-Joseph Goux, *Symbolic Economies: After Marx and Freud*, trans. Jennifer Curtiss Gage (Ithaca, N.Y.: Cornell University Press, 1990), 4.

39. Marc Shell, *Money, Language, and Thought: Literary and Philosophical Economies from the Medieval to the Modern Era* (Berkeley: University of California Press, 1982), 4.

40. "David Foster Wallace (*Brief Interviews with Hideous Men*)," interview by Michael Silverblatt, *Bookworm*, KCRW radio broadcast, August 3, 2000.

41. John Keats, *The Complete Poems*, ed. John Barnard, 3rd ed. (New York: Penguin, 1988), 459.

42. Katherine Rowe, *Dead Hands: Fictions of Agency, Renaissance to Modern* (Stanford, Calif.: Stanford University Press, 1999), 122.

43. David Graeber, *Debt: The First 5,000 Years* (Brooklyn, N.Y.: Melville House, 2011), 27.

44. Tom LeClair placed Wallace in the systems tradition, along with Richard Powers and William Vollmann, in one of the earliest articles on *Infinite Jest*. "The Prodigious Fiction of Richard Powers, William Vollmann, and David Foster Wallace," *Critique: Studies in Contemporary Fiction* 38, no. 1 (1996): 12–37. Wallace studied intently LeClair's book *In the Loop: Don DeLillo and the Systems Novel* (Urbana: University of Illinois Press, 1987), underlining numerous passages, including LeClair's summarizing assertion, "The pretense and power of large closed systems, their fake and therefore punishing 'certitudes,' are the constant foci of [DeLillo's] satire" (27). This line seems to me a solid assessment of the ambition of Wallace's own systems novels. The Ransom Center call number for Wallace's copy of *In the Loop* is PS3554.E4425 Z75 1987 DFW.

45. Thomas Tracey, elucidating David's relationship to the work of his father, the moral philosopher James D. Wallace, makes a similar point in citing the father's "Aristotelian view that ethics, the study of the good life, is a practical subject." "The Formative Years: David Foster Wallace's Philosophical Influences and *The Broom of the System*," in *Gesturing Toward Reality*, ed. Bolger and Korb, 163. Stephen J. Burn also links Wallace's moral project to his father's work. *David Foster Wallace's* Infinite Jest: *A Reader's Guide*, 2nd ed. (New York: Continuum, 2012), 5–6.

46. Alissa G. Karl, "Things Break Apart: James Kelman, Ali Smith, and the Neoliberal Novel," in *Reading Capitalist Realism*, ed. Alison Shonkwiler and Leigh Claire La Berge (Iowa City: University of Iowa Press, 2014), 65–66.

47. Adam Kirsch, "The Importance of Being Earnest," *New Republic* (July 28, 2011).

48. Andrew Hoberek, "Adultery, Crisis, Contract," in *Reading Capitalist Realism*, ed. Shonkwiler and La Berge, 55, 42.

49. Mark McGurl, "The Institution of Nothing: David Foster Wallace in the Program," *boundary 2* 41, no. 3 (2014): 50.

50. Michael Hardt and Antonio Negri, *Commonwealth* (Cambridge, Mass.: Harvard University Press, 2009), ix.

51. Lee Konstantinou, "No Bull: David Foster Wallace and Postironic Belief," in *The Legacy of David Foster Wallace*, ed. Cohen and Konstantinou, 105. In analysis drawing too sharp a divide between the political and ethical, McGurl is more harsh (and implicitly Foucauldian): in Wallace's work, "political questions" and "motives for political contestation" are "obediently dissolved into a series of ethical choices" ("The Institution of Nothing," 36).

52. Frederic Jameson, *Postmodernism, or, the Cultural Logic of Late Capitalism* (Durham, N.C.: Duke University Press, 1991), 49.

53. Shonkwiler and La Berge, "Introduction: A Theory of Capitalist Realism," in *Reading Capitalist Realism*, ed. Shonkwiler and La Berge, 3. For readings of Wallace making shrewd use of Jameson, see Connie Luther, "David Foster Wallace: Westward with Fredric Jameson," in *Consider David Foster Wallace: Critical Essays*, ed. Hering, 49–61; and, especially, Paul Quinn, "'Location's Location': Placing David Foster Wallace," in *A Companion to David Foster Wallace Studies*, ed. Boswell and Burn, 87–106.

54. Giles, "All Swallowed Up"; Josh Roiland, "Getting Away from It All: The Literary Journalism of David Foster Wallace and Nietzsche's Concept of Oblivion," in *The Legacy of David Foster Wallace*, ed. Cohen and Konstantinou, 25–52.

55. Andrew Hoberek, "The Novel After David Foster Wallace," in *A Companion to David Foster Wallace Studies*, ed. Boswell and Burn, 222; Burn, *David Foster Wallace's* Infinite Jest, 5; Kelly, "David Foster Wallace and the New Sincerity in American Fiction," 145.

56. Chuck Klosterman, "The Jonathan Franzen Award for Jaw-Dropping Literary Genius Goes to . . . Jonathan Franzen," *GQ* (December 2010). *The Corrections* (2001) was, according to Chad Harbach, "David Foster Wallace!" review of *Oblivion*, by David Foster Wallace, *n + 1* (Summer 2004), so influenced by *Infinite Jest* as to qualify as Wallace's own "next big novel."

57. Burn, *David Foster Wallace's* Infinite Jest, 4; and Toon Staes, "Rewriting the Author: A Narrative Approach to Empathy in *Infinite Jest* and *The Pale King*," *Studies in the Novel* 44, no. 4 (2012): 410, also connect Leonard to Wallace.

58. James Wood, *The Irresponsible Self: On Laughter and the Novel* (New York: Picador, 2005), 178.

59. Harbach, "David Foster Wallace!," calls *Infinite Jest* "the central American novel of the past thirty years."

1. COME TO WORK: CAPITALIST FANTASIES AND THE QUEST FOR BALANCE IN *THE BROOM OF THE SYSTEM*

1. D. T. Max, *Every Love Story Is a Ghost Story: A Life of David Foster Wallace* (New York: Viking, 2012), 187. Max's biography reports on Wallace's teenage job as a tennis instructor (9) and brief stints as a bus driver (while on leave from Amherst [23]), baker (in Tucson [112]), and health-club attendant (138), as well as long periods of poverty in which he scrambled for rent. But given his deep interest in work (particularly the humiliating kind) as philosophical subject, outside of teaching Wallace had little personal experience with bill-paying pursuits with which to compare writing—perhaps another reason for his distance from Marx and Marxism.

2. David Foster Wallace, "The Planet Trillaphon as It Stands in Relation to the Bad Thing," *Amherst Review* 7 (1984): 32. https://quomodocumque.files.wordpress.com/2008/09/wallace-amherst_review-the_planet.pdf.

3. Ronald K. Shelp, "Business Forum: Can Services Survive Without Manufacturing?; Giving the Service Economy a Bum Rap," *New York Times*, May 17, 1987.

4. Thomas Tracey regards both Wallace's Amherst philosophical training and his father's moral philosophy as the key substrates for the Deweyan pragmatism of *Broom*. "The Formative Years: David Foster Wallace's Philosophical Influences and *The Broom of the System*," in *Gesturing Toward Reality: David Foster Wallace and Philosophy*, ed. Robert K. Bolger and Scott Korb (New York: Bloomsbury, 2014), 157–176.

5. Shonkwiler and La Berge relate Harvey's claim in *The Postmodern Condition* to Giovanni Arrighi's similar sense (which I turn to in chapter 4) that accumulation changed fundamentally with financialization in the 1970s. In an elaboration of

Hardt and Negri, Shonkwiler and La Berge also argue that capital "deepen[s] and intensif[ies] already existing sites of capitalist valorization instead of expanding imperially through cartographic space." Alison Shonkwiler and Leigh Claire La Berge, "Introduction: A Theory of Capitalist Realism," in *Reading Capitalist Realism*, ed. Alison Shonkwiler and Leigh Claire La Berge (Iowa City: University of Iowa Press, 2014), 4.

6. Ronald Reagan, "Inaugural Address: January 20, 1981," in *Actor, Ideologue, Politician: The Public Speeches of Ronald Reagan*, ed. Davis W. Houck and Amos Kiewe (Westport, Conn.: Greenwood, 1993), 177.

7. D. T. Max, "In the D. F. W. Archives: An Unfinished Story About the Internet," *New Yorker* (October 11, 2012); Max, *Every Love Story*, 259.

8. Fredric Jameson, *Postmodernism, or, the Cultural Logic of Late Capitalism* (Durham, N.C.: Duke University Press, 1991), 314.

9. Patrick O'Donnell, "Almost a Novel: *The Broom of the System*," in *A Companion to David Foster Wallace Studies*, ed. Marshall Boswell and Stephen J. Burn (New York: Palgrave Macmillan, 2013), 12.

10. Max Weber, *The Protestant Ethic and the "Spirit" of Capitalism and Other Writings* (New York: Penguin, 2002), 77–78.

11. Thomas Pynchon, *Gravity's Rainbow* (1973; repr., New York: Penguin, 2000), 565; of the considerable scholarship on Pynchon's critique of the Puritan legacy, see the benchmarks of John M. Krafft ("'And How Far-Fallen': Puritan Themes in *Gravity's Rainbow*," *Critique* 18, no. 3 [1977]: 55–73) and Christopher Leise ("'Presto Change-o! Tyrone Slothrop's English Again!' Puritan Conversion, Imperfect Assurance, and the Salvific Sloth in *Gravity's Rainbow*," *Pynchon Notes* 56–57 [2009]: 127–143).

12. McHale calls *Broom* "abjectly imitative" of *The Crying of Lot 49*, though he gives Wallace "the benefit of the doubt" on his "implausible" claim not to have read *Lot 49* before writing *Broom* ("*The Pale King*, Or, The White Visitation," in *A Companion to David Foster Wallace Studies*, ed. Boswell and Burn, 194). But D. T. Max recounts a scene of Wallace first encountering *Lot 49* his junior year at Amherst ("The Unfinished: David Foster Wallace's Struggle to Surpass *Infinite Jest*," *New Yorker*, March 9, 2009).

13. Thomas Pynchon, *V.* (1963; repr., New York: Harper Perennial, 2005), 506.

14. *Oxford English Dictionary Online*, "cattle."

15. John Winthrop, "A Model of Christian Charity," in *The Journal of John Winthrop, 1630–1649*, ed. James Savage, Richard S. Dunn, and Laetitia Yaendle (Cambridge, Mass.: Harvard University Press, 1996), 10.

16. Reagan, "Farewell Address to the Nation: January 11, 1989," in *Actor, Ideologue, Politician*, ed. Houck and Kiewe, 327.

17. Don DeLillo, *White Noise* (New York: Penguin, 1985), 4.

18. In his paperback copy (from 1984) of *The Gift: Imagination and the Erotic Life of Property* (Hyde's original title), Wallace marked the copyright-page explanation of the cover image, the anonymous mid-nineteenth-century painting *Basket of Apples*, product of "the Shaker Community in Hancock, Massachusetts." That explanation continues, "The Shakers believed that they received their arts as gifts from the spiritual world. Persons who strove to become receptive of songs, dances, paintings, and so forth were said to be 'laboring for a gift,' and the works that they created circulated as gifts within the community" (and without an artist's name attached). While we cannot know when Wallace first read *The Gift* or marked that page, it is possible he did so before finishing *Broom*. The Ransom Center call number for Wallace's copy of *The Gift* is GN449.6.H93 1983b DFW.

19. John D. Caputo, *Demythologizing Heidegger* (Bloomington: Indiana University Press, 1993), 61.

20. Ludwig Wittgenstein, *Philosophical Investigations: The English Text of the Third Edition*, trans. G. E. M. Anscombe (Englewood Cliffs, N.J.: Prentice Hall, 1958), §241.

21. For readings of immanence in *Broom*, *Infinite Jest*, and "The Suffering Channel," by way of a comparison of Deleuze and Guattari's reading of Kafka with Wallace's, see my "'We've Been Inside What We Wanted All Along': David Foster Wallace's Immanent Structures," forthcoming in *Literature and the Encounter with Immanence*, ed. Brynnar Swenson (Amsterdam: Brill, 2016).

22. Marshall Boswell, *Understanding David Foster Wallace* (2003; repr., Columbia: University of South Carolina Press, 2009), 50. The tremendous meaning I show Wallace packing into initials throughout may derive from his love of *The Names*, the novel about an initials-driven cult that Wallace told DeLillo was both his introduction to the oeuvre and still among his three "favorites." Wallace to DeLillo, June 11, 1992, David Foster Wallace Papers, Harry Ransom Center, Austin.

23. *Broom*, a novel of "*almost*s," is rife with intentional formal gaps and incompletenesses, as Patrick O'Donnell argues ("Almost a Novel," 9–10), and there is meaning in the ways it stops short of symmetry. The book pays much attention to the sun and sundial images, and its plot, seemingly set up to extend much further in time, stops, amid apocalyptic events, on September 11. That date must have looked far different to Wallace in retrospect, but in context it is notably about twelve days shy of the traditional beginning of Libra's reign in the skies, September 23. As written, *Broom*'s 1990 plot runs eighteen days, from August 25, Rick's first journal date (*B* 32), to the night of September 11 (*B* 458). See chapters 3 and 6 for more on the importance of the dates Wallace's novels *fail* to reach.

24. This quotation is from Stanley Cavell, *This New Yet Unapproachable America: Lectures After Emerson After Wittgenstein* (1989; repr., Chicago: University of Chicago Press, 2013), 34.

25. Daniel 2:40–43 (New International Version).

26. Lance Olsen, "Termite Art, or Wallace's Wittgenstein," *Review of Contemporary Fiction* 13, no. 2 (1993): 201.

27. Wallace is also fond of neurological allegories, as Steven J. Burn notes of the Incandenza brothers ("'Webs of Nerves Pulsing and Firing': *Infinite Jest* and the Science of Mind," in *A Companion to David Foster Wallace Studies*, ed. Boswell and Burn, 68–69), and *Broom* suggests that the two sides of the brain need to be connected and brought into balance: Lenore's initial L makes her the left brain, commonly associated with rationality, while Rick (R) is the emotion-driven right brain.

28. David Lipsky and David Foster Wallace, *Although of Course You End Up Becoming Yourself: A Road Trip with David Foster Wallace* (New York: Broadway Books, 2010), 35.

29. O'Donnell ("Almost a Novel," 8) also places *Broom* in this genre. For a differing reading of *Broom*'s Wittgenstein/Derrida "conversation," claiming that *Broom* "asks what it means to write a novel in the wake of poststructuralism" and identifying Lenore and Bombardini with opposed forms of eschatology, see Bradley J. Fest, "'Then Out of the Rubble': David Foster Wallace's Early Fiction," in *David Foster Wallace and "The Long Thing": New Essays on the Novels*, ed. Marshall Boswell (New York: Bloomsbury, 2014), 87.

30. Giving a sense of how prominent Derrida was in Wallace's education, Max notes that at Amherst he "reveled in . . . 'The Double Session' and 'Plato's Pharmacy'" (*Every Love Story*, 38) and took a class focused on *Of Grammatology* at Arizona (56).

31. Sean Sayers, "Creative Activity and Alienation in Hegel and Marx," *Historical Materialism* 11, no. 1 (2003): 110.

32. This is the rendering of the first heading under "Observing Reason" by A. V. Miller in his highly regarded and much-used translation of Hegel's *Phenomenology*, first published in 1976.

33. Karl Marx, *Capital: A Critique of Political Economy*, trans. Ben Fowkes (New York: Vintage, 1977), 1:163.

34. This reference to medieval Scotland may be autobiographical for Wallace, who, according to Lipsky's interview, had a poster from the movie *Braveheart* (1995), an epic account of William Wallace, in his house. "That's my fucking *ancestor*," he says. "I think I saw that four times. Just to hear guys in kilts going, 'Wal-lace, Wal-lace!' . . . I *wept*, as he cried 'Freedom'" (*Although of Course*, 168). William

Wallace was "never cowardly . . . I couldn't *recognize* myself in him at all, you know?" (169). In *Broom*, such emotional attachment to ancestral example registers as an implicit yearning for a different economic order.

35. Dale Jacquette, *Wittgenstein's Thought in Transition* (West Lafayette, Ind.: Purdue University Press, 1998), 259.

36. Dale Peterson, an Amherst professor and Wallace's thesis advisor on *Broom*, notes in "The Start of Everything" that Wallace, in a 1983–1984 modern American literature course, submitted a "brilliant, spirited literary defense of [Frank] Norris' odd coupling of bizarre incident and semi-serious philosophizing" (a good description of *Broom*'s own mode!) when Peterson, after assigning it, disparaged *McTeague* in class. Rick refracts the murderous ending of *McTeague* when (having told his fable of a theoretical dentist) he handcuffs himself to Lenore in the G.O.D. In Norris, McTeague kills Trina, takes her lottery winnings, and escapes to Death Valley, where he is hunted by a vengeful Marcus, who handcuffs himself to McTeague before being killed by him. Rick—trying mimetically to make himself a literary character in a way opposed to the Lenorean peripheralization described earlier—sees himself as the ineffectual Marcus, rival to the masculine McTeague (i.e., Lang). Reading *Broom* in dialogue with literary naturalism underscores just how much brute male sexuality and possessiveness appear in the novel (and remain operative for Wallace up through *The Pale King*'s horrifying portrayal, in language indebted to the contemporary American naturalist Cormac McCarthy, of the multiple rape victim Toni Ware).

2. NEW DEALS: [THE] DEPRESSION AND DEVALUATION IN THE EARLY STORIES

1. Eric Gelman, "Does 1987 Equal 1929?" *New York Times*, October 20, 1987.

2. Paul Crosthwaite, "The Accident of Finance," in *Virilio Now: Current Perspectives in Virilio Studies*, ed. John Armitage (Cambridge: Polity, 2011), 178.

3. D. T. Max, *Every Love Story Is a Ghost Story: A Life of David Foster Wallace* (New York: Viking, 2012), 25; Max noted Wallace's childhood ambition to be a congressman in a presentation I attended at the David Foster Wallace Conference, Illinois State University, May 23, 2014.

4. In the preface to *Signifying Rappers* (1990; repr., New York: Back Bay, 2013), Mark Costello describes their co-composition of the book after Wallace became stalled: Costello wrote out replies to their conversations and "left [them] on his desk. It was Dave's idea to incorporate my responses and turn the essay into a coauthored

book" (xvi). The pair also cowrote a humor magazine at Amherst (Max, *Every Love Story*, 26). Costello describes Wallace as "intensely competitive everywhere" (*Signifying Rappers*, xiv)—why not in inventive analysis of New Deal economics as well?

5. Marshall Boswell, *Understanding David Foster Wallace* (2003; repr., Columbia: University of South Carolina Press, 2009), 65; Kasia Boddy, "A Fiction of Response: *Girl with Curious Hair* in Context," in *A Companion to David Foster Wallace Studies*, ed. Marshall Boswell and Stephen J. Burn (New York: Palgrave Macmillan, 2013), 23–24.

6. Jason Puskar, *Accident Society: Fiction, Collectivity, and the Production of Chance* (Stanford, Calif.: Stanford University Press, 2012), 14, 3.

7. Michael Szalay, *New Deal Modernism: American Literature and the Invention of the Welfare State* (Durham, N.C.: Duke University Press, 2000), 3.

8. David Foster Wallace, "Crash of '69," *Between C & D* (Winter 1989): 3. Hereafter cited parenthetically in the text.

9. In correspondence in his archive Wallace continues to refer to the story with the original title even after its publication in 1989, in the small journal *Between C & D* (which produced stories on a dot-matrix printer and placed them in plastic bags). The story was never collected, but Wallace did include it in original plans for both *Girl with Curious Hair* and *Brief Interviews with Hideous Men*, his correspondence with Nadell shows. Wallace to Nadell, September 20, 1987, and August 29, 1996, Bonnie Nadell Collection of David Foster Wallace, Harry Ransom Center, Austin.

10. The reference is to the famous aphorism (§125) of Nietzsche's *The Gay Science*: "God is dead. God remains dead. And we have killed him."

11. "It is no exaggeration to insist that going off the gold standard was the economic equivalent of the death of God," Mark C. Taylor argues in *Confidence Games: Money and Markets in a World Without Redemption* (Chicago: University of Chicago Press, 2004). "God functions in religious systems like gold functions in economic systems: God and gold are believed to be the firm foundations that provide a secure anchor for religious, moral, and economic values. When this foundation disappears, meaning and value become unmoored" (6).

12. Many became suspicious of Reagan's mental failures as early as his noticeable faltering in a 1984 debate. Wallace also took Reagan's mental health as a subject in the unfinished story "Wickedness," "from around 2000," which Max discovered among the *Pale King* materials: in it a tabloid reporter tries to "shoot pictures of Ronald Reagan [at a nursing home] beset by Alzheimer's." D. T. Max, "In the D.F.W. Archives: An Unfinished Story About the Internet," *New Yorker*, October 11, 2012.

13. The historical vertigo, proleptic of the confusions caused by Subsidized Time, also makes "Crash" a small-scale prototype for *Infinite Jest*.

14. David Foster Wallace, interview by Charlie Rose, televised on PBS, March 27, 1997.

15. One of the typescript drafts of "Crash" has Wallace's address on the title page as the University of Arizona English department. Wallace, "'Crash of '62,' typescripts, undated," box 27, folder 2, David Foster Wallace Papers, Harry Ransom Center, Austin.

16. Examples of such conventional notation can be found in Wallace's essay on fatalism: see page 191, for instance, in which he presents a series of rules that all use "= 1" to signify "is true." David Foster Wallace, *Fate, Time, and Language: An Essay on Free Will*, ed. Steven M. Cahn and Maureen Eckert (New York: Columbia University Press, 2011), 191. For technical explications of Wallace's attempted refutation of Richard Taylor's fatalism, see Steven M. Cahn and Maureen Eckert, eds., *Freedom and the Self: Essays on the Philosophy of David Foster Wallace* (New York: Columbia University Press, 2015), esp. William Hasker's chapter, "David Foster Wallace and the Fallacies of 'Fatalism,'" 16–25.

17. Wallace, interview by Charlie Rose.

18. Gen. 1:10 (New International Version).

19. Max (*Every Love Story*, 74) sees an homage to William Gass, Boddy ("A Fiction of Response," 25) makes connections to Cormac McCarthy, and Boswell (*Understanding*, 85–86) hears echoes of Faulkner and Joyce. But "John Billy" is also born of Steinbeck's great Dust Bowl novel, *The Grapes of Wrath*. Another source is De-Lillo's *The Names* and Owen Brademas's memories of his Depression-era Pentecostal congregation praying for rain and speaking in tongues, a scene played on in Tap's ending novel.

20. Martin Heidegger, *Being and Time*, trans. Joan Stambaugh (Albany: SUNY Press, 2010), 131–132.

21. In explaining "Westward" Wallace mentions his interest in "mediated myths" (*CW* 41). His understanding of myth in general is deeply indebted to Joseph Campbell, whose *Myths to Live By* he annotated. On the page of promotional material at the front of Wallace's edition is this sentence: "'The latest incarnation of Oedipus, the continued romance of Beauty and The Beast, stands this afternoon on the corner of 42nd Street and Fifth Avenue, waiting for the traffic light to change.'—Joseph Campbell." "This is my pt," Wallace writes in the margin. The Ransom Center call number for Wallace's copy of *Myths to Live By* is BL315.C27 1984 DFW.

22. Saul Bellow, *Herzog* (1964; repr., New York: Penguin, 2003), 75. Wallace says in a 1993 interview, "I like Bellow" (*CW* 20) and notably leaves him off a satiric list of U.S. fiction's "Great Male Narcissists" (*CL* 51).

23. J.D.'s perspective is connected to Stanley Cavell's "Being Odd, Getting Even (Descartes, Emerson, Poe)" in *In Quest of the Ordinary: Lines of Skepticism and Romanticism* (Chicago: University of Chicago Press, 1988), which seems to contain a seed of Wallace's critique of skepticism: in 1988, making notes for "The Empty Plenum," he underlines Cavell's remark, "I take skepticism not as the moral of a cautious science laboring to bring light into a superstitious, fanatical world, but as the recoil of a demonic reason, irrationally thinking to dominate the earth" (138). The Ransom Center call number for Wallace's copy of *In Quest of the Ordinary* is PS217.P45 C38 1988 DFW.

24. In less heightened terms, this "Reunion" reimagines the wildly successful Coca-Cola 1971 "Hilltop" commercial, featuring a multicultural cast holding Coke bottles and singing "I'd Like to Buy the World a Coke." Wallace refers to the iconic final crane shot when J.D. notes, regarding the LordAloft helicopter's arrival, "The camera's shots will be panoramic" (*GCH* 309).

25. For attention to Wallace and gender, see Clare Hayes-Brady, "'. . .': Language, Gender, and Modes of Power in the Work of David Foster Wallace," in *A Companion to David Foster Wallace Studies*, ed. Boswell and Burn, 131–150; and Kathleen Fitzpatrick, *The Anxiety of Obsolescence: The American Novel in the Age of Television* (Nashville, Tenn.: Vanderbilt University Press, 2006), 201–234. A notable exception to the general neglect of race in Wallace is Tara Morrisey and Lucas Thompson's interpretation of *Signifying Rappers* ("'The Rare White at the Window': A Reappraisal of Mark Costello and David Foster Wallace's *Signifying Rappers*," *Journal of American Studies* 49, no. 1 [2015]: 77–97) in relation to whiteness studies and Wallace's "commit[ment] to recording both subtle and unsubtle forms of racism" in *Infinite Jest* and other fiction (95). But this essay does not examine "Lyndon."

26. "Lyndon" refers subliminally to Coover when, just before the climactic homoerotic scene, a stirring passage about geography and nationhood asks the reader to "go as far west as the limit of the country lets you—Bodega Bay, not Whittier, California" (*GCH* 117), a town best known for being Nixon's birthplace and frequently mentioned in Coover's book. By contrast, Boswell (*Understanding*, 82) sees Wallace building on Coover's "curiously sympathetic portrayal" of Nixon by remaking Johnson.

27. Michael LeMahieu, *Fictions of Fact and Value: The Erasure of Logical Positivism in American Literature, 1940–1975* (New York: Oxford University Press, 2013), 12.

28. Mark McGurl, *The Program Era: Postwar Fiction and the Rise of Creative Writing* (Cambridge, Mass.: Harvard University Press, 2009), 417n76.

29. But Mark McGurl has, in a more recent article ("The Institution of Nothing: David Foster Wallace in the Program," *boundary 2* 41, no. 3 [2014]: 27–54), argued that Wallace is "a Program Man if ever there was one" (32), a writer whose work "marks a further step toward the thorough *normalization* of the emergent conditions of institutionalization" (31).

30. Boddy, though, employing some of *The Program Era*'s terms, claims that "Westward" shows "the creative writing class" to be "not a refuge from, but rather an example of, corporate capitalism" ("A Fiction of Response," 29).

31. Lewis Hyde, *The Gift: Creativity and the Artist in the Modern World*, 25th anniversary ed. (New York: Vintage, 2007), 4, 9, 12.

32. The impact of rising consumer debt among young American adults in the 1980s is another dimension of Wallace's economic allegory—and another sign of his prescience for the long-term effects of neoliberal principles.

33. David Graeber, *Debt: The First 5,000 Years* (Brooklyn, N.Y.: Melville House, 2011), 172.

34. I refer here again to A. V. Miller's well-known translation of Hegel's *Phenomenology of Spirit* (London: Oxford University Press, 1976), which renders *"Herrschaft und Knechtschaft"* in chapter 3 as "Lordship and Bondage."

3. *DEI GRATIA*: WORK ETHIC, GRACE, AND GIVING IN *INFINITE JEST*

1. Unpublished letter, quoted in Marshall Boswell, preface to *David Foster Wallace and "The Long Thing": New Essays on the Novels*, ed. Marshall Boswell (New York: Palgrave Macmillan, 2014), vii.

2. D. T. Max, *Every Love Story Is a Ghost Story: A Life of David Foster Wallace* (New York: Viking, 2012), 141.

3. Elizabeth Freudenthal, "Anti-Interiority: Compulsiveness, Objectification, and Identity in *Infinite Jest*," *New Literary History* 41, no. 1 (Winter 2010): 191.

4. Stephen J. Burn, *David Foster Wallace's* Infinite Jest: *A Reader's Guide*, 2nd ed. (New York: Continuum, 2012), 61–62.

5. Lawrence Buell, *The Dream of the Great American Novel* (Cambridge, Mass.: Harvard University Press, 2014).

6. "David Foster Wallace (*Infinite Jest*)," interview by Michael Silverblatt, *Bookworm*, KCRW radio broadcast, April 11, 1996.

7. Joseph Conte, *Design and Debris: A Chaotics of Postmodern American Fiction* (Tuscaloosa: University of Alabama Press, 2002), 29.

8. Thomas Pynchon, "Nearer, My Couch, to Thee," *New York Times Book Review*, June 6, 1993.

9. Luc Herman and Steven C. Weisenburger, Gravity's Rainbow, *Domination, and Freedom* (Athens: University of Georgia Press, 2013), 112.

10. Thomas Pynchon, *Gravity's Rainbow* (1973; repr., New York: Penguin, 2000), 179–180.

11. John Lingan, "William Gaddis, the Last Protestant," *Quarterly Conversation* 14 (2009).

12. William Gaddis, *The Rush for Second Place: Essays and Occasional Writings* (New York: Penguin, 2002), 46. Gaddis quotes from Ernst Troeltsch's *The Social Teaching of the Christian Churches*, trans. Olive Wyon (Louisville, Ky.: Westminster John Knox, 1992), 2:645.

13. William Gaddis, *J R* (1975; repr., New York: Penguin, 1993), 477.

14. For analysis of *J R* and other Gaddis works on the subject of Puritanism and the Protestant ethic, see Steven Moore, *William Gaddis* (New York: Twayne, 1989), 70–73. Brian McHale ("*The Pale King*, Or, The White Visitation," in *Companion*, ed. Boswell and Burn, 209n9) notes that in unpublished letters Wallace reveals he did not "read Gaddis until relatively late" in his career (McHale's source is Burn, who is preparing the letters for publication). But I use Gaddis as a guide to *Infinite Jest* in part because of Moore's description of an early typescript Wallace (his colleague at Illinois State) shared with him in 1993. Moore spots a few Gaddis allusions, mentions their "similar tastes in fiction (we both revere William Gaddis, for example)," and notes that Wallace taught *J R* "at ISU during this time" ("The First Draft Version of *Infinite Jest*," *The Howling Fantods*, September 20, 2008). On Wallace's reading of Gaddis's *A Frolic of His Own*, see chapter 5.

15. Along these same lines, A.F.R. members' paraplegic states, as caused by "*Le Jeu du Prochain Train*," are Wallace's attempts to vivify the process by which sadists are made (*IJ* 1058n304). For a treatment of the A.F.R. and other bodies in the more realistic terms of disability law, see Emily Russell, *Reading Embodied Citizenship: Disability, Narrative, and the Body Politic* (New Brunswick, N.J.: Rutgers University Press, 2011), 170–197.

16. Conley Wouters also recognizes that *Infinite Jest*'s characters "constantly and necessarily struggle to identify the most fundamental signs of their own interior selfhood, of proof that they exist." "'What Am I, a Machine?': Humans and Information in *The Pale King*," in *David Foster Wallace and "The Long Thing": New Essays on the Novels*, ed. Marshall Boswell (New York: Bloomsbury, 2014), 169.

17. David Lipsky and David Foster Wallace, *Although of Course You End Up Becoming Yourself: A Road Trip with David Foster Wallace* (New York: Broadway Books, 2010), 68.

18. Timothy Richard Aubry, *Reading as Therapy: What Contemporary Fiction Does for Middle-Class Americans* (Iowa City: University of Iowa Press, 2011), 104.

19. Mary K. Holland, "'The Art's Heart's Purpose': Braving the Narcissistic Loop of David Foster Wallace's *Infinite Jest*," *Critique: Studies in Contemporary Fiction* 47, no. 3 (2006): 221–223.

20. Michael Hardt and Antonio Negri, *Commonwealth* (Cambridge, Mass.: Harvard University Press, 2009), 30.

21. Mark Bresnan, "The Work of Play in David Foster Wallace's *Infinite Jest*," *Critique* 50, no. 1 (2008): 53, 58, 61.

22. Wallace is again exploring Depression-era lives: his (paternal) grandfather was a dentist, and, he says, "there was a lot more dental trivia in the first draft of the book." "The Jester Holds Court: An Interview with David Foster Wallace," by Valerie Stivers, *stim.com* 1, no. 1 (May 15, 1996), http://www.stim.com/Stim-x/0596May/Verbal/dfwmain.html.

23. Paul Quinn, "'Location's Location': Placing David Foster Wallace," in *Companion*, ed. Boswell and Burn, 91; Heather Houser, "*Infinite Jest*'s Environmental Case for Disgust," in *The Legacy of David Foster Wallace*, ed. Samuel Cohen and Lee Konstantinou (Iowa City: University of Iowa Press, 2012), 139.

24. Bradley J. Fest, "The Inverted Nuke in the Garden: Anti-Eschatology and Archival Emergence in David Foster Wallace's *Infinite Jest*," *boundary 2* 39, no. 3 (Fall 2012): 125–149; Daniel Grausam, "'It Is Only a Statement of the Power of What Comes After': Atomic Nostalgia and the Ends of Postmodernism," *American Literary History* 24, no. 2 (2012): 308–336.

25. "Transcript of the David Foster Wallace Interview," by David Wiley, *Minnesota Daily*, February 27, 1997, http://www.badgerinternet.com/~bobkat/jestwiley2.html.

26. James McCarthy, "Privatizing Conditions of Production: Trade Agreements as Neoliberal Environmental Governance," in *Neoliberal Environments: False Promises and Unnatural Consequences*, ed. Nik Heynen et al. (New York: Oxford University Press, 2007), 40.

27. In notes in his copy of DeLillo's *Ratner's Star* at the Ransom Center (its call number is PS3554.E4425 R386 1980 DFW), Wallace seems to be working out Steeply's name: at the top of the title page is a list in block capitals: "INGE / SLOTT / STEEPLY." Slott might have formed an internovel dialogue with the coin and sexual associations (females as slots) of *Broom*'s Evelyn Slotnik, whom Fieldbinder in "Love" uses for adulterous sex. In the Fieldbinder story there is thus a tension between a used Slotnik and Mr. Costigan ("cost," or even "cost, again"?), whose indeed costly urges toward Scott Slotnik foreshadow a Wallace theme in *Brief Interviews*—see chapter 4.

28. These qualities, as well as Marathe's agile manipulation of ideas, recall LaVache, whose name's resemblance to Marathe's (-a-a-he) is no coincidence. Adam Kelly ("David Foster Wallace and the Novel of Ideas," in *Long Thing*, ed. Boswell) ties together all three novels through the symmetries of the dialogue between LaVache and Lenore, that between Marathe and Steeply, and §19 of *The Pale King*.

29. Wallace, interview by Das ZDF-Interview, *Zweites Deutsches Fernsehen*, http://www.youtube.com/watch?v=FkxUYokxH80.

30. David Foster Wallace, "*Infinite Jest*: first two sections, typescript drafts and photocopy, undated," box 16, folder 3, David Foster Wallace Papers, Harry Ransom Center, Austin.

31. *Oxford English Dictionary Online*, 2nd ed., s.v. "addict."

32. Saidiya V. Hartman, *Scenes of Subjection: Terror, Slavery, and Self-Making in Nineteenth-Century America* (New York: Oxford University Press, 1997), 109.

33. Gompert, in her ungratified desire for more "shock" (*IJ* 72), is Wallace's rewriting of *The Bell Jar* by fellow McLean Hospital patient Sylvia Plath, a narrative culminating in electroshock therapy that Gompert reads (the unread Gately calls its author "Sylvia Plate" [*IJ* 591]). Himself's suicide clearly revisits Plath's as well. The note Gompert's doctor writes regarding her appeal for shock—"*Then what?*"—suggests that this therapeutic solution is, in contrast to AA's voluminous storytelling, an antinarrative choice (*IJ* 78). On Wallace's own fears about the courses of electroshock therapy he received, see Max (*Every Love Story*, 300).

34. For Wallace's anxieties about the United States "*really* setting [itself] up for repression and fascism," see Lipsky and Wallace (*Although of Course*, 158). In 2006 Wallace warns of U.S. fascism again, worried over corporate power in politics ("'A Frightening Time in America': An Interview with David Foster Wallace," by Ostap Karmodi, *NYR Blog* [June 13, 2011]). On *Infinite Jest*'s critique of the liberal subject's autonomy, see N. Katherine Hayles, "The Illusion of Autonomy and the Fact of Recursivity: Virtual Ecologies, Entertainment, and *Infinite Jest*," *New Literary History* 30, no. 3 (1999): 675–697.

35. Karmodi, "'A Frightening Time in America.'"

36. David Foster Wallace, "*Infinite Jest*: handwritten drafts, undated," box 15, folder 6, David Foster Wallace Papers, Harry Ransom Center, Austin. Alongside this pennies passage, run together on the same handwritten pages, are prototypes of passages in the eventual novel, including the first description of Lyle (127–128 in the novel) and Hal's "We are all dying to give our lives away" monologue (900 in the novel). Wallace typed up a revised version of the pennies passage, calling it an essay by Hal for his mother's "Expository But Errorless Composition" class, but did not include it in the published novel. David Foster Wallace, "*Infinite Jest*:

typescript draft fragments, undated," box 16, folder 7, David Foster Wallace Papers, Harry Ransom Center, Austin.

37. Critics who quote from these sections include Iannis Goerlandt, "'Put the Book Down and Slowly Walk Away': Irony and David Foster Wallace's *Infinite Jest*," *Critique: Studies in Contemporary Fiction* 47, no. 3 (2006): 310–311; Holland, "'Art's Heart's Purpose,'" 223; and Bresnan, "Work of Play," 64–66.

38. Sigmund Freud, *The Standard Edition of the Complete Psychological Works of Sigmund Freud*, trans. James Strachey et al. (London: Hogarth, 1953–1974), 12:187.

39. On Wallace's interest in Buddhism and other "Eastern religious practices," including sitting meditation, see Max (*Every Love Story*, 257). Max dates the origin of this interest to a woman Wallace met in Syracuse, where in 1992 he worked intensively on *Infinite Jest* (181).

40. For a Lacanian reading of the whole novel, see Marshall Boswell, *Understanding David Foster Wallace* (2003; repr., Columbia: University of South Carolina Press, 2009), 128–133.

41. Lee Konstantinou, "No Bull: David Foster Wallace and Postironic Belief," in *Legacy*, ed. Cohen and Konstantinou, 86.

42. David H. Evans, "'The Chains of Not Choosing': Free Will and Faith in William James and David Foster Wallace," in *Companion*, ed. Boswell and Burn, 185.

43. David Foster Wallace, "Quo Vadis – Introduction," *Review of Contemporary Fiction* 16, no. 1 (1996): 7–8.

44. Max Weber, *The Protestant Ethic and the "Spirit" of Capitalism and Other Writings* (New York: Penguin, 2002), 38.

45. For arguments relating Wallace to pragmatism, see Thomas Tracey, "The Formative Years: David Foster Wallace's Philosophical Influences and *The Broom of the System*," in *Gesturing Toward Reality: David Foster Wallace and Philosophy*, ed. Robert K. Bolger and Scott Korb (New York: Bloomsbury, 2014); Clare Hayes-Brady, "The Book, the Broom and the Ladder: Philosophical Groundings in the Work of David Foster Wallace," in *Consider David Foster Wallace: Critical Essays*, ed. David Hering (Los Angeles: Sideshow Media Group, 2010), 31–33; and Evans, "'The Chains of Not Choosing.'"

46. For several other punning dimensions of the morpheme "Ennet," including those suggesting entrapment and immanence, see my "'We've Been Inside What We Wanted All Along': David Foster Wallace's Immanent Structures," forthcoming in *Literature and the Encounter with Immanence*, ed. Brynnar Swenson (Amsterdam: Brill, 2016).

47. Michael North, *Machine-Age Comedy* (Oxford: Oxford University Press, 2009), 168.

48. Jackson Lears, *Something for Nothing: Luck in America* (New York: Penguin, 2004), 2. Randy Ramal suggests that Wallace "would have liked" Roquentin, the hero of *Nausea*, and his view of a life that "does not carry a preconceived essential meaning to be appropriated and followed" ("Beyond Philosophy: David Foster Wallace on Literature, Wittgenstein, and the Dangers of Theorizing," in *Gesturing Toward Reality*, ed. Bolger and Korb, 180), while Allard den Dulk finds "Sartrean virtues" throughout *Infinite Jest* ("Boredom, Irony, and Anxiety: Wallace and the Kierkegaardian View of the Self," in *Long Thing*, ed. Boswell). Wallace calls *Nausea* a "work[] of genius" in "The Empty Plenum" (*BF* 75). Much work remains to be done on Wallace's rich relationship to existentialist novelists, including Camus in *The Pale King*.

49. Max writes of Gately's real-life model having "a Dostoevskian gloss to him, the redeemed criminal" (*Every Love Story*, 141). Raskolnikov in *Crime and Punishment* is one model: the associations include an unplanned killing (DuPlessis), a hallucinatory stint in a hospital, Joelle's parallels with Sonya, and the Revere ADA's with Porfiry. For a comparison of *Infinite Jest* to *The Brothers Karamazov*, see Timothy Jacobs, "The Brothers Incandenza: Translating Ideology in Fyodor Dostoevsky's *The Brothers Karamazov* and David Foster Wallace's *Infinite Jest*," *Texas Studies in Literature and Language* 49, no. 3 (2007): 265–292.

50. Jacques Derrida, *Given Time: I. Counterfeit Money*, trans. Peggy Kamuf (Chicago: University of Chicago Press, 1992), 26–27.

51. Adam Kelly, "David Foster Wallace and the New Sincerity in American Fiction," in *Consider*, ed. Hering, 139, 138.

52. Charles B. Harris, "David Foster Wallace: 'That Distinctive Singular Stamp of Himself,'" *Critique* 51, no. 2 (2010): 172.

53. Lewis Hyde, *The Gift: Imagination and the Erotic Life of Property* (1984), 50. See chapter 1, n. 18.

54. Wallace's notes come in Hyde's final chapter, on Ezra Pound, and mention Marathe, Steeply, Hal, and Pemulis (Hyde [1984], 243, 247, 249).

55. Jonathan Lethem, "*The Gift*: Comments and Reviews," blurb, *Lewishyde.com*, http://www.lewishyde.com/publications/the-gift/comments-reviews/.

56. Jonathan Lethem, *The Ecstasy of Influence: Nonfictions, Etc.* (New York: Vintage, 2011), 115, 117.

57. Paul Giles, "All Swallowed Up: David Foster Wallace and American Literature," in *Legacy*, ed. Cohen and Konstantinou, 7–9.

58. Jonathan Lethem, *Chronic City* (2009; repr., New York: Vintage, 2010), 12.

59. Jamie Clarke, ed., *Conversations with Jonathan Lethem* (Jackson: University Press of Mississippi, 2011), 173, 174. That this January 2010 interview occurred four months before Lethem was officially announced as Wallace's successor as Disney

Professor of Creative Writing at Pomona may also influence these no-disrespect-intended caveats.

60. The fact that Roy Tony, abuser of Wardine, *does* get the help of AA (he enforces hugging [*IJ* 505–507]) but his nominal kin Poor Tony does not is another example of a karmic injustice. Class is a largely untouched topic in Wallace criticism, but Buell does identify in the "ethnographies" of E.T.A. and Ennet House "contrast[s] between privileged and downscale, elect and preterite" (*Dream of the Great American Novel*, 455).

61. John Barth, "The Literature of Exhaustion," in *The Friday Book: Essays and Other Nonfiction* (Baltimore, Md.: Johns Hopkins University Press, 1997), 64.

62. Wallace Stevens, *The Collected Poems of Wallace Stevens* (New York: Vintage, 1990), 503.

63. Making his case for prescriptive grammar, Wallace in "Authority and American Usage" lightly objects to implications of another aspect of Chomsky's argument, the idea "that there exists a Universal Grammar beneath and common to all languages" and "imprinted" on the human brain (*CL* 92). On Wallace's extensive reading in cognitive science, see Stephen J. Burn, "'Webs of Nerves Pulsing and Firing': *Infinite Jest* and the Science of Mind," in *Companion*, ed. Boswell and Burn.

64. Boswell, *Understanding*, 112.

65. David Foster Wallace, "*Infinite Jest*: handwritten drafts, undated," box 15, folder 5, David Foster Wallace Papers, Harry Ransom Center, Austin.

4. OTHER MATH: HUMAN COSTS, FRACTIONAL SELVES, AND NEOLIBERAL CRISIS IN *BRIEF INTERVIEWS WITH HIDEOUS MEN*

1. "Other Math" appeared in the *Western Humanities Review* (Summer 1987). In a letter of August 29, 1996, to Nadell (Bonnie Nadell Collection of David Foster Wallace, Harry Ransom Center, Austin), Wallace includes "Other Math" among stories for a possible collection: *much* changed over the next few years, this is the book that would become *Brief Interviews*.

2. Tom LeClair, "The Non-Silence of the Un-Lamblike," review of *Brief Interviews with Hideous Men*, by David Foster Wallace, *The Nation*, July 19, 1999.

3. Giovanni Arrighi, *The Long Twentieth Century: Money, Power, and the Origins of Our Times* (New York: Verso, 1994), 217.

4. David Harvey, *A Brief History of Neoliberalism* (London: Oxford University Press, 2005), 33.

5. Patrick O'Donnell, "Almost a Novel: *The Broom of the System*," in *A Companion to David Foster Wallace Studies*, ed. Marshall Boswell and Stephen J. Burn (New York: Palgrave Macmillan, 2013), 4.

6. D. T. Max, *Every Love Story Is a Ghost Story: A Life of David Foster Wallace* (New York: Viking, 2012), 248; ellipses in the original.

7. Holland also sees the collection "assert[ing] a kind of integrity" but finds the linchpin to be a "consistent structural monovocality" ("Mediated Immediacy in *Brief Interviews with Hideous Men*," in *Companion*, ed. Boswell and Burn, 109). In his chapter on the collection, Marshall Boswell calls *Brief Interviews* a "carefully constructed . . . story cycle" and sees its binding theme as "the 'interview' and . . . interrogation in general." *Understanding David Foster Wallace* (2003; repr., Columbia: University of South Carolina Press, 2009), 182.

8. Gérard Genette, *Paratexts, Thresholds of Interpretation*, trans. Jane E. Lewin (Cambridge: Cambridge University Press, 2001), 16–17.

9. Howard Brick, *Age of Contradiction: American Thought and Culture in the 1960s* (Ithaca, N.Y.: Cornell University Press, 2000), 54.

10. Zadie Smith, *Changing My Mind: Occasional Essays* (New York: Penguin, 2009), 288.

11. Wallace confirms his attention to such meanings when, after noting that "observing a quantum phenomenon's been proven to alter the phenomenon," he tells McCaffery that understanding of fiction must catch up to physics: "We're not keen on the idea of the story sharing its valence with the reader" (*CW* 40).

12. Wendy Brown, *Edgework: Critical Essays on Knowledge and Politics* (Princeton, N.J.: Princeton University Press, 2005), 40.

13. Michael Taussig, *The Devil and Commodity Fetishism in South America* (1980; repr., Chapel Hill: University of North Carolina Press, 2010), 11.

14. The man's race grants further power to the son's assertion (about his father's uniform), "I wear nothing white. Not one white thing" (*BI* 90).

15. Don DeLillo, *End Zone* (1972; repr., New York: Penguin, 1986), 88.

16. Søren Kierkegaard, *A Kierkegaard Anthology*, ed. Robert Bretall (Princeton, N.J.: Princeton University Press, 1973), 103. On Wallace being inspired by Kierkegaard, see Allard den Dulk, who quotes unpublished personal correspondence in which Wallace states, "I too believe that most of the problems of what might be called 'the tyranny of irony' in today's West can be explained almost perfectly in terms of Kierkegaard's distinction between the aesthetic and the ethical life" ("Boredom, Irony, and Anxiety: Wallace and the Kierkegaardian View of the Self," in *David Foster Wallace and "The Long Thing": New Essays on the Novels*, ed. Marshall Boswell [New York: Bloomsbury, 2014], 59). See also Boswell, *Understanding*, 137–145.

17. For just three examples of synthetic readings of Wallace that make significant use of "Octet," see Lee Konstantinou, "No Bull: David Foster Wallace and Postironic

Belief," in *The Legacy of David Foster Wallace*, ed. Samuel Cohen and Lee Konstantinou (Iowa City: University of Iowa Press, 2012); Adam Kelly, "David Foster Wallace and the New Sincerity in American Fiction," in *Consider David Foster Wallace: Critical Essays*, ed. David Hering (Los Angeles: Sideshow Media Group, 2010); and Timothy Richard Aubry, *Reading as Therapy: What Contemporary Fiction Does for Middle-Class Americans* (Iowa City: University of Iowa Press, 2011).

18. Boswell, *Understanding*, 180.

19. "Everything and More: *The Pale King* by David Foster Wallace," panel discussion with Laura Miller, Michael Pietsch, Rick Moody, and Sandro Veronesi, PEN World Voices Festival video (April 26, 2011), http://www.pen.org/video /everything-and-more-pale-king-david-foster-wallace.

20. J. Peder Zane, *The Top Ten: Writers Pick Their Favorite Books* (New York: Norton, 2007), 128.

21. Tom McCarthy, *Remainder* (New York: Vintage, 2007), 64.

22. Tom McCarthy, "The *New Yorker*'s D. T. Max and Novelist Tom McCarthy Discuss David Foster Wallace," YouTube video, 1:05:53, posted by "Strand Bookstore" (November 28, 2012), https://www.youtube.com/watch?v=Xc_UlODoowU.

23. Plato, *The Symposium*, trans. Christopher Gill (London: Penguin, 1999), 24.

24. Stephen J. Burn, "'Webs of Nerves Pulsing and Firing': *Infinite Jest* and the Science of Mind," in *Companion*, ed. Boswell and Burn, 71.

25. Naomi Klein, *The Shock Doctrine: The Rise of Disaster Capitalism* (New York: Random House, 2007), 318.

26. My account of the stochastic is generally indebted to James Owen Weatherall, *The Physics of Wall Street: A Brief History of Predicting the Unpredictable* (New York: Houghton Mifflin, 2013), 1–48.

27. "David Foster Wallace (*Infinite Jest*)," interview by Michael Silverblatt, *Bookworm*, KCRW radio broadcast, April 11, 1996.

28. Wallace shows in his philosophy thesis that Richard Taylor makes a "category mistake," writes Leland de la Durantaye: Taylor uses semantic arguments to reach a metaphysical conclusion endorsing fatalism and calling free will an illusion. This "counterintuitive" argument, de la Durantaye claims, "was focused more on saving logic than saving the phenomena" ("The Subsurface Unity of All Things, or David Foster Wallace's Free Will," in *Gesturing Toward Reality: David Foster Wallace and Philosophy*, ed. Robert K. Bolger and Scott Korb [New York: Bloomsbury, 2014], 22). Wallace's fiction, particularly in its intuitive "innit" dimensions, often moves characters from maintaining logical structures such as graphed points to saving the phenomena.

29. Surprisingly, in 2004, Wallace called "Little Expressionless Animals" the "single thing I like best" among his writings; perhaps he was compelled to return to its

form in later works. "David Foster Wallace: In Conversation with David Kipen," *City Arts & Lectures* (2004), https://www.youtube.com/watch?v=mfjjSj9c0A0.

30. In both the essay I quote ("Fictional Futures") and "Little Expressionless Animals," Wallace may refer obliquely to John Barth's inclusion of a graphic version of Freitag's Triangle in *Lost in the Funhouse* (1968; repr., New York: Anchor, 2014), 95.

31. Thomas Pynchon, *The Crying of Lot 49* (New York: Harper Perennial, 2006), 181.

32. E.g., Iannis Goerlandt, "'Put the Book Down and Slowly Walk Away': Irony and David Foster Wallace's *Infinite Jest*," *Critique: Studies in Contemporary Fiction* 47, no. 3 (2006): 321.

33. Teddy Wayne, *Kapitoil: A Novel* (New York: Harper Perennial, 2010), 87.

34. In a column on language shortening, Wayne writes of "'I can't with' (the short form of 'I can't deal with'), which has been around for at least a few decades, including in a 1987 David Foster Wallace short story." "On Internet Slang, IMHO," *New York Times*, March 28, 2014. Wayne leaves it unnamed, but he means "Here and There."

35. With the window image Wayne is likely referring specifically to not just Gramma Beadsman's broom but Wallace's claim that *Infinite Jest* is structured like a "pretty pane of glass that has been dropped off the twentieth story of a building" (*CW* 57).

36. "Memories of David Foster Wallace," *McSweeney's Internet Tendency*, http://www.mcsweeneys.net/pages/memories-of-david-foster-wallace.

37. Zadie Smith, *NW* (2012; repr., New York: Penguin, 2013), 135, 198.

38. Along with Dave Eggers's *The Circle* (see chapter 6), *NW* is also the first major *Pale King*–influenced work. A hideous man at a college party who makes short films "about boredom" (and misunderstands Wallace's subject) badgers a woman: "It's the only subject left. We're all bored. Aren't you bored?" (*NW*, 237). The critic Helen Small evokes *NW*'s commonality with *The Pale King* when she claims regarding Leah's lottery work that Smith's novel undoes the traditional "opposition between proceduralism and imaginative exploration, economic accounting and novelistic recounting" ("Fully Accountable," *New Literary History* 44, no. 4 [2013]: 554).

5. HIS CAPITAL FLUSH: DESPAIRING OVER WORK AND VALUE IN *OBLIVION*

1. Philip Mirowski, *Never Let a Serious Crisis Go to Waste: How Neoliberalism Survived the Financial Meltdown* (London: Verso, 2013), 59.

2. Dave Eggers explains that Wallace asked to have "Mister Squishy" published in *McSweeney's* under the pen name, "for the life of me I now can't remember why"—

but the move fits for an author contemplating modes of self-erasure ("Memories of David Foster Wallace," *McSweeney's Internet Tendency*).

3. Wallace here distorts the lawsuit he faced over naming Kate Gompert after a fellow junior tennis player, satirized in the attempts to not name "R - - d©" (obviously, Raid) as the product responsible for Mother's disfiguring (*O* 185). Also germane are the legal delays of *Girl* over the naming of celebrities and corporations. For analysis of these legal problems, see chapter 6.

4. The "Oblivion" typescript draft with the Justice epigraph is in box 24, folder 8, David Foster Wallace Papers, Harry Ransom Center, Austin. A photocopy of Justice's essay is also among Wallace's creative-nonfiction teaching materials; Wallace stars the passage I have as my epigraph and places quote marks around the "What glories . . ." sentence, presumably planning to use it as an epigraph. See "Taught essays and writing topics," box 32, folder 8, David Foster Wallace Papers, Harry Ransom Center, Austin.

5. Walter Kirn, "Staring Either Absently or Intently," review of *Oblivion*, by David Foster Wallace, *New York Times*, June 27, 2004.

6. Wallace to DeLillo, May 20, 1997, David Foster Wallace Papers, Harry Ransom Center, Austin.

7. Brian McHale, "*The Pale King*, Or, The White Visitation," in *A Companion to David Foster Wallace Studies*, ed. Marshall Boswell and Stephen J. Burn (New York: Palgrave Macmillan, 2013), 204.

8. Sheryl Gay Stolberg, "The Decider," *New York Times*, December 24, 2006.

9. Tor Nørretranders, *The User Illusion: Cutting Consciousness Down to Size*, trans. Jonathan Sydenham (New York: Viking, 1998), 125. Wallace's copy of *The User Illusion* is, as noted on the Ransom Center's bibliographic entry (the call number is BF311.N675 1998p DFW), the "Advanced Uncorrected Proofs" of the first English translation, from 1998. Stephen J. Burn ("'A Paradigm for the Life of Consciousness': *The Pale King*," in *David Foster Wallace and "The Long Thing": New Essays on the Novels*, ed. Marshall Boswell [New York: Bloomsbury, 2014], 164) cites the book as an influence on *The Pale King*. For an account of Wallace's allusions to *The User Illusion*, see my "Cutting Consciousness Down to Size: David Foster Wallace, Exformation, and the Scale of Encyclopedic Fiction," forthcoming in *Size and Scale in Literature and Culture*, ed. David Wittenberg and Michael Tavel Clarke.

10. Marshall Boswell, "'The Constant Monologue Inside Your Head': *Oblivion* and the Nightmare of Consciousness," in *A Companion to David Foster Wallace Studies*, ed. Marshall Boswell and Stephen J. Burn (New York: Palgrave Macmillan, 2013), 166.

11. David Letzler, "Encyclopedic Novels and the Cruft of Fiction: *Infinite Jest*'s Endnotes," in *Long Thing*, ed. Boswell.

12. Marc Shell, *Money, Language, and Thought: Literary and Philosophical Economies from the Medieval to the Modern Era* (Berkeley: University of California Press, 1982), 14.

13. *Oxford English Dictionary Online*, 3rd ed., s.v. "coin."

14. Stephen J. Burn, "'Webs of Nerves Pulsing and Firing': *Infinite Jest* and the Science of Mind," in *Companion*, ed. Boswell and Burn, 65.

15. David Foster Wallace, "Order and Flux in Northampton," *Conjunctions* 17 (Fall 1991): 106.

16. Wallace makes one explicit State Farm reference in his fiction: the claims adjuster who laughs over Glynn's bricklaying fiasco in *Infinite Jest* is a State Farm employee from Bloomington (*IJ* 138–140), and as Pat Montesian later cuts through "the red tape at Health" to gain hospital admission for Glynn despite "insurance fraud on his yellow sheet," the gift-driven AA network becomes an alternative form of insurance in the novel (*IJ* 824).

17. Ursula K. Heise, *Sense of Place and Sense of Planet: The Environmental Imagination of the Global* (Oxford: Oxford University Press, 2008), 160–177.

18. Mirowski (*Serious Crisis*, 120), writing of the broader economy and undermining neoliberalism's adoration of capitalist "risk-takers," identifies risk as "entirely a cultural construct" that, especially in finance, is manipulated to justify disaster-prone systems as the natural cost of entrepreneurial freedom.

19. Sweaty David Cusk will also repeat Roosevelt's famous line to himself in assessing his nervousness in *The Pale King* (95–96).

20. "Everything and More: *The Pale King* by David Foster Wallace," panel discussion with Laura Miller, Michael Pietsch, Rick Moody, and Sandro Veronesi, PEN World Voices Festival video (April 26, 2011), http://www.pen.org/video/everything-and-more-pale-king-david-foster-wallace.

21. Burn, "'A Paradigm for the Life of Consciousness,'" 151, 166n5.

22. David Harvey, *A Brief History of Neoliberalism* (London: Oxford University Press, 2005), 79–80.

23. Paul Giles, "Sentimental Posthumanism: David Foster Wallace," *Twentieth Century Literature* 53, no. 3 (Fall 2007): 339.

24. Wallace, "'Oblivion': handwritten draft, undated," box 24, folder 7, David Foster Wallace Papers, Harry Ransom Center, Austin.

25. Kurt Eichenwald, *Serpent on the Rock* (1995; repr., New York: Broadway Books, 2007), 94.

26. A copy of *Serpent on the Rock* is unfortunately not among the Wallace books preserved at the Ransom Center.

27. Given his attention to the 1930s, Wallace may reply here to the Clinton-approved repeal in 1999 of the Glass-Steagall Act, which in 1933 placed safeguard limits

on combinations of securities firms and commercial banks. Widely regarded as a contributing cause of the 2008 financial crisis, repealing Glass-Steagall was another neoliberal victory of flexible capital.

28. D. T. Max, *Every Love Story Is a Ghost Story: A Life of David Foster Wallace* (New York: Viking, 2012), 215.

29. Laurel's thoughts track closely with a Gordon W. Allport quotation, circled by Wallace in his copy of William Ian Miller's *The Anatomy of Disgust* (Cambridge, Mass.: Harvard University Press, 1997): "Think first of swallowing the saliva in your mouth, or do so," Miller quotes from Allport. "Then imagine expectorating it into a tumbler and drinking it! What seemed natural and 'mine' suddenly becomes disgusting and alien" (97). The Ransom Center call number for Wallace's copy of Miller is BF575.A886 M55 1997 DFW. Miller's source is Gordon W. Allport, *Becoming: Basic Considerations for a Psychology of Personality* (New Haven, Conn.: Yale University Press, 1955), 43.

30. Elizabeth Anker ("Allegories of Falling and the 9/11 Novel," *American Literary History* 23, no. 3 [2011]: 471) also sees an oblique reference to 9/11 in the man climbing the Chicago office tower in "Mister Squishy." "The Suffering Channel" has led to several critical essays on its relationship to 9/11, the best of which is by Annie McClanahan ("Future's Shock: Plausibility, Preemption, and the Fiction of 9/11," *symplokē* 17, no. 1–2 [2009]: 41–62).

31. Marshall Boswell, *Understanding David Foster Wallace* (2003; repr., Columbia: University of South Carolina Press, 2009), 5.

32. Immanuel Kant, *Critique of Judgment*, trans. James Creed Meredith, ed. Nicholas Walker (Oxford: Oxford University Press, 2008), §45.

33. Kai Hammermeister, *The German Aesthetic Tradition* (Cambridge: Cambridge University Press, 2002), 35.

34. Lewis Hyde, *The Gift: Imagination and the Erotic Life of Property* (1984), 229. See chapter 1, n. 18.

35. Toon Staes, "'Only Artists Can Transfigure': Kafka's Artists and the Possibility of Redemption in the Novellas of David Foster Wallace," *Orbis Litterarum: International Review of Literary Studies* 65, no. 6 (2010): 473–478.

6. *E PLURIBUS UNUM*: RITUAL, CURRENCY, AND THE EMBODIED VALUES OF *THE PALE KING*

1. D. T. Max notes chiropractor visits by Wallace; the spine imagery throughout his corpus seems partly based in a chronic issue for him (*Every Love Story Is a Ghost Story: A Life of David Foster Wallace* [New York: Viking, 2012], 301).

2. Examining §19 (but not Nichols's ideas in particular), Emily J. Hogg explores the "subjective" nature of politics for Wallace, claiming *The Pale King* probes "the troubled intersection of the inner world and politics" ("Subjective Politics in *The Pale King*," *English Studies* 95, no. 1 [2014]: 60).

3. Ralph Clare, "The Politics of Boredom and the Boredom of Politics in *The Pale King*," in *David Foster Wallace and "The Long Thing": New Essays on the Novels*, ed. Marshall Boswell (New York: Bloomsbury, 2014), 199.

4. Richard Godden and Michael Szalay, "The Bodies in the Bubble: David Foster Wallace's *The Pale King*," *Textual Practice* 28, no. 7 (2014): 1274.

5. Marshall Boswell, "Trickle-Down Citizenship: Taxes and Civic Responsibility in *The Pale King*," in *Long Thing*, ed. Boswell, 217.

6. Adam Kelly, "David Foster Wallace and the Novel of Ideas," in *Long Thing*, ed. Boswell, 15.

7. Stephen J. Burn, "'A Paradigm for the Life of Consciousness': *The Pale King*," in *Long Thing*, ed. Boswell, 162–163.

8. Jacques Derrida, *Spurs: Nietzsche's Styles*, trans. Barbara Harlow (Chicago: University of Chicago Press, 1979), 37.

9. David Lipsky and David Foster Wallace, *Although of Course You End Up Becoming Yourself: A Road Trip with David Foster Wallace* (New York: Broadway Books, 2010), 258.

10. In an e-mail reply to my query, Amherst College archivist Christina E. Barber confirms that classes ended on May 10 and Wallace's graduation occurred on May 17, 1985. Wallace's thesis panel graded *Broom* in "late spring of 1985" (Max, *Every Love Story*, 48).

11. The fantastical structure of *The Pale King*—in which ghosts play a role and trauma produces odd powers—might be indebted to the kinds of books Wallace found immersive in his youth, particularly *Lord of the Rings*, which he read five times as a teen (Lipsky and Wallace, *Although of Course*, 221) and calls a "bitchingly good read" (*LI* 46).

12. Unpublished letter, quoted in D. T. Max, "In the D.F.W. Archives: An Unfinished Story About the Internet," *New Yorker* (October 11, 2012).

13. Greg Carlisle, *Elegant Complexity: A Study of David Foster Wallace's* Infinite Jest (Los Angeles: Sideshow Media Group, 2007), 54.

14. Zadie Smith, *Changing My Mind: Occasional Essays* (New York: Penguin, 2009), 297.

15. George Saunders, "Informal Remarks from the David Foster Wallace Memorial Service in New York on October 23, 2008," in *The Legacy of David Foster Wallace*, ed. Samuel Cohen and Lee Konstantinou (Iowa City: University of Iowa Press, 2012), 53.

16. Don DeLillo, *End Zone* (1972; repr., New York: Penguin, 1986), 42.

17. Amy Hungerford, *Postmodern Belief: American Literature and Religion Since 1960* (Princeton, N.J.: Princeton University Press, 2010), xiv.

18. Paul Giles, "All Swallowed Up: David Foster Wallace and American Literature," in *The Legacy of David Foster Wallace*, ed. Cohen and Konstantinou, 11.

19. This poor Toni has the same name as her birthplace, Anthony, Illinois (*PK* 59, 62). Max notes that one of the novel's several working titles was *What Is Peoria For?* (*Every Love Story*, 323n17), a question that might have given this novel even more connections to Heideggerian criticisms of technology. Toni's witchlike powers are predicted by one more pun: were- as in werewolf.

20. The bracketed insertion and ellipsis here are Wallace's; the quotation (*BF* 234–235n30) is from Joseph Campbell, *The Hero with a Thousand Faces*, 3rd ed. (Novato, Calif.: New World Library, 2008), 10–11.

21. Søren Kierkegaard, *A Kierkegaard Anthology*, ed. Robert Bretall (Princeton, N.J.: Princeton University Press, 1973), 119–20.

22. See chapter 4, n. 16.

23. Matt. 21:31 (New International Version).

24. Falling forty days after Easter, Pentecost does at times occur much closer to May 15. Smith's notes on "Church Not Made with Hands" (*Changing My Mind*, 297) show that Wallace mined that title from Acts of the Apostles, which also contains the description of the first Pentecost (see Acts 2:1–13). The suspended revelation at the end of Pynchon's *Lot 49* is another possible inspiration. Sylvanshine comes to Peoria having "forgotten to wash the shampoo from his hair," giving "him the flame-shaped coiffure" (*PK* 338). Might Wallace be, in his cheeky way, evoking Acts 2:3? "They saw what seemed to be tongues of fire that separated and came to rest on each of them."

25. "Everything and More: *The Pale King* by David Foster Wallace," panel discussion with Laura Miller, Michael Pietsch, Rick Moody, and Sandro Veronesi, PEN World Voices Festival video (April 26, 2011), http://www.pen.org/video/everything-and-more-pale-king-david-foster-wallace.

26. Such textual effects could be put into dialogue with the digital networks of "Infinite Summer" that Fitzpatrick examines ("Infinite Summer: Reading, Empathy, and the Social Network," in *The Legacy of David Foster Wallace*, ed. Cohen and Konstantinou, 182–207). Godden and Szalay read this scene pessimistically, as an illustration of the examiners becoming machine-like ("The Bodies in the Bubble," 1297–1298).

27. *Oxford English Dictionary Online*, 2nd ed., s.v. "fogle."

28. Jimmy Carter, "Report to the American People: Remarks from the White House Library. February 2, 1977," *Public Papers of the Presidents of the United States,*

Jimmy Carter, 1977–1981 (Washington, D.C.: U.S. Government Printing Office), 69–71.

29. "Everything and More" panel discussion.

30. "Welt" pays tribute to Wallace's own father-in-fiction, DeLillo: in his glowing letter after reading the *Underworld* typescript, Wallace praises the "line where Nick tosses off 'welt of his shoe' so many years after his shoe-lesson from Paulus (there was something about that that just tore my liver out)." David Foster Wallace to DeLillo, January 19, 1997, David Foster Wallace Papers, Harry Ransom Center, Austin. Father Paulus's shoe talk is also a prime intertext for Wallace's tax teacher's speech, and both Wallace and DeLillo clearly draw on Joyce's *Portrait of the Artist.*

31. This moment may encapsulate Wallace's two attempts to join the Catholic Church: "I always flunk the period of inquiry," he said in 1999. "They don't really want inquiries. They really just want you to learn responses" (*CW* 99).

32. David Foster Wallace, "Amherst College: essays and exams, 1980–1981, undated," box 31, folder 6, David Foster Wallace Papers, Harry Ransom Center, Austin. Stephen Shapiro sees other, more abstract "parallels to *Moby Dick*" and, in the examiners' drudgery, to "Bartleby the Scrivener" ("From Capitalist to Communist Abstraction: *The Pale King*'s Cultural Fix," *Textual Practice* 28, no. 7 [2014]: 1267–1268).

33. Lee Konstantinou, "No Bull: David Foster Wallace and Postironic Belief," in *The Legacy of David Foster Wallace*, ed. Cohen and Konstantinou, 104.

34. Dave Eggers, *The Circle* (2013; repr., New York: Vintage, 2014), 198.

35. Brian McHale says Wallace's title refers to Nabokov, "though exactly how *The Pale King* might be related to *Pale Fire* is harder to say" ("*The Pale King*, Or, The White Visitation," in *A Companion to David Foster Wallace Studies*, ed. Marshall Boswell and Stephen J. Burn [New York: Palgrave Macmillan, 2013], 193). But might tensions between David Wallace and Fogle have proven, in a finished novel, to be akin to those between poet John Shade and critic Charles Kinbote, whose "Foreword" and "Commentary" seem a model for §9? Wallace may have even been trying to recreate *Pale Fire*'s ambiguity (covered in a vast critical literature) over who exactly writes the novel's various parts and who is concealing his identity. As I suggest later, the Author sections have an intentional awkwardness that introduces doubt about their provenance. Wallace has played with *Pale Fire* before: the name of Molly Notkin, who tells tales about a dead artist's intentions, echoes the problem of distinguishing Kinbote and Botkin that Nabokov critics face, and, like *Pale Fire*, *Infinite Jest* shares its name with a controversial, posthumous work within the novel. On other Wallace engagements with Nabokov,

see Marshall Boswell, *Understanding David Foster Wallace* (2003; repr., Columbia: University of South Carolina Press, 2009).

36. Marshall Boswell, "Author Here: The Legal Fiction of David Foster Wallace's *The Pale King,*" *English Studies* 95, no. 1 (2014): 37n46.

37. When the lawyer for Time Warner claimed *Infinite Jest* was protected by its futuristic setting and the usual disclaimers, Gompert's lawyer shot back that the phrase "your own troubled imagination" was "anything but boilerplate" and clearly "a 'taunt' of his client" ("Fact Meets Fiction in Truly Novel Dispute," *The Recorder* [September 8, 1998]).

38. Wallace to DeLillo, November 25, 1998, David Foster Wallace Papers, Harry Ransom Center, Austin.

39. Jonathan Franzen, "Mr. Difficult," in *How to Be Alone: Essays* (2002; repr., New York: Farrar Straus & Giroux, 2003), 240.

40. William Gaddis, *J R* (1975; repr., New York: Penguin, 1993), 393.

41. Ludwig Wittgenstein, *Philosophical Investigations: The English Text of the Third Edition*, trans. G. E. M. Anscombe (Englewood Cliffs, N.J.: Prentice Hall, 1958), §241. By contrast, Andrew Warren, examining narratological modes, sees a community-building force in what he terms Wallace's "Contracted Realism," which "aims to render reality's fine print legible" ("Modeling Community and Narrative in *Infinite Jest* and *The Pale King,*" in *Long Thing*, ed. Boswell, 63).

42. Don DeLillo, *Libra* (1988; repr., New York: Penguin, 1991), 181. Wallace says in his first letter to DeLillo (June 11, 1992, David Foster Wallace Papers, Harry Ransom Center, Austin), "I have little doubt that your best and most comprehensive novel is <u>Libra</u>, but I read it in galleys when I was trying to do some fiction-work of my own in the transfiguration of real U.S. fact and myth, and jealousy kept me from being able to love <u>Libra</u>, and I've been afraid to reread it." What specific "fiction-work" Wallace means here remains a mystery, but I suspect *The Pale King* was his effort finally to engage with DeLillo's analysis of government agents (and agency), massive archives of "fact," and American myths.

43. Eliot Caroom, "fact-checking" Wallace, confirms that the IRS "doesn't have an official motto. What it does have on the face of its building in Washington, is a quote from Justice Oliver Wendell Holmes: 'Taxes are what we pay for a civilized society'" ("'The Pale King's' Depiction of IRS Gets Fact Checked," *The Daily Beast* [April 17, 2012]).

44. Sigmund Freud, *The Standard Edition of the Complete Psychological Works of Sigmund Freud*, trans. James Strachey et al. (London: Hogarth, 1953–1974), 9:174.

45. Conley Wouters, "'What Am I, a Machine?': Humans and Information in *The Pale King,*" in *Long Thing*, ed. Boswell, 182.

46. §1 appeared under the title "Peoria (4)" in *TriQuarterly* in 2002.

47. Marc Shell, *Money, Language, and Thought: Literary and Philosophical Economies from the Medieval to the Modern Era* (Berkeley: University of California Press, 1982), 40–41.

48. Marc Shell, *Art and Money* (Chicago: University of Chicago Press, 1995), 16.

49. For accounts of the interdependence of debt repayment and the neoliberal status quo, see David Graeber, *Debt: The First 5,000 Years* (Brooklyn, N.Y.: Melville House, 2011); and Maurizio Lazzarato, *The Making of the Indebted Man: Essays on the Neoliberal Condition*, trans. Joshua David Jordan (Los Angeles: Semiotext(e), 2012). For a reading relating Wallace's vision to these two theorists, see Mark McGurl, "The Institution of Nothing: David Foster Wallace in the Program," *boundary 2* 41, no. 3 (2014): 54. Godden and Szalay dazzlingly situate Bondurant's story of Fat Marcus and service in Vietnam in the context of Nixon's 1971 decision to remove the U.S. dollar from the gold standard, avoiding bankruptcy and enabling continued funding for Vietnam (and future wars) ("The Bodies in the Bubble," 1292–1293). In Godden and Szalay's hands, *The Pale King* seems like an expanded version of "Crash of '69," whose evocations of Nixon in 1971 I analyzed in chapter 2.

50. Emily J. Hogg also sees a link to Ayn Rand ("Subjective Politics in *The Pale King*," *English Studies* 95, no. 1 [2014]: 62).

51. Glendenning is called "a man of style" for his dress (*PK* 436), but that word, always metafictional for Wallace, suggests that encyclopedic novel writing and organizational administration are similar tasks: note that *DeWitt G*lendenning shares three capital letters with "D.W. Gately" (*IJ* 57), who grows through his administration of Ennet House (§48 of *The Pale King* also shows Glendenning hospitalized, another leader felled in a work-related attack). These similar characters are images of their many-character-administering creator, who shares the first two initials.

52. On another possible source for Fogle's nickname, see my "David Foster Wallace, James Wood, and a Source for 'Irrelevant' Chris Fogle," *The Explicator* 73, no. 2 (2015): 129–132. For an extensive reading of Wallace's relationship to Borges, see Lucas Thompson, "Programming Literary Influence: David Foster Wallace's 'B.I. #59,'" *Texas Studies in Literature and Language* 56, no. 2 (2014): 113–134.

53. Granada House has now done so: in 2013 Madras Press published §22 as *The Awakening of My Interest in Advanced Tax* (echoing the title of James Incandenza's memoir), with proceeds benefiting Granada House.

54. Tor Nørretranders, *The User Illusion: Cutting Consciousness Down to Size*, trans. Jonathan Sydenham (New York: Viking, 1998), 30–31. Wallace's copy of *The User Illusion* is, as noted on the Ransom Center's bibliographic entry (the call number

is BF311.N675 1998p DFW), the "Advanced Uncorrected Proofs" of the first English translation, from 1998.

CONCLUSION: IN LINE FOR THE CASH REGISTER WITH WALLACE

1. Don DeLillo, *White Noise* (New York: Penguin, 1985), 326.
2. Wallace, "*Infinite Jest*: handwritten drafts, undated," box 15, folder 6, David Foster Wallace Papers, Harry Ransom Center, Austin.
3. Amy Wallace Havens, "Amy Wallace Havens on Her Brother," interview by Anne Strainchamps, *To the Best of Our Knowledge*, PRI radio broadcast (August 23, 2009), http://www.ttbook.org/book/amy-wallace-havens-her-brother.
4. D. T. Max, *Every Love Story Is a Ghost Story: A Life of David Foster Wallace* (New York: Viking, 2012), 54.
5. Hubert Dreyfus and Sean Dorrance Kelly, *All Things Shining: Reading the Western Classics to Find Meaning in a Secular Age* (New York: Free Press, 2011), 47.
6. Jonathan Franzen, "Informal Remarks from the David Foster Wallace Memorial Service in New York on October 23, 2008," in *The Legacy of David Foster Wallace*, ed. Samuel Cohen and Lee Konstantinou (Iowa City: University of Iowa Press, 2012), 177.
7. For a nuanced take on the idea of "reading" Wallace's suicide alongside his texts, see Lee Konstantinou, "No Bull: David Foster Wallace and Postironic Belief," in *The Legacy of David Foster Wallace*, ed. Cohen and Konstantinou, 104.
8. Lee Konstantinou, "The World of David Foster Wallace," *boundary 2* 40, no. 3 (2013): 68.

BIBLIOGRAPHY

Allport, Gordon W. *Becoming: Basic Considerations for a Psychology of Personality*. New Haven, Conn.: Yale University Press, 1955.

Andersen, Tore Rye. "Pay Attention! David Foster Wallace and His Real Enemies." *English Studies* 95, no. 1 (2014): 7–24.

Anker, Elizabeth. "Allegories of Falling and the 9/11 Novel." *American Literary History* 23, no. 3 (2011): 463–482.

Arrighi, Giovanni. *The Long Twentieth Century: Money, Power, and the Origins of Our Times*. New York: Verso, 1994.

Aubry, Timothy Richard. *Reading as Therapy: What Contemporary Fiction Does for Middle-Class Americans*. Iowa City: University of Iowa Press, 2011.

Ballantyne, Nathan, and Justin Tosi. "David Foster Wallace and the Good Life." In *Freedom and the Self*, ed. Cahn and Eckert, 133–168.

Barth, John. *The Floating Opera and The End of the Road*. 1967. Reprint, New York: Anchor, 1988.

———. "The Literature of Exhaustion." In *The Friday Book: Essays and Other Nonfiction*, 62–76. Baltimore, Md.: Johns Hopkins University Press, 1997.

———. *Lost in the Funhouse*. 1968. Reprint, New York: Anchor, 2014.

Bellow, Saul. *Herzog*. 1964. Reprint, New York: Penguin, 2003.

Boddy, Kasia. "A Fiction of Response: *Girl with Curious Hair* in Context." In *A Companion to David Foster Wallace Studies*, ed. Boswell and Burn, 23–42.

Bolger, Robert K., and Scott Korb, eds. *Gesturing Toward Reality: David Foster Wallace and Philosophy*. New York: Bloomsbury, 2014.

Boswell, Marshall. "Author Here: The Legal Fiction of David Foster Wallace's *The Pale King.*" *English Studies* 95, no. 1 (2014): 25–39.

——. "'The Constant Monologue Inside Your Head': *Oblivion* and the Nightmare of Consciousness." In *A Companion to David Foster Wallace Studies*, ed. Boswell and Burn, 151–170.

——, ed. *David Foster Wallace and "The Long Thing": New Essays on the Novels.* New York: Bloomsbury, 2014.

——. "Preface: David Foster Wallace and 'The Long Thing.'" In *David Foster Wallace and "The Long Thing": New Essays on the Novels*, ed. Boswell, vi–xii.

——. "Trickle-Down Citizenship: Taxes and Civic Responsibility in *The Pale King.*" In *David Foster Wallace and "The Long Thing": New Essays on the Novels*, ed. Boswell, 209–225.

——. *Understanding David Foster Wallace.* 2003. Reprint, Columbia: University of South Carolina Press, 2009.

Boswell, Marshall, and Stephen J. Burn. Preface to *A Companion to David Foster Wallace Studies*, ed. Boswell and Burn, ix–xii.

Boswell, Marshall, and Stephen J. Burn, eds. *A Companion to David Foster Wallace Studies.* New York: Palgrave Macmillan, 2013.

Bresnan, Mark. "The Work of Play in David Foster Wallace's *Infinite Jest.*" *Critique* 50, no. 1 (2008): 51–68.

Brick, Howard. *Age of Contradiction: American Thought and Culture in the 1960s.* Ithaca, N.Y.: Cornell University Press, 2000.

Brown, Wendy. *Edgework: Critical Essays on Knowledge and Politics.* Princeton, N.J.: Princeton University Press, 2005.

Buell, Lawrence. *The Dream of the Great American Novel.* Cambridge, Mass.: Harvard University Press, 2014.

Burn, Stephen J. "'A Paradigm for the Life of Consciousness': *The Pale King.*" In *David Foster Wallace and "The Long Thing": New Essays on the Novels*, ed. Boswell, 149–168.

——, ed. *Conversations with David Foster Wallace.* Jackson: University Press of Mississippi, 2012.

——. *David Foster Wallace's* Infinite Jest: *A Reader's Guide.* 2nd ed. New York: Continuum, 2012.

——. Review of *Consider David Foster Wallace: Critical Essays*, by David Hering. *Modernism/modernity* 18, no. 2 (2011): 465–468.

——. "Toward a General Theory of Vision in Wallace's Fiction." *English Studies* 95, no. 1 (2014): 85–93.

——. "'Webs of Nerves Pulsing and Firing': *Infinite Jest* and the Science of Mind." In *A Companion to David Foster Wallace Studies*, ed. Boswell and Burn, 59–86.

Bustillos, Maria. "Inside David Foster Wallace's Private Self-Help Library." *The Awl*, April 5, 2011. http://www.theawl.com/2011/04/inside-david-foster-wallaces-private-self-help-library.

Cahn, Steven M., and Maureen Eckert, eds. *Freedom and the Self: Essays on the Philosophy of David Foster Wallace.* New York: Columbia University Press, 2015.

Campbell, Joseph. *The Hero with a Thousand Faces.* 3rd ed. Novato, Calif.: New World Library, 2008.

———. *Myths to Live By.* 1972. Reprint, New York: Bantam Books, 1984.

Caputo, John D. *Demythologizing Heidegger.* Bloomington: Indiana University Press, 1993.

———. *The Mystical Element in Heidegger's Thought.* New York: Fordham University Press, 1986.

Carlisle, Greg. *Elegant Complexity: A Study of David Foster Wallace's* Infinite Jest. Los Angeles: Sideshow Media Group, 2007.

Caroom, Eliot. "'The Pale King's' Depiction of IRS Gets Fact Checked." *The Daily Beast*, April 17, 2012.

Carter, Jimmy. "Report to the American People: Remarks from the White House Library. February 2, 1977." *Public Papers of the Presidents of the United States, Jimmy Carter, 1977–1981.* U.S. Government Printing Office, Washington, D.C, pp. 69–71.

Cavell, Stanley. *Disowning Knowledge in Six Plays of Shakespeare.* 1987. Reprint, Cambridge: Cambridge University Press, 2003.

———. *In Quest of the Ordinary: Lines of Skepticism and Romanticism.* Chicago: University of Chicago Press, 1988.

———. *This New yet Unapproachable America: Lectures After Emerson After Wittgenstein.* 1989. Reprint, Chicago: University of Chicago Press, 2013.

Clare, Ralph. "The Politics of Boredom and the Boredom of Politics in *The Pale King*." In *David Foster Wallace and "The Long Thing": New Essays on the Novels*, ed. Boswell, 187–207.

Clarke, Jaime, ed. *Conversations with Jonathan Lethem.* Jackson: University Press of Mississippi, 2011.

Cohen, Samuel, and Lee Konstantinou, eds. *The Legacy of David Foster Wallace.* Iowa City: University of Iowa Press, 2012.

Conte, Joseph. *Design and Debris: A Chaotics of Postmodern American Fiction.* Tuscaloosa: University of Alabama Press, 2002.

Crosthwaite, Paul. "The Accident of Finance." In *Virilio Now: Current Perspectives in Virilio Studies*, ed. John Armitage, 177–199. Cambridge: Polity, 2011.

De la Durantaye, Leland. "The Subsurface Unity of All Things, or David Foster Wallace's Free Will." In *Gesturing Toward Reality*, ed. Bolger and Korb, 19–30.

DeLillo, Don. *End Zone*. 1972. Reprint, New York: Penguin, 1986.

———. *Libra*. 1988. Reprint, New York: Penguin, 1991.

———. *Ratner's Star*. 1976. Reprint, New York: Vintage, 1980.

———. *White Noise*. New York: Penguin, 1985.

Den Dulk, Allard. "Boredom, Irony, and Anxiety: Wallace and the Kierkegaardian View of the Self." In *David Foster Wallace and "The Long Thing": New Essays on the Novels*, ed. Boswell, 43–60.

———. "Good Faith and Sincerity: Sartrean Virtues of Self-Becoming in David Foster Wallace's *Infinite Jest*." In *Gesturing Toward Reality*, ed. Bolger and Korb, 199–220.

Derrida, Jacques. *Given Time: I. Counterfeit Money*. Translated by Peggy Kamuf. Chicago: University of Chicago Press, 1992.

———. *Spurs: Nietzsche's Styles*. Translated by Barbara Harlow. Chicago: University of Chicago Press, 1979.

Dreyfus, Hubert, and Sean Dorrance Kelly. *All Things Shining: Reading the Western Classics to Find Meaning in a Secular Age*. New York: Free Press, 2011.

Eggers, Dave. *The Circle*. 2013. Reprint, New York: Vintage, 2014.

Eichenwald, Kurt. *Serpent on the Rock*. 1995. Reprint, New York: Broadway Books, 2007.

Evans, David H. "'The Chains of Not Choosing': Free Will and Faith in William James and David Foster Wallace." In *A Companion to David Foster Wallace Studies*, ed. Boswell and Burn, 171–190.

"Everything and More: *The Pale King* by David Foster Wallace." Panel discussion with Laura Miller, Michael Pietsch, Rick Moody, and Sandro Veronesi. PEN World Voices Festival video. Filmed April 26, 2011. http://www.pen.org/video/everything-and-more-pale-king-david-foster-wallace.

"Fact Meets Fiction in Truly Novel Dispute." *The Recorder*, September 8, 1998.

Fest, Bradley J. "The Inverted Nuke in the Garden: Anti-Eschatology and Archival Emergence in David Foster Wallace's *Infinite Jest*." *boundary 2* 39, no. 3 (Fall 2012): 125–149.

———. "'Then Out of the Rubble': David Foster Wallace's Early Fiction." In *David Foster Wallace and "The Long Thing": New Essays on the Novels*, ed. Boswell, 85–105.

Fitzpatrick, Kathleen. *The Anxiety of Obsolescence: The American Novel in the Age of Television*. Nashville, Tenn.: Vanderbilt University Press, 2006.

———. "Infinite Summer: Reading, Empathy, and the Social Network." In *The Legacy of David Foster Wallace*, ed. Cohen and Konstantinou, 182–207.

Franzen, Jonathan. *Freedom: A Novel*. New York: Farrar, Straus, and Giroux, 2010.

———. "Informal Remarks from the David Foster Wallace Memorial Service in New York on October 23, 2008." In *The Legacy of David Foster Wallace*, ed. Cohen and Konstantinou, 177–181.

———. "Mr. Difficult." In *How to Be Alone: Essays*. 2002. Reprint, New York: Farrar Straus & Giroux, 2003. 238–269.

Freud, Sigmund. *The Standard Edition of the Complete Psychological Works of Sigmund Freud*. Translated by James Strachey et al. 24 vols. London: Hogarth, 1953–1974.

Freudenthal, Elizabeth. "Anti-Interiority: Compulsiveness, Objectification, and Identity in *Infinite Jest*." *New Literary History* 41, no. 1 (Winter 2010): 191–211.

Gaddis, William. *J R*. 1975. Reprint, New York: Penguin, 1993.

———. *The Rush for Second Place: Essays and Occasional Writings*. New York: Penguin, 2002.

Gelman, Eric. "Does 1987 Equal 1929?" *New York Times*, October 20, 1987.

Genette, Gérard. *Paratexts, Thresholds of Interpretation*. Translated by Jane E. Lewin. Cambridge: Cambridge University Press, 2001.

Giles, Paul. "All Swallowed Up: David Foster Wallace and American Literature." In *The Legacy of David Foster Wallace*, ed. Cohen and Konstantinou, 3–22.

———. "Sentimental Posthumanism: David Foster Wallace." *Twentieth Century Literature* 53, no. 3 (Fall 2007): 327–344.

Godden, Richard, and Michael Szalay. "The Bodies in the Bubble: David Foster Wallace's *The Pale King*." *Textual Practice* 28, no. 7 (2014): 1273–1322.

Goerlandt, Iannis. "'Put the Book Down and Slowly Walk Away': Irony and David Foster Wallace's *Infinite Jest*." *Critique: Studies in Contemporary Fiction* 47, no. 3 (2006): 309–328.

Goux, Jean-Joseph. *Symbolic Economies: After Marx and Freud*. Translated by Jennifer Curtiss Gage. Ithaca, N.Y.: Cornell University Press, 1990.

Graeber, David. *Debt: The First 5,000 Years*. Brooklyn, N.Y.: Melville House, 2011.

Grausam, Daniel. "'It Is Only a Statement of the Power of What Comes After': Atomic Nostalgia and the Ends of Postmodernism." *American Literary History* 24, no. 2 (2012): 308–336.

Hammermeister, Kai. *The German Aesthetic Tradition*. Cambridge: Cambridge University Press, 2002.

Harbach, Chad. *The Art of Fielding: A Novel*. New York: Back Bay Books, 2013.

———. "David Foster Wallace!" Review of *Oblivion*, by David Foster Wallace. *n + 1* (Summer 2004).

Hardt, Michael, and Antonio Negri. *Commonwealth*. Cambridge, Mass.: Harvard University Press, 2009.

———. *Empire*. Cambridge, Mass.: Harvard University Press, 2001.

Harris, Charles B. "David Foster Wallace: 'That Distinctive Singular Stamp of Himself.'" *Critique* 51, no. 2 (2010): 168–176.

Hartman, Saidiya V. *Scenes of Subjection: Terror, Slavery, and Self-Making in Nineteenth-Century America*. New York: Oxford University Press, 1997.

Harvey, David. *A Brief History of Neoliberalism*. London: Oxford University Press, 2005.

———. *The Condition of Postmodernity*. 1990. Reprint, Oxford: Blackwell, 1991.

Hasker, William. "David Foster Wallace and the Fallacies of 'Fatalism.'" In *Freedom and the Self*, ed. Cahn and Eckert, 1–30.

Hayes-Brady, Clare. "The Book, the Broom and the Ladder: Philosophical Groundings in the Work of David Foster Wallace." In *Consider David Foster Wallace*, ed. Hering, 24–36.

———. "'. . .': Language, Gender, and Modes of Power in the Work of David Foster Wallace." In *A Companion to David Foster Wallace Studies*, ed. Boswell and Burn, 131–150.

———. *The Unspeakable Failures of David Foster Wallace: Language, Identity, and Resistance*. New York: Bloomsbury, 2016.

Hayles, N. Katherine. "The Illusion of Autonomy and the Fact of Recursivity: Virtual Ecologies, Entertainment, and *Infinite Jest*." *New Literary History* 30, no. 3 (1999): 675–697.

Hegel, G. W. F. *The Phenomenology of Spirit*. Translated by A. V. Miller. London: Oxford University Press, 1976.

Heidegger, Martin. *Being and Time*. Translated by Joan Stambaugh. Albany: SUNY Press, 2010.

Heise, Ursula K. *Sense of Place and Sense of Planet: The Environmental Imagination of the Global*. Oxford: Oxford University Press, 2008.

Hering, David, ed. *Consider David Foster Wallace: Critical Essays*. Los Angeles: Sideshow Media Group, 2010.

Herman, Luc, and Steven C. Weisenburger. Gravity's Rainbow*, Domination, and Freedom*. Athens: University of Georgia Press, 2013.

Hoberek, Andrew. "Adultery, Crisis, Contract." In *Reading Capitalist Realism*, ed. Shonkwiler and La Berge, 41–63.

———. "The Novel After David Foster Wallace." In *A Companion to David Foster Wallace Studies*, ed. Boswell and Burn, 211–227.

Hogg, Emily J. "Subjective Politics in *The Pale King*." *English Studies* 95, no. 1 (2014): 59–69.

Holland, Mary K. "'The Art's Heart's Purpose': Braving the Narcissistic Loop of David Foster Wallace's *Infinite Jest*." *Critique: Studies in Contemporary Fiction* 47, no. 3 (2006): 218–242.

———. "Mediated Immediacy in *Brief Interviews with Hideous Men*." In *A Companion to David Foster Wallace Studies*, ed. Boswell and Burn, 107–130.

———. *Succeeding Postmodernism: Language and Humanism in Contemporary American Literature*. New York: Bloomsbury, 2013.

Houser, Heather. "*Infinite Jest*'s Environmental Case for Disgust." In *The Legacy of David Foster Wallace*, ed. Cohen and Konstantinou, 118–142.

Huehls, Mitchum. *After Critique: Twenty-First-Century Fiction in a Neoliberal Age*. New York: Oxford University Press, 2016.

Hungerford, Amy. *Postmodern Belief: American Literature and Religion Since 1960*. Princeton, N.J.: Princeton University Press, 2010.

Hyde, Lewis. *The Gift: Creativity and the Artist in the Modern World*. 25th Anniversary ed. New York: Vintage, 2007.

——. *The Gift: Imagination and the Erotic Life of Property*. 1983. Reprint, New York: Vintage, 1984.

Jacobs, Timothy. "The Brothers Incandenza: Translating Ideology in Fyodor Dostoevsky's *The Brothers Karamazov* and David Foster Wallace's *Infinite Jest*." *Texas Studies in Literature and Language* 49, no. 3 (2007): 265–292.

Jacquette, Dale. *Wittgenstein's Thought in Transition*. West Lafayette, Ind.: Purdue University Press, 1998.

Jameson, Fredric. *Postmodernism, or The Cultural Logic of Late Capitalism*. Durham, N.C.: Duke University Press, 1991.

Jones, Robert C. "The Lobster Considered." In *Gesturing Toward Reality*, ed. Bolger and Korb, 85–102.

Justice, Donald. "Oblivion: Variations on a Theme." In *Oblivion: On Writers and Writing*, 52–68. Ashland, Ore.: Story Line, 1998.

Kant, Immanuel. *Critique of Judgment*. Translated by James Creed Meredith. Edited by Nicholas Walker. Oxford: Oxford University Press, 2008.

Karl, Alissa G. "Things Break Apart: James Kelman, Ali Smith, and the Neoliberal Novel." In *Reading Capitalist Realism*, ed. Shonkwiler and La Berge, 64–88.

Karmodi, Ostap. "'A Frightening Time in America': An Interview with David Foster Wallace." *NYR Blog*, June 13, 2011. http://www.nybooks.com/daily/2011/06/13/david-foster-wallace-russia-interview/.

——. "June 13th, 2011." *Ostap Karmodi* (blog), June 13, 2011. http://ostap.livejournal.com/799511.html.

Keats, John. *The Complete Poems*. Edited by John Barnard. 3rd ed. New York: Penguin, 1988.

Kelly, Adam. "David Foster Wallace and the New Sincerity in American Fiction." In *Consider David Foster Wallace*, ed. Hering, 131–146.

——. "David Foster Wallace and the Novel of Ideas." In *David Foster Wallace and "The Long Thing": New Essays on the Novels*, ed. Boswell, 3–22.

Kierkegaard, Søren. *A Kierkegaard Anthology*. Edited by Robert Bretall. Princeton, N.J.: Princeton University Press, 1973.

Kirn, Walter. "Staring Either Absently or Intently." Review of *Oblivion*, by David Foster Wallace. *New York Times*, June 27, 2004.

Kirsch, Adam. "The Importance of Being Earnest." *New Republic*, July 28, 2011.

Klein, Naomi. *The Shock Doctrine: The Rise of Disaster Capitalism.* New York: Random House, 2007.

Klosterman, Chuck. "The Jonathan Franzen Award for Jaw-Dropping Literary Genius Goes to . . . Jonathan Franzen." *GQ*, December 2010.

Konstantinou, Lee. *Cool Characters: Irony and American Fiction.* Cambridge, Mass.: Harvard University Press, 2016.

——. "No Bull: David Foster Wallace and Postironic Belief." In *The Legacy of David Foster Wallace*, ed. Cohen and Konstantinou, 83–112.

——. "The World of David Foster Wallace." *boundary 2* 40, no. 3 (2013): 59–86.

Krafft, John M. "'And How Far-Fallen': Puritan Themes in *Gravity's Rainbow*." *Critique* 18, no. 3 (1977): 55–73.

La Berge, Leigh Claire. *Scandals and Abstraction: Financial Fiction of the Long 1980s.* New York: Oxford University Press, 2015.

Lazzarato, Maurizio. *The Making of the Indebted Man: Essays on the Neoliberal Condition.* Translated by Joshua David Jordan. Los Angeles: Semiotext(e), 2012.

Lears, Jackson. *Something for Nothing: Luck in America.* New York: Penguin, 2004.

LeClair, Tom. *In the Loop: Don DeLillo and the Systems Novel.* Urbana: University of Illinois Press, 1987.

——. "The Non-Silence of the Un-Lamblike." Review of *Brief Interviews with Hideous Men*, by David Foster Wallace. *The Nation*, July 19, 1999.

——. "The Prodigious Fiction of Richard Powers, William Vollmann, and David Foster Wallace." *Critique: Studies in Contemporary Fiction* 38, no. 1 (1996): 12–37.

Leise, Christopher. "'Presto Change-o! Tyrone Slothrop's English Again!' Puritan Conversion, Imperfect Assurance, and the Salvific Sloth in *Gravity's Rainbow*." *Pynchon Notes* 56–57 (2009): 127–143.

LeMahieu, Michael. *Fictions of Fact and Value: The Erasure of Logical Positivism in American Literature, 1940–1975.* New York: Oxford University Press, 2013.

Lethem, Jonathan. *Chronic City.* 2009. Reprint, New York: Vintage, 2010.

——. *The Ecstasy of Influence: Nonfictions, Etc.* New York: Vintage, 2011.

——. "*The Gift: Comments and Reviews.*" Blurb. *Lewishyde.com.* http://www.lewishyde.com/publications/the-gift/comments-reviews/.

——. "Jonathan Lethem on Chronic City." Filmed March 30, 2010. *The Guardian* video. http://www.theguardian.com/books/video/2010/mar/22/jonathan-lethem-chronic-city-fiction.

Letzler, David. "Encyclopedic Novels and the Cruft of Fiction: *Infinite Jest*'s Endnotes." In *David Foster Wallace and "The Long Thing": New Essays on the Novels*, ed. Boswell, 127–147.

Lingan, John. "William Gaddis, the Last Protestant." *Quarterly Conversation* 14 (2009).

Lipsky, David, and David Foster Wallace. *Although of Course You End Up Becoming Yourself: A Road Trip with David Foster Wallace.* New York: Broadway Books, 2010.

Luther, Connie. "David Foster Wallace: Westward with Fredric Jameson." In *Consider David Foster Wallace,* ed. Hering, 49–61.

Lyotard, Jean-François. *The Postmodern Condition: A Report on Knowledge.* Translated by Geoff Bennington and Brian Massumi. Minneapolis: University of Minnesota Press, 1984.

Marx, Karl. *Capital: A Critique of Political Economy.* Translated by Ben Fowkes. Vol. 1. New York: Vintage, 1977.

Max, D. T. *Every Love Story Is a Ghost Story: A Life of David Foster Wallace.* New York: Viking, 2012.

——. "In the D.F.W. Archives: An Unfinished Story About the Internet." *New Yorker,* October 11, 2012.

——. "The Unfinished: David Foster Wallace's Struggle to Surpass 'Infinite Jest.'" *New Yorker,* March 9, 2009.

McCarthy, James. "Privatizing Conditions of Production: Trade Agreements as Neoliberal Environmental Governance." In *Neoliberal Environments: False Promises and Unnatural Consequences,* edited by Nik Heynen et al., 38–50. New York: Oxford University Press, 2007.

McCarthy, Tom. "The *New Yorker*'s D. T. Max and Novelist Tom McCarthy Discuss David Foster Wallace." YouTube video. Posted by "Strand Bookstore," November 28, 2012. https://www.youtube.com/watch?v=Xc_UlODoowU.

——. *Remainder.* New York: Vintage, 2007.

McClanahan, Annie. "Future's Shock: Plausibility, Preemption, and the Fiction of 9/11." *symplokē* 17, no. 1–2 (2009): 41–62.

McGurl, Mark. "The Institution of Nothing: David Foster Wallace in the Program." *boundary 2* 41, no. 3 (2014): 27–54.

——. *The Program Era: Postwar Fiction and the Rise of Creative Writing.* Cambridge, Mass.: Harvard University Press, 2009.

McHale, Brian. "*The Pale King*, Or, The White Visitation." In *A Companion to David Foster Wallace Studies,* ed. Boswell and Burn, 191–210.

——. *Postmodernist Fiction.* 1987. Reprint, New York: Routledge, 2003.

McLaughlin, Robert L. "Post-Postmodern Discontent: Contemporary Fiction and the Social World." *symplokē* 12, no. 1–2 (2004): 53–68.

Melville, Herman. *Moby-Dick.* Edited by Hershel Parker and Harrison Hayford. 2nd ed. New York: Norton, 2002.

"Memories of David Foster Wallace." *McSweeney's Internet Tendency.* http://www.mcsweeneys.net/pages/memories-of-david-foster-wallace.

Miller, William Ian. *The Anatomy of Disgust.* Cambridge, Mass.: Harvard University Press, 1997.

Mirowski, Philip. *Never Let a Serious Crisis Go to Waste: How Neoliberalism Survived the Financial Meltdown*. London: Verso, 2013.

Mishra, Pankaj. "The Postmodern Moralist." Review of *Consider the Lobster*, by David Foster Wallace. *New York Times*, March 12, 2006.

Moore, Steven. "The First Draft Version of *Infinite Jest*." *The Howling Fantods*, September 20, 2008.

——. *William Gaddis*. New York: Twayne, 1989.

Morrisey, Tara, and Lucas Thompson. "'The Rare White at the Window': A Reappraisal of Mark Costello and David Foster Wallace's *Signifying Rappers*." *Journal of American Studies* 49, no. 1 (2015): 77–97.

Nadell, Bonnie. Bonnie Nadell Collection of David Foster Wallace. Harry Ransom Center, Austin.

Nietzsche, Friedrich. *The Gay Science: With a Prelude in Rhymes and an Appendix of Songs*. Translated by Walter Kaufmann. New York: Vintage, 1974.

Nørretranders, Tor. *The User Illusion: Cutting Consciousness Down to Size*. Translated by Jonathan Sydenham. New York: Viking, 1998.

North, Michael. *Machine-Age Comedy*. Oxford: Oxford University Press, 2009.

O'Donnell, Patrick. "Almost a Novel: *The Broom of the System*." In *A Companion to David Foster Wallace Studies*, ed. Boswell and Burn, 1–22.

Olsen, Lance. "Termite Art, or Wallace's Wittgenstein." *Review of Contemporary Fiction* 13, no. 2 (1993): 199–215.

Peterson, Dale. "The Start of Everything That Followed." *Amherst Magazine*, Winter 2009. https://www.amherst.edu/aboutamherst/magazine/issues/2009winter/dfw/peterson/node/97025.

Plato. *The Symposium*. Translated by Christopher Gill. London: Penguin, 1999.

Poovey, Mary. *A History of the Modern Fact: Problems of Knowledge in the Sciences*. Chicago: University of Chicago Press, 1998.

Puskar, Jason. *Accident Society: Fiction, Collectivity, and the Production of Chance*. Stanford, Calif.: Stanford University Press, 2012.

Pynchon, Thomas. *The Crying of Lot 49*. 1966. Reprint, New York: Harper Perennial, 2006.

——. *Gravity's Rainbow*. 1973. Reprint, New York: Penguin, 2000.

——. "Nearer, My Couch, to Thee." *New York Times Book Review*, June 6, 1993.

——. *V*. 1963. Reprint, New York: Harper Perennial, 2005.

Quinn, Paul. "'Location's Location': Placing David Foster Wallace." In *A Companion to David Foster Wallace Studies*, ed. Boswell and Burn, 87–106.

Ramal, Randy. "Beyond Philosophy: David Foster Wallace on Literature, Wittgenstein, and the Dangers of Theorizing." In *Gesturing Toward Reality*, ed. Bolger and Korb, 177–198.

Rando, David P. "David Foster Wallace and Lovelessness." *Twentieth Century Literature* 59, no. 4 (2013): 575–595.

Reagan, Ronald. "Inaugural Address: January 20, 1981." In *Actor, Ideologue, Politician: The Public Speeches of Ronald Reagan*, ed. Davis W. Houck and Amos Kiewe, 176–180. Westport, Conn.: Greenwood, 1993.

——. "Farewell Address to the Nation: January 11, 1989." In *Actor, Ideologue, Politician*, ed. Houck and Kiewe, 322–327.

Roiland, Josh. "Getting Away from It All: The Literary Journalism of David Foster Wallace and Nietzsche's Concept of Oblivion." In *The Legacy of David Foster Wallace*, ed. Cohen and Konstantinou, 25–52.

Rowe, Katherine. *Dead Hands: Fictions of Agency, Renaissance to Modern*. Stanford, Calif.: Stanford University Press, 1999.

Russell, Emily. *Reading Embodied Citizenship: Disability, Narrative, and the Body Politic*. New Brunswick, N.J.: Rutgers University Press, 2011.

Saunders, George. "Informal Remarks from the David Foster Wallace Memorial Service in New York on October 23, 2008." In *The Legacy of David Foster Wallace*, ed. Cohen and Konstantinou, 53–58.

Sayers, Sean. "Creative Activity and Alienation in Hegel and Marx." *Historical Materialism* 11, no. 1 (2003): 107–128.

Scott, A. O. "The Panic of Influence." *New York Review of Books*, February 10, 2010.

Severs, Jeffrey. "Cutting Consciousness Down to Size: David Foster Wallace, Exformation, and the Scale of Encyclopedic Fiction." Forthcoming in *Size and Scale in Literature and Culture*, ed. David Wittenberg and Michael Tavel Clarke.

——. "David Foster Wallace, James Wood, and a Source for 'Irrelevant' Chris Fogle." *The Explicator* 73, no. 2 (2015): 129–132.

——. "'We've Been Inside What We Wanted All Along': David Foster Wallace's Immanent Structures." Forthcoming in *Literature and the Encounter with Immanence*, ed. Brynnar Swenson. Amsterdam: Brill, 2016.

Shapiro, Stephen. "From Capitalist to Communist Abstraction: *The Pale King*'s Cultural Fix." *Textual Practice* 28, no. 7 (2014): 1249–1271.

Shell, Marc. *Art and Money*. Chicago: University of Chicago Press, 1995.

——. *Money, Language, and Thought: Literary and Philosophical Economies from the Medieval to the Modern Era*. Berkeley: University of California Press, 1982.

Shelp, Ronald K. "Business Forum: Can Services Survive Without Manufacturing? Giving the Service Economy a Bum Rap." *New York Times*, May 17, 1987.

Shonkwiler, Alison, and Leigh Claire La Berge. "Introduction: A Theory of Capitalist Realism." In *Reading Capitalist Realism*, ed. Shonkwiler and La Berge, 1–25.

——, eds. *Reading Capitalist Realism*. Iowa City: University of Iowa Press, 2014.

Small, Helen. "Fully Accountable." *New Literary History* 44, no. 4 (2013): 539–560.

Smith, Zadie. *Changing My Mind: Occasional Essays*. New York: Penguin, 2009.

——. *NW*. 2012. Reprint, New York: Penguin, 2013.

Staes, Toon. "'Only Artists Can Transfigure': Kafka's Artists and the Possibility of Redemption in the Novellas of David Foster Wallace." *Orbis Litterarum: International Review of Literary Studies* 65, no. 6 (2010): 459–480.

——. "Rewriting the Author: A Narrative Approach to Empathy in *Infinite Jest* and *The Pale King*." *Studies in the Novel* 44, no. 4 (2012): 409–427.

Stevens, Wallace. *The Collected Poems of Wallace Stevens*. New York: Vintage, 1990.

Stolberg, Sheryl Gay. "The Decider." *New York Times*, December 24, 2006.

Szalay, Michael. *New Deal Modernism: American Literature and the Invention of the Welfare State*. Durham, N.C.: Duke University Press, 2000.

Taussig, Michael. *The Devil and Commodity Fetishism in South America*. 1980. Reprint, Chapel Hill: University of North Carolina Press, 2010.

Taylor, Mark C. *Confidence Games: Money and Markets in a World Without Redemption*. Chicago: University of Chicago Press, 2004.

Thompson, Lucas. "Programming Literary Influence: David Foster Wallace's 'B.I. #59.'" *Texas Studies in Literature and Language* 56, no. 2 (2014): 113–134.

Troeltsch, Ernst. *The Social Teaching of the Christian Churches*. Translated by Olive Wyon. Vol. 2. Louisville, Ky.: Westminster John Knox, 1992.

Tracey, Thomas. "The Formative Years: David Foster Wallace's Philosophical Influences and *The Broom of the System*." In *Gesturing Toward Reality*, ed. Bolger and Korb, 157–176.

Wallace Havens, Amy. "Amy Wallace Havens on Her Brother." Interview by Anne Strainchamps. *To The Best of Our Knowledge*. PRI radio broadcast, August 23, 2009. http://www.ttbook.org/book/amy-wallace-havens-her-brother.

Wallace, David Foster. "All That." *New Yorker*, December 14, 2009. http://www.new yorker.com/magazine/2009/12/14/all-that-2.

——. *The Awakening of My Interest in Advanced Tax*. Westborough, Mass.: Madras, 2013.

——. *Both Flesh and Not: Essays*. New York: Little, Brown, 2012.

——. "Brief Interviews with Hideous Men." *Harper's* (October 1998): 41–56.

——. *Brief Interviews with Hideous Men*. 1999. Reprint, New York: Little, Brown, 2007.

——. *The Broom of the System*. 1987. Reprint, New York: Avon, 1993.

——. *Consider the Lobster and Other Essays*. New York: Little, Brown, 2005.

——. "Le Conversazioni 2006." YouTube video. Posted by "Dazzle Communication," May 26, 2007. https://www.youtube.com/watch?v=MsziSppMUS4.

——. "Crash of '69." *Between C & D* (Winter 1989): 3–12.

——. "David Foster Wallace." Interview by Charlie Rose. *Charlie Rose.* PBS. March 27, 1997.

——. "David Foster Wallace: In Conversation with David Kipen." Interview. *City Arts & Lectures.* 2004. https://www.youtube.com/watch?v=mfjjSj9coAo.

——. "David Foster Wallace (*Brief Interviews With Hideous Men*)." Interview by Michael Silverblatt. *Bookworm.* KCRW radio broadcast. August 3, 2000.

——. "David Foster Wallace (*Consider the Lobster*)." Interview by Michael Silverblatt. *Bookworm.* KCRW radio broadcast. March 2, 2006.

——. "David Foster Wallace (*Infinite Jest*)." Interview by Michael Silverblatt. *Bookworm.* KCRW radio broadcast. April 11, 1996.

——. *David Foster Wallace: The Last Interview and Other Conversations.* Brooklyn, N.Y.: Melville House, 2012.

——. David Foster Wallace Papers. Harry Ransom Center, Austin.

——. *Everything and More: A Compact History of Infinity.* 2003. Reprint, New York: Norton, 2010.

——. *Fate, Time, and Language: An Essay on Free Will.* Edited by Steven M. Cahn and Maureen Eckert. New York: Columbia University Press, 2011.

——. "*The Gift: Comments and Reviews.*" Blurb. Lewishyde.com. http://www.lewishyde.com/publications/the-gift/comments-reviews/.

——. *Girl with Curious Hair.* New York: Norton, 1989.

——. *Infinite Jest.* 10th Anniversary ed. New York: Back Bay, 2006.

——. Interview by Das ZDF-Interview. *Zweites Deutsches Fernsehen.* http://www.youtube.com/watch?v=FkxUYokxH8o.

——. "The Jester Holds Court: An Interview with David Foster Wallace." By Valerie Stivers. *stim.com* 1, no. 1 (May 15, 1996). http://www.stim.com/Stim-x/0596May/Verbal/dfwmain.html.

——. "Laughing with Kafka." *Harper's* (July 1998): 23, 26–27.

——. *Oblivion.* New York: Little, Brown, 2004.

——. "Order and Flux in Northampton." *Conjunctions* 17 (Fall 1991): 91–118.

——. "Other Math." *Western Humanities Review* (Summer 1987): 287–289.

——. *The Pale King: An Unfinished Novel.* 2011. Reprint, New York: Back Bay, 2012.

——. "Peoria (4)." *TriQuarterly* 112 (2002): 131.

——. "The Planet Trillaphon as It Stands in Relation to the Bad Thing." *The Amherst Review* 7 (1984): 26–33. https://quomodocumque.files.wordpress.com/2008/09/wallace-amherst_review-the_planet.pdf.

——. "Quo Vadis – Introduction." *Review of Contemporary Fiction* 16, no. 1 (1996): 7–8.

——. *A Supposedly Fun Thing I'll Never Do Again: Essays and Arguments.* New York: Little, Brown, 1997.

———. *This Is Water: Some Thoughts, Delivered on a Significant Occasion, About Living a Compassionate Life*. New York: Little, Brown, 2009.

———. "Transcript of the David Foster Wallace Interview." By David Wiley. *Minnesota Daily*, February 27, 1997. http://www.badgerinternet.com/~bobkat/jestwiley2.html.

Wallace, David Foster, and Mark Costello. *Signifying Rappers*. 1990. Reprint, New York: Back Bay, 2013.

Warren, Andrew. "Modeling Community and Narrative in *Infinite Jest* and *The Pale King*." In *David Foster Wallace and "The Long Thing": New Essays on the Novels*, ed. Boswell, 61–82.

Wayne, Teddy. "Addiction to Itself: Self-Consciousness in David Foster Wallace's *Infinite Jest*." AB Thesis, Harvard, 2001.

———. *Kapitoil: A Novel*. New York: Harper Perennial, 2010.

———. "On Internet Slang, IMHO." *New York Times*, March 28, 2014.

Weatherall, James Owen. *The Physics of Wall Street: A Brief History of Predicting the Unpredictable*. New York: Houghton Mifflin, 2013.

Weber, Bruce. "David Foster Wallace, Influential Writer, Dies at 46." *New York Times*, September 14, 2008.

Weber, Max. *The Protestant Ethic and the "Spirit" of Capitalism and Other Writings*. New York: Penguin, 2002.

Winthrop, John. "A Model of Christian Charity." In *The Journal of John Winthrop, 1630–1649*, ed. James Savage, Richard S. Dunn, and Laetitia Yaendle, 1–11. Cambridge, Mass.: Harvard University Press, 1996.

Wittgenstein, Ludwig. *Tractatus Logico-Philosophicus*. Trans. D. F. Pears and B. F. McGuinness. Rev. ed. New York: Routledge, 1974.

———. *Philosophical Investigations: The English Text of the Third Edition*. Translated by G. E. M. Anscombe. Englewood Cliffs, N.J.: Prentice Hall, 1958.

Wood, James. *The Irresponsible Self: On Laughter and the Novel*. New York: Picador, 2005.

Wouters, Conley. "'What Am I, a Machine?': Humans and Information in *The Pale King*." In *David Foster Wallace and "The Long Thing": New Essays on the Novels*, ed. Boswell, 169–186.

Zane, J. Peder. *The Top Ten: Writers Pick Their Favorite Books*. New York: Norton, 2007.

INDEX